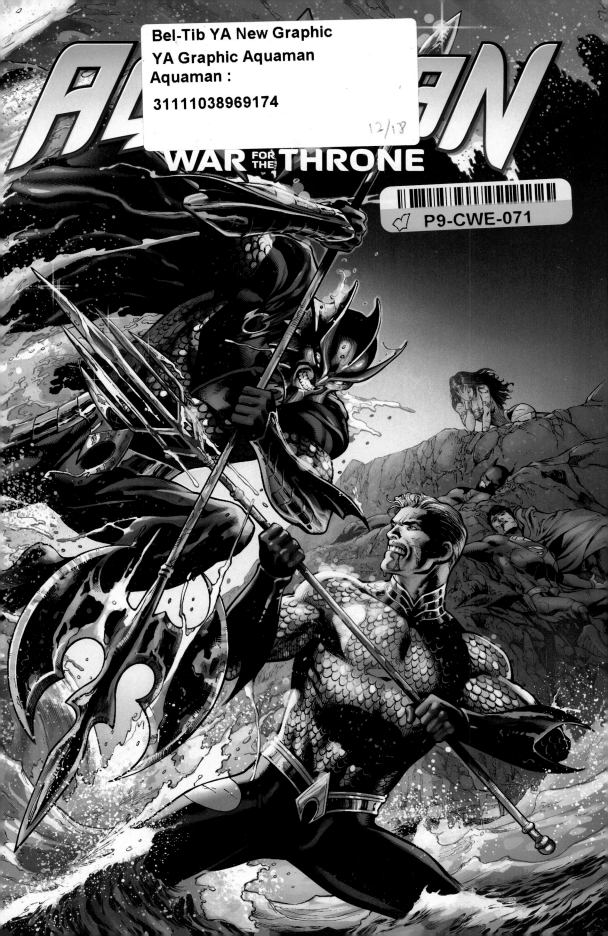

Bel-Tib YA New Graphic
YA Graphic Aquaman
Aquaman :
31111038969174

12/18

P9-CWE-071

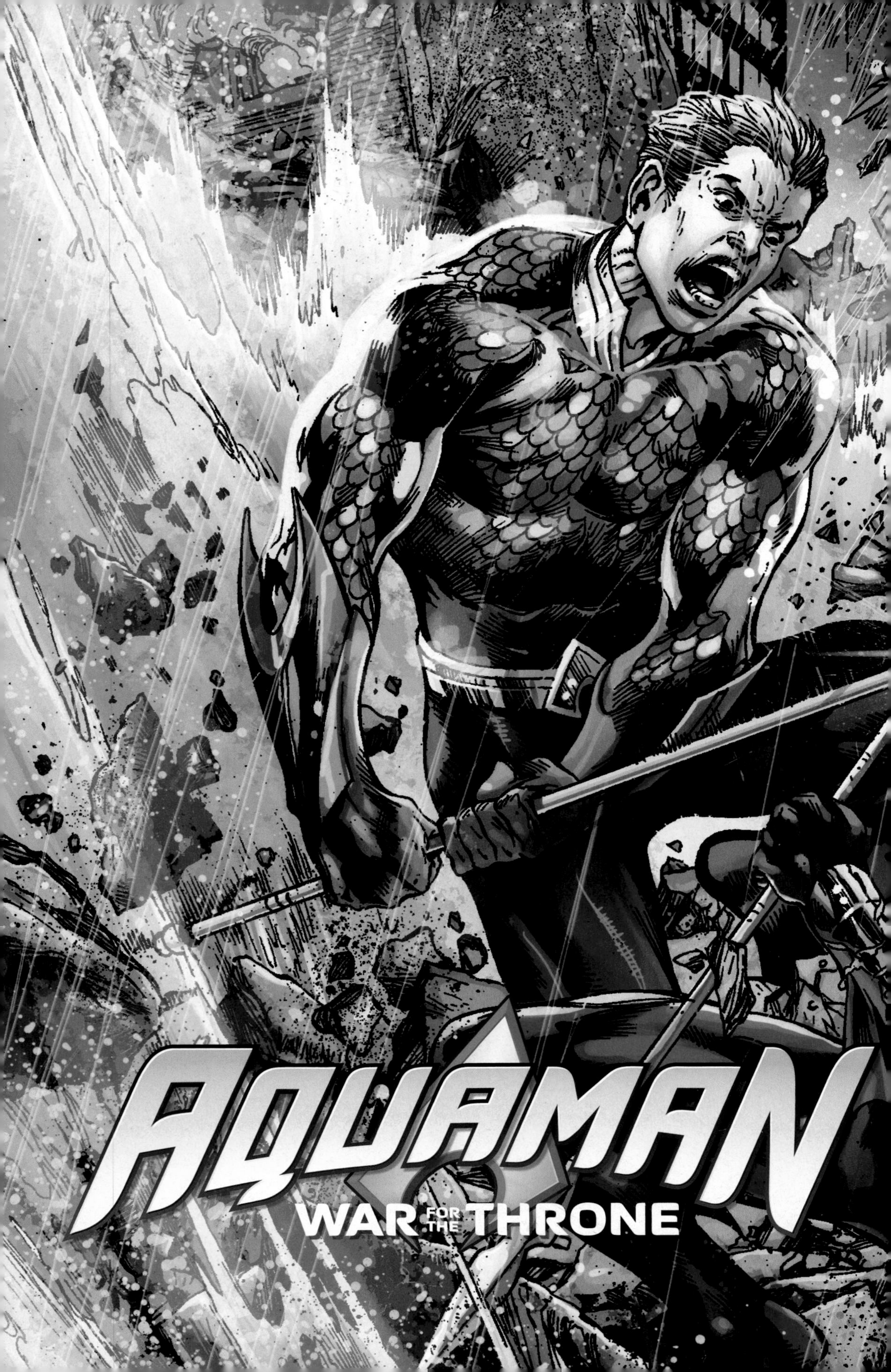
AQUAMAN
WAR FOR THE THRONE

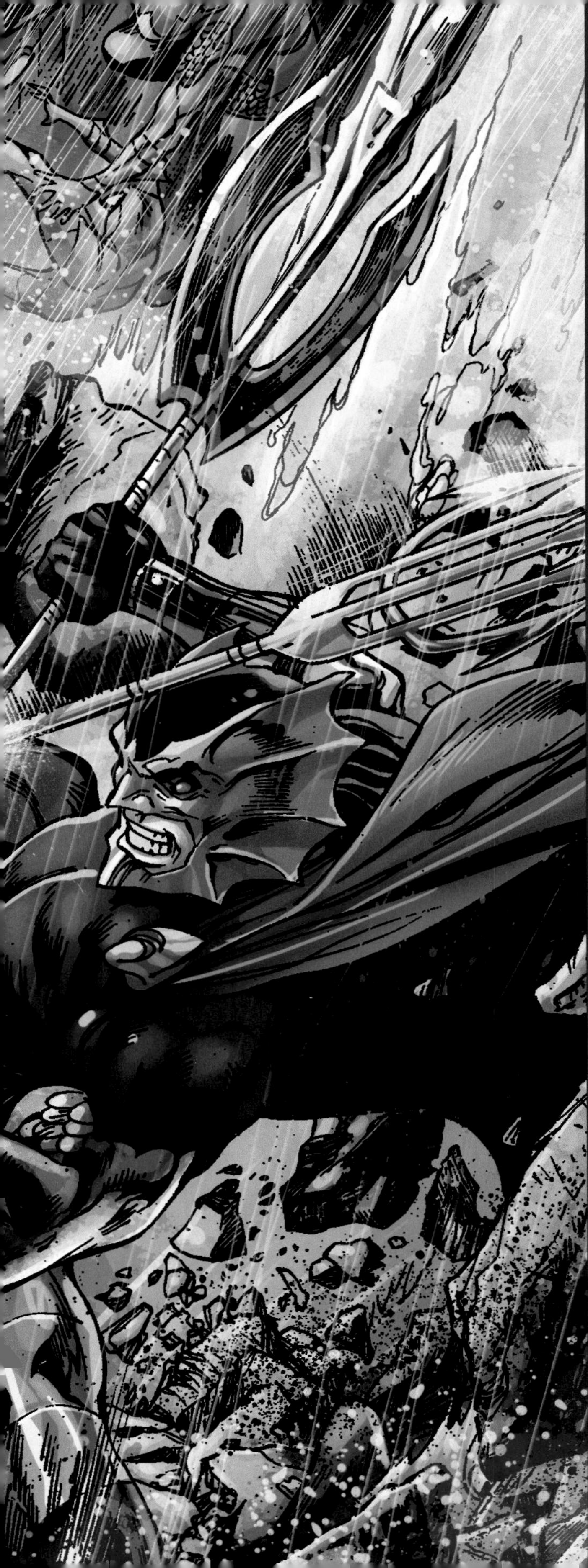

GEOFF JOHNS
write

PAUL PELLETIER
IVAN REIS
PETE WOODS
PERE PÉREZ
pencillers

JOE PRADO
SEAN PARSONS
ART THIBERT
OCLAIR ALBERT
MARLO ALQUIZA
RUY JOSE
KARL KESEL
PERE PÉREZ
IVAN REIS
CAM SMITH
inkers

ROD REIS
TONY AVIÑA
NATHAN EYRING
colorists

NICK J. NAPOLITANO
DEZI SIENTY
DAVE SHARPE
letterers

AQUAMAN created by
PAUL NORRIS

SUPERMAN created by
JERRY SIEGEL
and **JOE SHUSTER**
By special arrangement
with the Jerry Siegel family

BRIAN CUNNINGHAM   PAT McCALLUM
Editors – Original Series

KATIE KUBERT   CHRIS CONROY
Associate Editors – Original Series

KATE STEWART
Assistant Editor – Original Series

JEB WOODARD
Group Editor – Collected Editions

ROBIN WILDMAN
Editor – Collected Edition

STEVE COOK
Design Director – Books

CURTIS KING JR.
Publication Design

BOB HARRAS
Senior VP – Editor-in-Chief, DC Comics

PAT McCALLUM
Executive Editor, DC Comics

DAN DiDIO
Publisher

JIM LEE
Publisher & Chief Creative Officer

AMIT DESAI
*Executive VP – Business & Marketing Strategy,
Direct to Consumer & Global Franchise Management*

BOBBIE CHASE
*VP & Executive Editor,
Young Reader & Talent Development*

MARK CHIARELLO
Senior VP – Art, Design & Collected Editions

JOHN CUNNINGHAM
Senior VP – Sales & Trade Marketing

BRIAR DARDEN
VP – Business Affairs

ANNE DePIES
*Senior VP – Business Strategy,
Finance & Administration*

DON FALLETTI
VP – Manufacturing Operations

LAWRENCE GANEM
VP – Editorial Administration & Talent Relations

ALISON GILL
Senior VP – Manufacturing & Operations

JASON GREENBERG
VP – Business Strategy & Finance

HANK KANALZ
Senior VP – Editorial Strategy & Administration

JAY KOGAN
Senior VP – Legal Affairs

NICK J. NAPOLITANO
VP – Manufacturing Administration

LISETTE OSTERLOH
VP – Digital Marketing & Events

EDDIE SCANNELL
VP – Consumer Marketing

COURTNEY SIMMONS
Senior VP – Publicity & Communications

JIM (SKI) SOKOLOWSKI
VP – Comic Book Specialty Sales & Trade Marketing

NANCY SPEARS
VP – Mass, Book, Digital Sales & Trade Marketing

MICHELE R. WELLS
VP – Content Strategy

Cover art by **LUCIO PARRILLO**

AQUAMAN: WAR FOR THE THRONE

Published by DC Comics. Compilation and all new
material Copyright © 2018 DC Comics. All Rights
Reserved. Originally published in single magazine
form in AQUAMAN 0, 14-16, JUSTICE LEAGUE 15-17.
Copyright © 2012, 2013 DC Comics. All Rights
Reserved. All characters, their distinctive likenesses
and related elements featured in this publication are
trademarks of DC Comics. The stories, characters and
incidents featured in this publication are entirely
fictional. DC Comics does not read or accept
unsolicited submissions of ideas, stories or artwork.

DC Comics
2900 West Alameda Ave., Burbank, CA 91505
Printed by LSC Communications,
Kendallville, IN, USA. 10/19/18.
First Printing. ISBN: 978-1-4012-8358-2

Library of Congress
Cataloging-in-Publication Data is available.

PEFC Certified

Printed on paper from
sustainably managed
forests, controlled
sources

PEFC/29-31-337   www.pefc.org

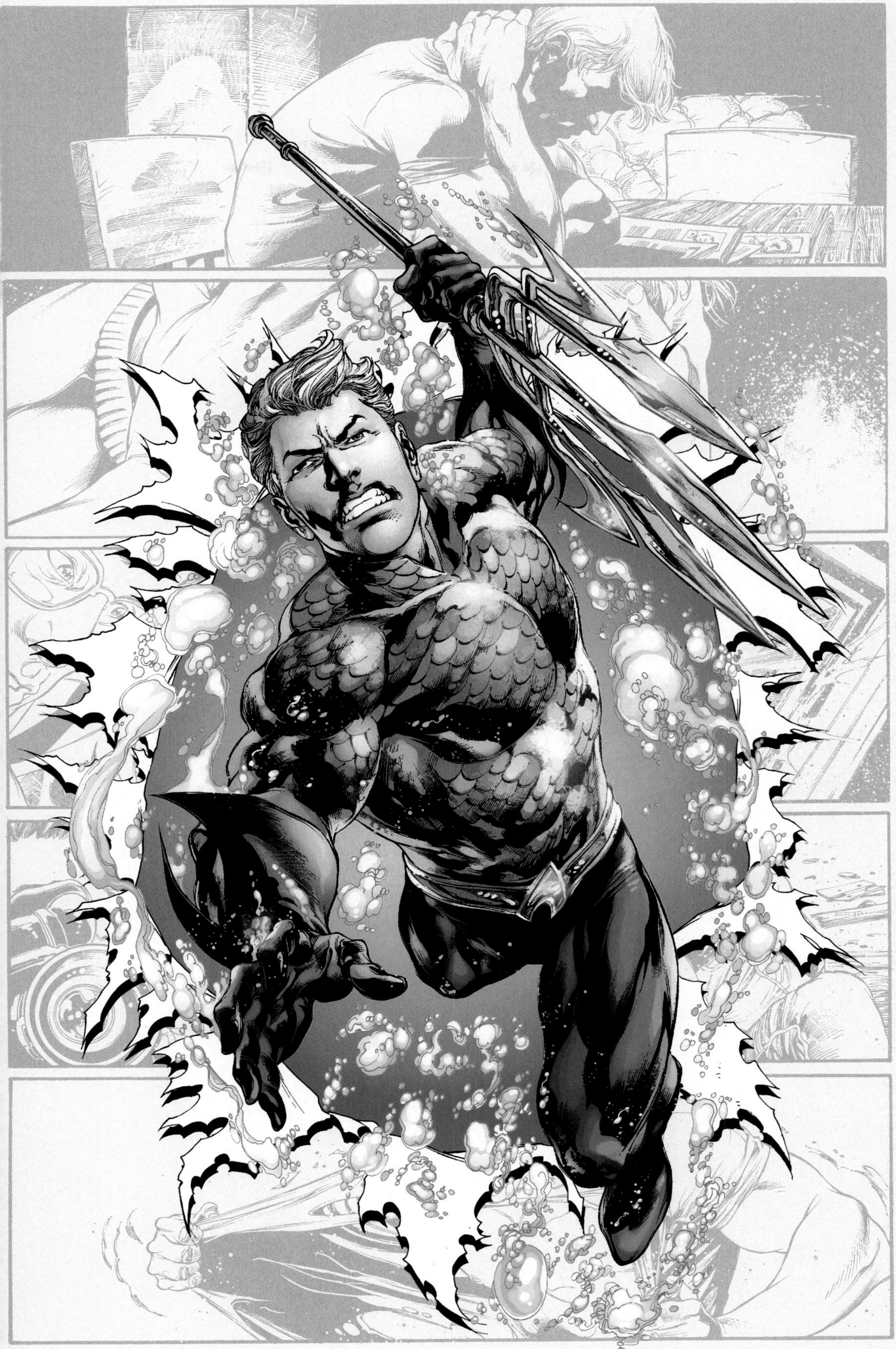

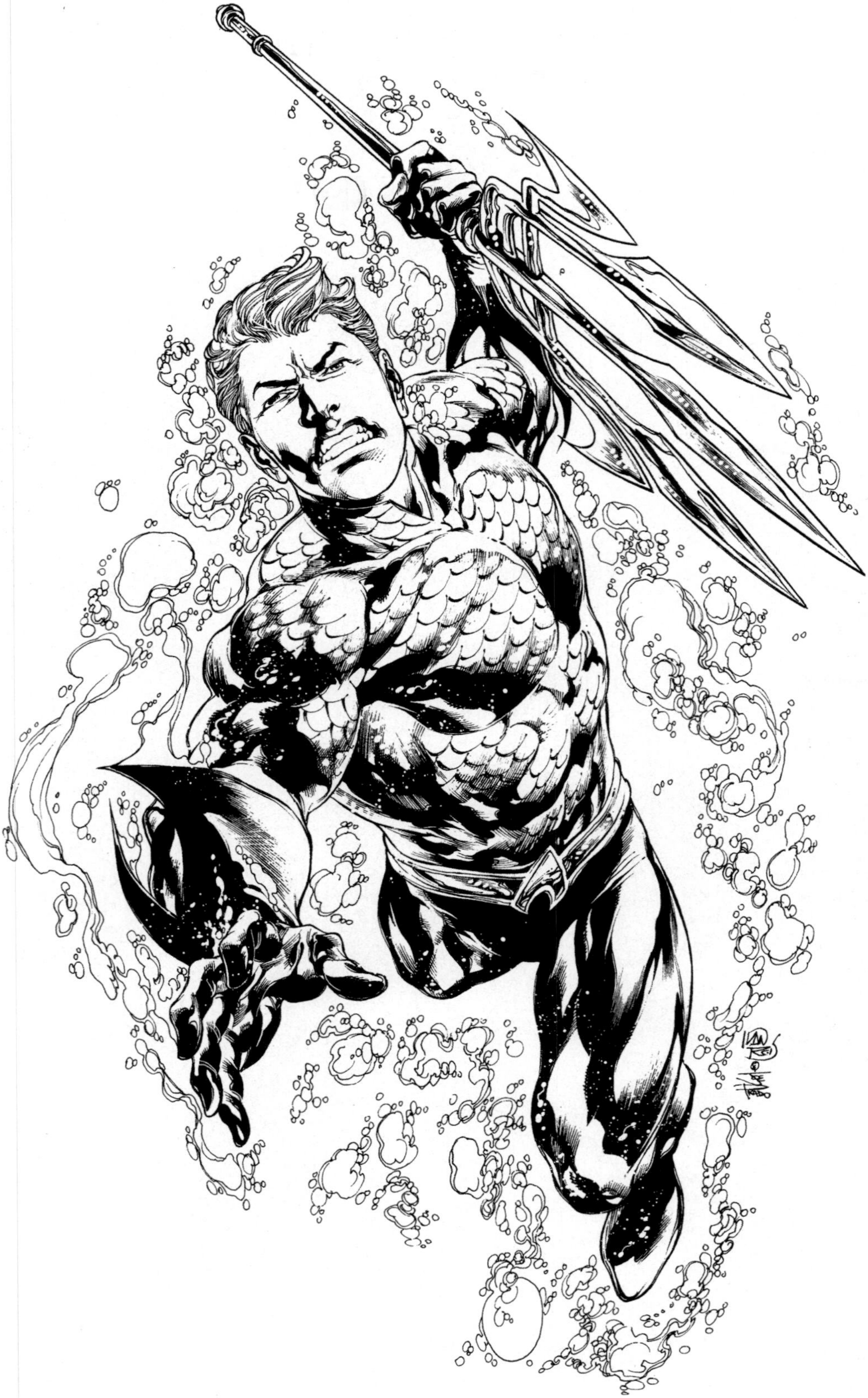

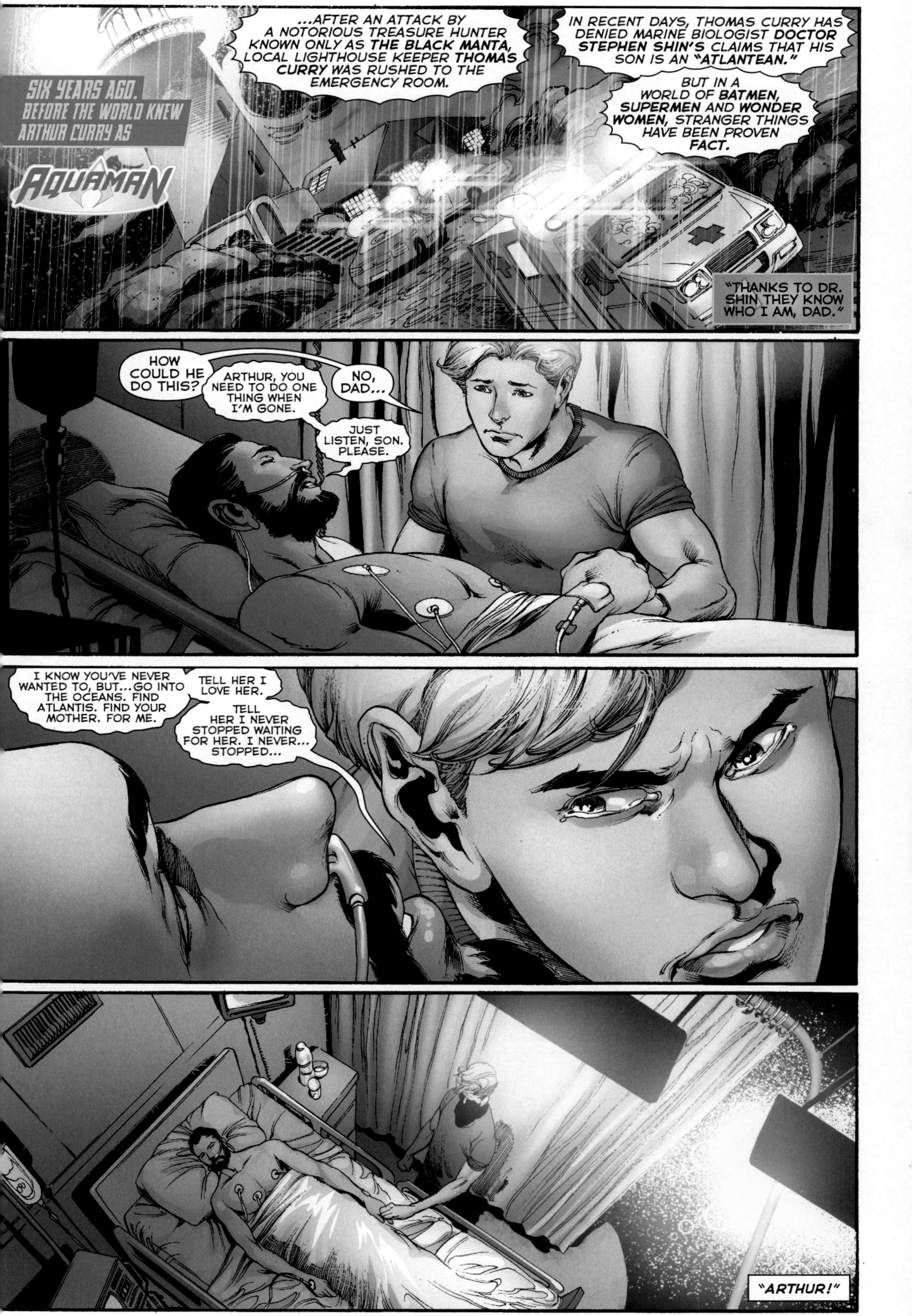
SIX YEARS AGO. BEFORE THE WORLD KNEW ARTHUR CURRY AS
AQUAMAN
...AFTER AN ATTACK BY A NOTORIOUS TREASURE HUNTER KNOWN ONLY AS THE BLACK MANTA, LOCAL LIGHTHOUSE KEEPER THOMAS CURRY WAS RUSHED TO THE EMERGENCY ROOM.
IN RECENT DAYS, THOMAS CURRY HAS DENIED MARINE BIOLOGIST DOCTOR STEPHEN SHIN'S CLAIMS THAT HIS SON IS AN "ATLANTEAN."
BUT IN A WORLD OF BATMEN, SUPERMEN AND WONDER WOMEN, STRANGER THINGS HAVE BEEN PROVEN FACT.
"THANKS TO DR. SHIN THEY KNOW WHO I AM, DAD."
HOW COULD HE DO THIS?
NO, DAD...
ARTHUR, YOU NEED TO DO ONE THING WHEN I'M GONE.
JUST LISTEN, SON. PLEASE.
I KNOW YOU'VE NEVER WANTED TO, BUT...GO INTO THE OCEANS. FIND ATLANTIS. FIND YOUR MOTHER. FOR ME.
TELL HER I LOVE HER.
TELL HER I NEVER STOPPED WAITING FOR HER. I NEVER... STOPPED...
"ARTHUR!"

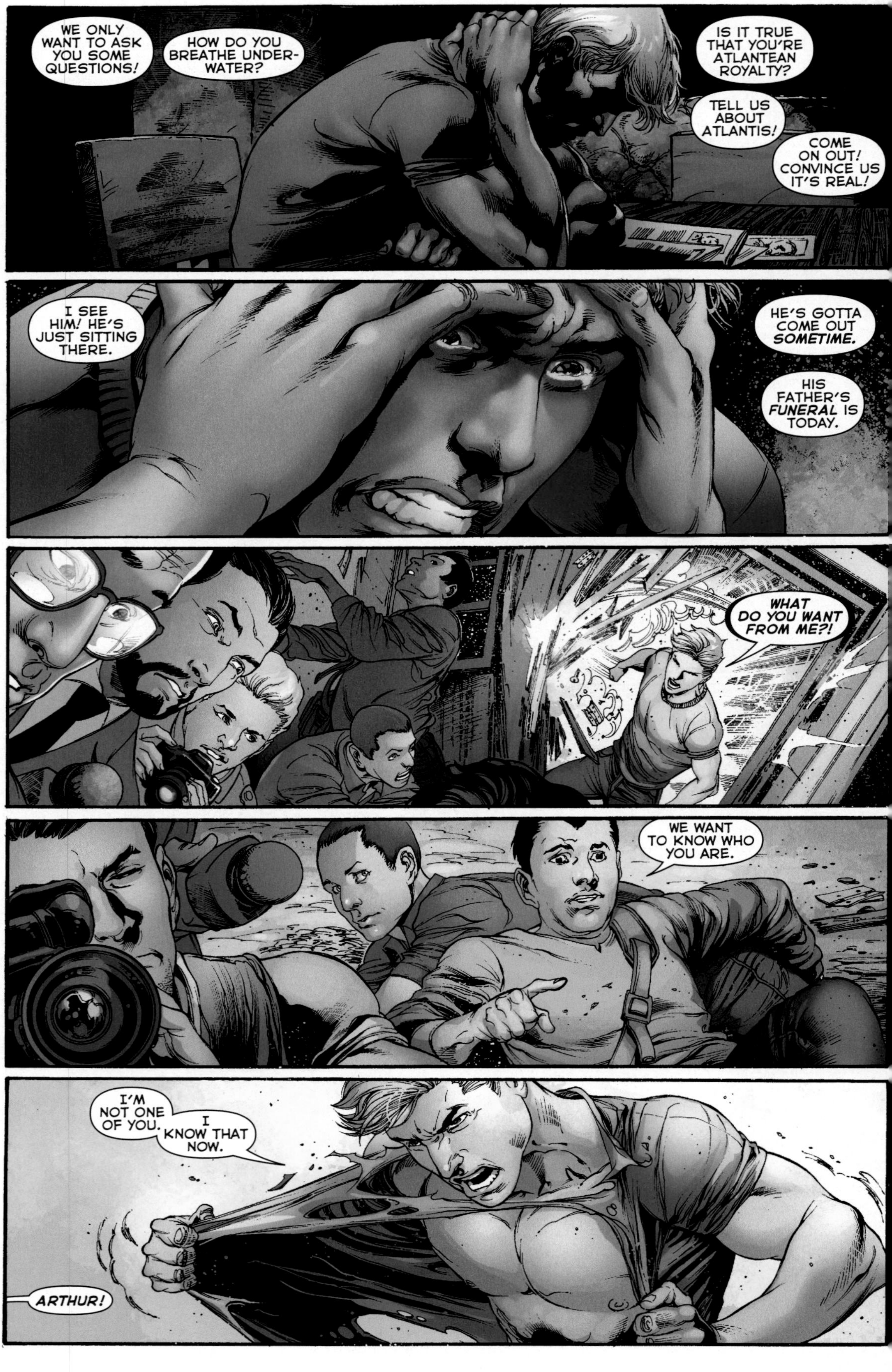

WE ONLY WANT TO ASK YOU SOME QUESTIONS!
HOW DO YOU BREATHE UNDER-WATER?
IS IT TRUE THAT YOU'RE ATLANTEAN ROYALTY?
TELL US ABOUT ATLANTIS!
COME ON OUT! CONVINCE US IT'S REAL!
I SEE HIM! HE'S JUST SITTING THERE.
HE'S GOTTA COME OUT *SOMETIME.*
HIS FATHER'S *FUNERAL* IS TODAY.
WHAT DO YOU WANT FROM ME?!
WE WANT TO KNOW WHO YOU ARE.
I'M NOT ONE OF YOU.
I KNOW THAT NOW.
ARTHUR!

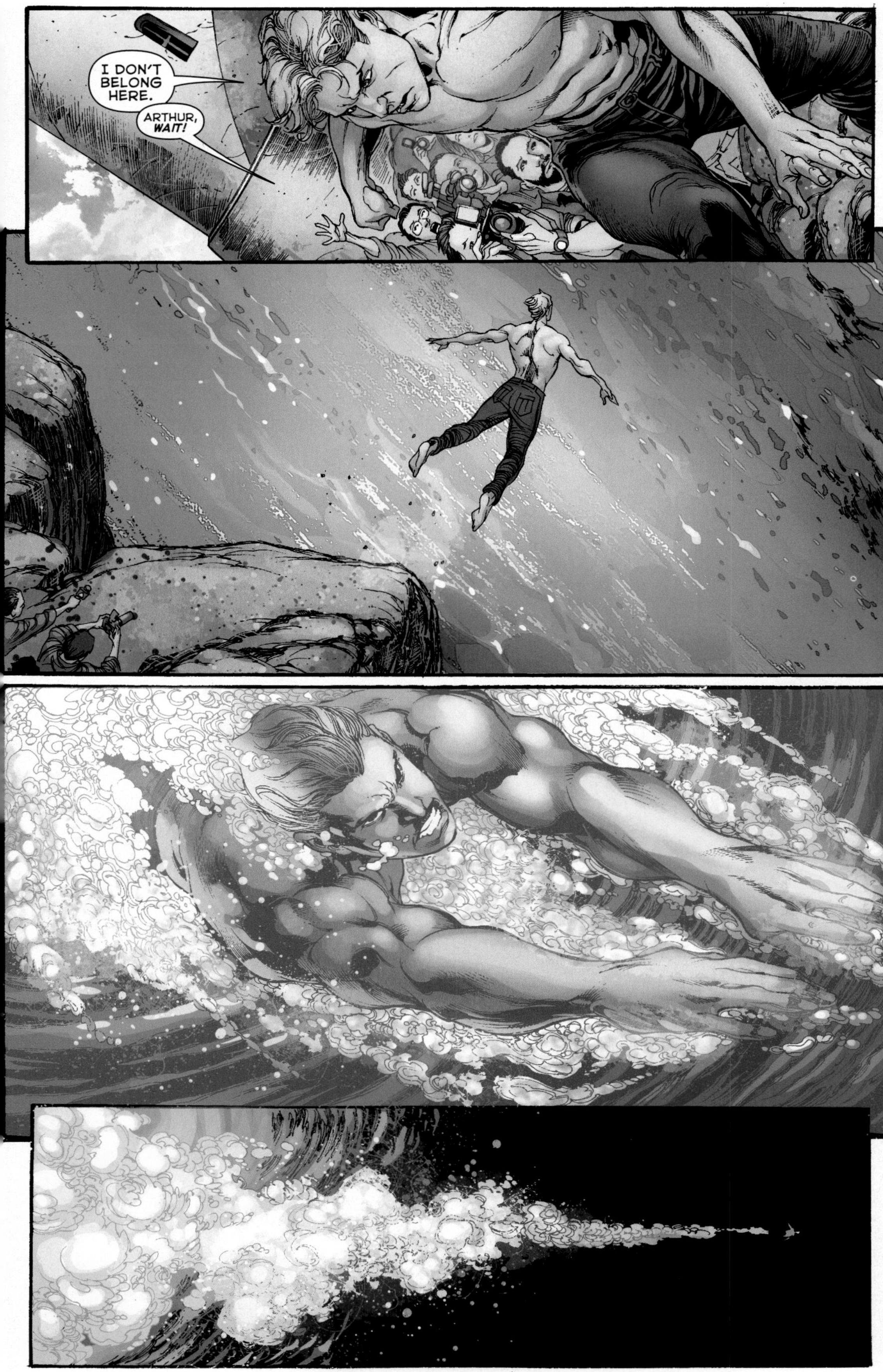
I DON'T BELONG HERE.
ARTHUR, WAIT!

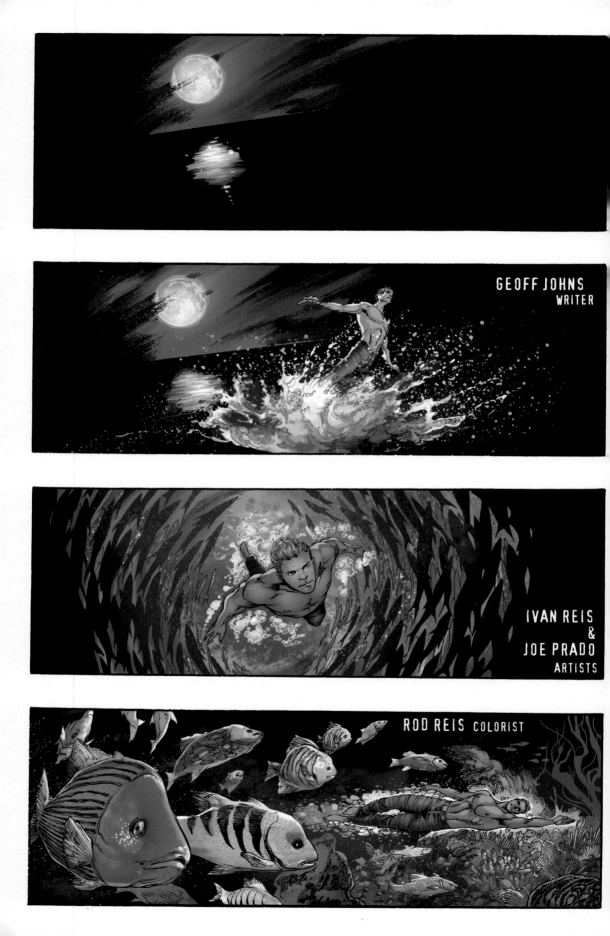

GEOFF JOHNS
WRITER

IVAN REIS
&
JOE PRADO
ARTISTS

ROD REIS COLORIST

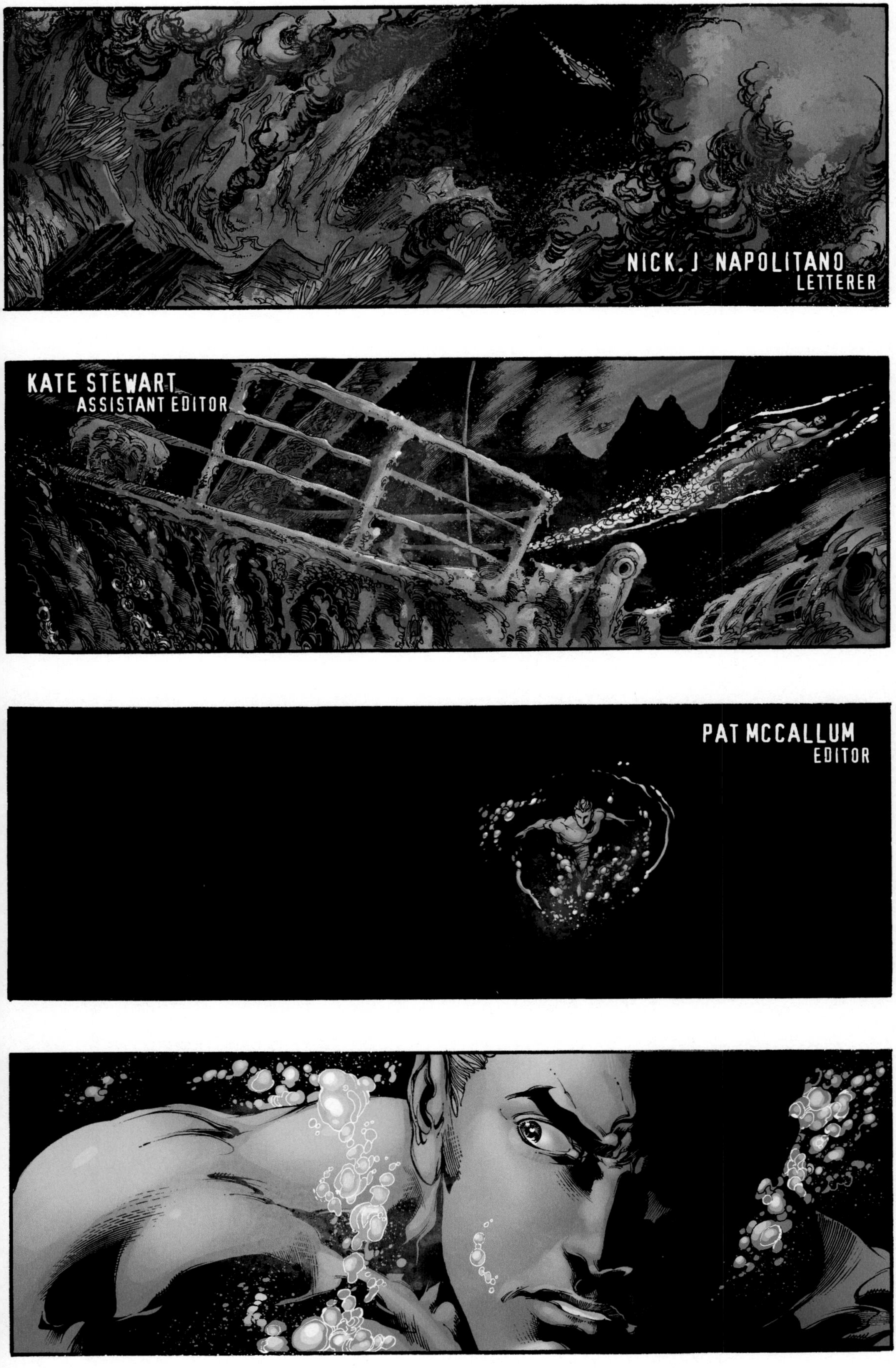
NICK. J NAPOLITANO
LETTERER
KATE STEWART
ASSISTANT EDITOR
PAT MCCALLUM
EDITOR

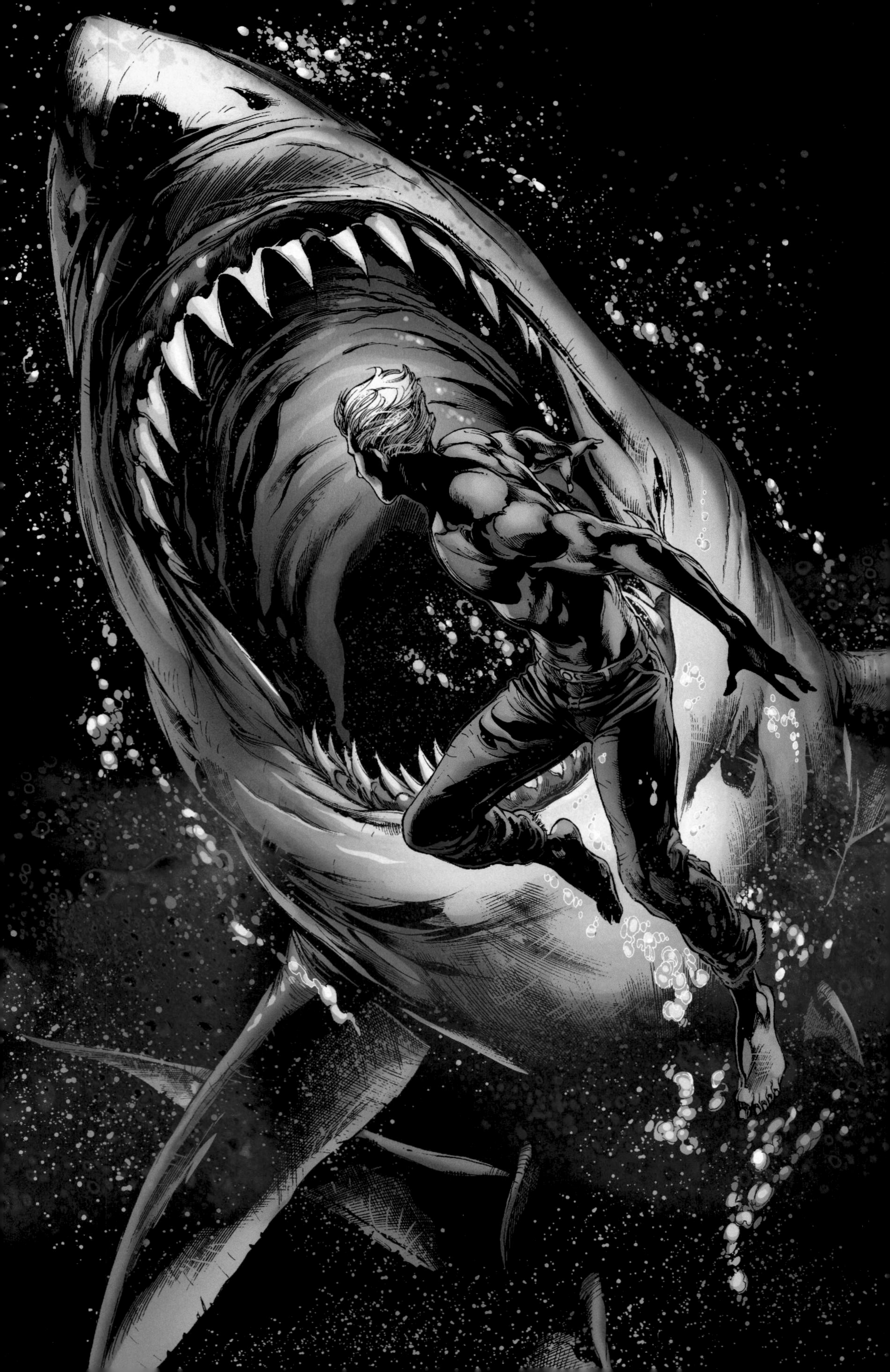

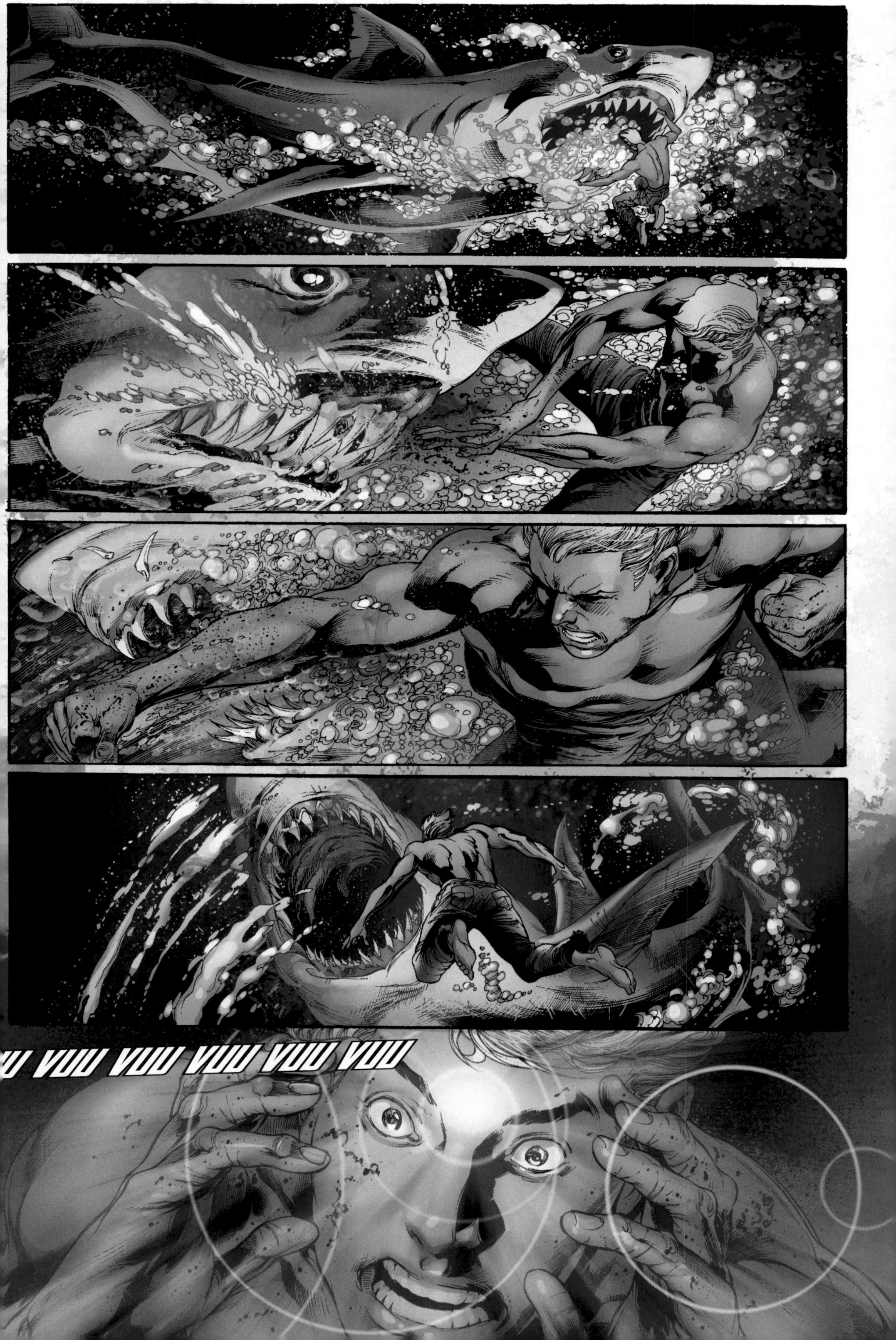
VUU VUU VUU VUU VUU VUU

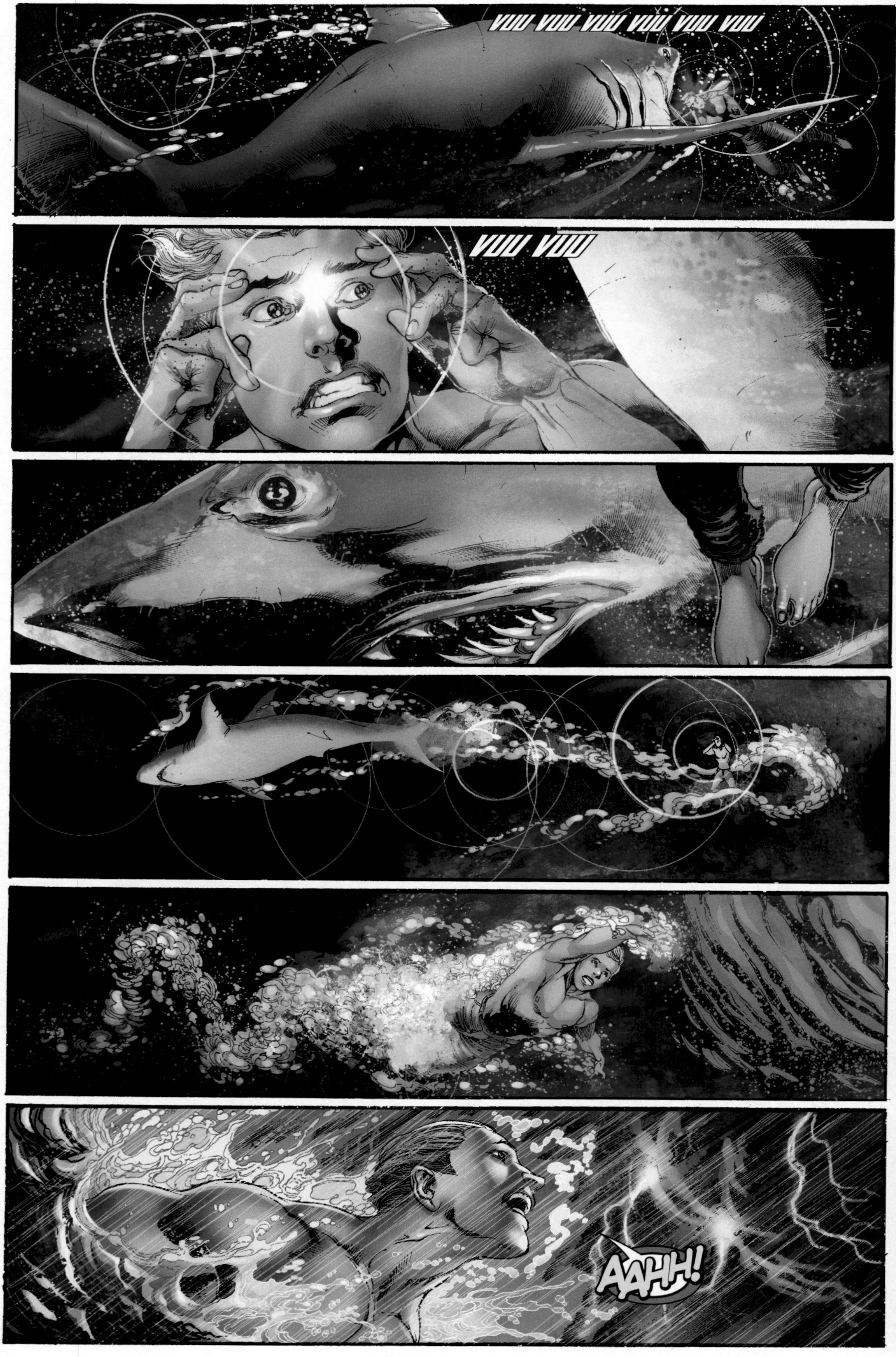
VUU VUU VUU VUU VUU VUU
VUU VUU
AAHH!

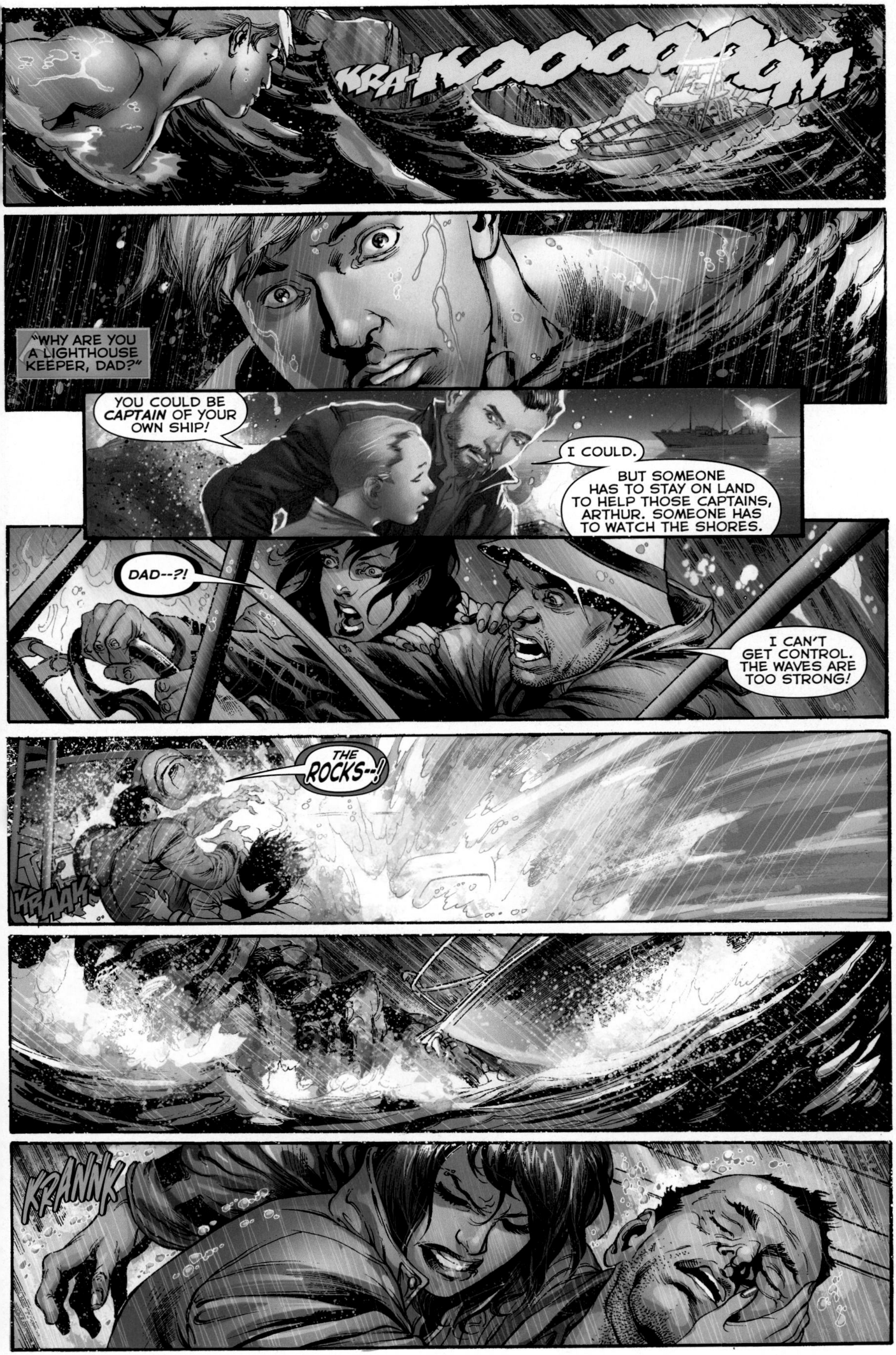

KRA-KOOOOOOOM
"WHY ARE YOU A LIGHTHOUSE KEEPER, DAD?"
YOU COULD BE CAPTAIN OF YOUR OWN SHIP!
I COULD.
BUT SOMEONE HAS TO STAY ON LAND TO HELP THOSE CAPTAINS, ARTHUR. SOMEONE HAS TO WATCH THE SHORES.
DAD--?!
I CAN'T GET CONTROL. THE WAVES ARE TOO STRONG!
THE ROCKS--!
KRAAK
KRANNK

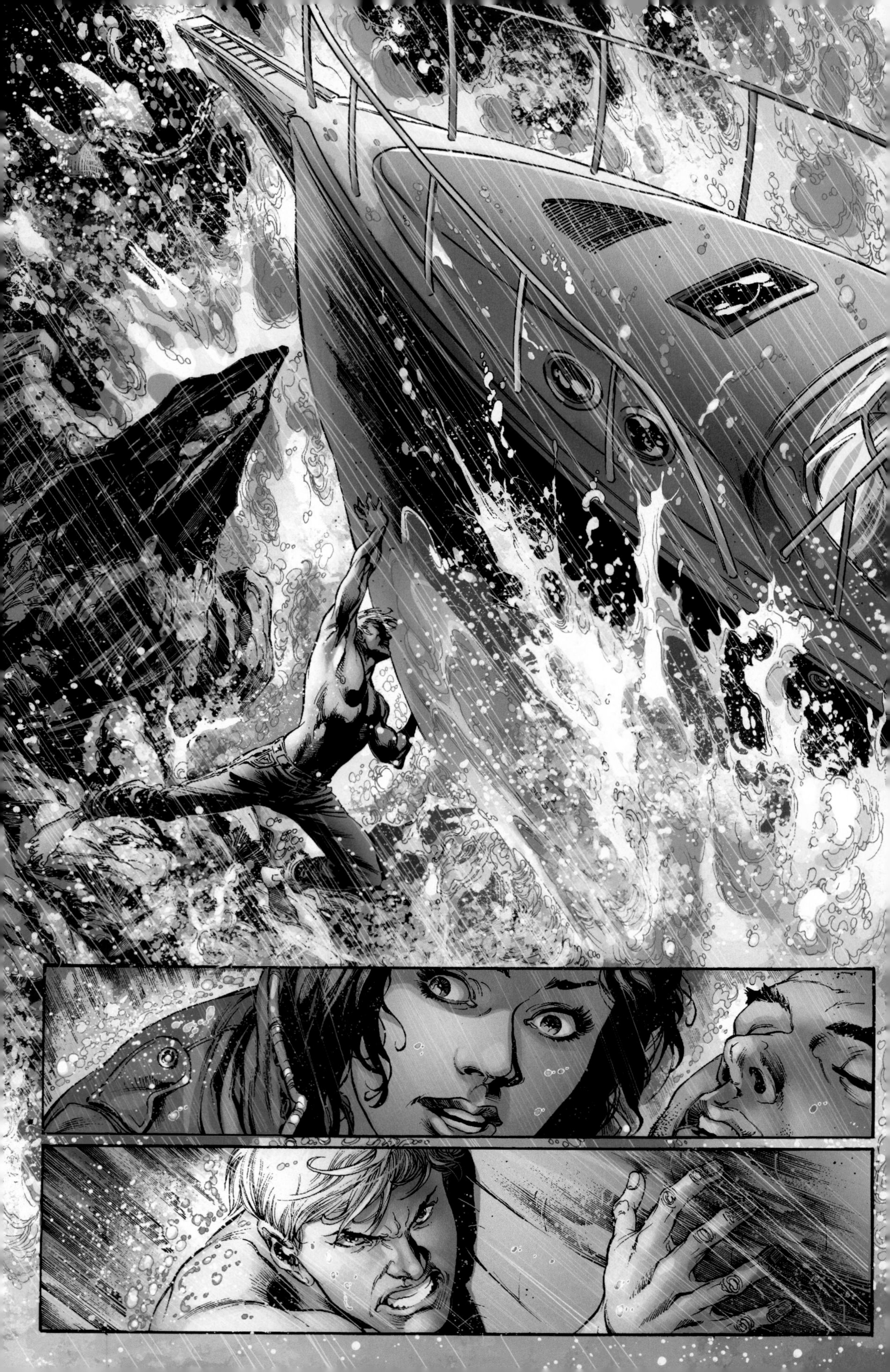

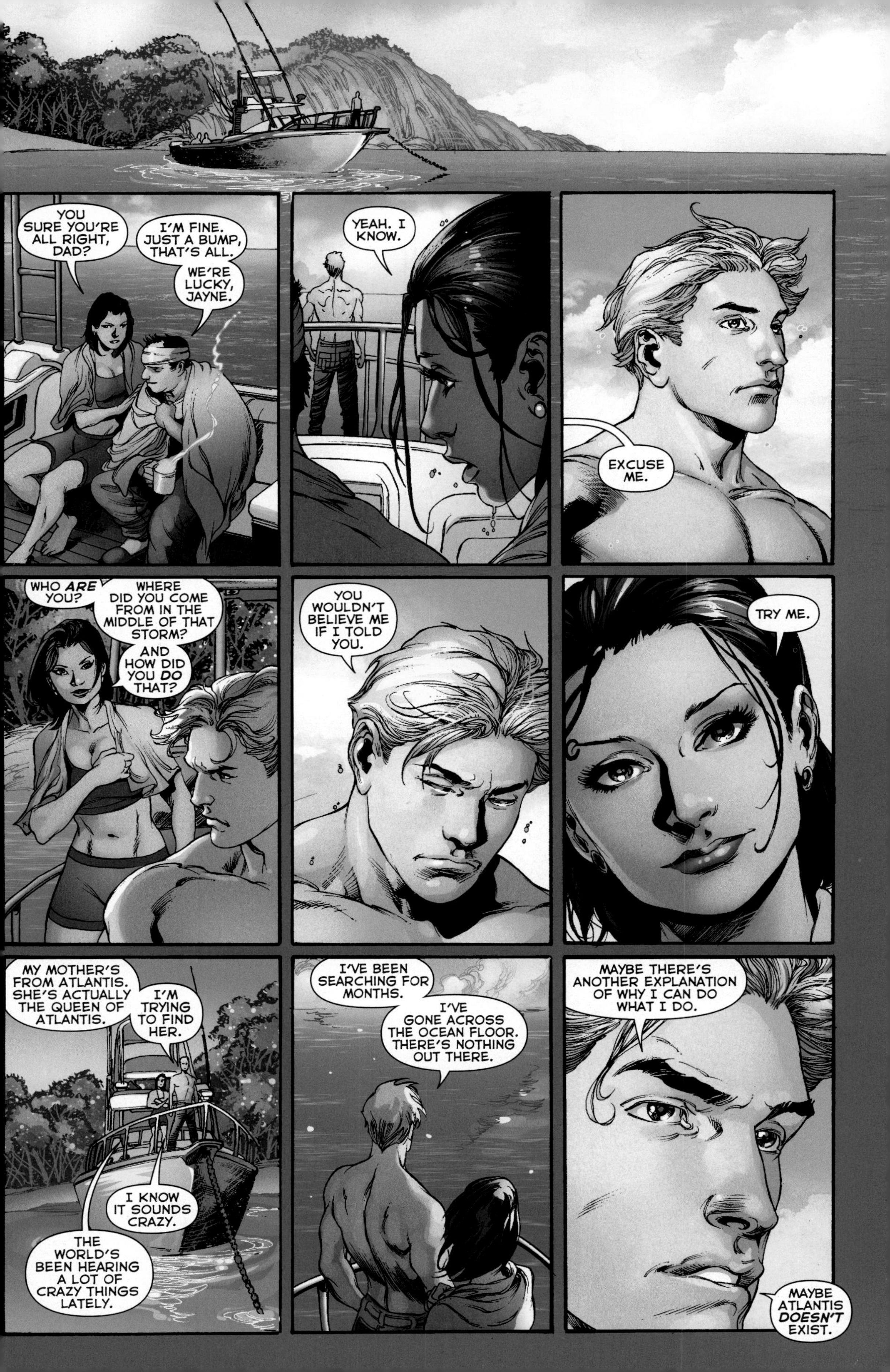
YOU SURE YOU'RE ALL RIGHT, DAD?
I'M FINE. JUST A BUMP, THAT'S ALL.
WE'RE LUCKY, JAYNE.
YEAH. I KNOW.
EXCUSE ME.
WHO ARE YOU?
WHERE DID YOU COME FROM IN THE MIDDLE OF THAT STORM?
AND HOW DID YOU DO THAT?
YOU WOULDN'T BELIEVE ME IF I TOLD YOU.
TRY ME.
MY MOTHER'S FROM ATLANTIS. SHE'S ACTUALLY THE QUEEN OF ATLANTIS.
I'M TRYING TO FIND HER.
I KNOW IT SOUNDS CRAZY.
THE WORLD'S BEEN HEARING A LOT OF CRAZY THINGS LATELY.
I'VE BEEN SEARCHING FOR MONTHS.
I'VE GONE ACROSS THE OCEAN FLOOR. THERE'S NOTHING OUT THERE.
MAYBE THERE'S ANOTHER EXPLANATION OF WHY I CAN DO WHAT I DO.
MAYBE ATLANTIS DOESN'T EXIST.

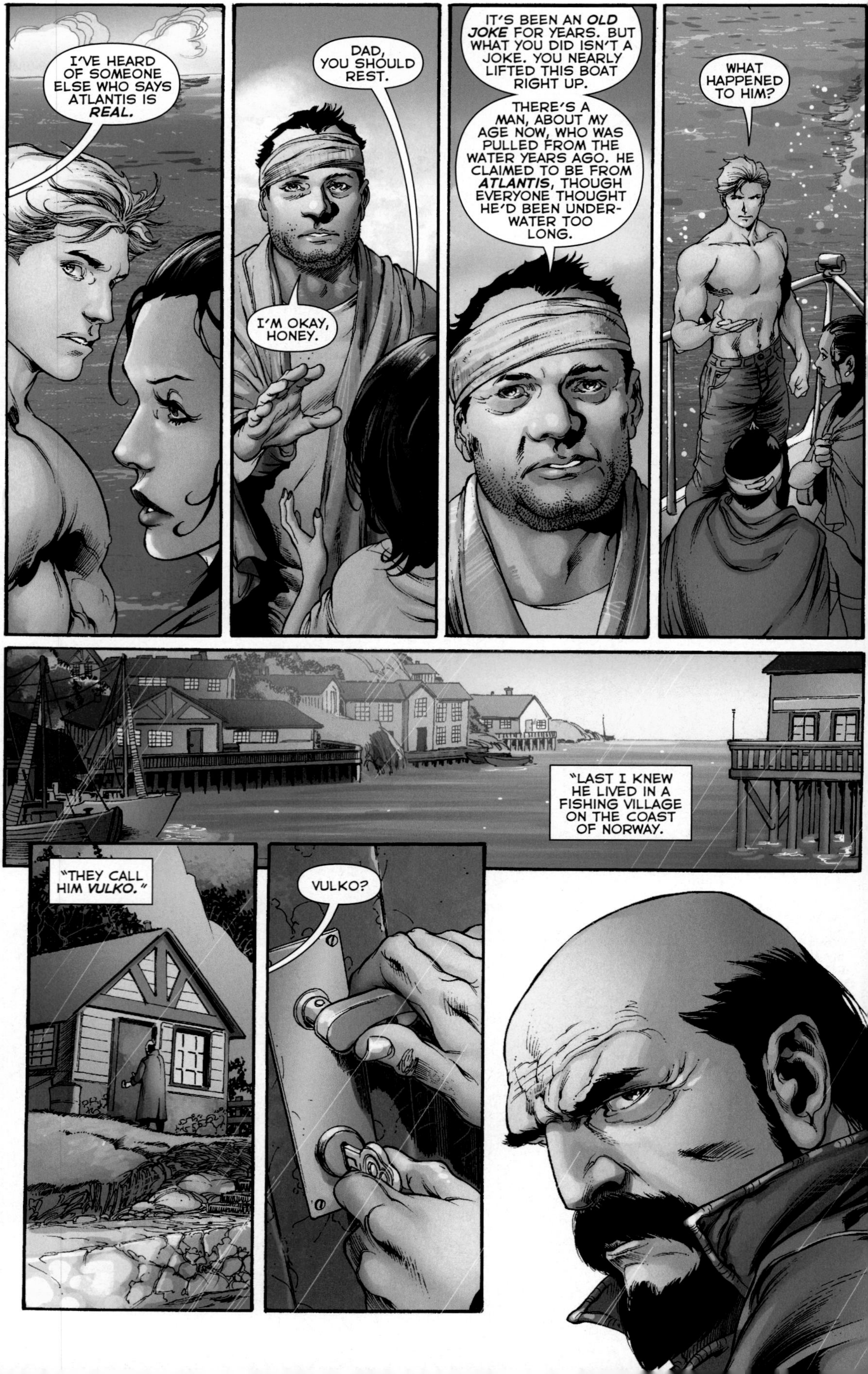
I'VE HEARD OF SOMEONE ELSE WHO SAYS ATLANTIS IS *REAL.*
DAD, YOU SHOULD REST.
I'M OKAY, HONEY.
IT'S BEEN AN *OLD JOKE* FOR YEARS. BUT WHAT YOU DID ISN'T A JOKE. YOU NEARLY LIFTED THIS BOAT RIGHT UP.
THERE'S A MAN, ABOUT MY AGE NOW, WHO WAS PULLED FROM THE WATER YEARS AGO. HE CLAIMED TO BE FROM *ATLANTIS*, THOUGH EVERYONE THOUGHT HE'D BEEN UNDER-WATER TOO LONG.
WHAT HAPPENED TO HIM?
"LAST I KNEW HE LIVED IN A FISHING VILLAGE ON THE COAST OF NORWAY.
"THEY CALL HIM *VULKO.*"
VULKO?

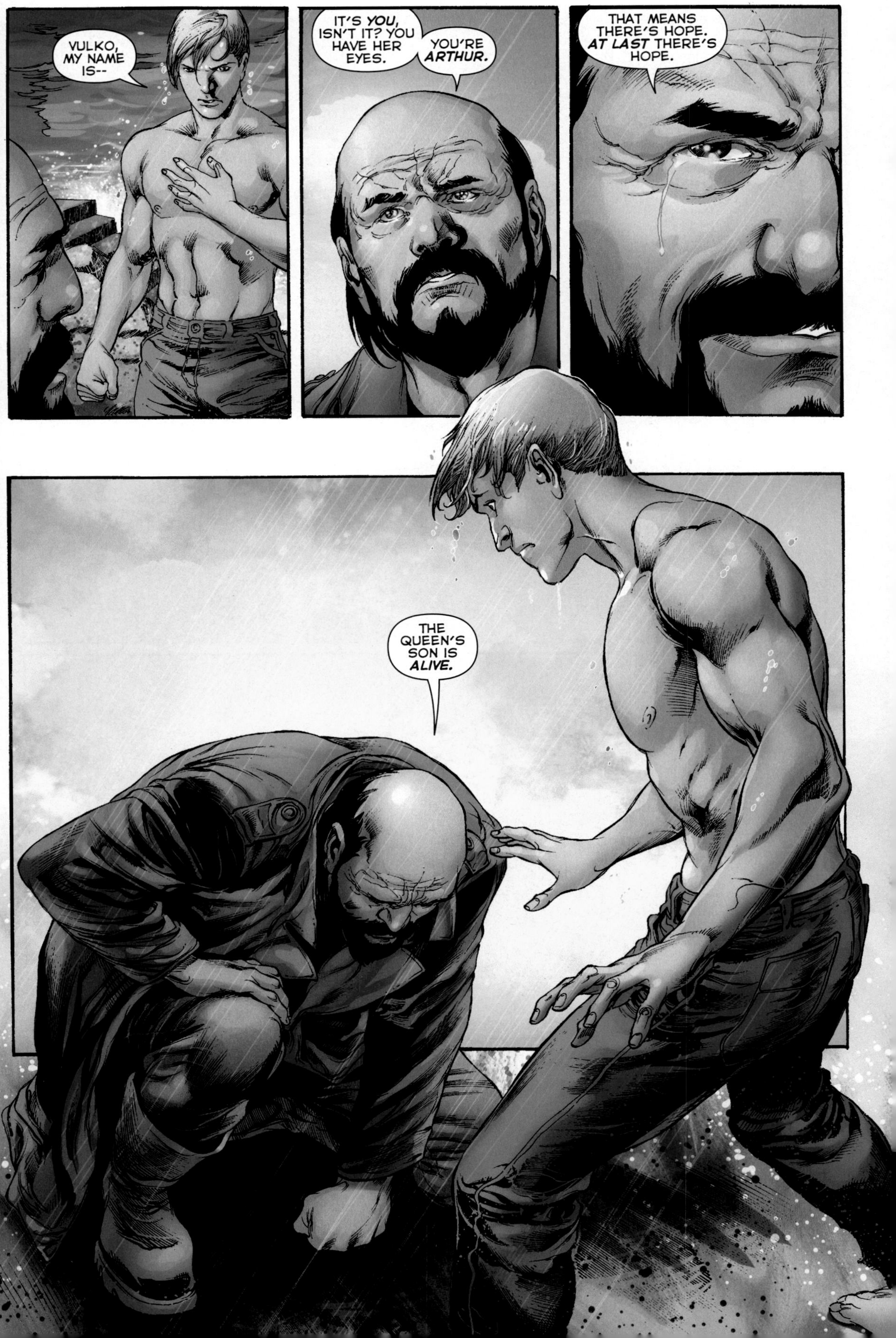
VULKO, MY NAME IS--
IT'S *YOU*, ISN'T IT? YOU HAVE HER EYES.
YOU'RE *ARTHUR.*
THAT MEANS THERE'S HOPE. *AT LAST* THERE'S HOPE.
THE QUEEN'S SON IS *ALIVE.*

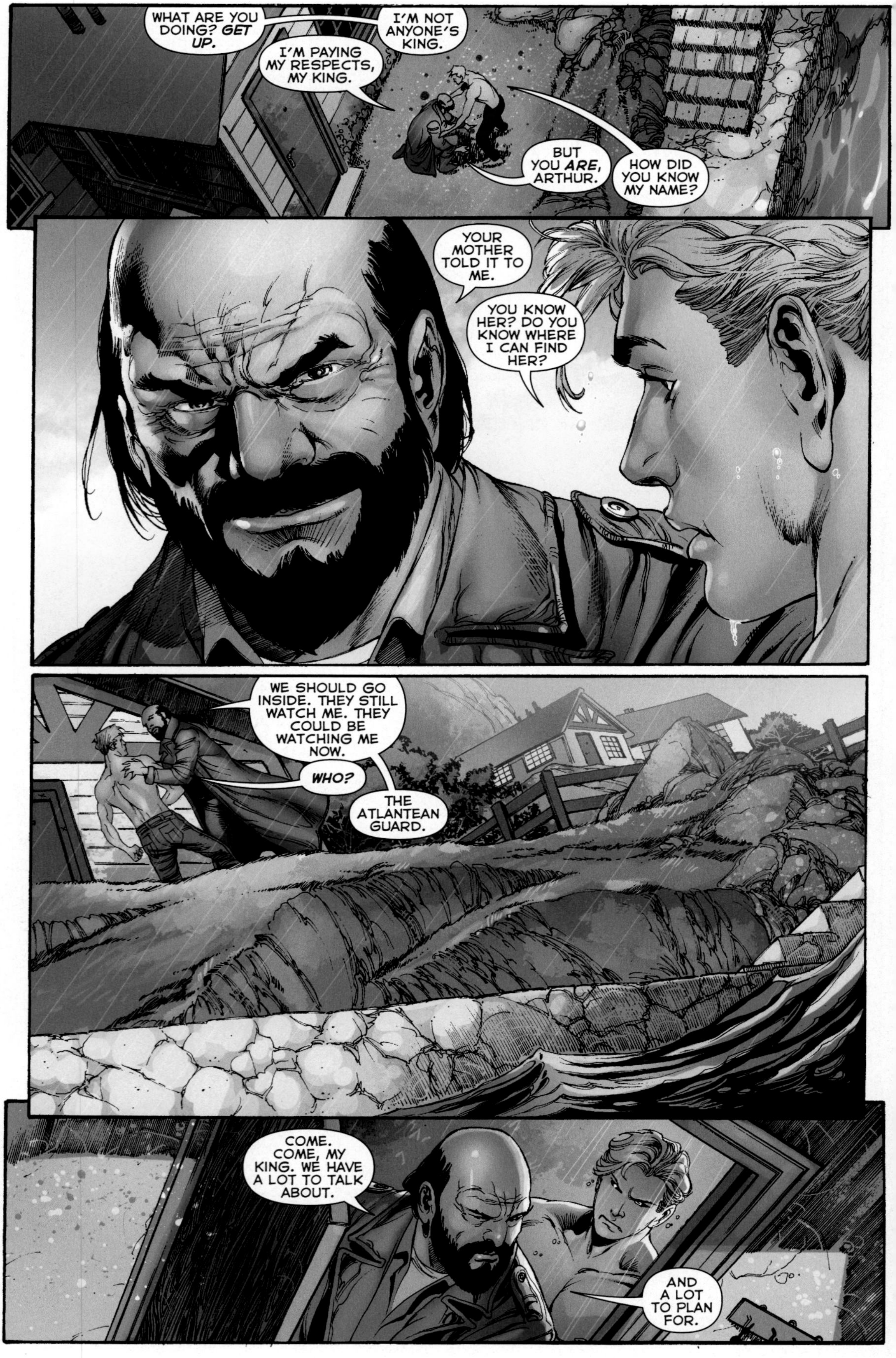
WHAT ARE YOU DOING? GET UP.
I'M PAYING MY RESPECTS, MY KING.
I'M NOT ANYONE'S KING.
BUT YOU ARE, ARTHUR.
HOW DID YOU KNOW MY NAME?
YOUR MOTHER TOLD IT TO ME.
YOU KNOW HER? DO YOU KNOW WHERE I CAN FIND HER?
WE SHOULD GO INSIDE. THEY STILL WATCH ME. THEY COULD BE WATCHING ME NOW.
WHO?
THE ATLANTEAN GUARD.
COME. COME, MY KING. WE HAVE A LOT TO TALK ABOUT.
AND A LOT TO PLAN FOR.

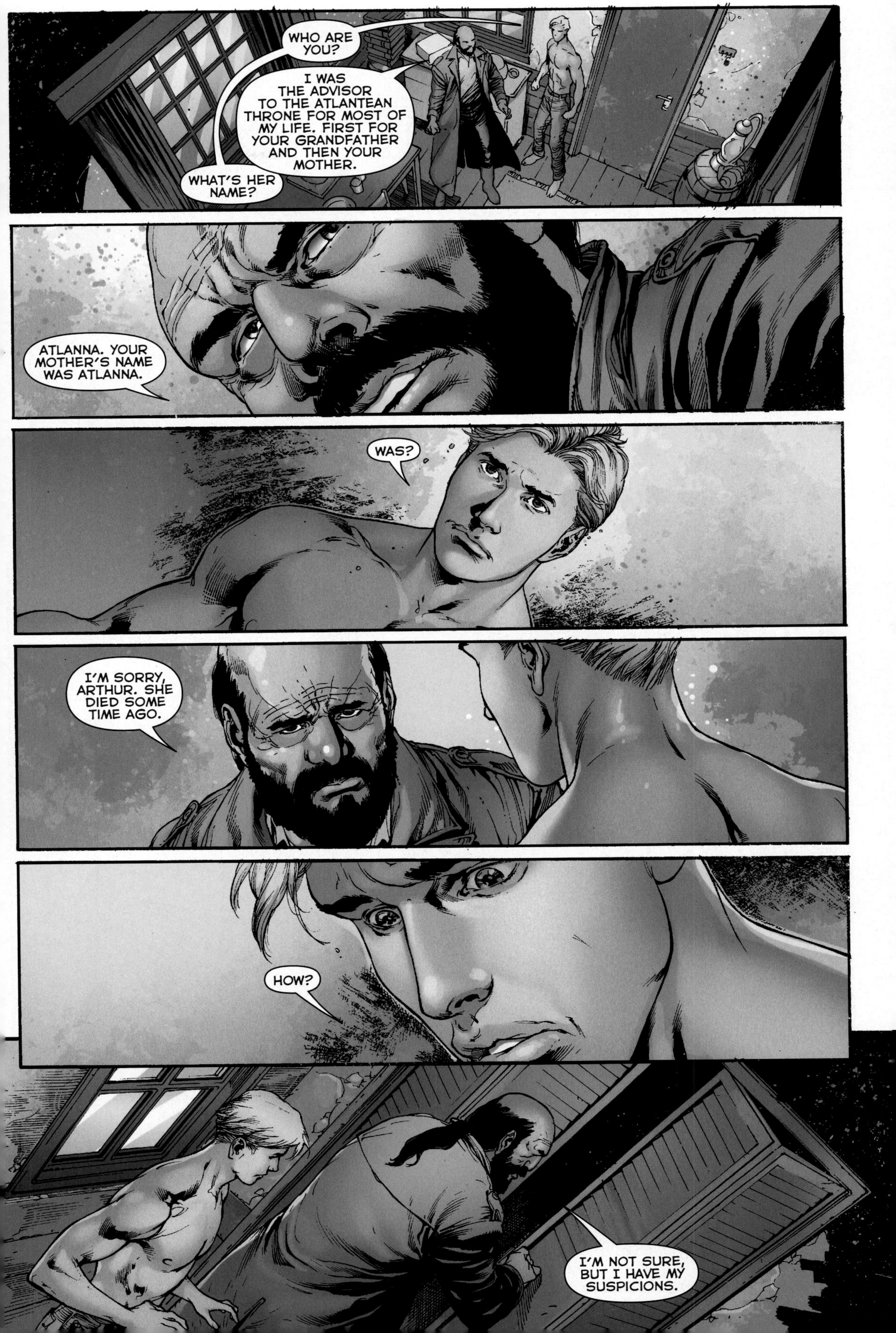
WHO ARE YOU?
I WAS THE ADVISOR TO THE ATLANTEAN THRONE FOR MOST OF MY LIFE. FIRST FOR YOUR GRANDFATHER AND THEN YOUR MOTHER.
WHAT'S HER NAME?
ATLANNA. YOUR MOTHER'S NAME WAS ATLANNA.
WAS?
I'M SORRY, ARTHUR. SHE DIED SOME TIME AGO.
HOW?
I'M NOT SURE, BUT I HAVE MY SUSPICIONS.

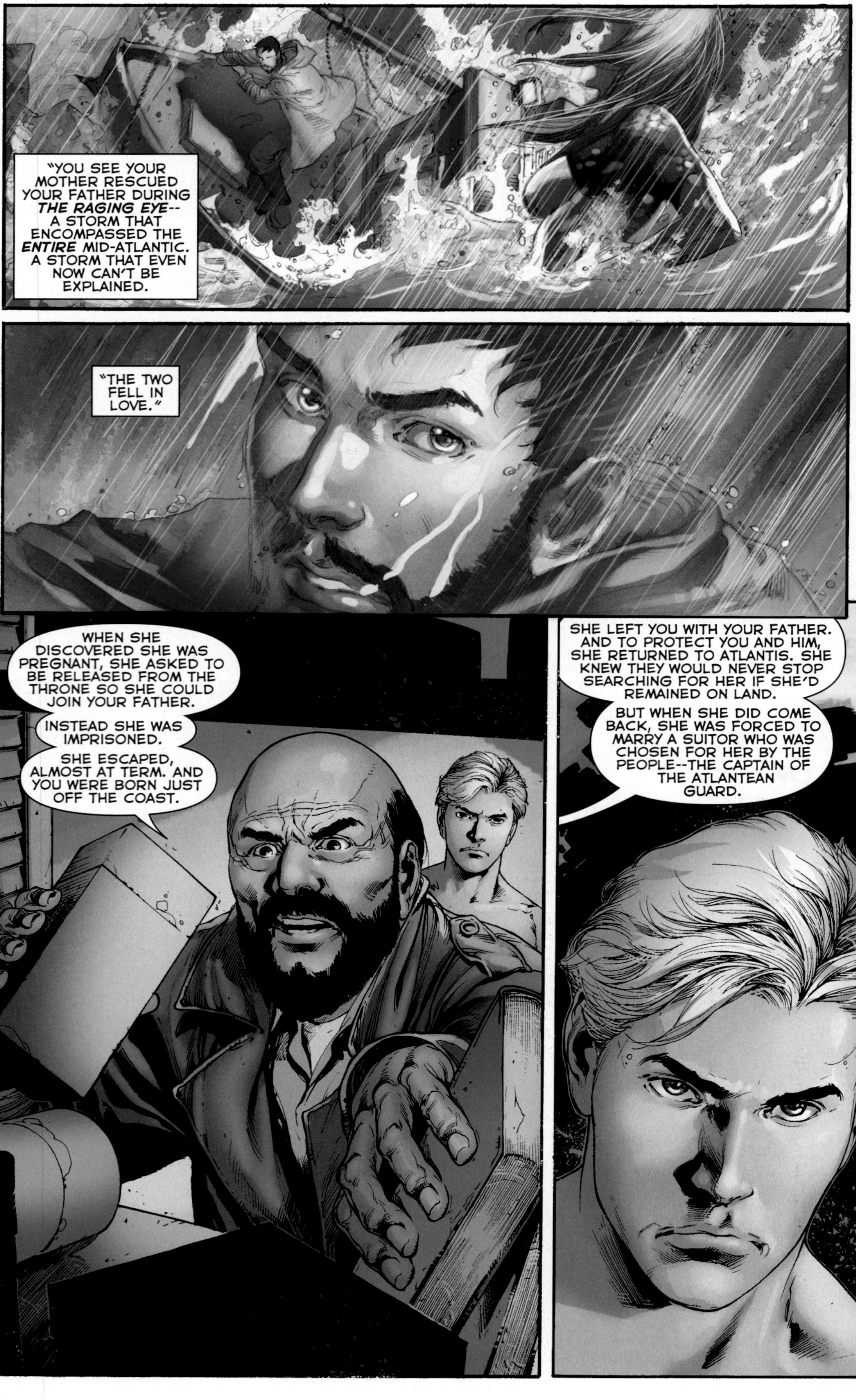

"YOU SEE YOUR MOTHER RESCUED YOUR FATHER DURING *THE RAGING EYE*-- A STORM THAT ENCOMPASSED THE *ENTIRE* MID-ATLANTIC. A STORM THAT EVEN NOW CAN'T BE EXPLAINED.
"THE TWO FELL IN LOVE."
WHEN SHE DISCOVERED SHE WAS PREGNANT, SHE ASKED TO BE RELEASED FROM THE THRONE SO SHE COULD JOIN YOUR FATHER.
INSTEAD SHE WAS IMPRISONED.
SHE ESCAPED, ALMOST AT TERM. AND YOU WERE BORN JUST OFF THE COAST.
SHE LEFT YOU WITH YOUR FATHER. AND TO PROTECT YOU AND HIM, SHE RETURNED TO ATLANTIS. SHE KNEW THEY WOULD NEVER STOP SEARCHING FOR HER IF SHE'D REMAINED ON LAND.
BUT WHEN SHE DID COME BACK, SHE WAS FORCED TO MARRY A SUITOR WHO WAS CHOSEN FOR HER BY THE PEOPLE--THE CAPTAIN OF THE ATLANTEAN GUARD.

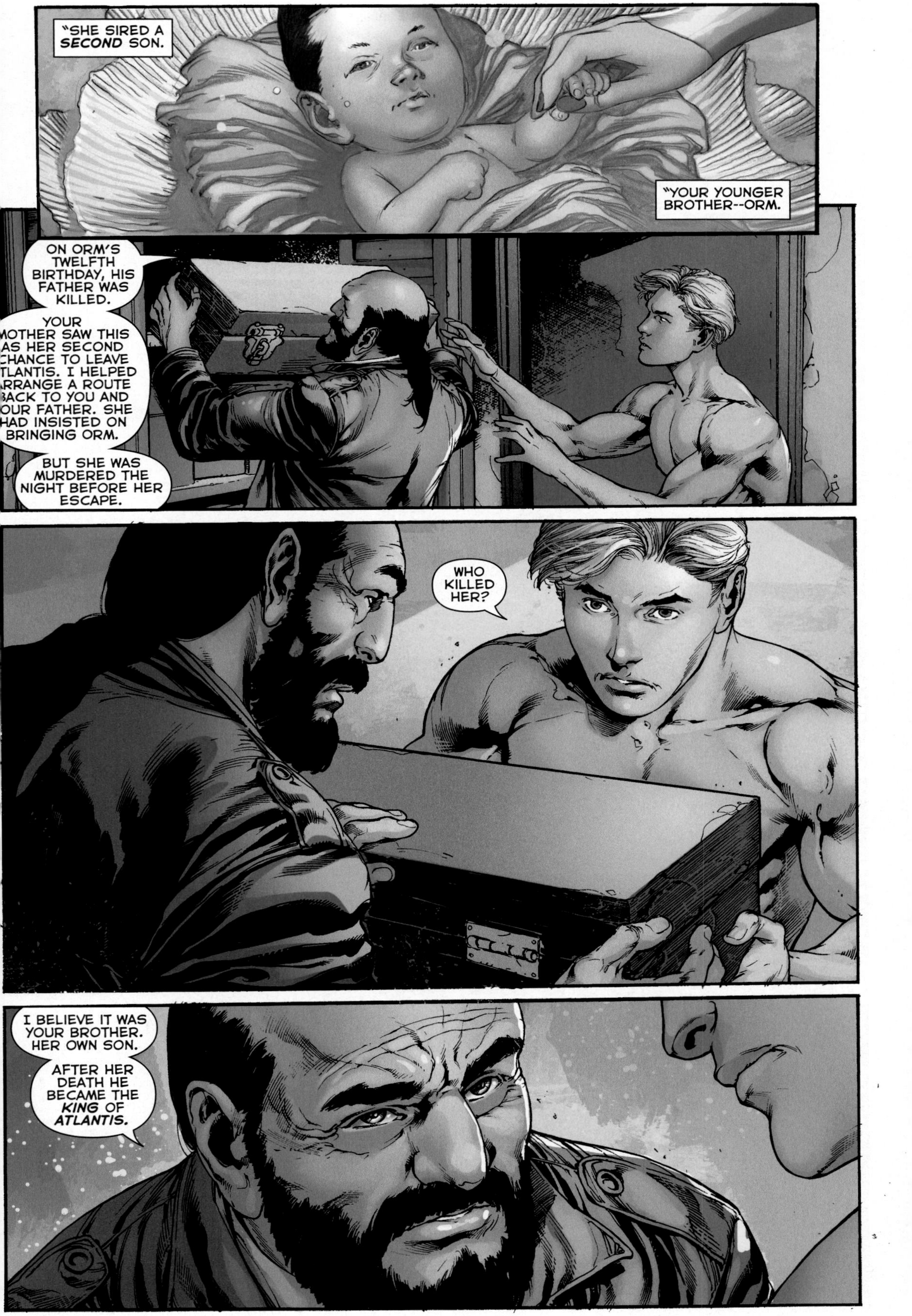
"SHE SIRED A SECOND SON.
"YOUR YOUNGER BROTHER--ORM.
ON ORM'S TWELFTH BIRTHDAY, HIS FATHER WAS KILLED.
YOUR MOTHER SAW THIS AS HER SECOND CHANCE TO LEAVE TLANTIS. I HELPED RRANGE A ROUTE BACK TO YOU AND OUR FATHER. SHE HAD INSISTED ON BRINGING ORM.
BUT SHE WAS MURDERED THE NIGHT BEFORE HER ESCAPE.
WHO KILLED HER?
I BELIEVE IT WAS YOUR BROTHER. HER OWN SON.
AFTER HER DEATH HE BECAME THE KING OF ATLANTIS.

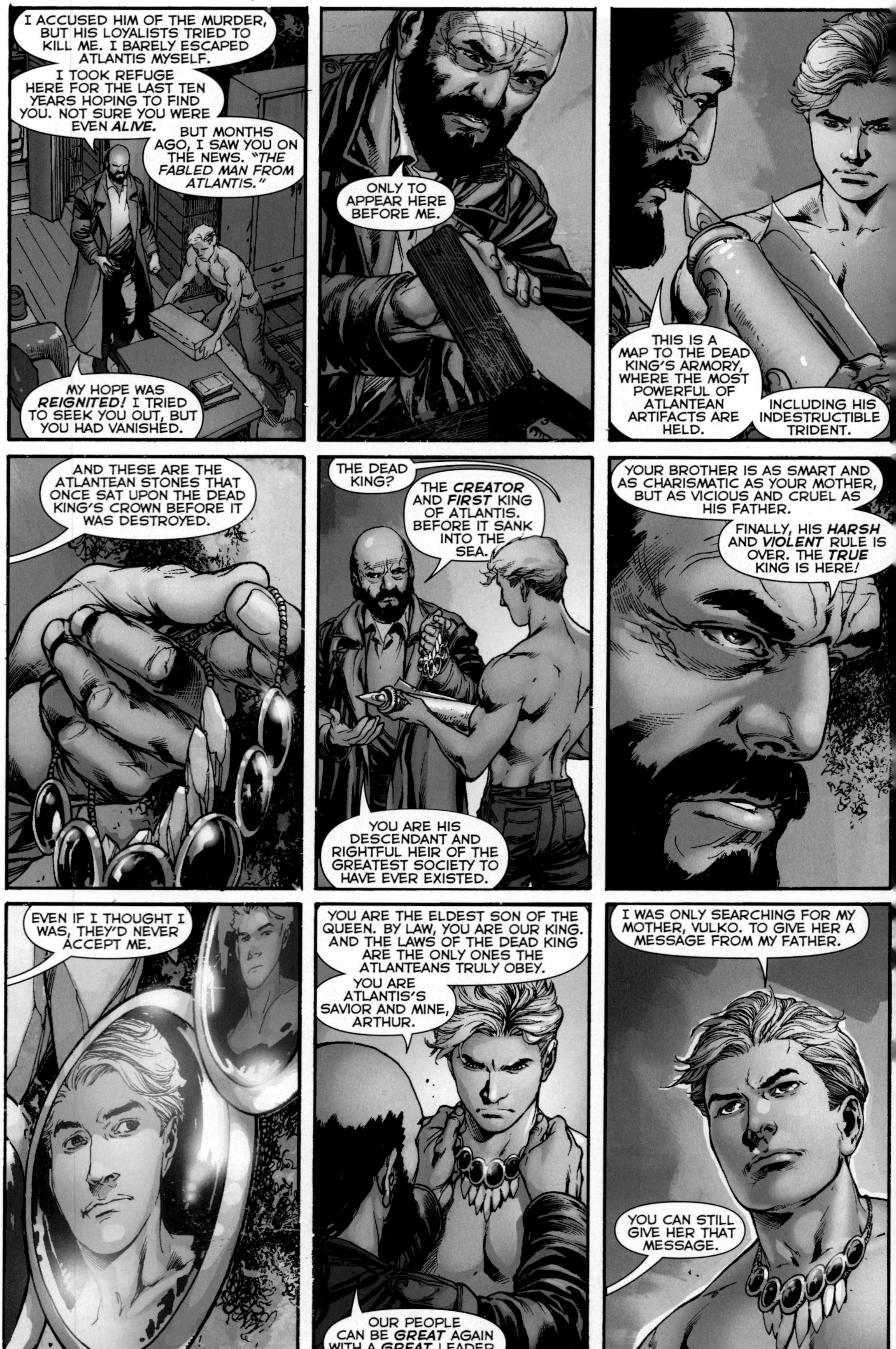
I ACCUSED HIM OF THE MURDER, BUT HIS LOYALISTS TRIED TO KILL ME. I BARELY ESCAPED ATLANTIS MYSELF.
I TOOK REFUGE HERE FOR THE LAST TEN YEARS HOPING TO FIND YOU. NOT SURE YOU WERE EVEN ALIVE.
BUT MONTHS AGO, I SAW YOU ON THE NEWS. "THE FABLED MAN FROM ATLANTIS."
MY HOPE WAS REIGNITED! I TRIED TO SEEK YOU OUT, BUT YOU HAD VANISHED.
ONLY TO APPEAR HERE BEFORE ME.
THIS IS A MAP TO THE DEAD KING'S ARMORY, WHERE THE MOST POWERFUL OF ATLANTEAN ARTIFACTS ARE HELD.
INCLUDING HIS INDESTRUCTIBLE TRIDENT.
AND THESE ARE THE ATLANTEAN STONES THAT ONCE SAT UPON THE DEAD KING'S CROWN BEFORE IT WAS DESTROYED.
THE DEAD KING?
THE CREATOR AND FIRST KING OF ATLANTIS. BEFORE IT SANK INTO THE SEA.
YOU ARE HIS DESCENDANT AND RIGHTFUL HEIR OF THE GREATEST SOCIETY TO HAVE EVER EXISTED.
YOUR BROTHER IS AS SMART AND AS CHARISMATIC AS YOUR MOTHER, BUT AS VICIOUS AND CRUEL AS HIS FATHER.
FINALLY, HIS HARSH AND VIOLENT RULE IS OVER. THE TRUE KING IS HERE!
EVEN IF I THOUGHT I WAS, THEY'D NEVER ACCEPT ME.
YOU ARE THE ELDEST SON OF THE QUEEN. BY LAW, YOU ARE OUR KING. AND THE LAWS OF THE DEAD KING ARE THE ONLY ONES THE ATLANTEANS TRULY OBEY.
YOU ARE ATLANTIS'S SAVIOR AND MINE, ARTHUR.
OUR PEOPLE CAN BE GREAT AGAIN WITH A GREAT LEADER.
I WAS ONLY SEARCHING FOR MY MOTHER, VULKO. TO GIVE HER A MESSAGE FROM MY FATHER.
YOU CAN STILL GIVE HER THAT MESSAGE.

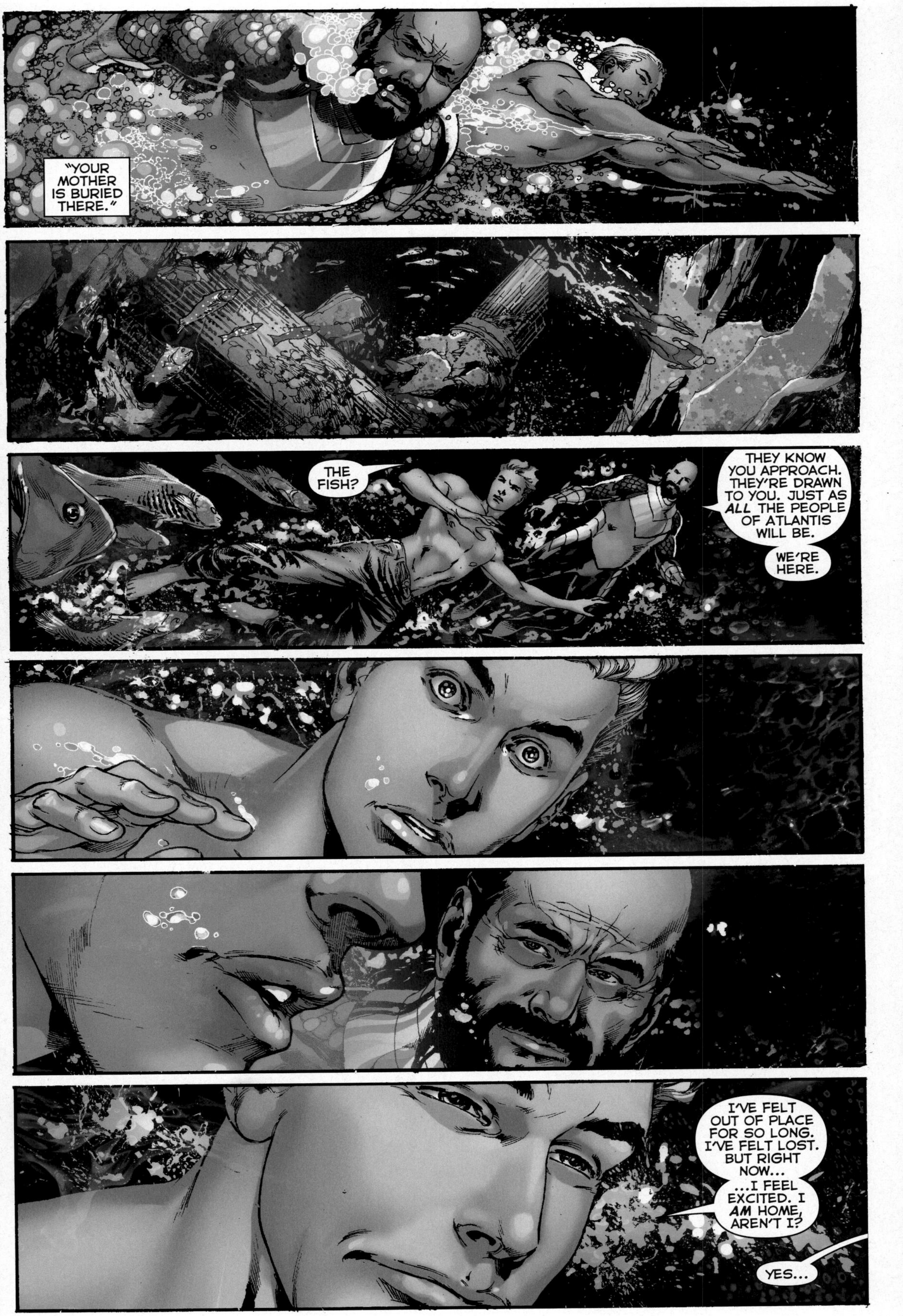
"YOUR MOTHER IS BURIED THERE."
THE FISH?
THEY KNOW YOU APPROACH. THEY'RE DRAWN TO YOU. JUST AS ALL THE PEOPLE OF ATLANTIS WILL BE.
WE'RE HERE.
I'VE FELT OUT OF PLACE FOR SO LONG. I'VE FELT LOST. BUT RIGHT NOW...
...I FEEL EXCITED. I AM HOME, AREN'T I?
YES...

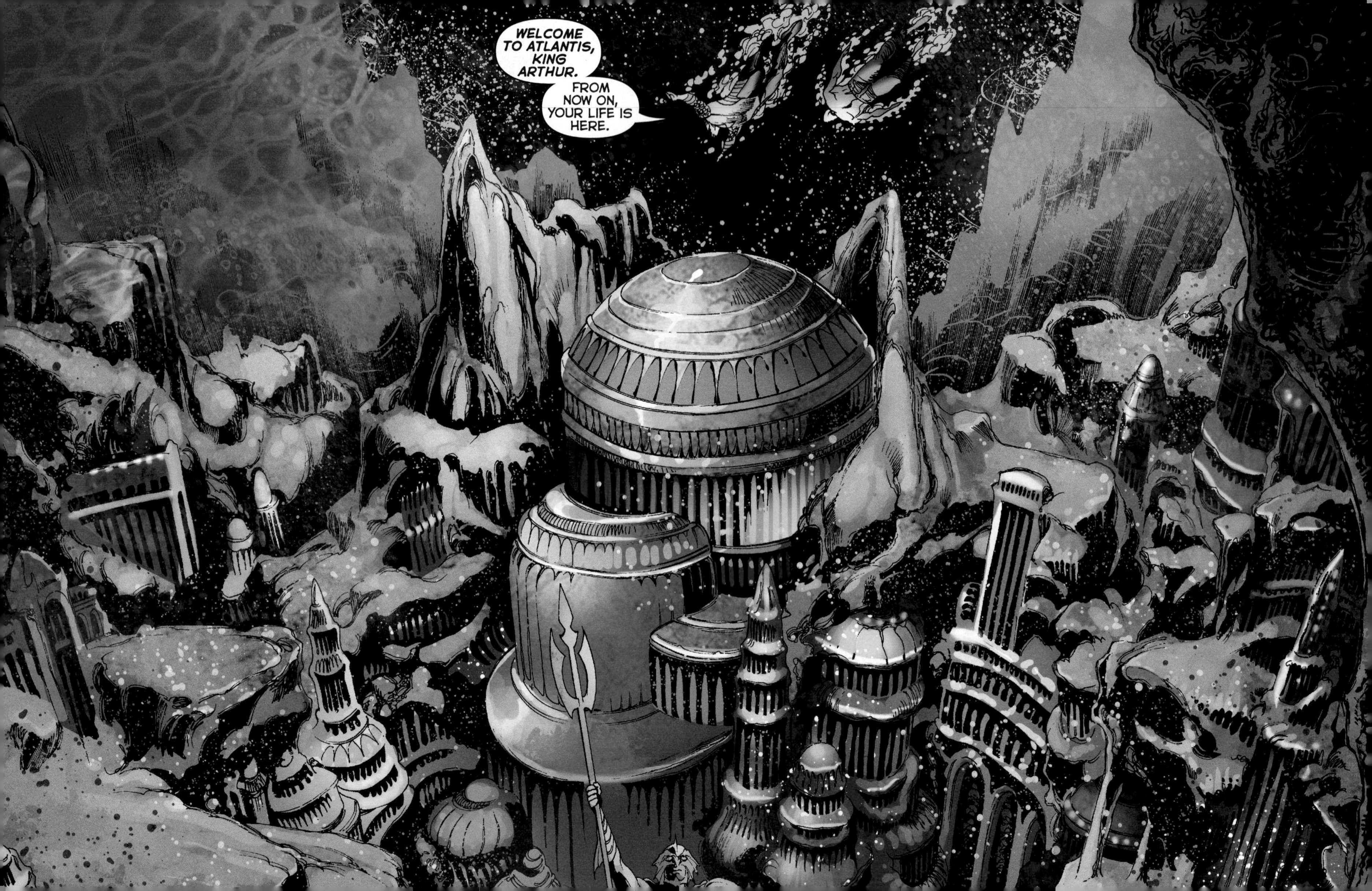
WELCOME TO ATLANTIS, KING ARTHUR.
FROM NOW ON, YOUR LIFE IS HERE.

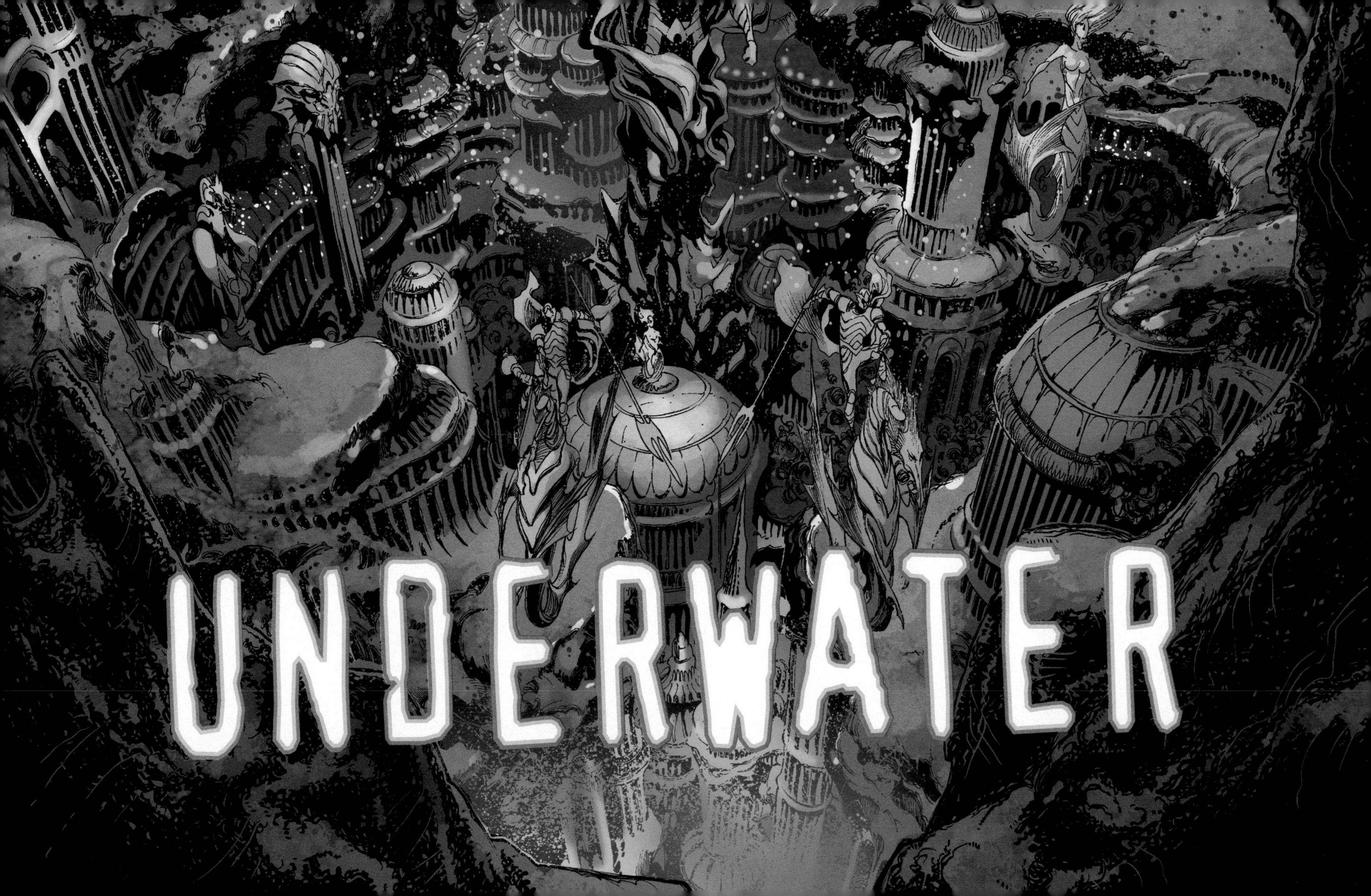
UNDERWATER

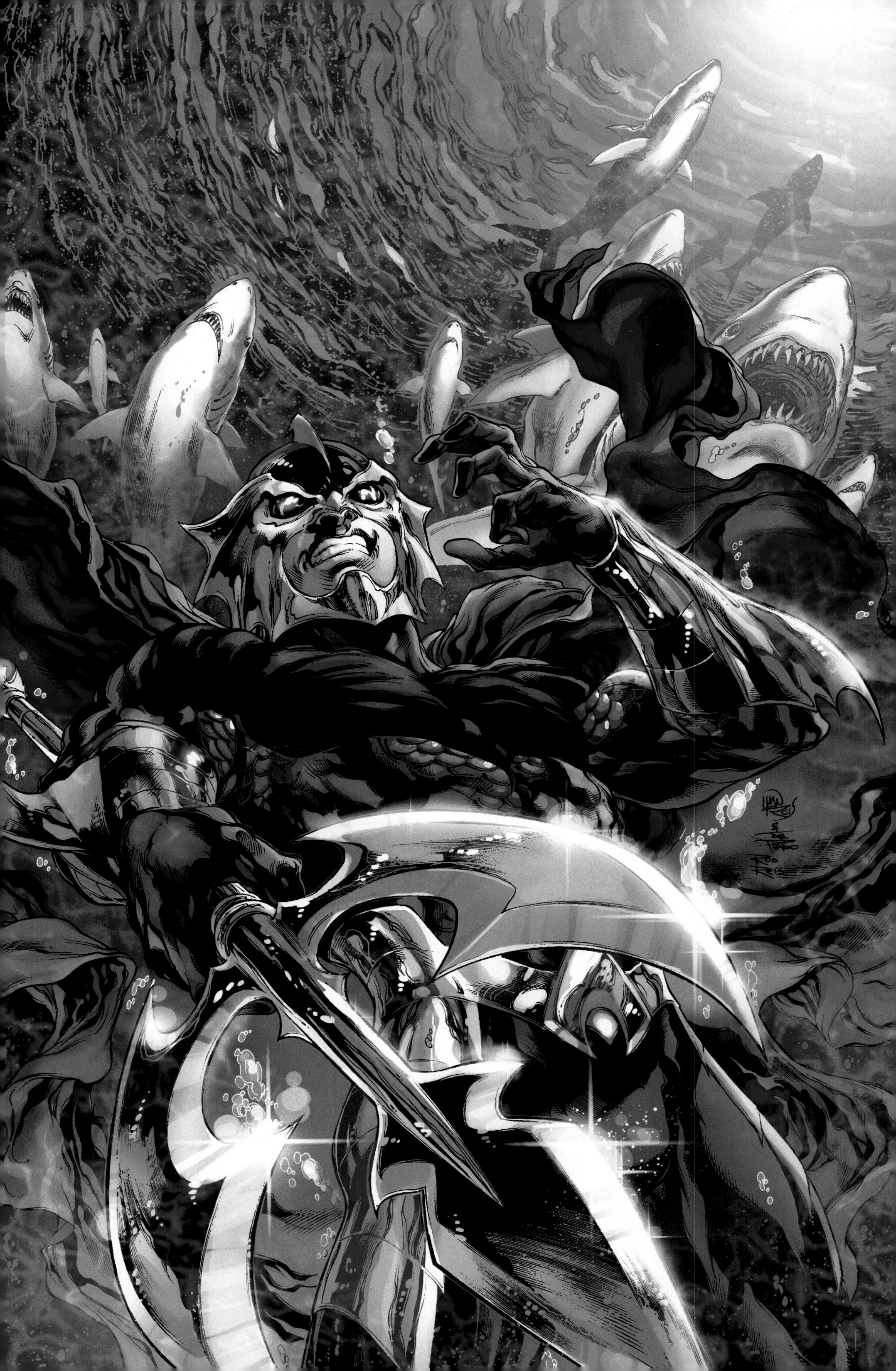

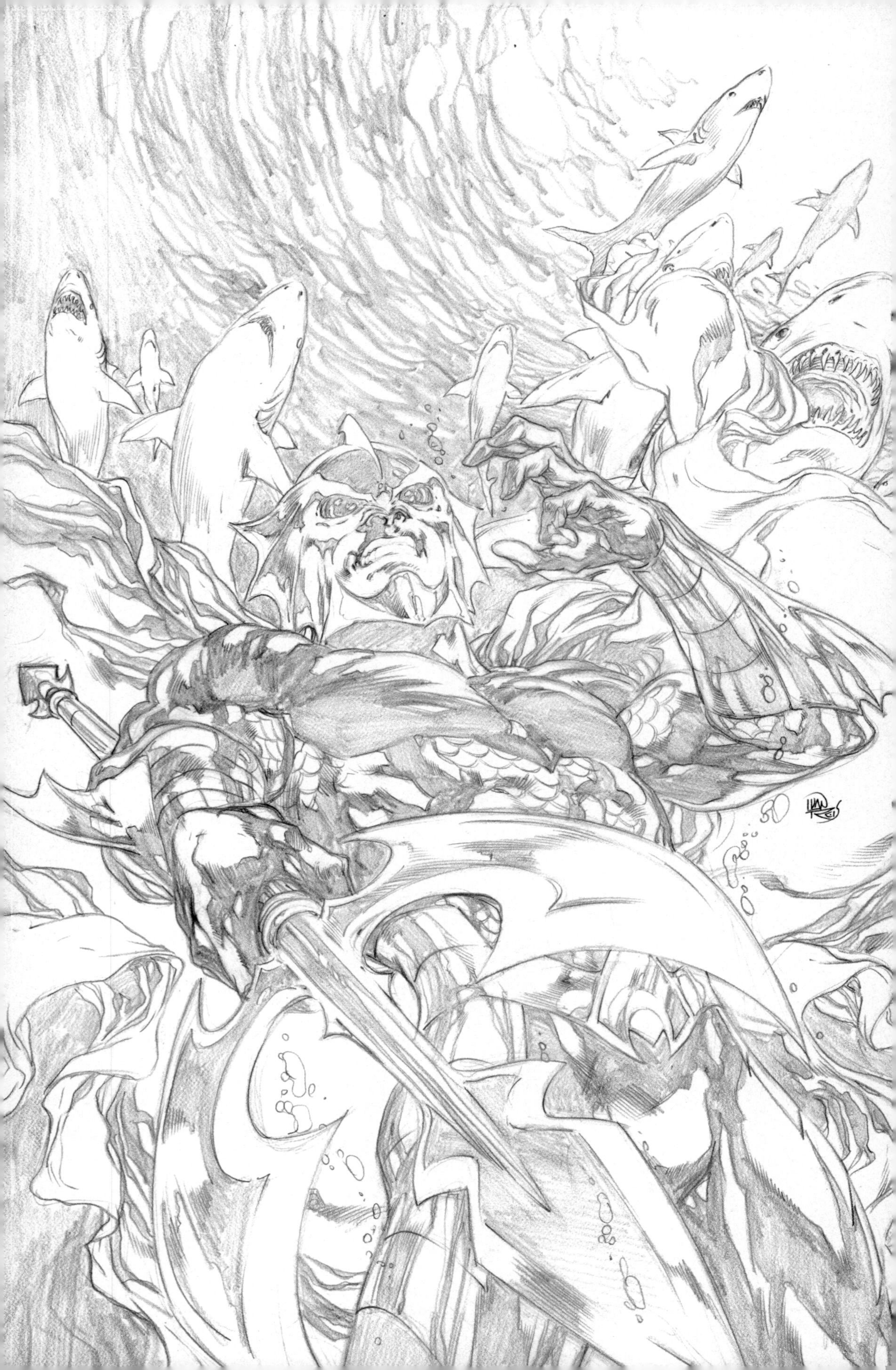

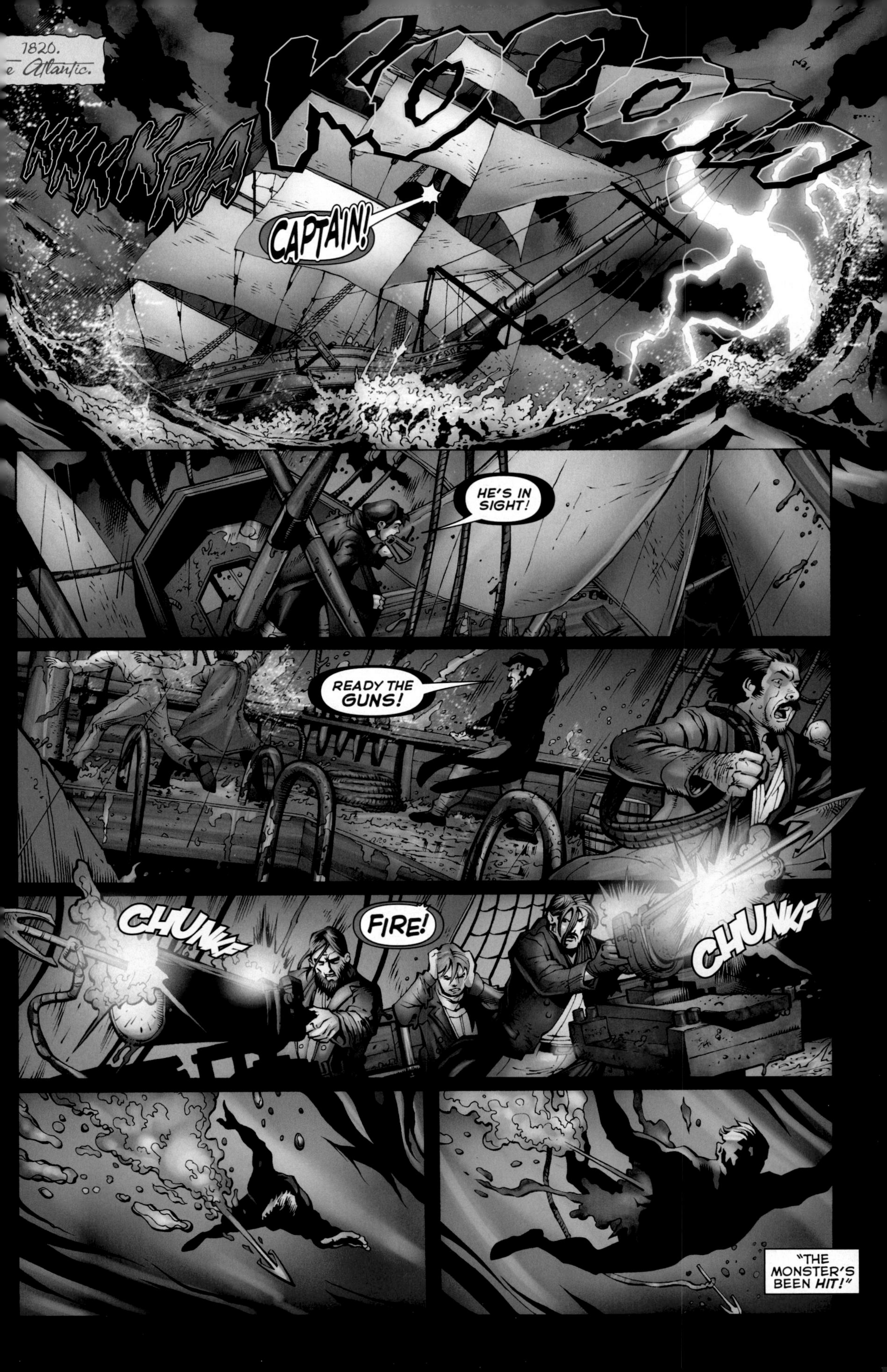
1820.
e Atlantic.
KKKKRA KOOOOOM
CAPTAIN!
HE'S IN SIGHT!
READY THE GUNS!
CHUNKF
FIRE!
CHUNKF
"THE MONSTER'S BEEN HIT!"

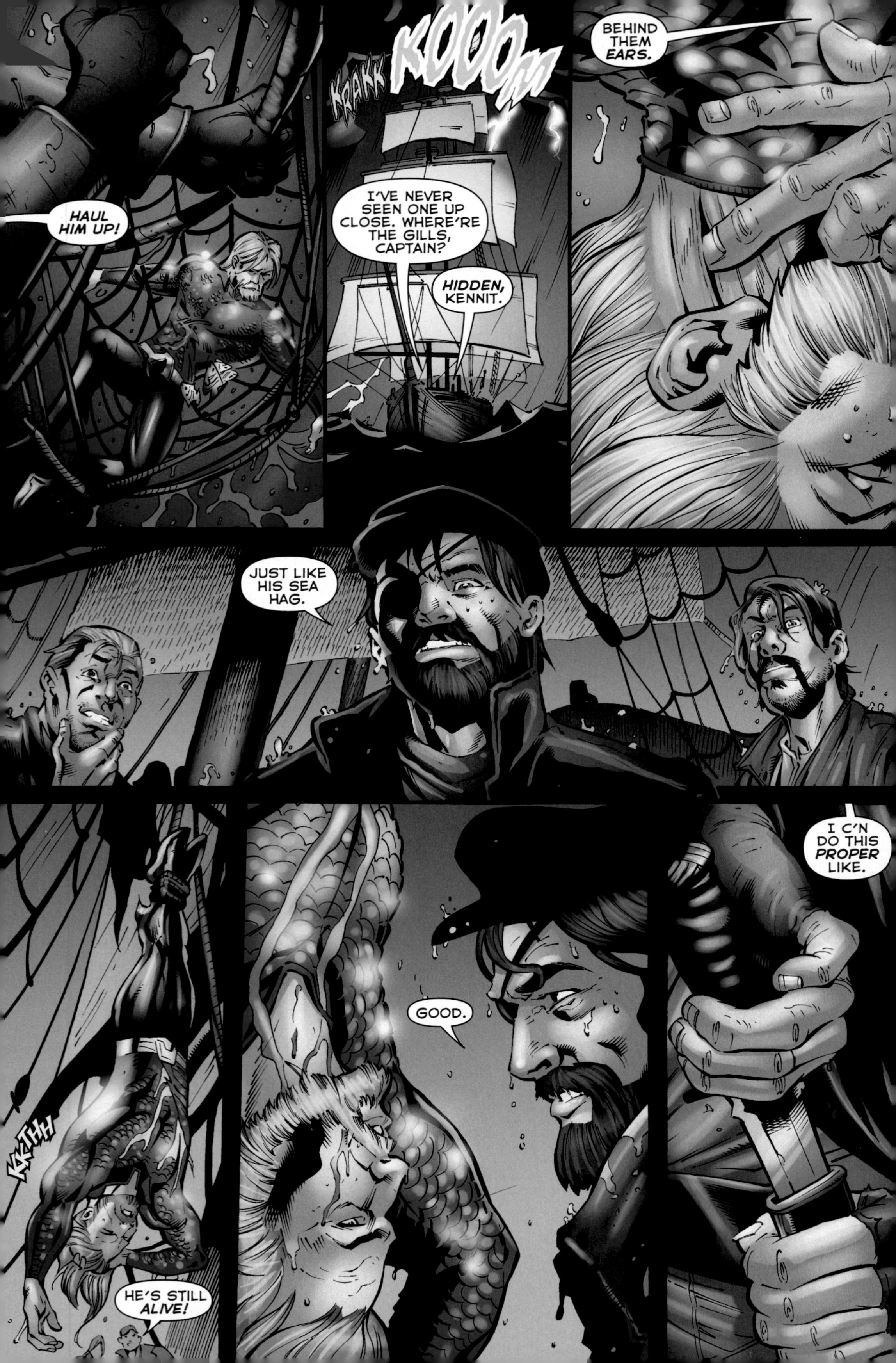
HAUL HIM UP!
KRAKK KOOOM
I'VE NEVER SEEN ONE UP CLOSE. WHERE'RE THE GILLS, CAPTAIN?
HIDDEN, KENNIT.
BEHIND THEM EARS.
JUST LIKE HIS SEA HAG.
KKTHH
HE'S STILL ALIVE!
GOOD.
I C'N DO THIS PROPER LIKE.

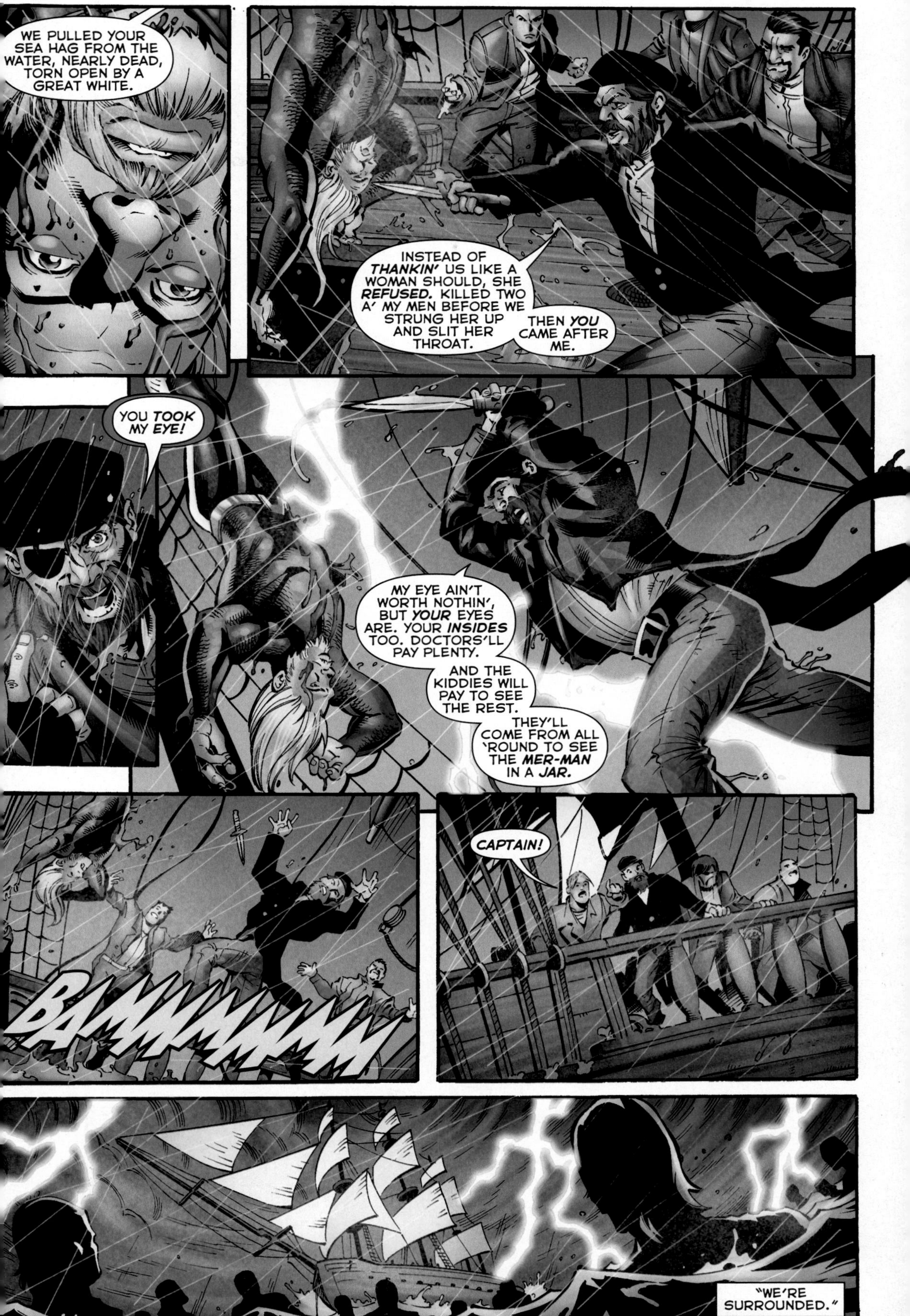
WE PULLED YOUR SEA HAG FROM THE WATER, NEARLY DEAD, TORN OPEN BY A GREAT WHITE.
INSTEAD OF THANKIN' US LIKE A WOMAN SHOULD, SHE REFUSED. KILLED TWO A' MY MEN BEFORE WE STRUNG HER UP AND SLIT HER THROAT.
THEN YOU CAME AFTER ME.
YOU TOOK MY EYE!
MY EYE AIN'T WORTH NOTHIN', BUT YOUR EYES ARE. YOUR INSIDES TOO. DOCTORS'LL PAY PLENTY.
AND THE KIDDIES WILL PAY TO SEE THE REST.
THEY'LL COME FROM ALL 'ROUND TO SEE THE MER-MAN IN A JAR.
BAMMMMMM
CAPTAIN!
"WE'RE SURROUNDED."

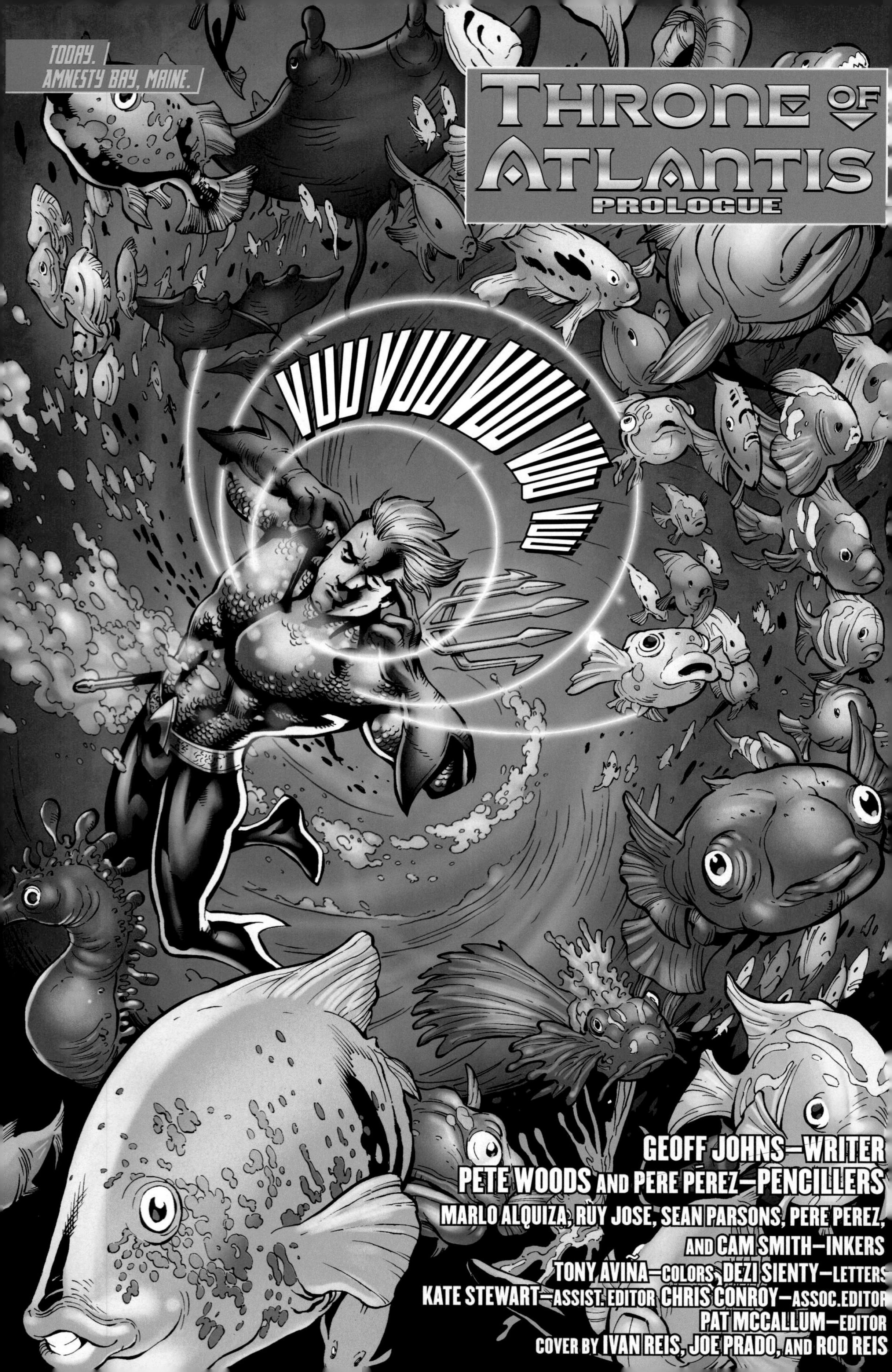
TODAY.
AMNESTY BAY, MAINE.
THRONE OF ATLANTIS
PROLOGUE
VUUVUUVUUVUUVUU
GEOFF JOHNS—WRITER
PETE WOODS AND PERE PÉREZ—PENCILLERS
MARLO ALQUIZA, RUY JOSE, SEAN PARSONS, PERE PEREZ,
AND CAM SMITH—INKERS
TONY AVIÑA—COLORS, DEZI SIENTY—LETTERS
KATE STEWART—ASSIST. EDITOR CHRIS CONROY—ASSOC.EDITOR
PAT MCCALLUM—EDITOR
COVER BY IVAN REIS, JOE PRADO, AND ROD REIS

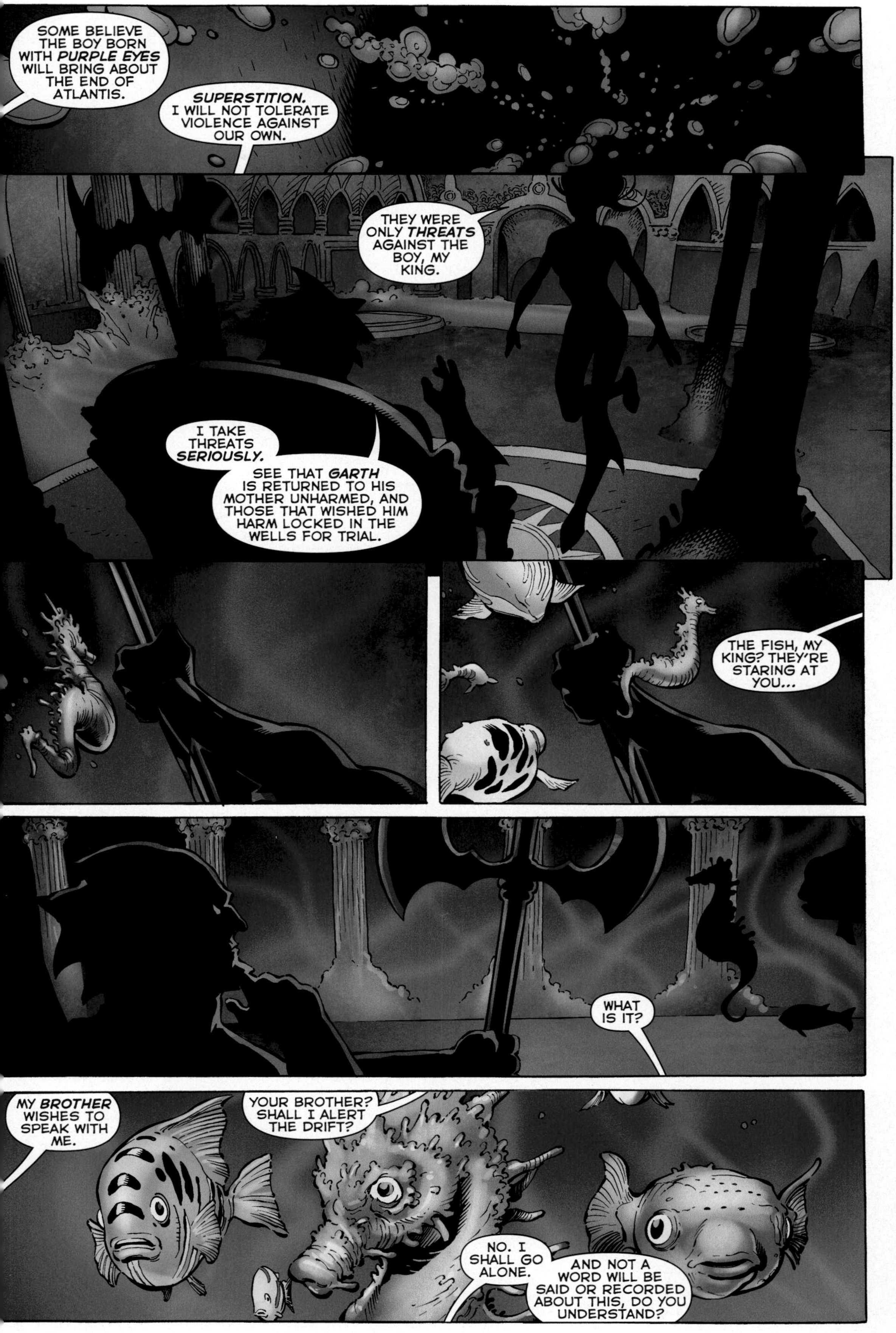
SOME BELIEVE THE BOY BORN WITH PURPLE EYES WILL BRING ABOUT THE END OF ATLANTIS.
SUPERSTITION. I WILL NOT TOLERATE VIOLENCE AGAINST OUR OWN.
THEY WERE ONLY THREATS AGAINST THE BOY, MY KING.
I TAKE THREATS SERIOUSLY.
SEE THAT GARTH IS RETURNED TO HIS MOTHER UNHARMED, AND THOSE THAT WISHED HIM HARM LOCKED IN THE WELLS FOR TRIAL.
THE FISH, MY KING? THEY'RE STARING AT YOU...
WHAT IS IT?
MY BROTHER WISHES TO SPEAK WITH ME.
YOUR BROTHER? SHALL I ALERT THE DRIFT?
NO. I SHALL GO ALONE.
AND NOT A WORD WILL BE SAID OR RECORDED ABOUT THIS, DO YOU UNDERSTAND?

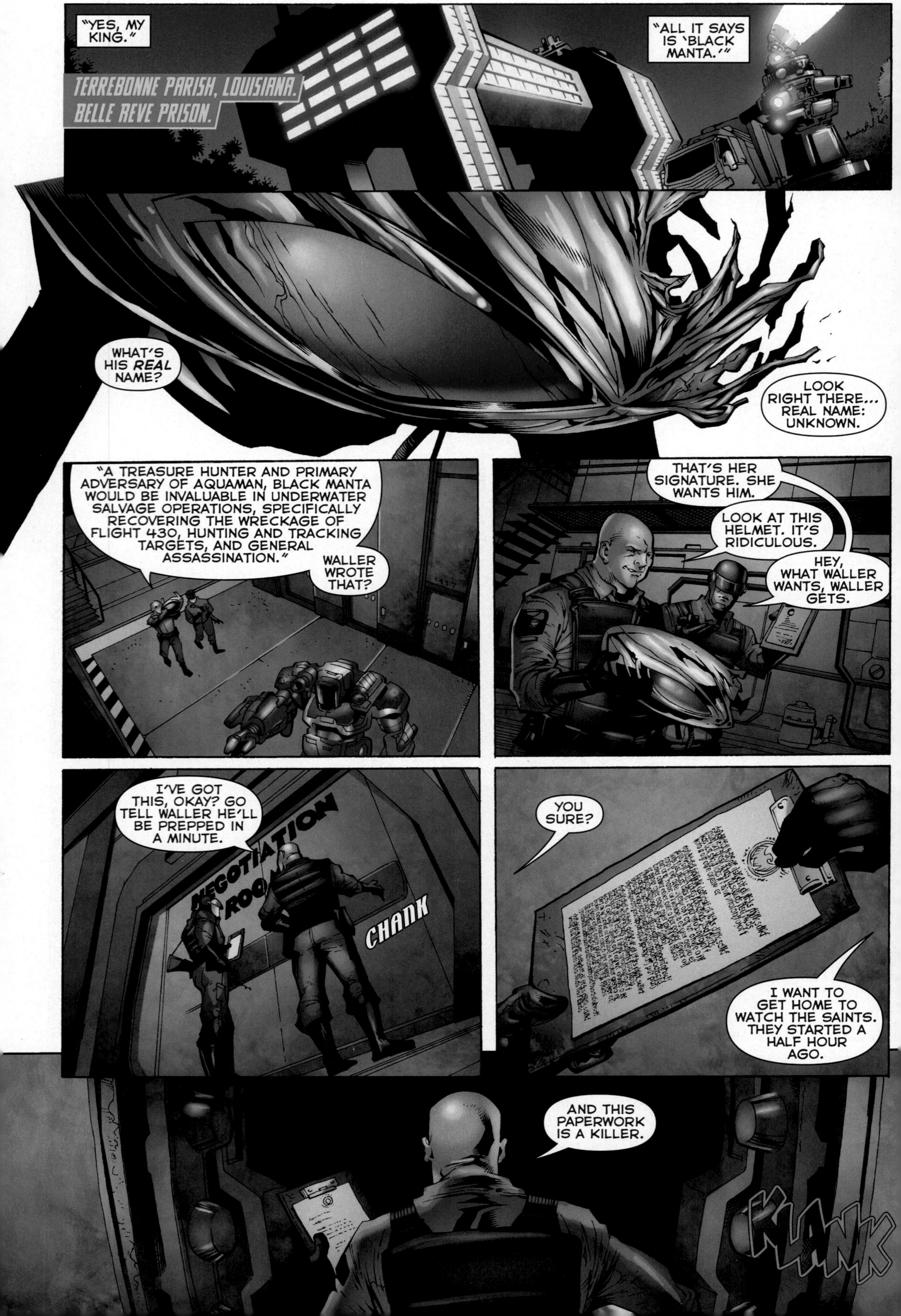
"YES, MY KING."
TERREBONNE PARISH, LOUISIANA. BELLE REVE PRISON.
"ALL IT SAYS IS 'BLACK MANTA.'"
WHAT'S HIS REAL NAME?
LOOK RIGHT THERE... REAL NAME: UNKNOWN.
"A TREASURE HUNTER AND PRIMARY ADVERSARY OF AQUAMAN, BLACK MANTA WOULD BE INVALUABLE IN UNDERWATER SALVAGE OPERATIONS, SPECIFICALLY RECOVERING THE WRECKAGE OF FLIGHT 430, HUNTING AND TRACKING TARGETS, AND GENERAL ASSASSINATION."
WALLER WROTE THAT?
THAT'S HER SIGNATURE. SHE WANTS HIM.
LOOK AT THIS HELMET. IT'S RIDICULOUS.
HEY, WHAT WALLER WANTS, WALLER GETS.
I'VE GOT THIS, OKAY? GO TELL WALLER HE'LL BE PREPPED IN A MINUTE.
NEGOTIATION ROOM
CHANK
YOU SURE?
I WANT TO GET HOME TO WATCH THE SAINTS. THEY STARTED A HALF HOUR AGO.
AND THIS PAPERWORK IS A KILLER.
KLANK

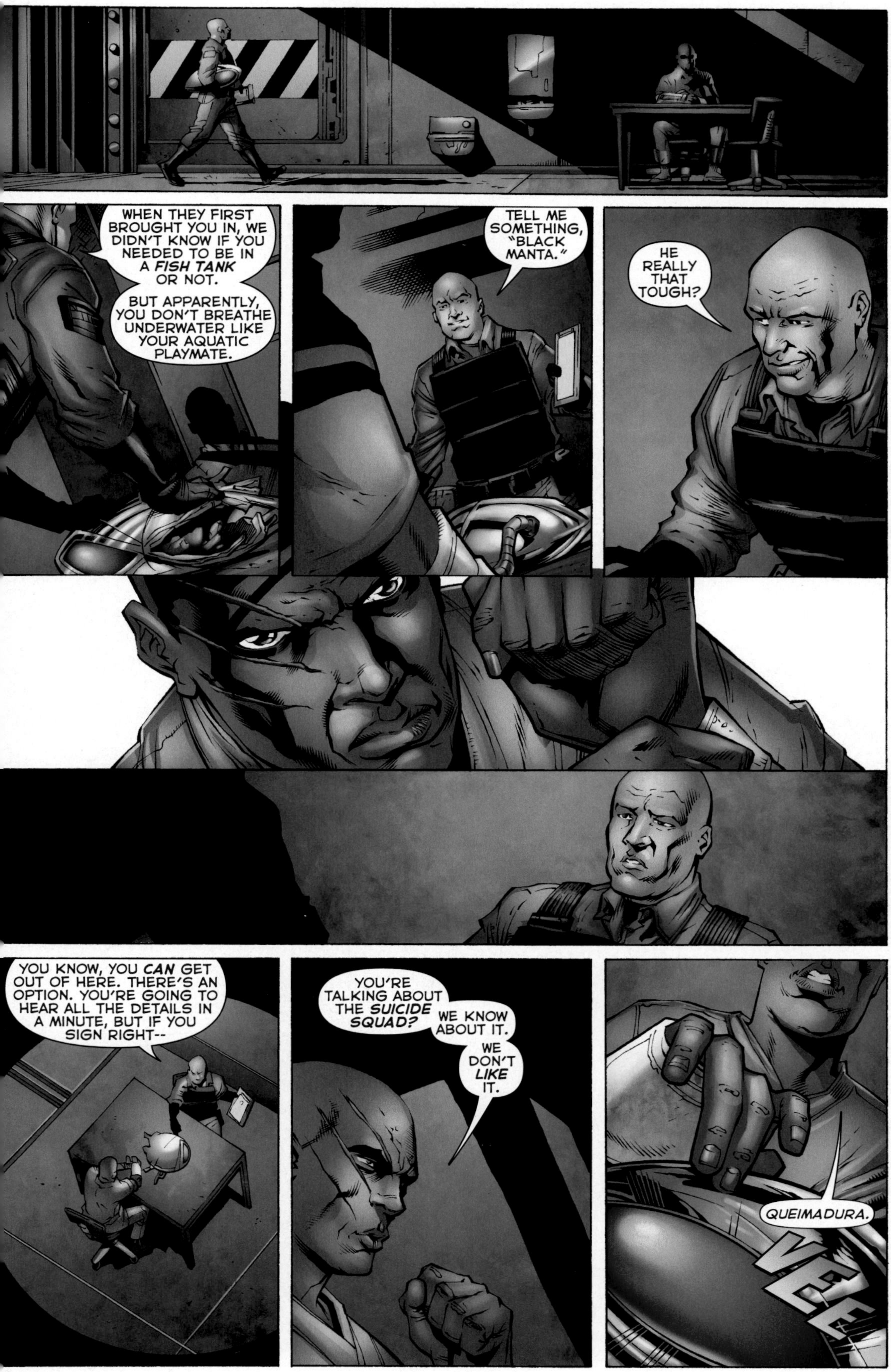
WHEN THEY FIRST BROUGHT YOU IN, WE DIDN'T KNOW IF YOU NEEDED TO BE IN A *FISH TANK* OR NOT.
BUT APPARENTLY, YOU DON'T BREATHE UNDERWATER LIKE YOUR AQUATIC PLAYMATE.
TELL ME SOMETHING, "BLACK MANTA."
HE REALLY THAT TOUGH?
YOU KNOW, YOU *CAN* GET OUT OF HERE. THERE'S AN OPTION. YOU'RE GOING TO HEAR ALL THE DETAILS IN A MINUTE, BUT IF YOU SIGN RIGHT--
YOU'RE TALKING ABOUT THE *SUICIDE SQUAD?*
WE KNOW ABOUT IT.
WE DON'T *LIKE* IT.
QUEIMADURA.
VEE

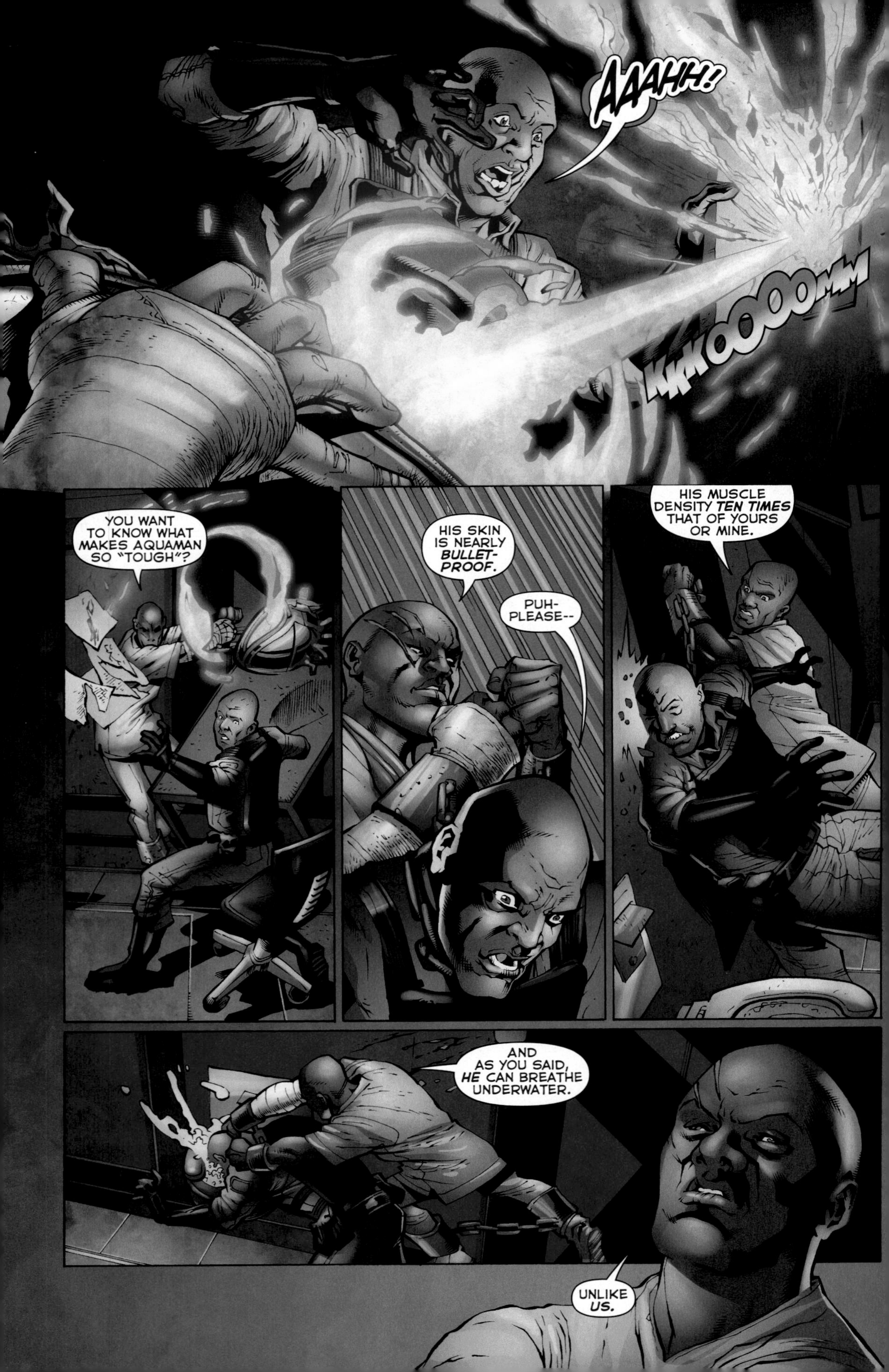

AAAHH!
KKKOOOOMMM
YOU WANT TO KNOW WHAT MAKES AQUAMAN SO "TOUGH"?
HIS SKIN IS NEARLY BULLET-PROOF.
PUH-PLEASE--
HIS MUSCLE DENSITY TEN TIMES THAT OF YOURS OR MINE.
AND AS YOU SAID, HE CAN BREATHE UNDERWATER.
UNLIKE US.

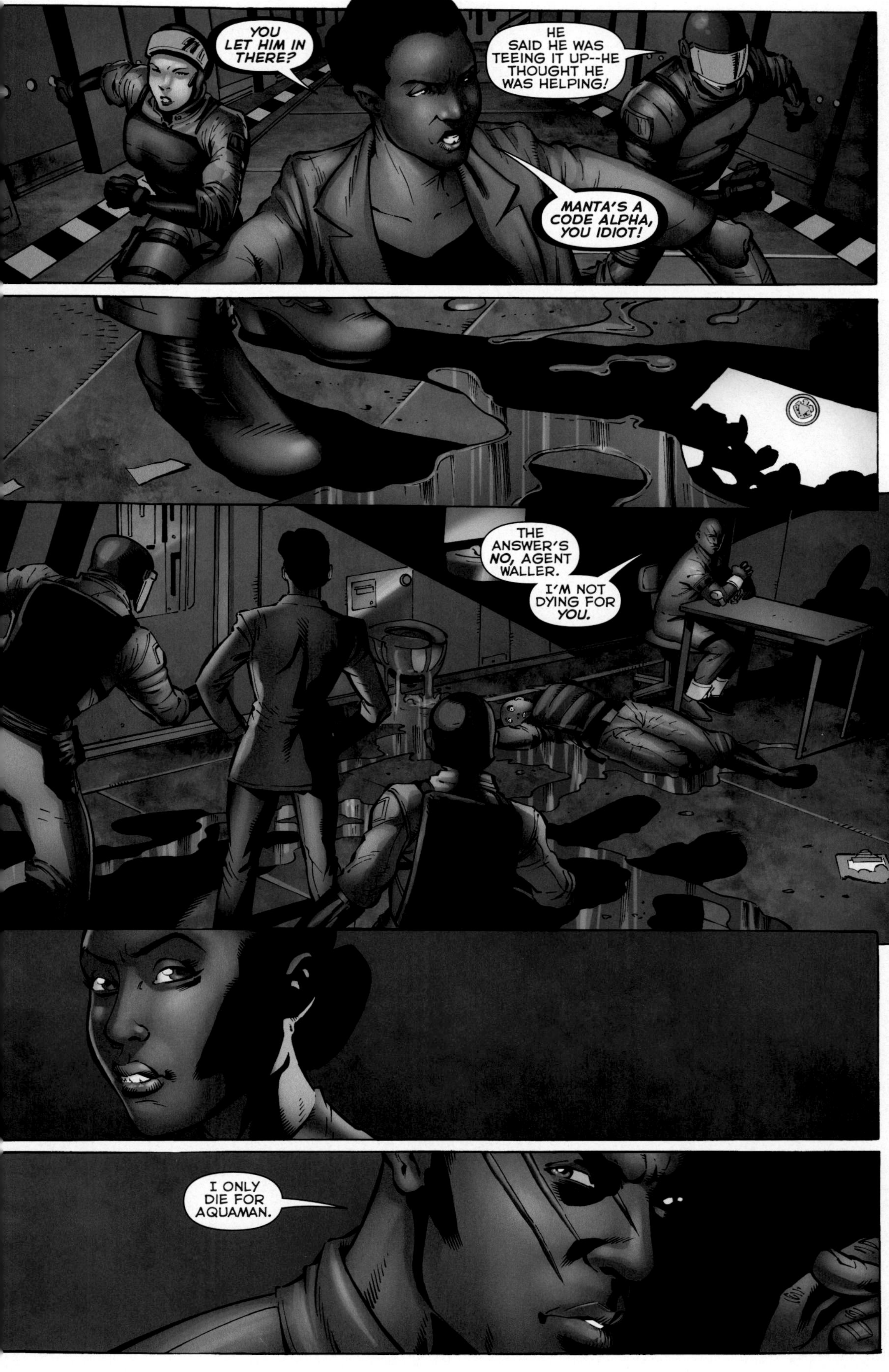
YOU LET HIM IN THERE?
HE SAID HE WAS TEEING IT UP--HE THOUGHT HE WAS HELPING!
MANTA'S A CODE ALPHA, YOU IDIOT!
THE ANSWER'S NO, AGENT WALLER. I'M NOT DYING FOR YOU.
I ONLY DIE FOR AQUAMAN.

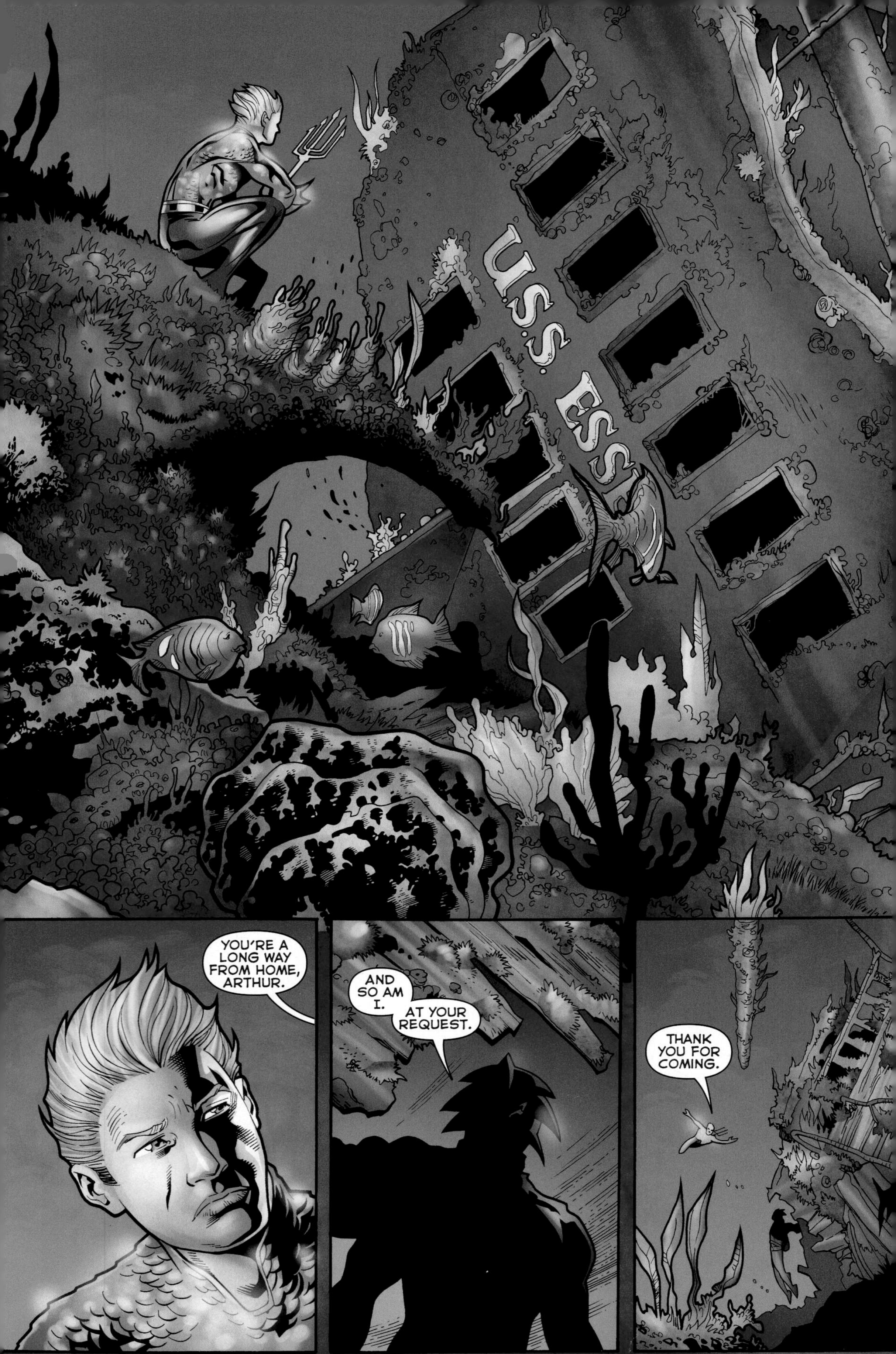
U.S.S. ESS
YOU'RE A LONG WAY FROM HOME, ARTHUR.
AND SO AM I.
AT YOUR REQUEST.
THANK YOU FOR COMING.

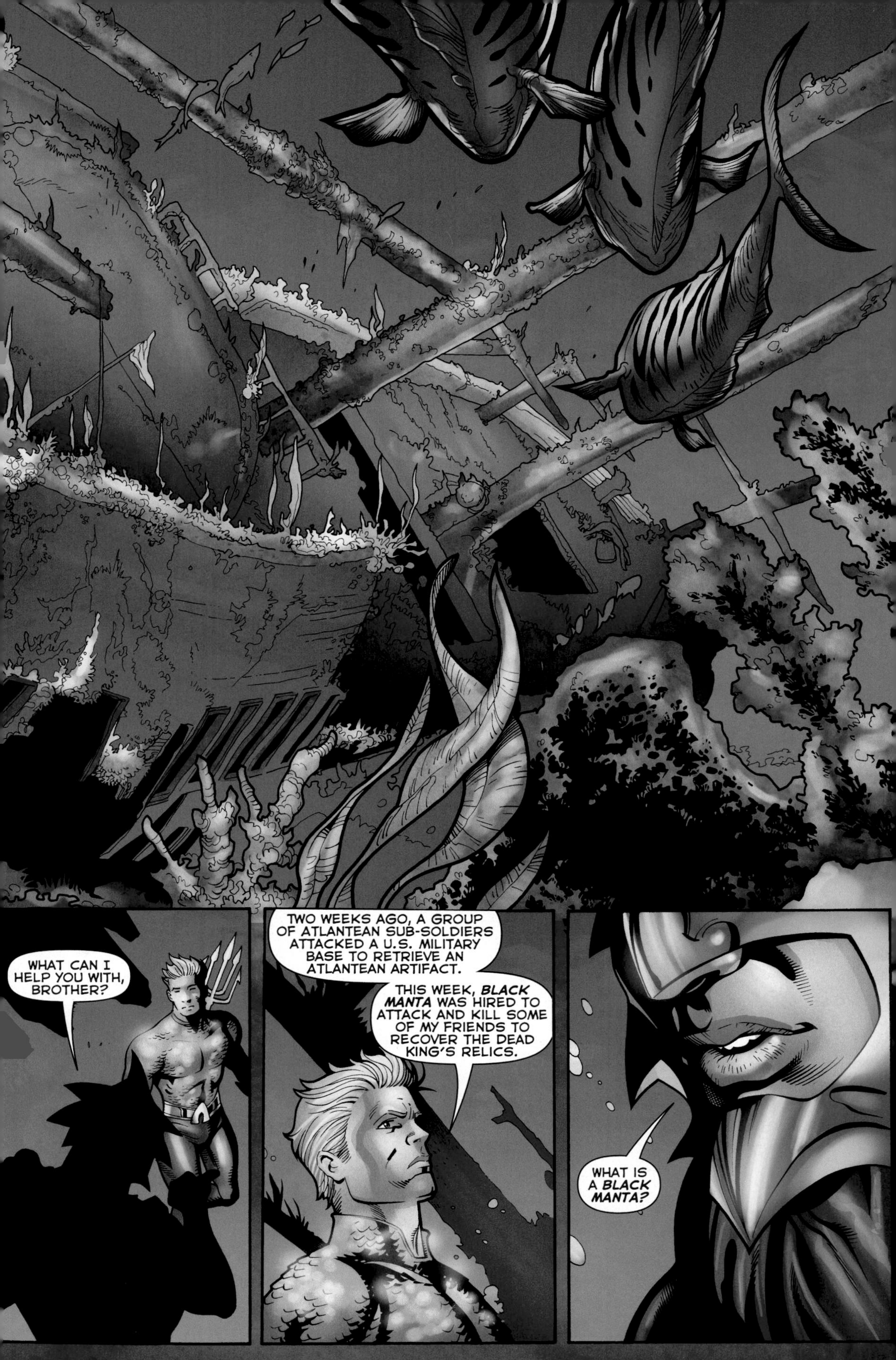
WHAT CAN I HELP YOU WITH, BROTHER?
TWO WEEKS AGO, A GROUP OF ATLANTEAN SUB-SOLDIERS ATTACKED A U.S. MILITARY BASE TO RETRIEVE AN ATLANTEAN ARTIFACT.
THIS WEEK, *BLACK MANTA* WAS HIRED TO ATTACK AND KILL SOME OF MY FRIENDS TO RECOVER THE DEAD KING'S RELICS.
WHAT IS A *BLACK MANTA?*

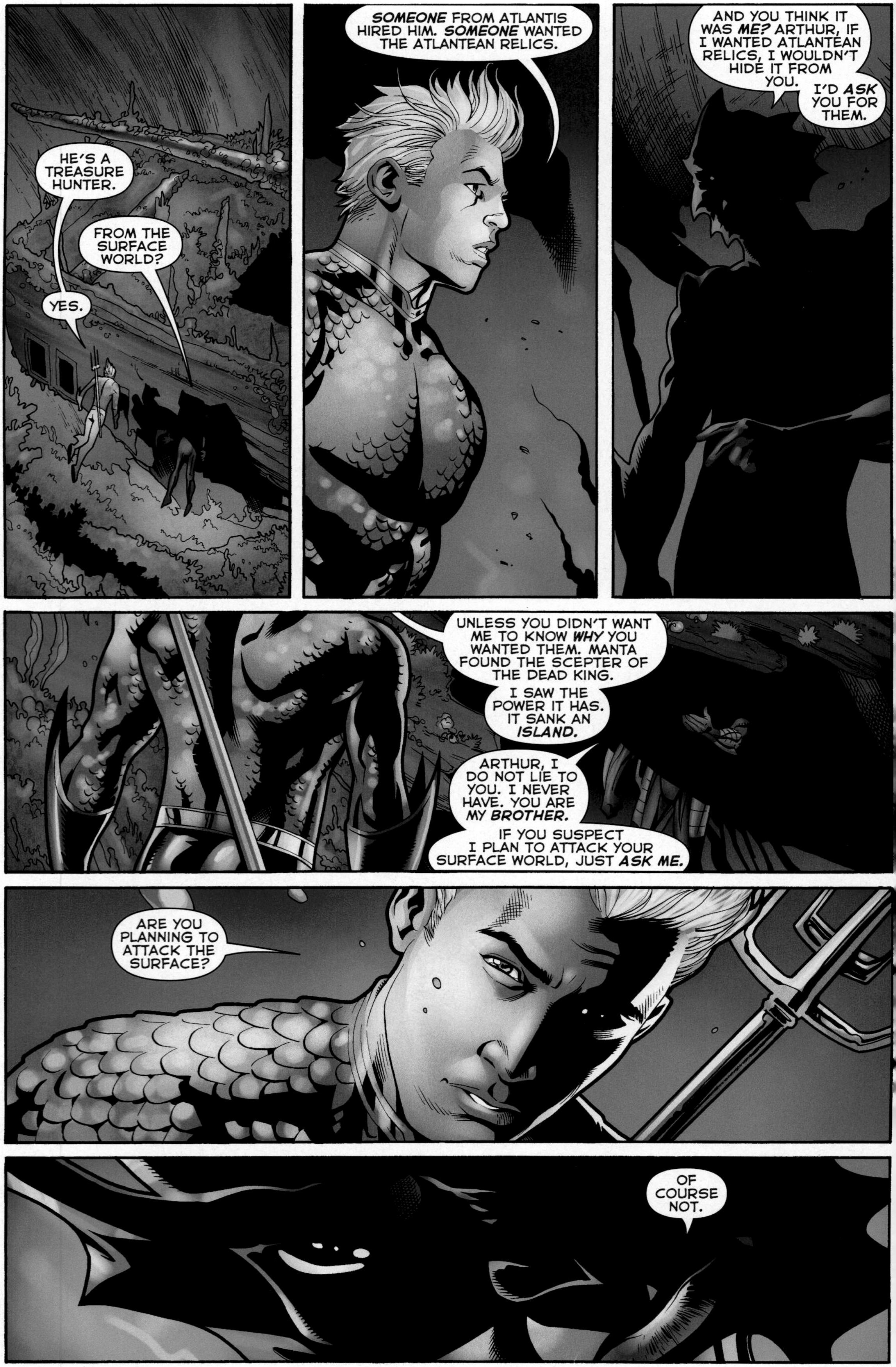
HE'S A TREASURE HUNTER.
FROM THE SURFACE WORLD?
YES.
SOMEONE FROM ATLANTIS HIRED HIM. SOMEONE WANTED THE ATLANTEAN RELICS.
AND YOU THINK IT WAS ME? ARTHUR, IF I WANTED ATLANTEAN RELICS, I WOULDN'T HIDE IT FROM YOU.
I'D ASK YOU FOR THEM.
UNLESS YOU DIDN'T WANT ME TO KNOW WHY YOU WANTED THEM. MANTA FOUND THE SCEPTER OF THE DEAD KING.
I SAW THE POWER IT HAS. IT SANK AN ISLAND.
ARTHUR, I DO NOT LIE TO YOU. I NEVER HAVE. YOU ARE MY BROTHER.
IF YOU SUSPECT I PLAN TO ATTACK YOUR SURFACE WORLD, JUST ASK ME.
ARE YOU PLANNING TO ATTACK THE SURFACE?
OF COURSE NOT.

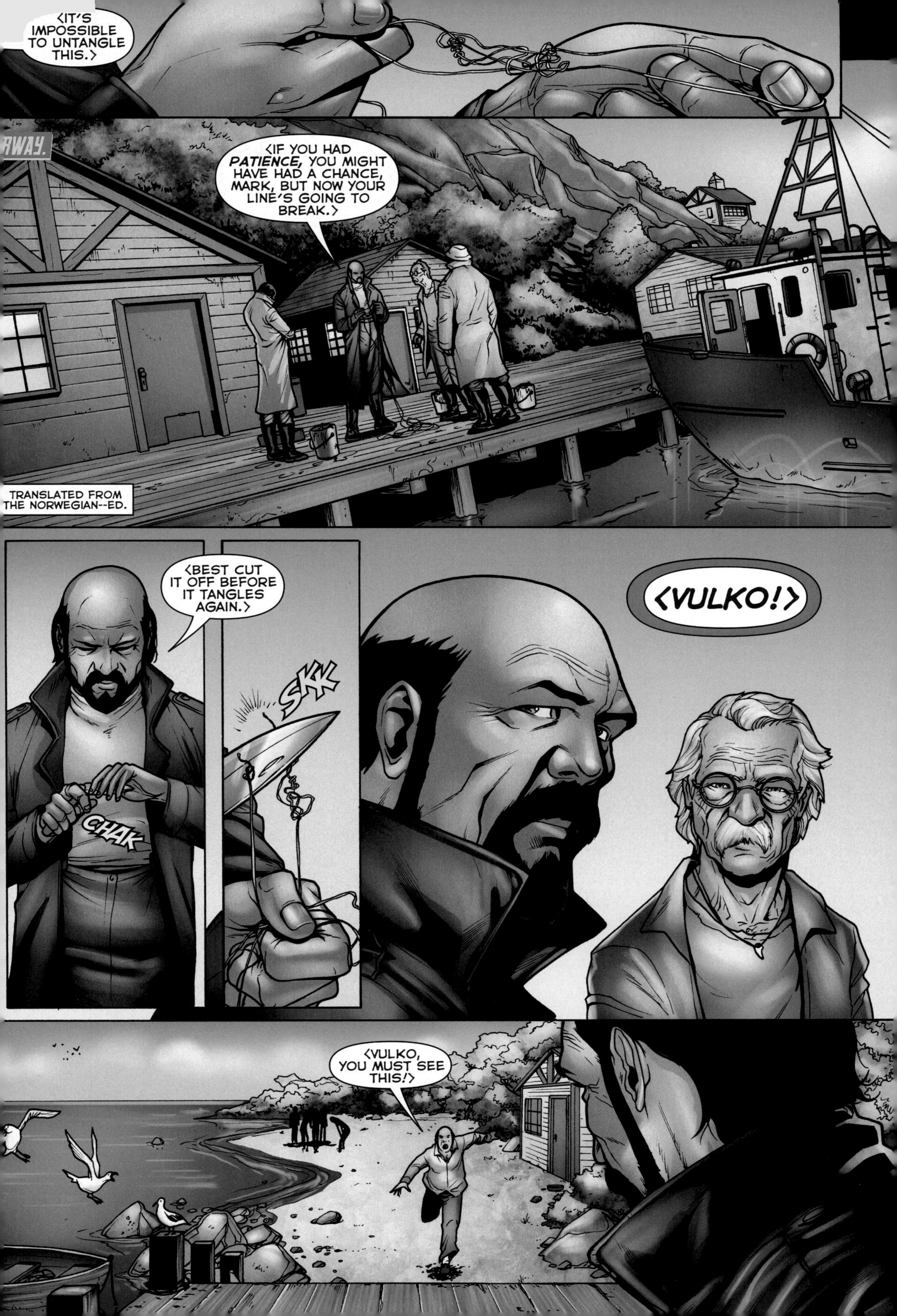

<IT'S IMPOSSIBLE TO UNTANGLE THIS.>
RWAY.
<IF YOU HAD PATIENCE, YOU MIGHT HAVE HAD A CHANCE, MARK, BUT NOW YOUR LINE'S GOING TO BREAK.>
TRANSLATED FROM THE NORWEGIAN--ED.
<BEST CUT IT OFF BEFORE IT TANGLES AGAIN.>
CHAK
SKK
<VULKO!>
<VULKO, YOU MUST SEE THIS!>

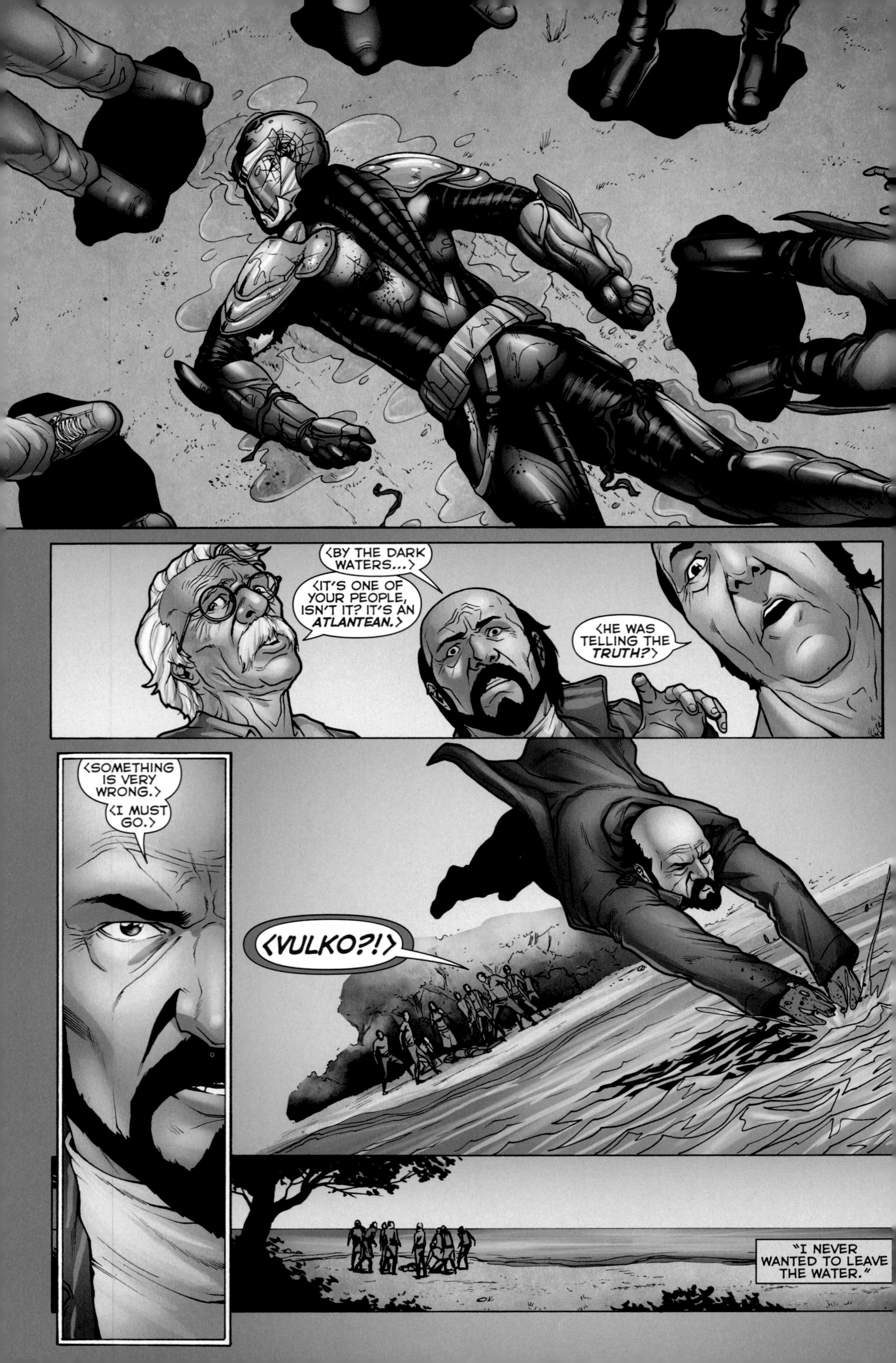
<BY THE DARK WATERS...>
<IT'S ONE OF YOUR PEOPLE, ISN'T IT? IT'S AN *ATLANTEAN.*>
<HE WAS TELLING THE *TRUTH?*>
<SOMETHING IS VERY WRONG.>
<I MUST GO.>
<VULKO?!>
"I NEVER WANTED TO LEAVE THE WATER."

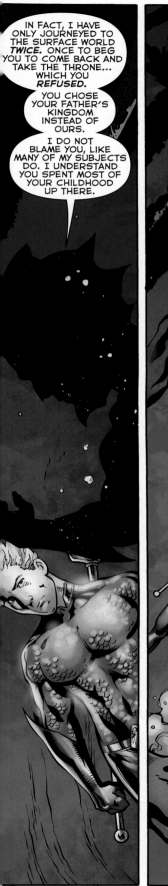

IN FACT, I HAVE ONLY JOURNEYED TO THE SURFACE WORLD *TWICE.* ONCE TO BEG YOU TO COME BACK AND TAKE THE THRONE... WHICH YOU *REFUSED.*

YOU CHOSE YOUR FATHER'S KINGDOM INSTEAD OF OURS.

I DO NOT BLAME YOU, LIKE MANY OF MY SUBJECTS DO. I UNDERSTAND YOU SPENT MOST OF YOUR CHILDHOOD UP THERE.

BREATHING THAT AIR.

PINNED TO THE GROUND.

HOW HORRIBLE IT MUST HAVE BEEN.

THE WORLD UP THERE ISN'T THE NIGHTMARE YOU THINK IT IS.

I AM SURE YOU HAVE IMPROVED IT, ARTHUR. JUST AS I HAVE IMPROVED ATLANTIS.

I ONCE THOUGHT WE WOULD DO THAT *TOGETHER.* NOW WE ARE LITERALLY WORLDS APART.

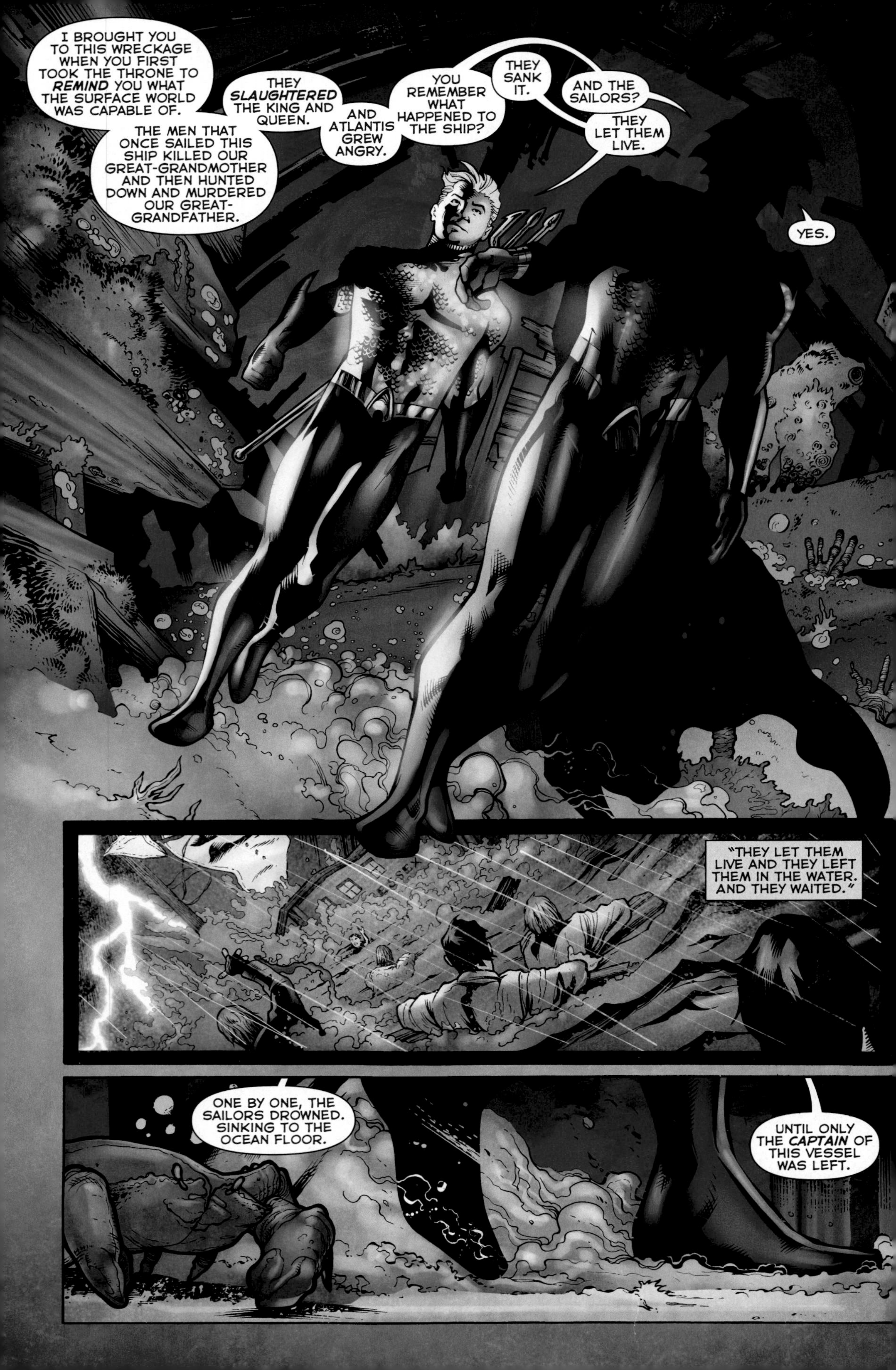
I BROUGHT YOU TO THIS WRECKAGE WHEN YOU FIRST TOOK THE THRONE TO *REMIND* YOU WHAT THE SURFACE WORLD WAS CAPABLE OF.
THE MEN THAT ONCE SAILED THIS SHIP KILLED OUR GREAT-GRANDMOTHER AND THEN HUNTED DOWN AND MURDERED OUR GREAT-GRANDFATHER.
THEY *SLAUGHTERED* THE KING AND QUEEN.
AND ATLANTIS GREW ANGRY.
YOU REMEMBER WHAT HAPPENED TO THE SHIP?
THEY SANK IT.
AND THE SAILORS?
THEY LET THEM LIVE.
YES.
"THEY LET THEM LIVE AND THEY LEFT THEM IN THE WATER. AND THEY WAITED."
ESSEX
ONE BY ONE, THE SAILORS DROWNED. SINKING TO THE OCEAN FLOOR.
UNTIL ONLY THE *CAPTAIN* OF THIS VESSEL WAS LEFT.

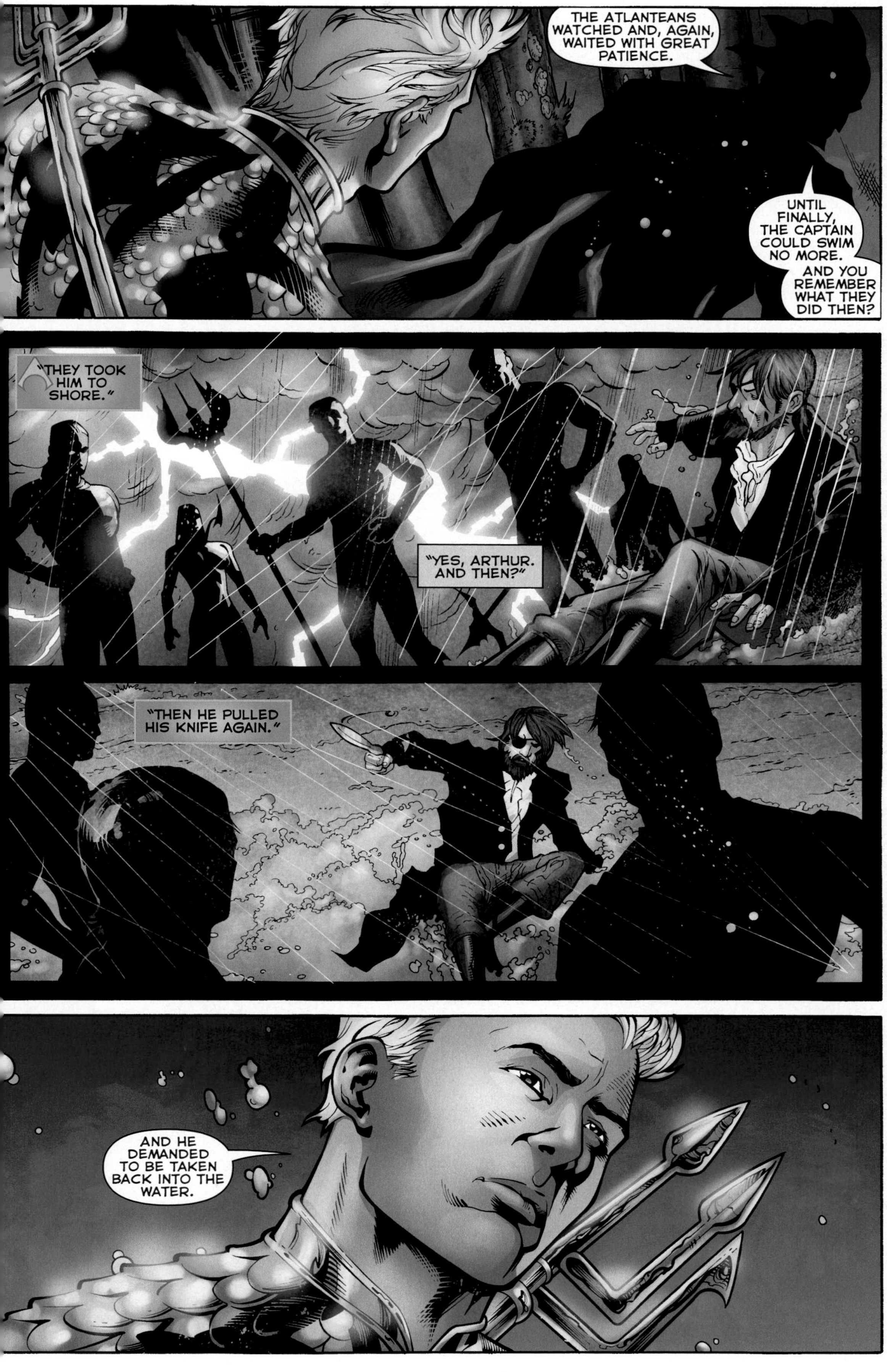
THE ATLANTEANS WATCHED AND, AGAIN, WAITED WITH GREAT PATIENCE.
UNTIL FINALLY, THE CAPTAIN COULD SWIM NO MORE.
AND YOU REMEMBER WHAT THEY DID THEN?
"THEY TOOK HIM TO SHORE."
"YES, ARTHUR. AND THEN?"
"THEN HE PULLED HIS KNIFE AGAIN."
AND HE DEMANDED TO BE TAKEN BACK INTO THE WATER.

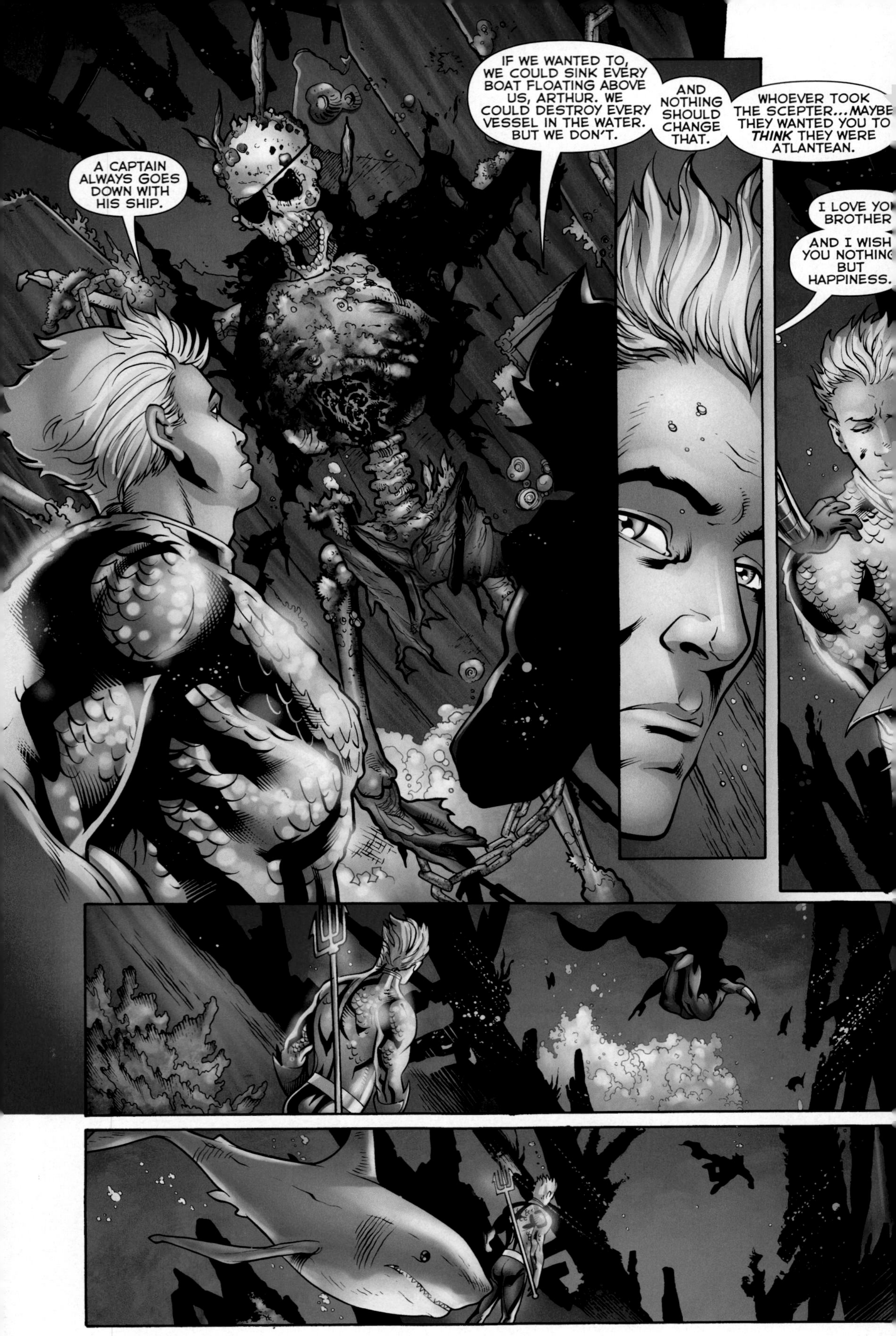

A CAPTAIN ALWAYS GOES DOWN WITH HIS SHIP.
IF WE WANTED TO, WE COULD SINK EVERY BOAT FLOATING ABOVE US, ARTHUR. WE COULD DESTROY EVERY VESSEL IN THE WATER. BUT WE DON'T.
AND NOTHING SHOULD CHANGE THAT.
WHOEVER TOOK THE SCEPTER...MAYBE THEY WANTED YOU TO THINK THEY WERE ATLANTEAN.
I LOVE YOU BROTHER.
AND I WISH YOU NOTHING BUT HAPPINESS.

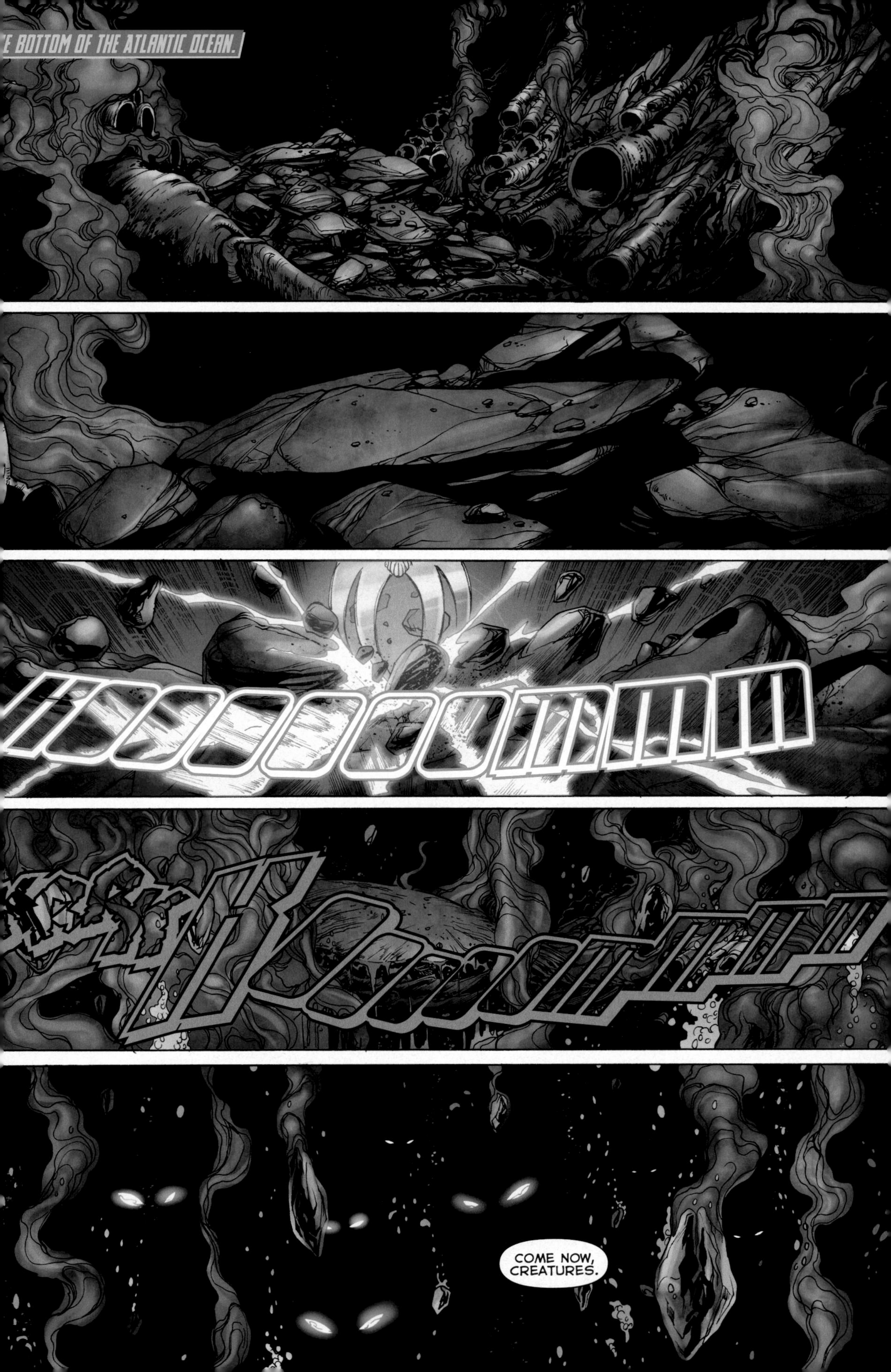
E BOTTOM OF THE ATLANTIC OCEAN.
COME NOW, CREATURES.

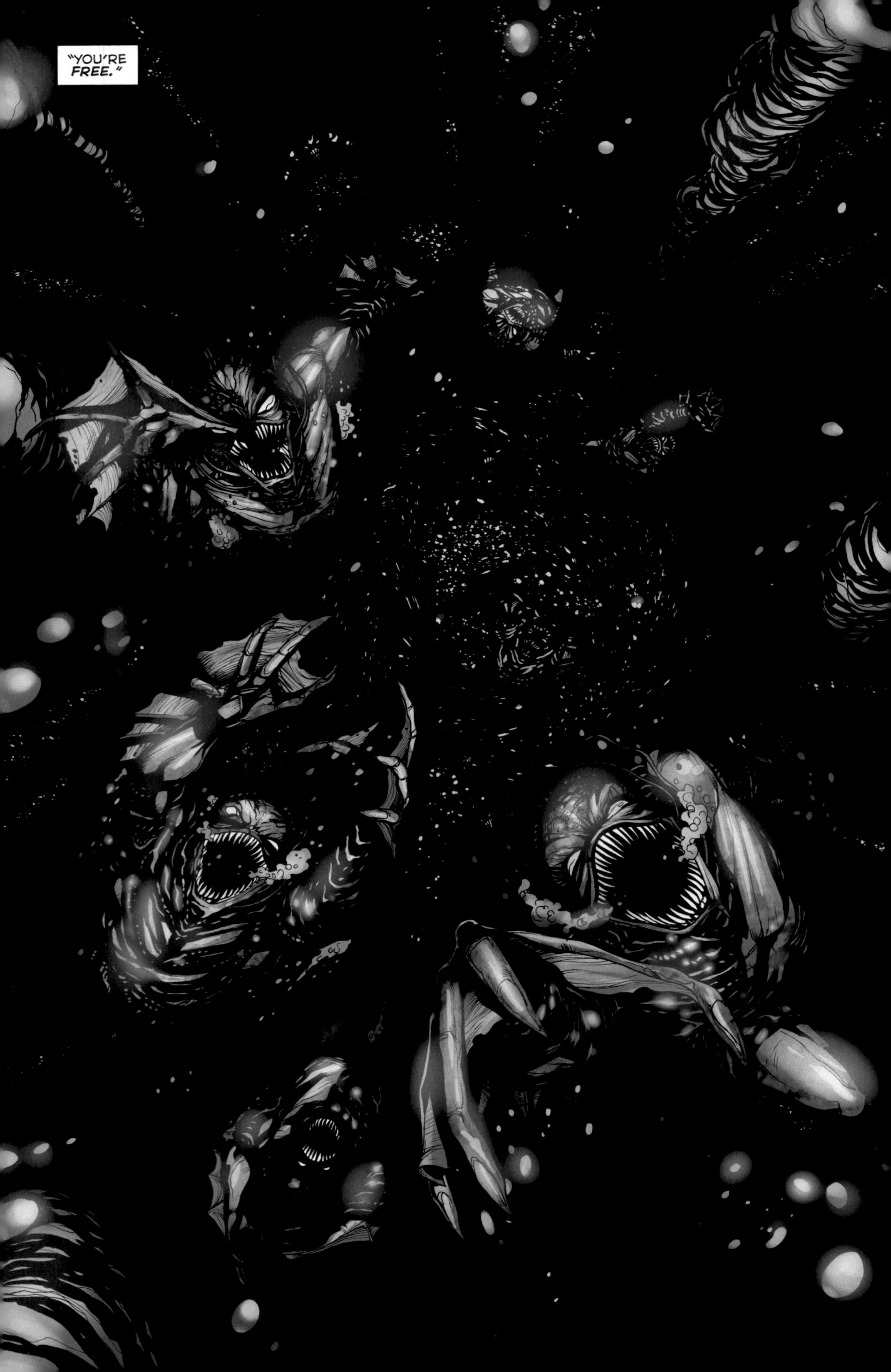
"YOU'RE FREE."

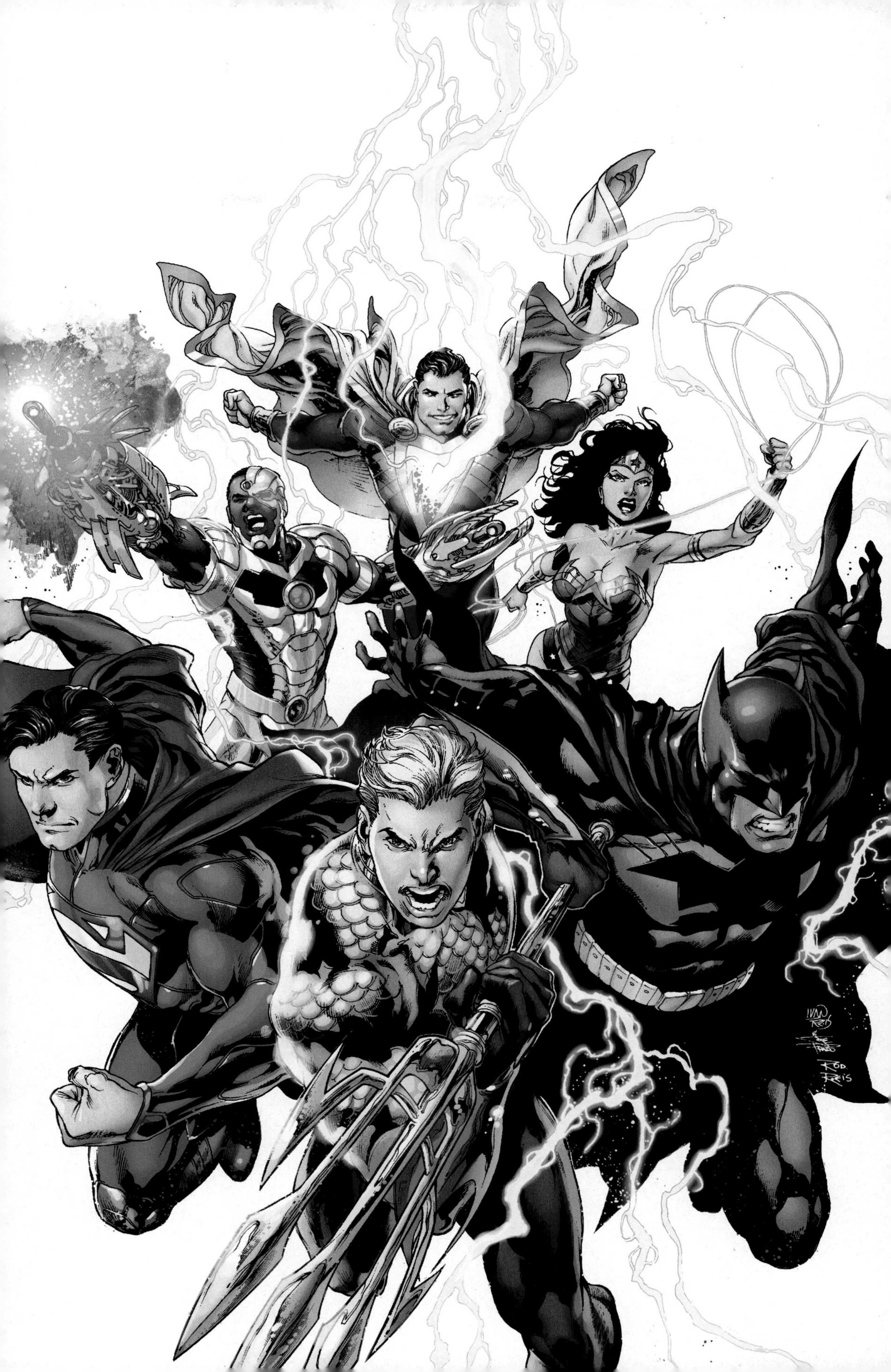

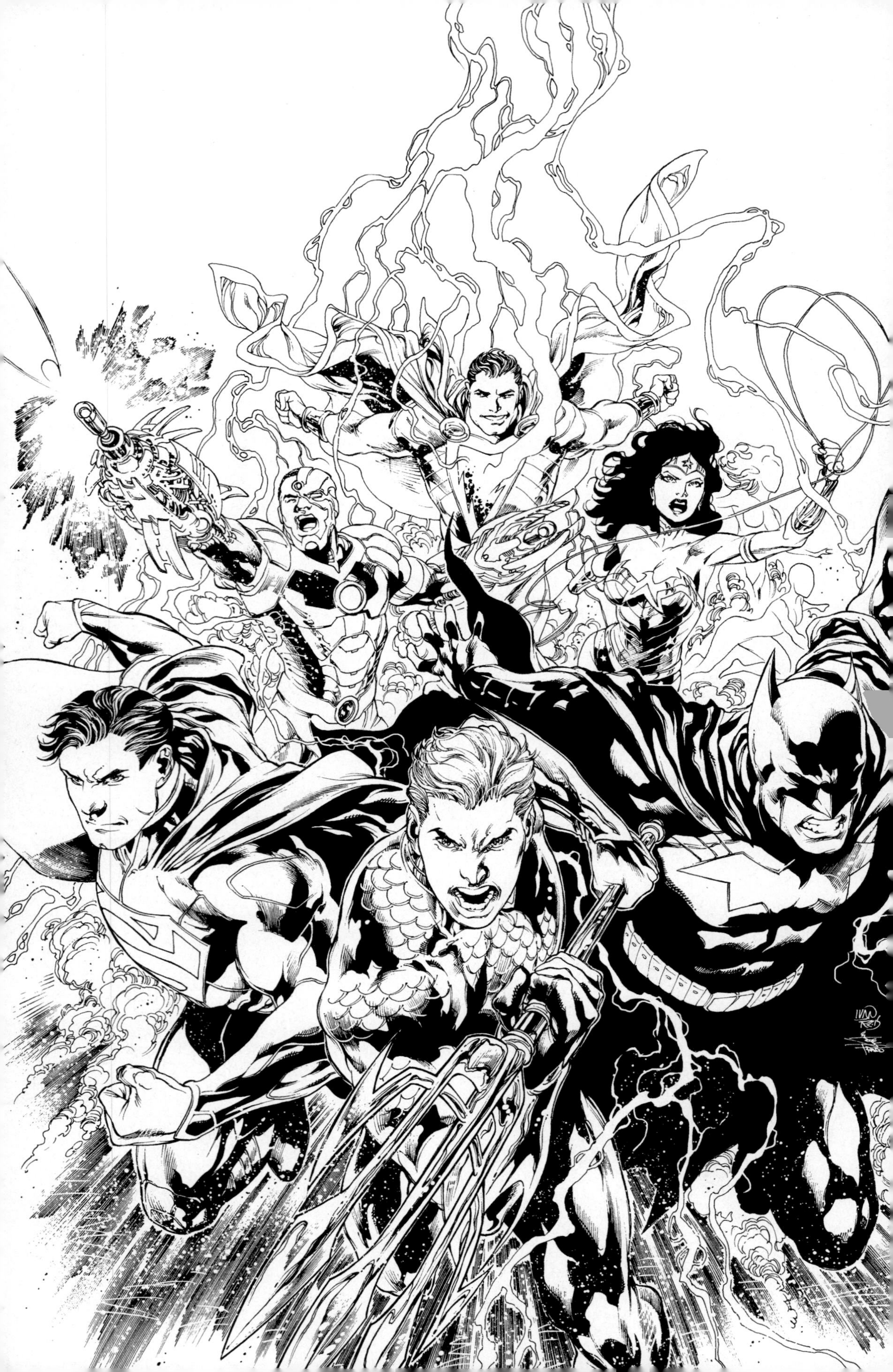

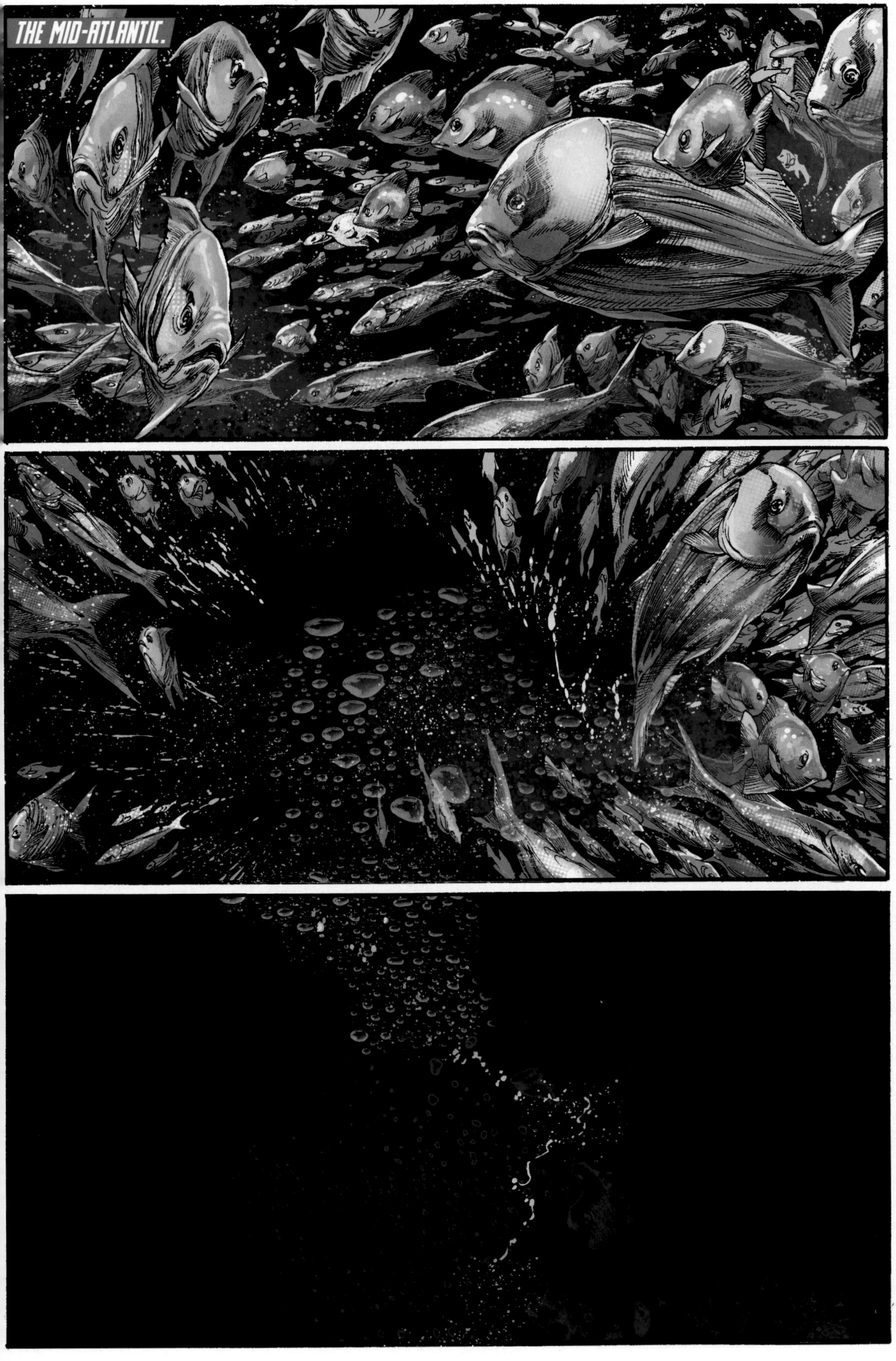
THE MID-ATLANTIC.

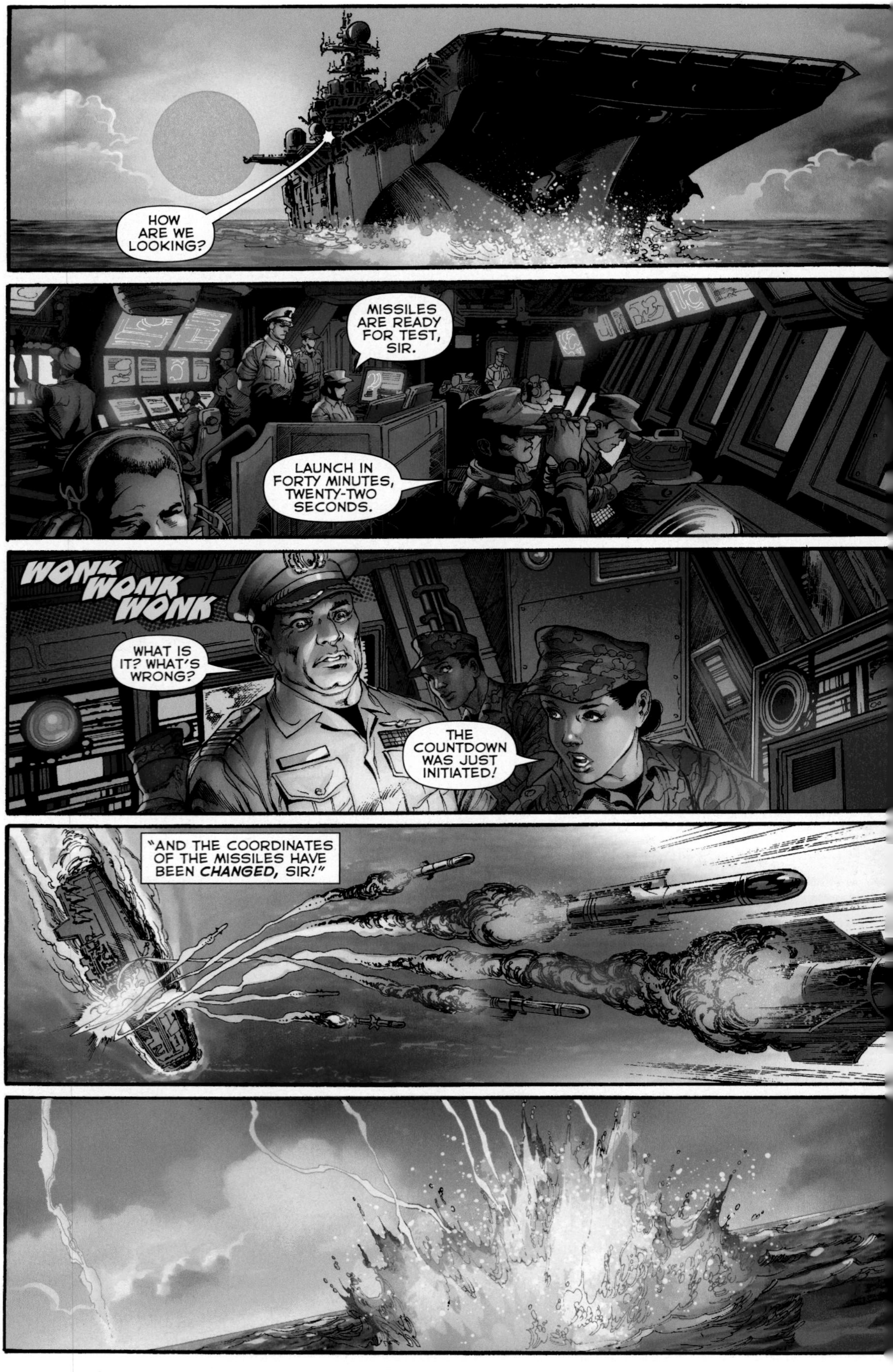
HOW ARE WE LOOKING?
MISSILES ARE READY FOR TEST, SIR.
LAUNCH IN FORTY MINUTES, TWENTY-TWO SECONDS.
WONK WONK WONK
WHAT IS IT? WHAT'S WRONG?
THE COUNTDOWN WAS JUST INITIATED!
"AND THE COORDINATES OF THE MISSILES HAVE BEEN CHANGED, SIR!"

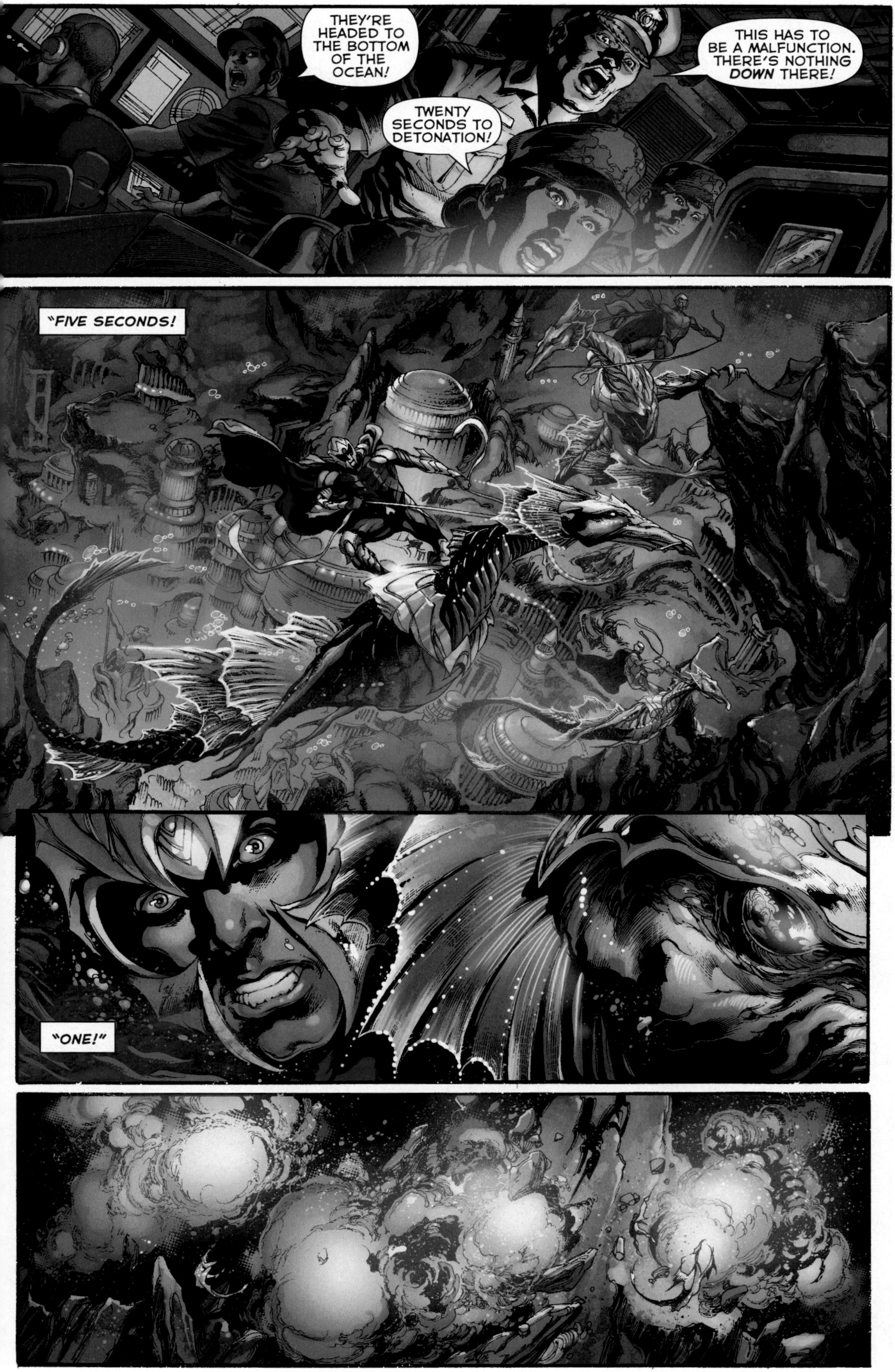
THEY'RE HEADED TO THE BOTTOM OF THE OCEAN!
THIS HAS TO BE A MALFUNCTION. THERE'S NOTHING DOWN THERE!
TWENTY SECONDS TO DETONATION!
"FIVE SECONDS!
"ONE!"

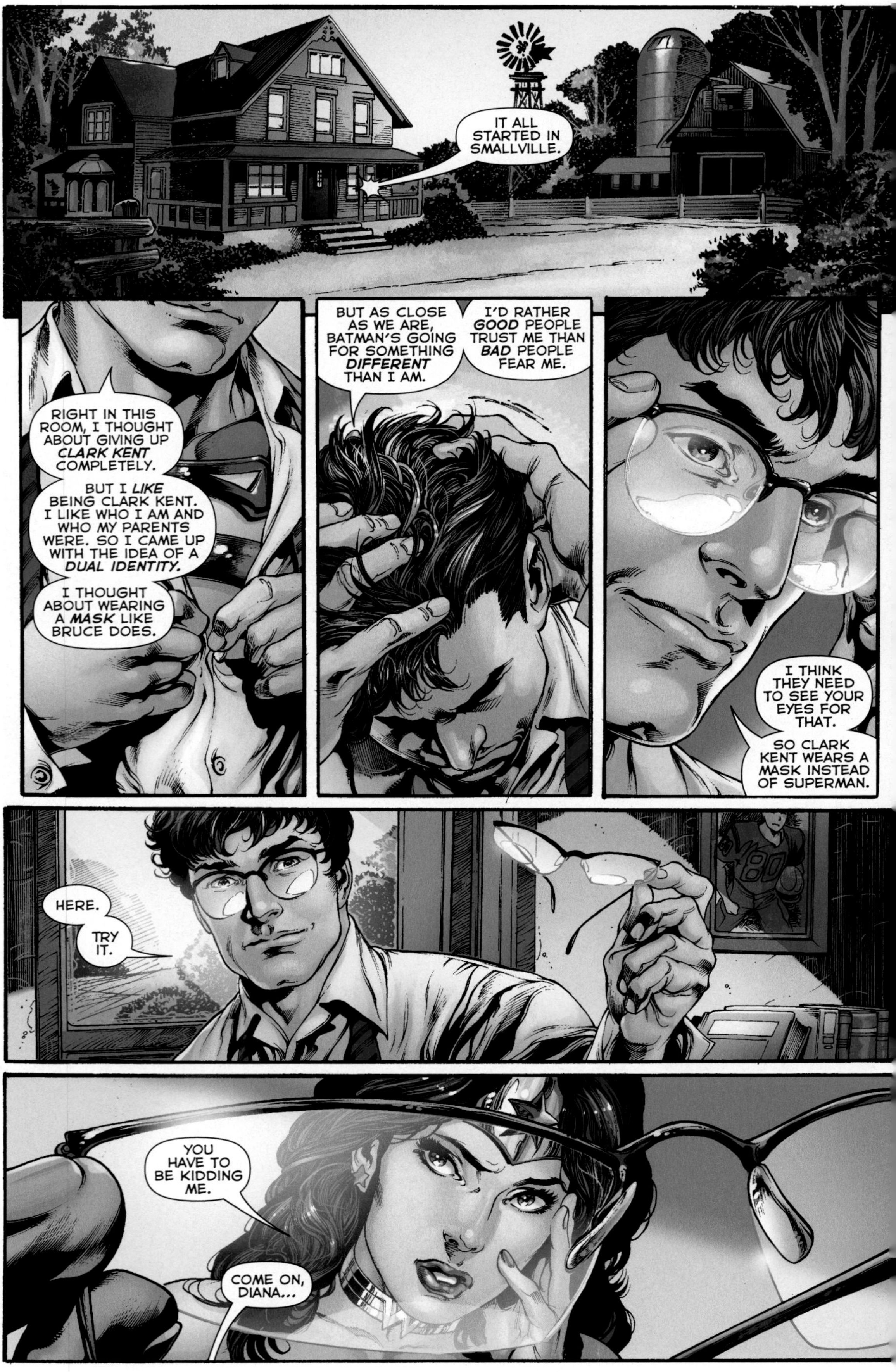
IT ALL STARTED IN SMALLVILLE.
RIGHT IN THIS ROOM, I THOUGHT ABOUT GIVING UP CLARK KENT COMPLETELY.
BUT I LIKE BEING CLARK KENT. I LIKE WHO I AM AND WHO MY PARENTS WERE. SO I CAME UP WITH THE IDEA OF A DUAL IDENTITY.
I THOUGHT ABOUT WEARING A MASK LIKE BRUCE DOES.
BUT AS CLOSE AS WE ARE, BATMAN'S GOING FOR SOMETHING DIFFERENT THAN I AM.
I'D RATHER GOOD PEOPLE TRUST ME THAN BAD PEOPLE FEAR ME.
I THINK THEY NEED TO SEE YOUR EYES FOR THAT.
SO CLARK KENT WEARS A MASK INSTEAD OF SUPERMAN.
HERE.
TRY IT.
YOU HAVE TO BE KIDDING ME.
COME ON, DIANA...

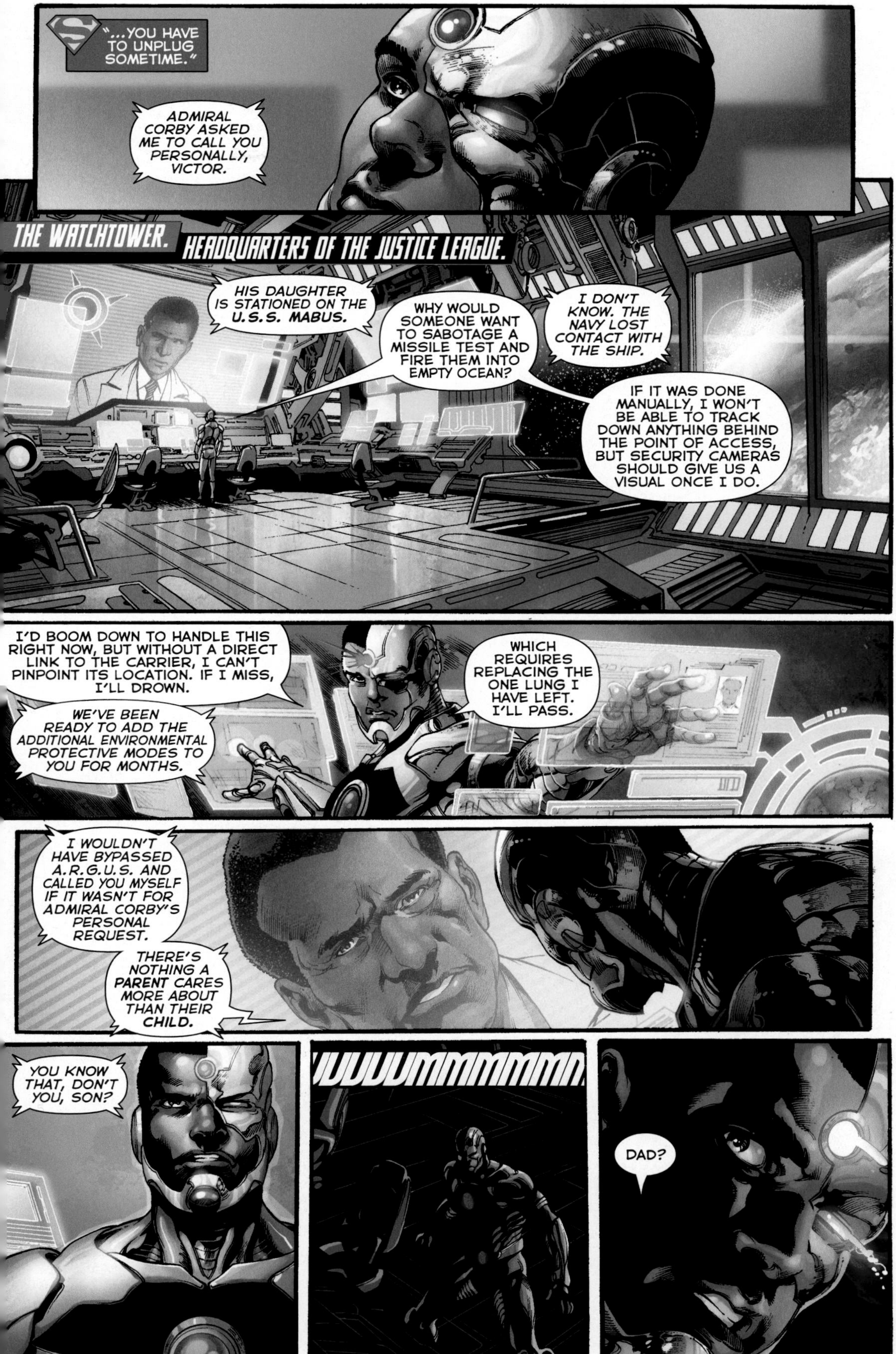

"...YOU HAVE TO UNPLUG SOMETIME."
ADMIRAL CORBY ASKED ME TO CALL YOU PERSONALLY, VICTOR.
THE WATCHTOWER.
HEADQUARTERS OF THE JUSTICE LEAGUE.
HIS DAUGHTER IS STATIONED ON THE U.S.S. MABUS.
WHY WOULD SOMEONE WANT TO SABOTAGE A MISSILE TEST AND FIRE THEM INTO EMPTY OCEAN?
I DON'T KNOW. THE NAVY LOST CONTACT WITH THE SHIP.
IF IT WAS DONE MANUALLY, I WON'T BE ABLE TO TRACK DOWN ANYTHING BEHIND THE POINT OF ACCESS, BUT SECURITY CAMERAS SHOULD GIVE US A VISUAL ONCE I DO.
I'D BOOM DOWN TO HANDLE THIS RIGHT NOW, BUT WITHOUT A DIRECT LINK TO THE CARRIER, I CAN'T PINPOINT ITS LOCATION. IF I MISS, I'LL DROWN.
WE'VE BEEN READY TO ADD THE ADDITIONAL ENVIRONMENTAL PROTECTIVE MODES TO YOU FOR MONTHS.
WHICH REQUIRES REPLACING THE ONE LUNG I HAVE LEFT. I'LL PASS.
I WOULDN'T HAVE BYPASSED A.R.G.U.S. AND CALLED YOU MYSELF IF IT WASN'T FOR ADMIRAL CORBY'S PERSONAL REQUEST.
THERE'S NOTHING A PARENT CARES MORE ABOUT THAN THEIR CHILD.
YOU KNOW THAT, DON'T YOU, SON?
VVVVVMMMMMMMM
DAD?

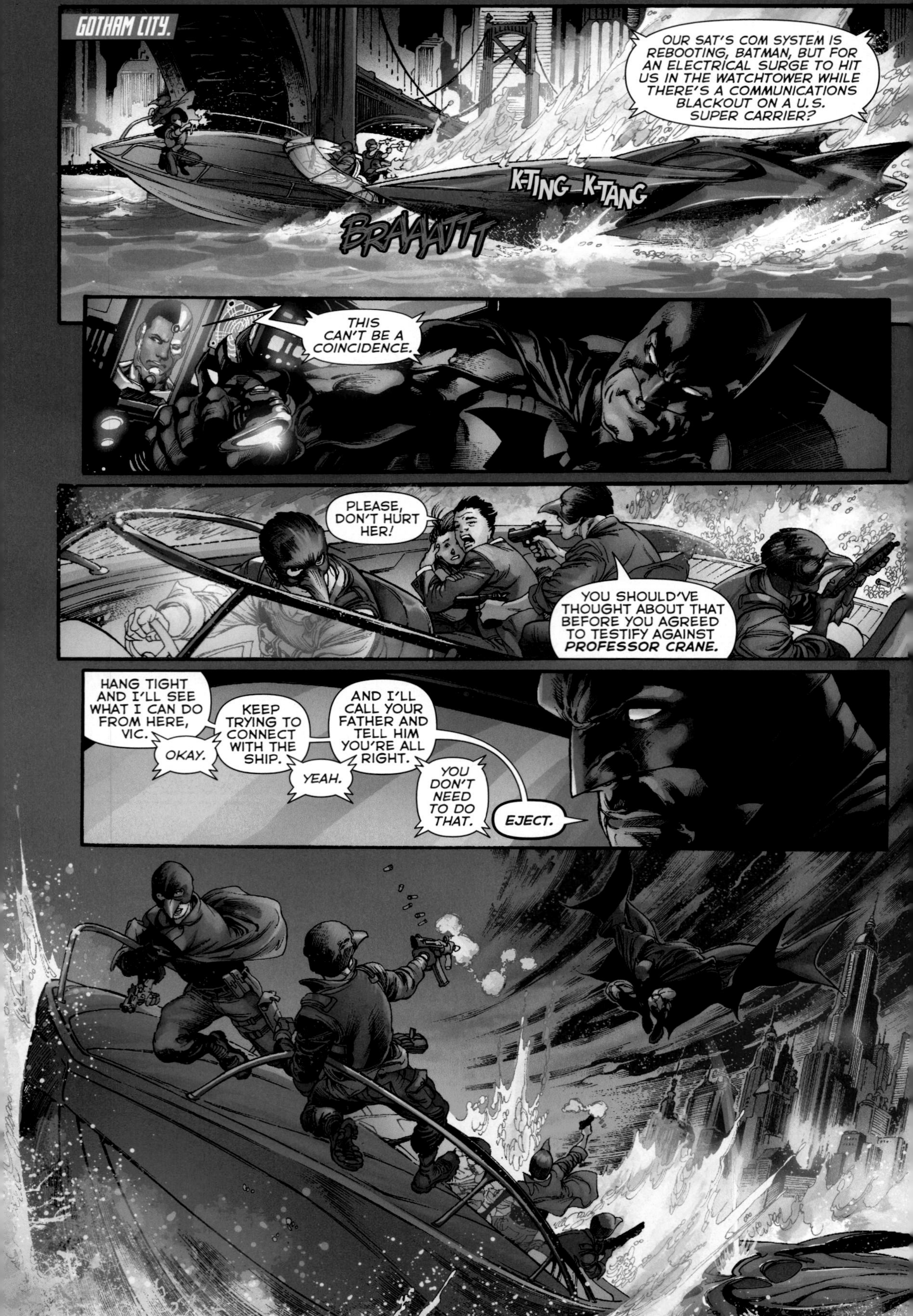
GOTHAM CITY.
OUR SAT'S COM SYSTEM IS REBOOTING, BATMAN, BUT FOR AN ELECTRICAL SURGE TO HIT US IN THE WATCHTOWER WHILE THERE'S A COMMUNICATIONS BLACKOUT ON A U.S. SUPER CARRIER?
K-TING K-TANG
BRAAATTT
THIS CAN'T BE A COINCIDENCE.
PLEASE, DON'T HURT HER!
YOU SHOULD'VE THOUGHT ABOUT THAT BEFORE YOU AGREED TO TESTIFY AGAINST PROFESSOR CRANE.
HANG TIGHT AND I'LL SEE WHAT I CAN DO FROM HERE, VIC.
OKAY.
KEEP TRYING TO CONNECT WITH THE SHIP.
YEAH.
AND I'LL CALL YOUR FATHER AND TELL HIM YOU'RE ALL RIGHT.
YOU DON'T NEED TO DO THAT.
EJECT.

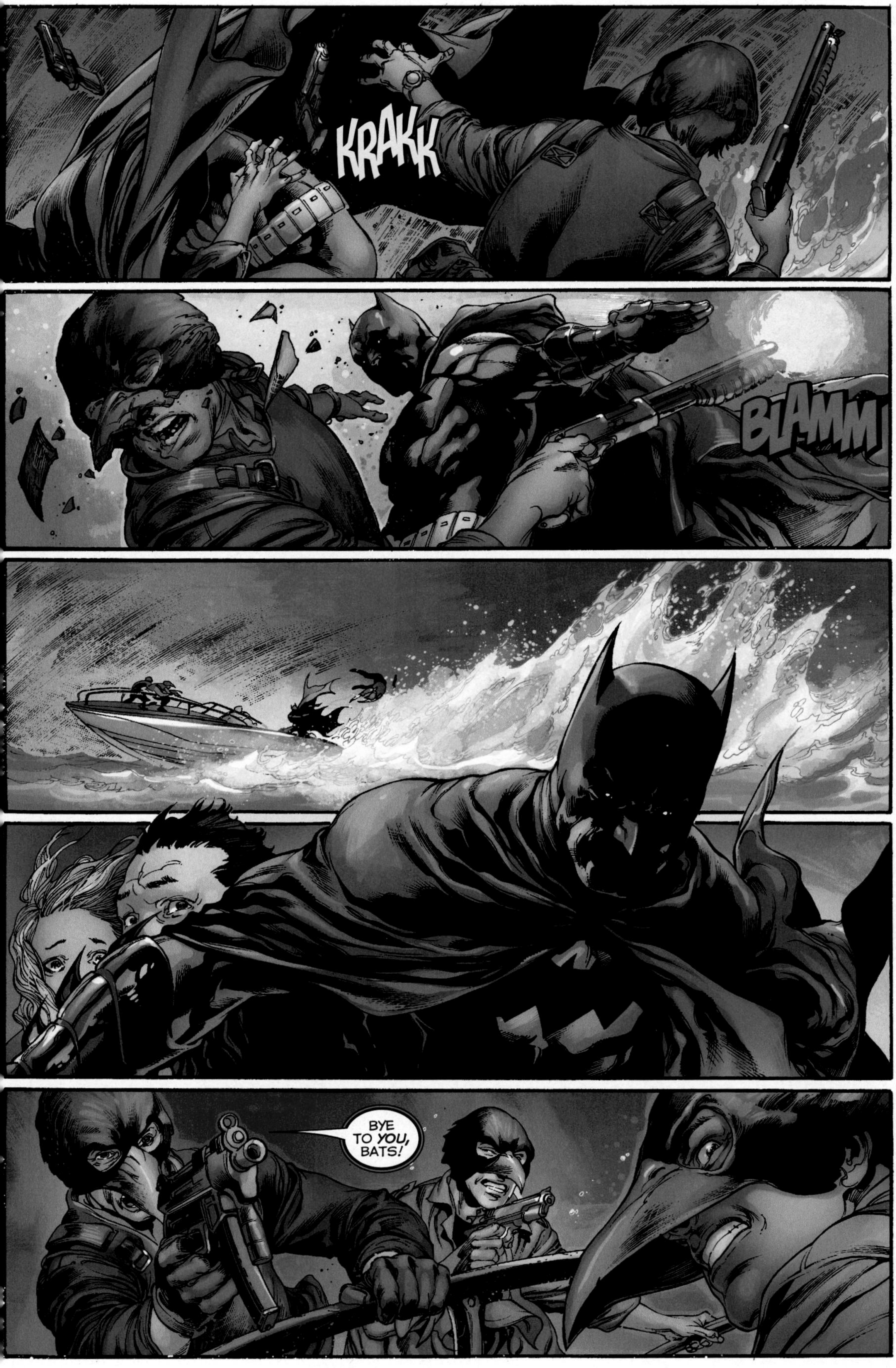
KRAKK
BLAMM
BYE TO YOU, BATS!

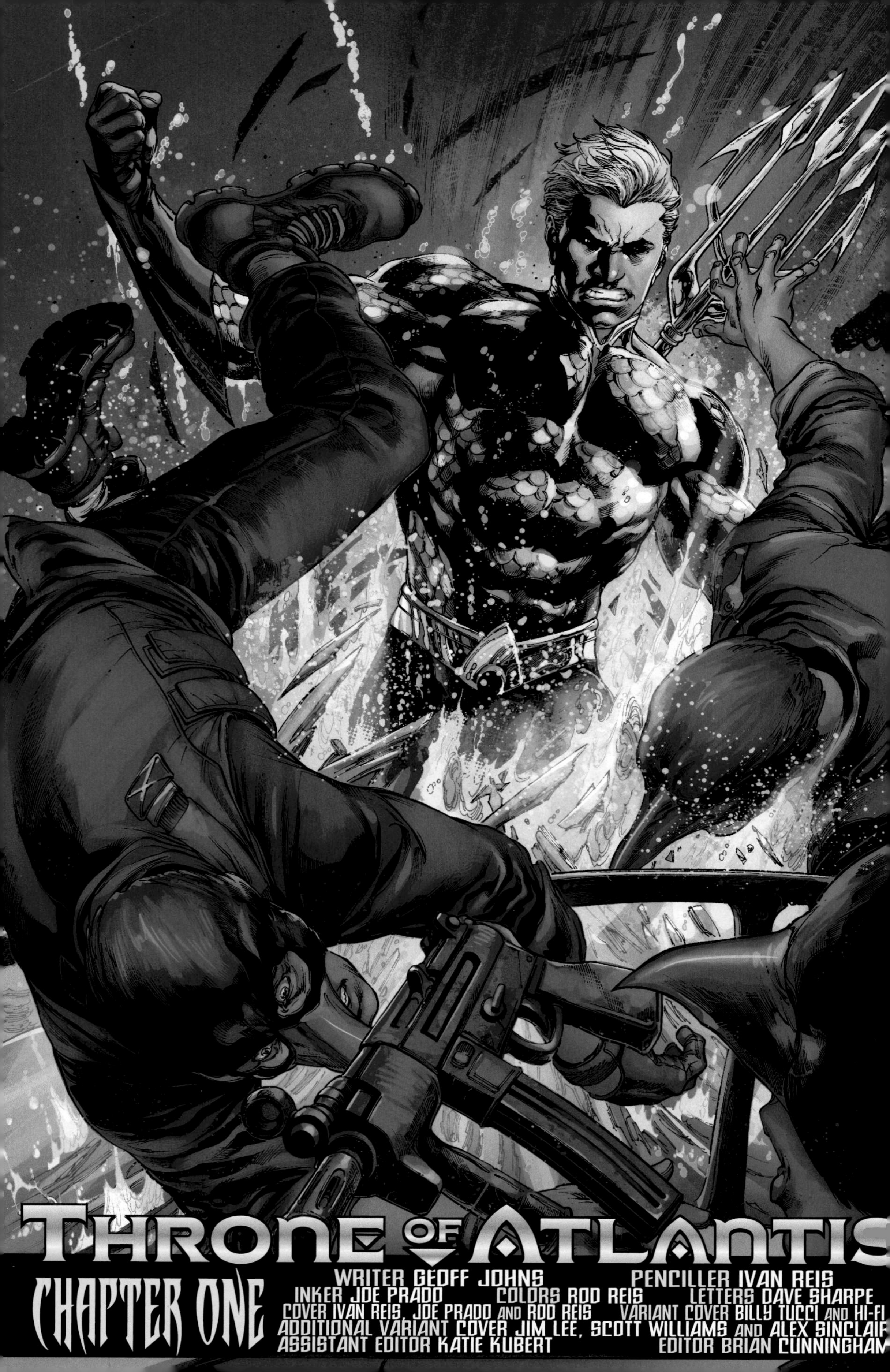
THRONE OF ATLANTIS
CHAPTER ONE
WRITER GEOFF JOHNS
PENCILLER IVAN REIS
INKER JOE PRADO
COLORS ROD REIS
LETTERS DAVE SHARPE
COVER IVAN REIS, JOE PRADO AND ROD REIS
VARIANT COVER BILLY TUCCI AND HI-FI
ADDITIONAL VARIANT COVER JIM LEE, SCOTT WILLIAMS AND ALEX SINCLAIR
ASSISTANT EDITOR KATIE KUBERT
EDITOR BRIAN CUNNINGHAM

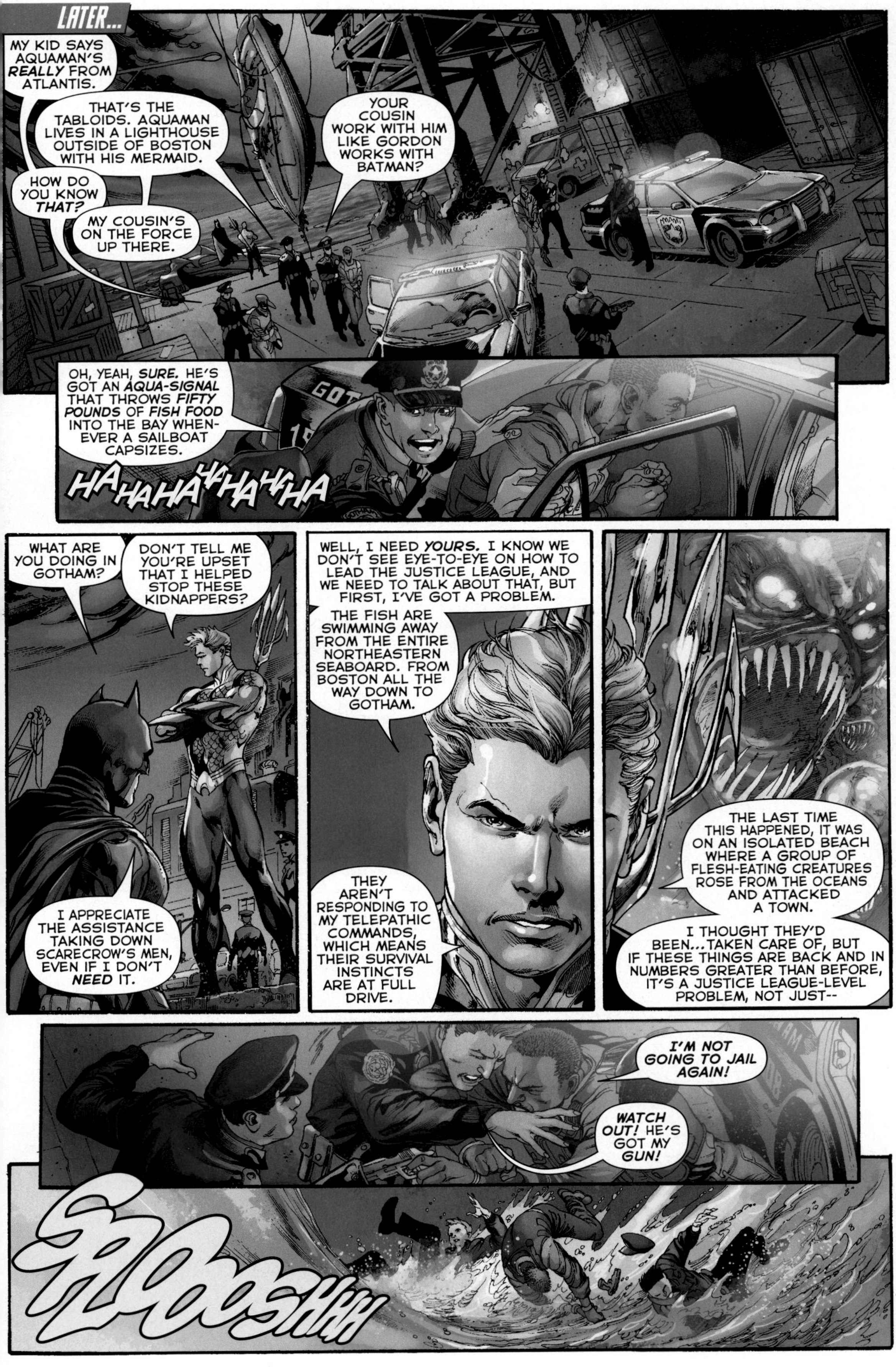
LATER...
MY KID SAYS AQUAMAN'S REALLY FROM ATLANTIS.
THAT'S THE TABLOIDS. AQUAMAN LIVES IN A LIGHTHOUSE OUTSIDE OF BOSTON WITH HIS MERMAID.
HOW DO YOU KNOW THAT?
MY COUSIN'S ON THE FORCE UP THERE.
YOUR COUSIN WORK WITH HIM LIKE GORDON WORKS WITH BATMAN?
OH, YEAH, SURE. HE'S GOT AN AQUA-SIGNAL THAT THROWS FIFTY POUNDS OF FISH FOOD INTO THE BAY WHEN-EVER A SAILBOAT CAPSIZES.
HAHAHAHAHAHAHAHA
WHAT ARE YOU DOING IN GOTHAM?
DON'T TELL ME YOU'RE UPSET THAT I HELPED STOP THESE KIDNAPPERS?
I APPRECIATE THE ASSISTANCE TAKING DOWN SCARECROW'S MEN, EVEN IF I DON'T NEED IT.
WELL, I NEED YOURS. I KNOW WE DON'T SEE EYE-TO-EYE ON HOW TO LEAD THE JUSTICE LEAGUE, AND WE NEED TO TALK ABOUT THAT, BUT FIRST, I'VE GOT A PROBLEM.
THE FISH ARE SWIMMING AWAY FROM THE ENTIRE NORTHEASTERN SEABOARD. FROM BOSTON ALL THE WAY DOWN TO GOTHAM.
THEY AREN'T RESPONDING TO MY TELEPATHIC COMMANDS, WHICH MEANS THEIR SURVIVAL INSTINCTS ARE AT FULL DRIVE.
THE LAST TIME THIS HAPPENED, IT WAS ON AN ISOLATED BEACH WHERE A GROUP OF FLESH-EATING CREATURES ROSE FROM THE OCEANS AND ATTACKED A TOWN.
I THOUGHT THEY'D BEEN...TAKEN CARE OF, BUT IF THESE THINGS ARE BACK AND IN NUMBERS GREATER THAN BEFORE, IT'S A JUSTICE LEAGUE-LEVEL PROBLEM, NOT JUST--
I'M NOT GOING TO JAIL AGAIN!
WATCH OUT! HE'S GOT MY GUN!
SPLOOSHHH

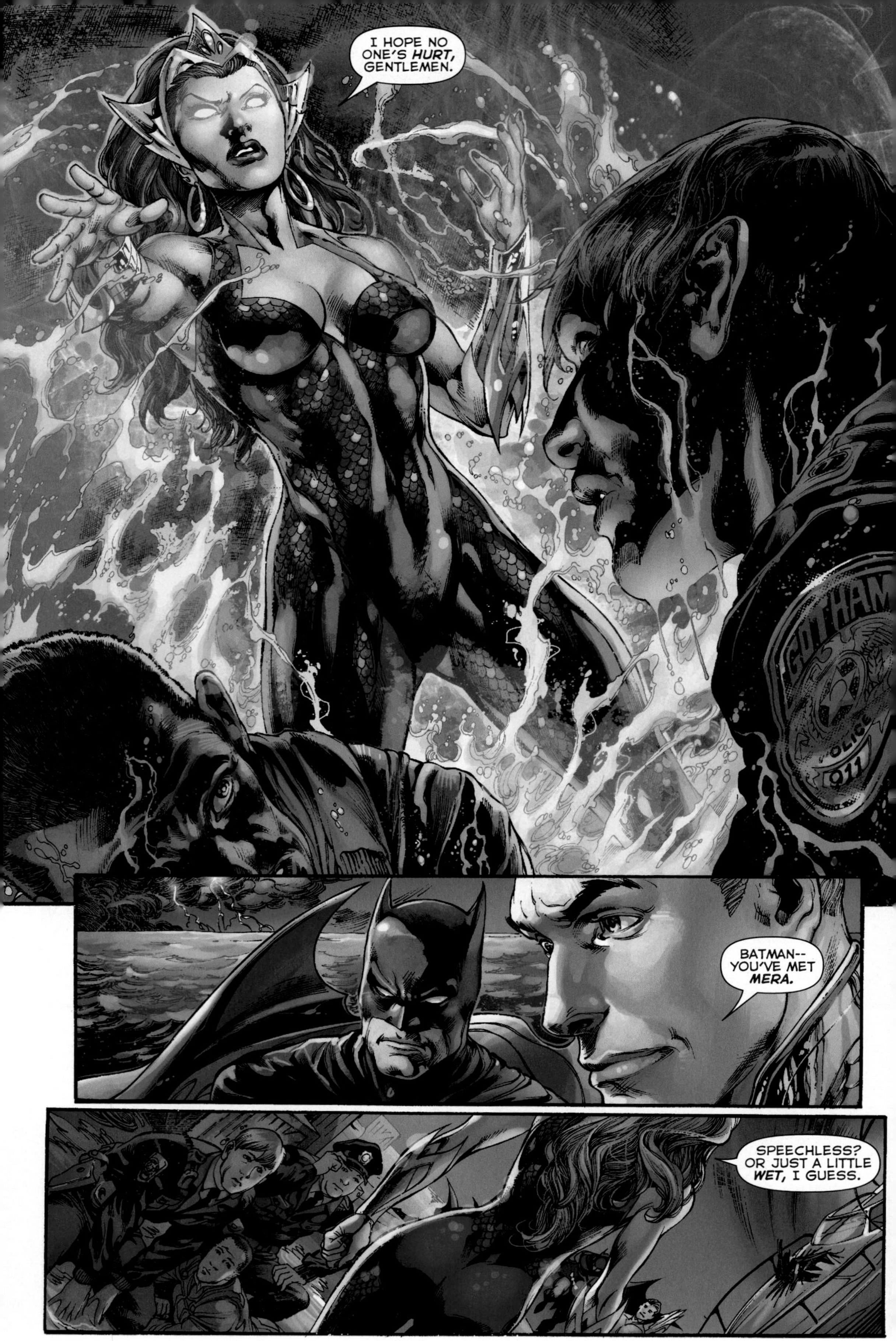
I HOPE NO ONE'S *HURT*, GENTLEMEN.
BATMAN-- YOU'VE MET *MERA.*
SPEECHLESS? OR JUST A LITTLE *WET,* I GUESS.

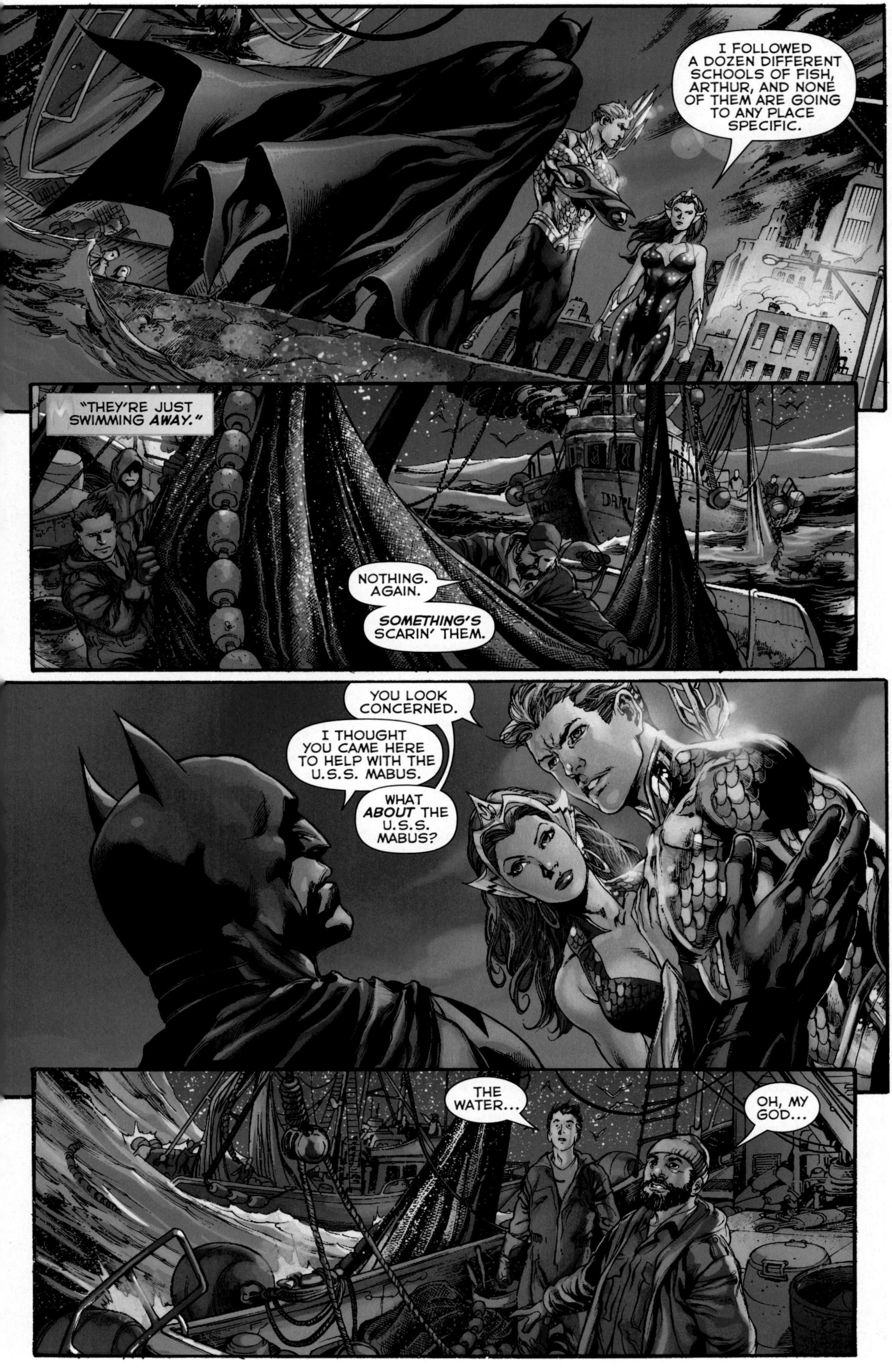
I FOLLOWED A DOZEN DIFFERENT SCHOOLS OF FISH, ARTHUR, AND NONE OF THEM ARE GOING TO ANY PLACE SPECIFIC.
"THEY'RE JUST SWIMMING *AWAY.*"
NOTHING. AGAIN.
SOMETHING'S SCARIN' THEM.
YOU LOOK CONCERNED.
I THOUGHT YOU CAME HERE TO HELP WITH THE U.S.S. MABUS.
WHAT *ABOUT* THE U.S.S. MABUS?
THE WATER...
OH, MY GOD...

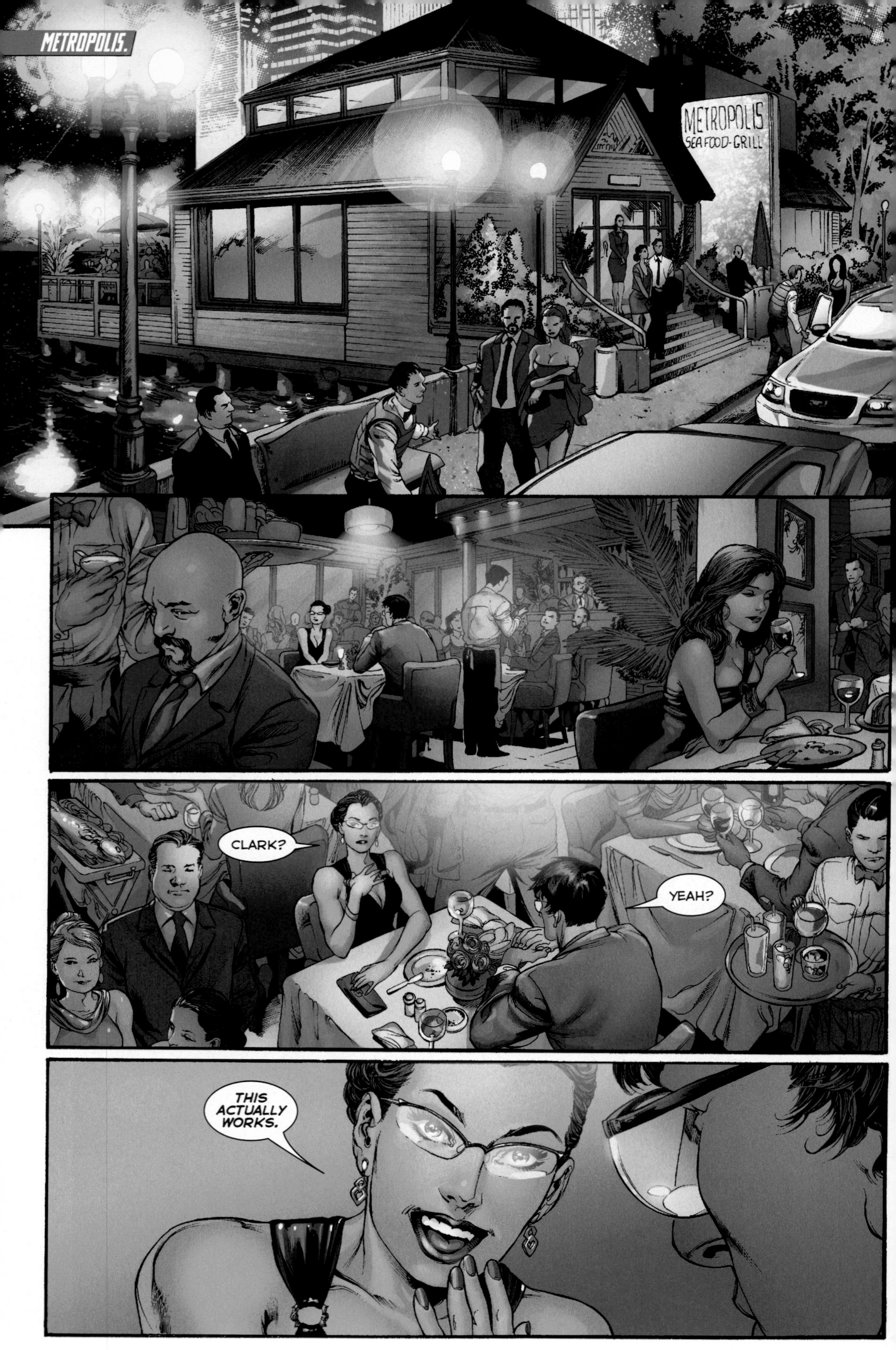
METROPOLIS.
METROPOLIS SEAFOOD-GRILL
CLARK?
YEAH?
THIS ACTUALLY WORKS.

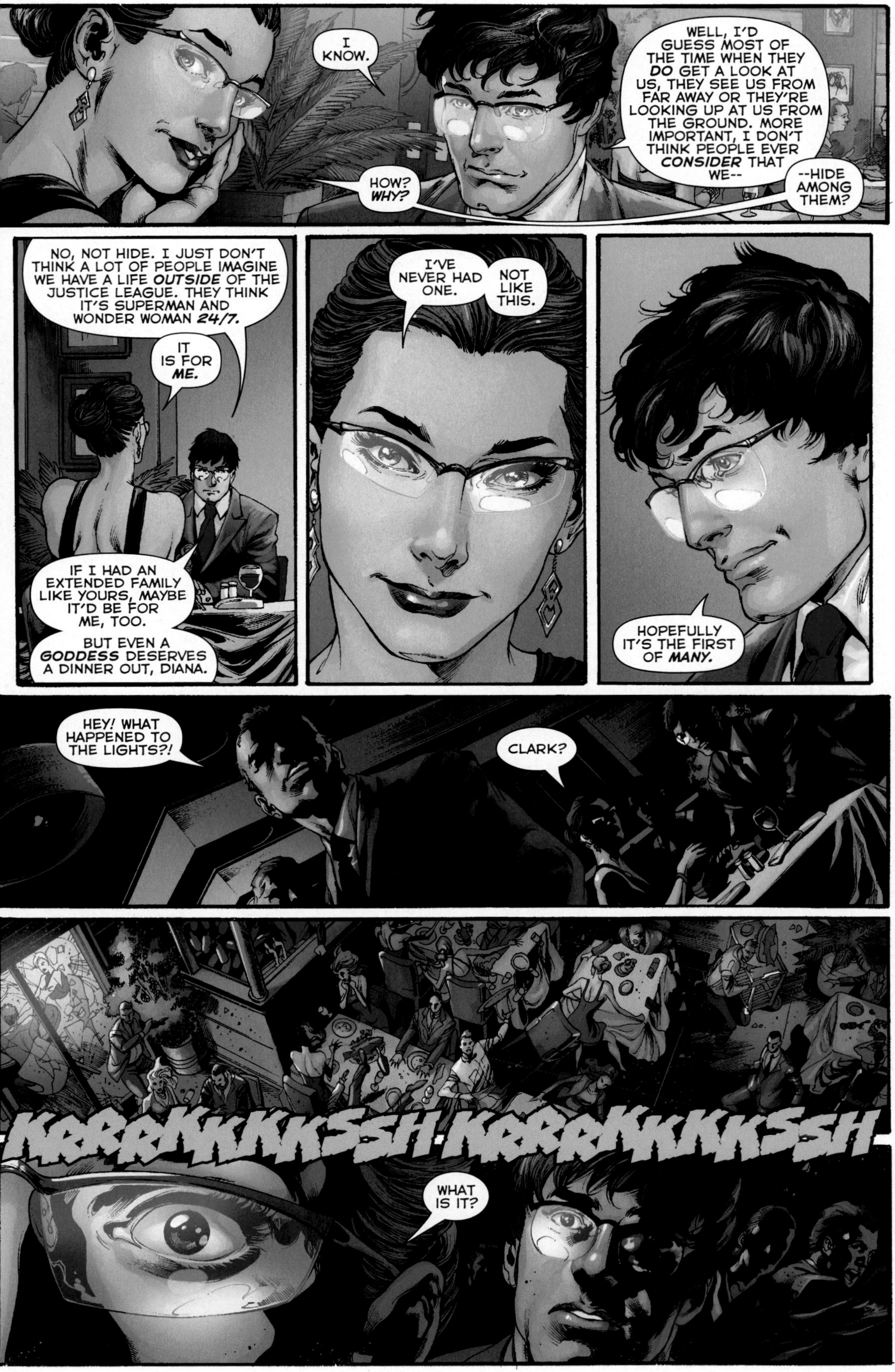
I KNOW.
HOW? WHY?
WELL, I'D GUESS MOST OF THE TIME WHEN THEY DO GET A LOOK AT US, THEY SEE US FROM FAR AWAY OR THEY'RE LOOKING UP AT US FROM THE GROUND. MORE IMPORTANT, I DON'T THINK PEOPLE EVER CONSIDER THAT WE--
--HIDE AMONG THEM?
NO, NOT HIDE. I JUST DON'T THINK A LOT OF PEOPLE IMAGINE WE HAVE A LIFE OUTSIDE OF THE JUSTICE LEAGUE. THEY THINK IT'S SUPERMAN AND WONDER WOMAN 24/7.
IT IS FOR ME.
IF I HAD AN EXTENDED FAMILY LIKE YOURS, MAYBE IT'D BE FOR ME, TOO.
BUT EVEN A GODDESS DESERVES A DINNER OUT, DIANA.
I'VE NEVER HAD ONE.
NOT LIKE THIS.
HOPEFULLY IT'S THE FIRST OF MANY.
HEY! WHAT HAPPENED TO THE LIGHTS?!
CLARK?
KRRRKKKKSSH KRRRKKKKSSH
WHAT IS IT?

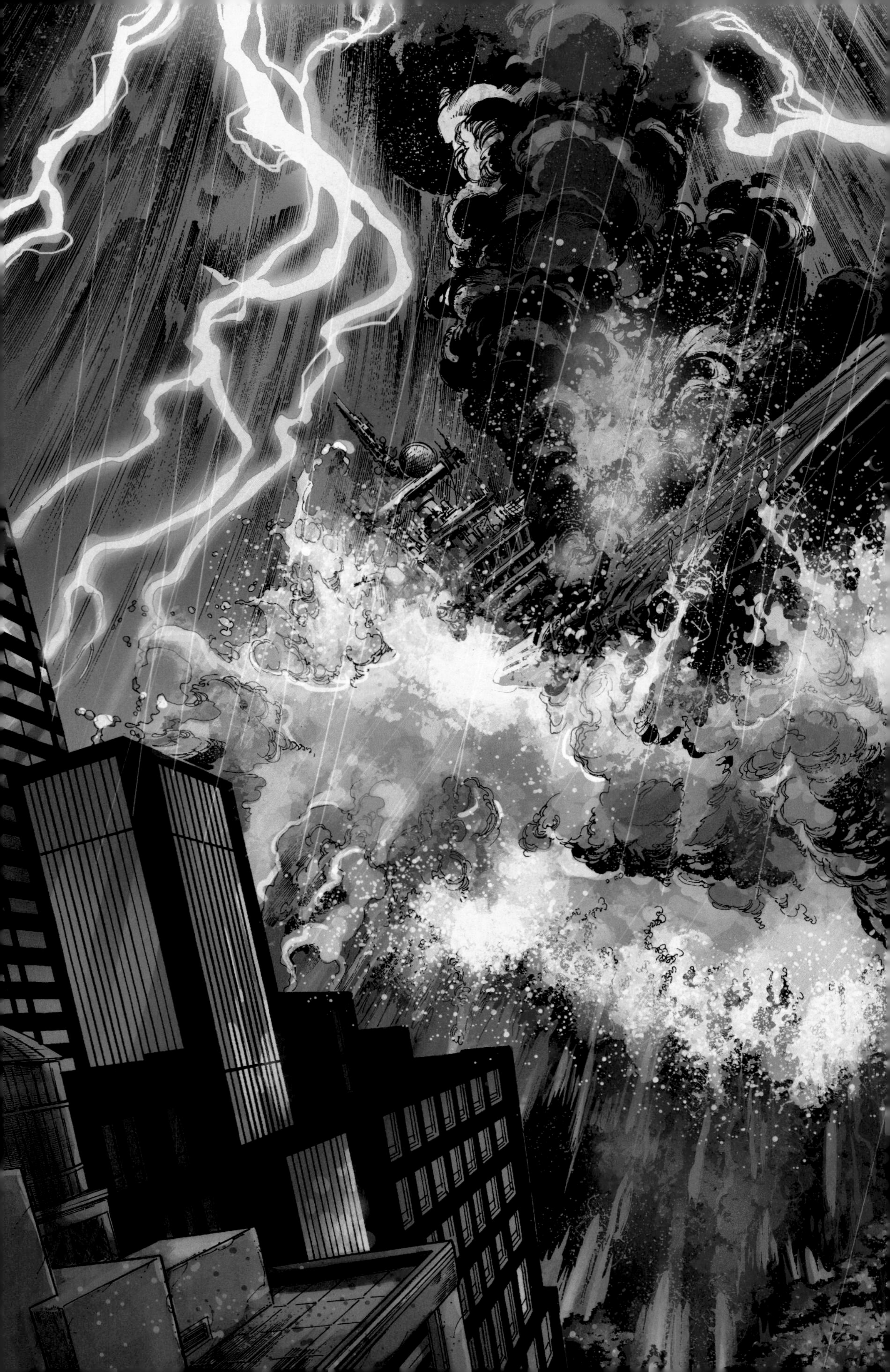

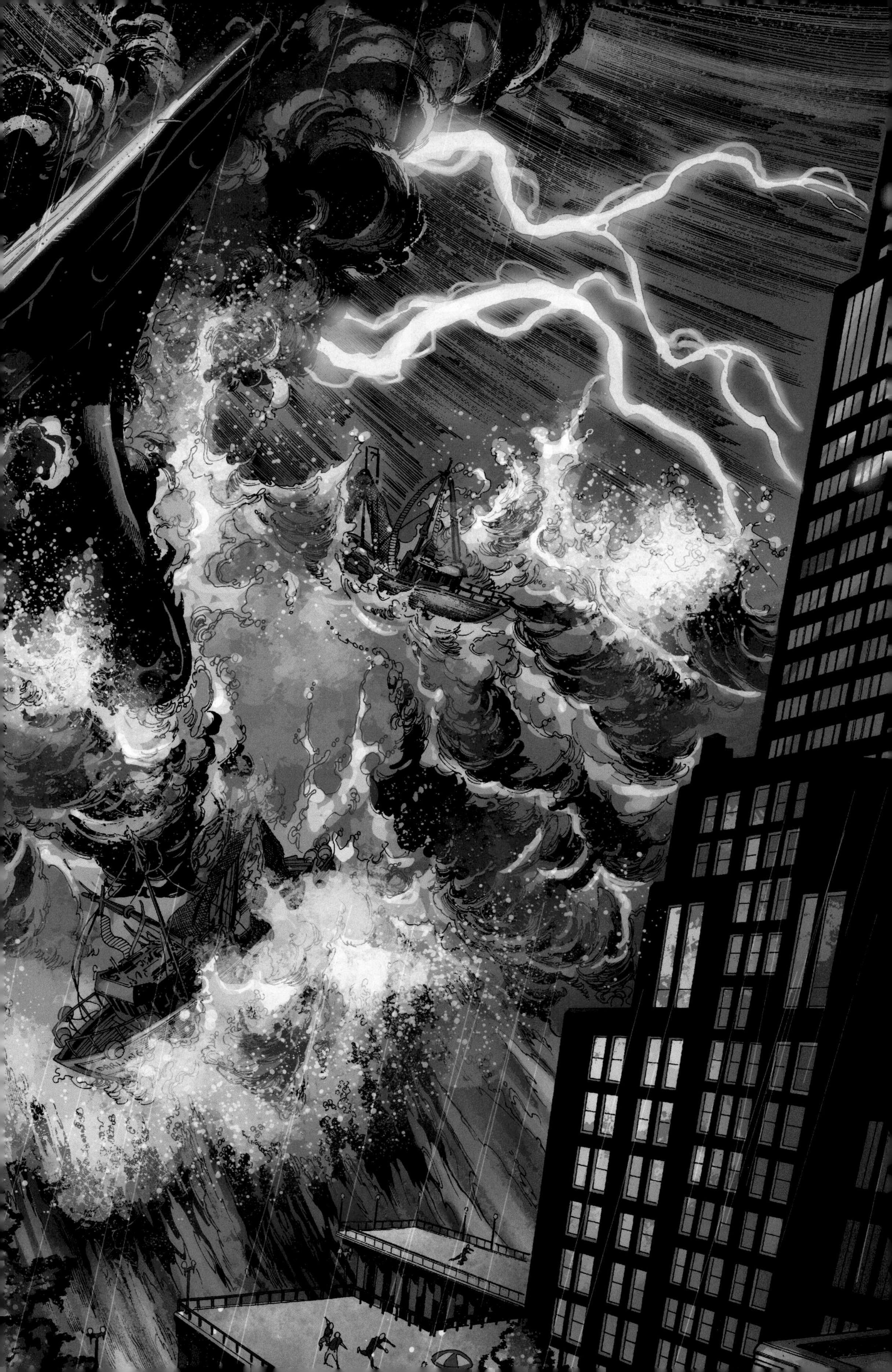

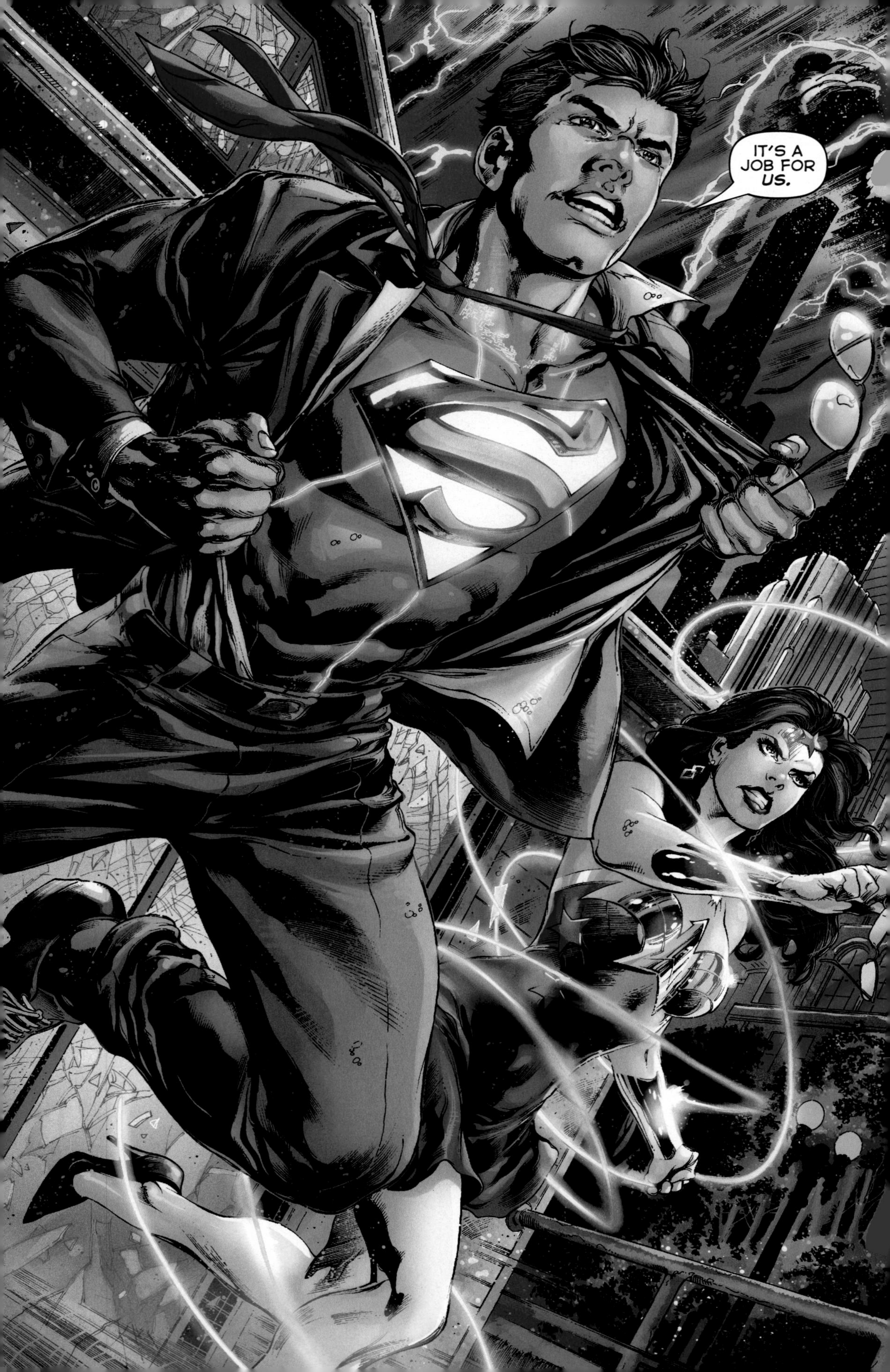
IT'S A JOB FOR US.

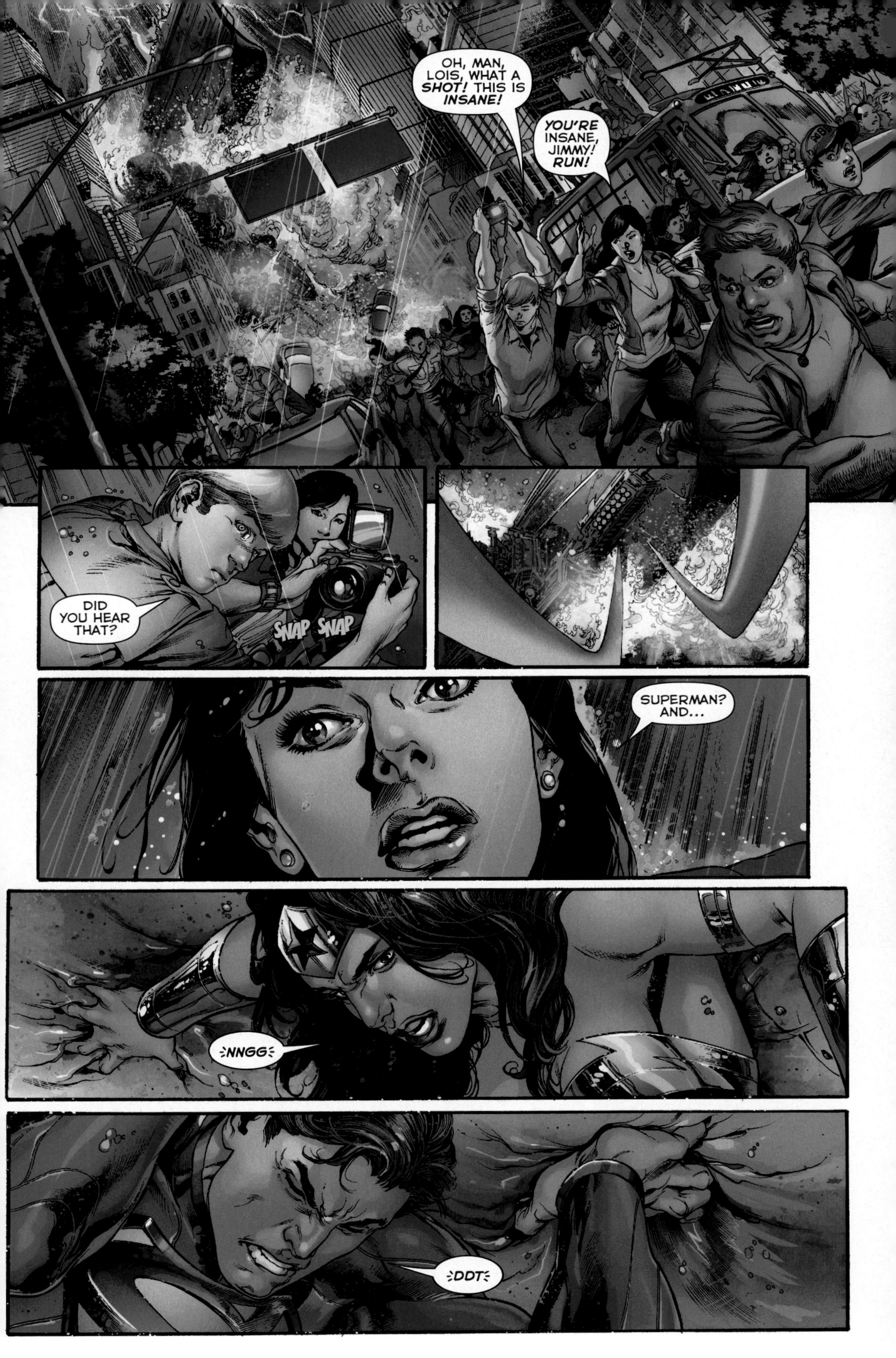
OH, MAN, LOIS, WHAT A SHOT! THIS IS INSANE!
YOU'RE INSANE, JIMMY! RUN!
DID YOU HEAR THAT?
SNAP SNAP
SUPERMAN? AND...
NNGG
DDT

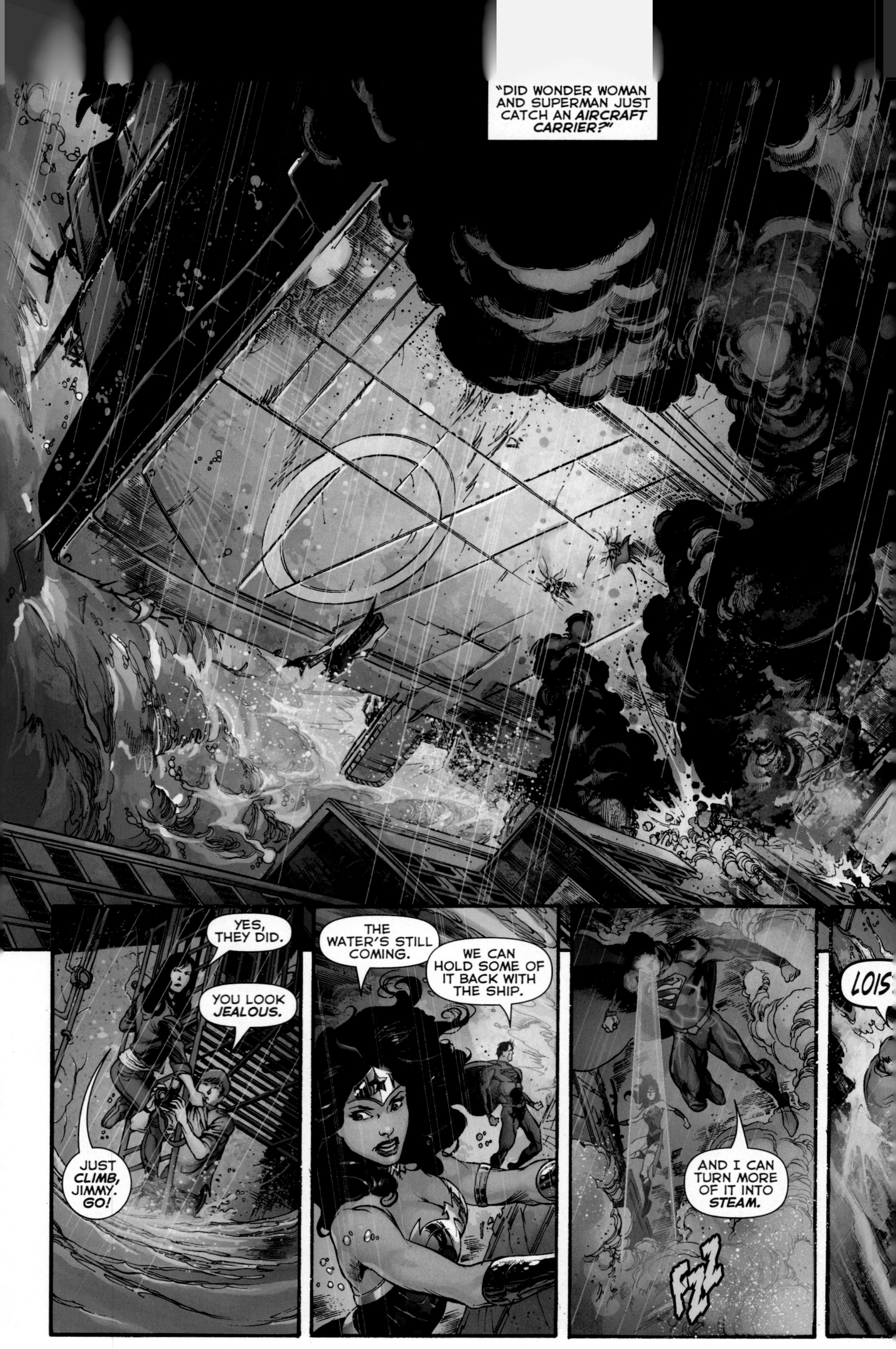
"DID WONDER WOMAN AND SUPERMAN JUST CATCH AN *AIRCRAFT CARRIER?*"
YES, THEY DID.
YOU LOOK *JEALOUS.*
JUST *CLIMB,* JIMMY. *GO!*
THE WATER'S STILL COMING.
WE CAN HOLD SOME OF IT BACK WITH THE SHIP.
AND I CAN TURN MORE OF IT INTO *STEAM.*
FZZ
LOIS

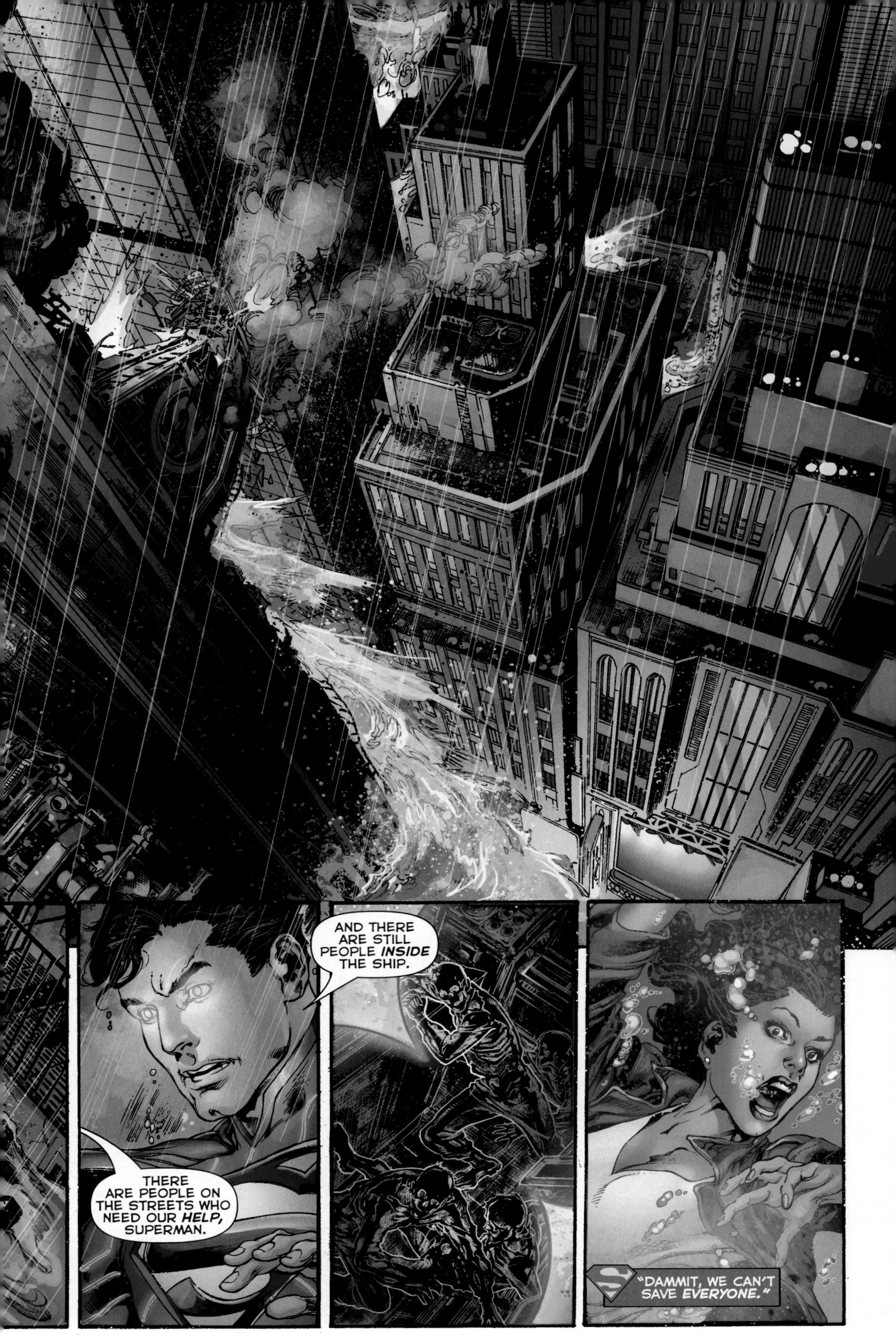
AND THERE ARE STILL PEOPLE *INSIDE* THE SHIP.
THERE ARE PEOPLE ON THE STREETS WHO NEED OUR *HELP*, SUPERMAN.
"DAMMIT, WE CAN'T SAVE *EVERYONE*."

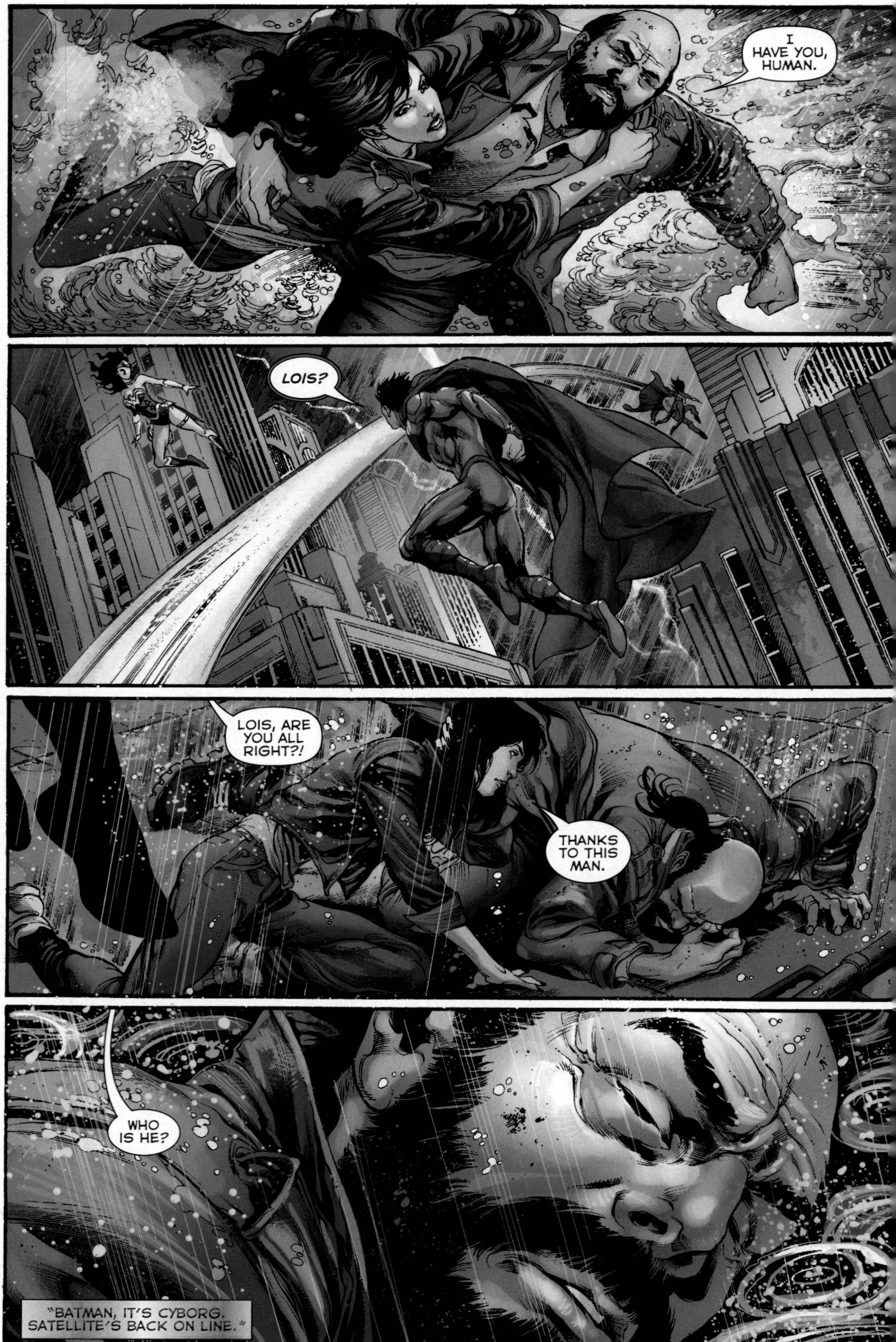
I HAVE YOU, HUMAN.
LOIS?
LOIS, ARE YOU ALL RIGHT?!
THANKS TO THIS MAN.
WHO IS HE?
"BATMAN, IT'S CYBORG. SATELLITE'S BACK ON LINE."

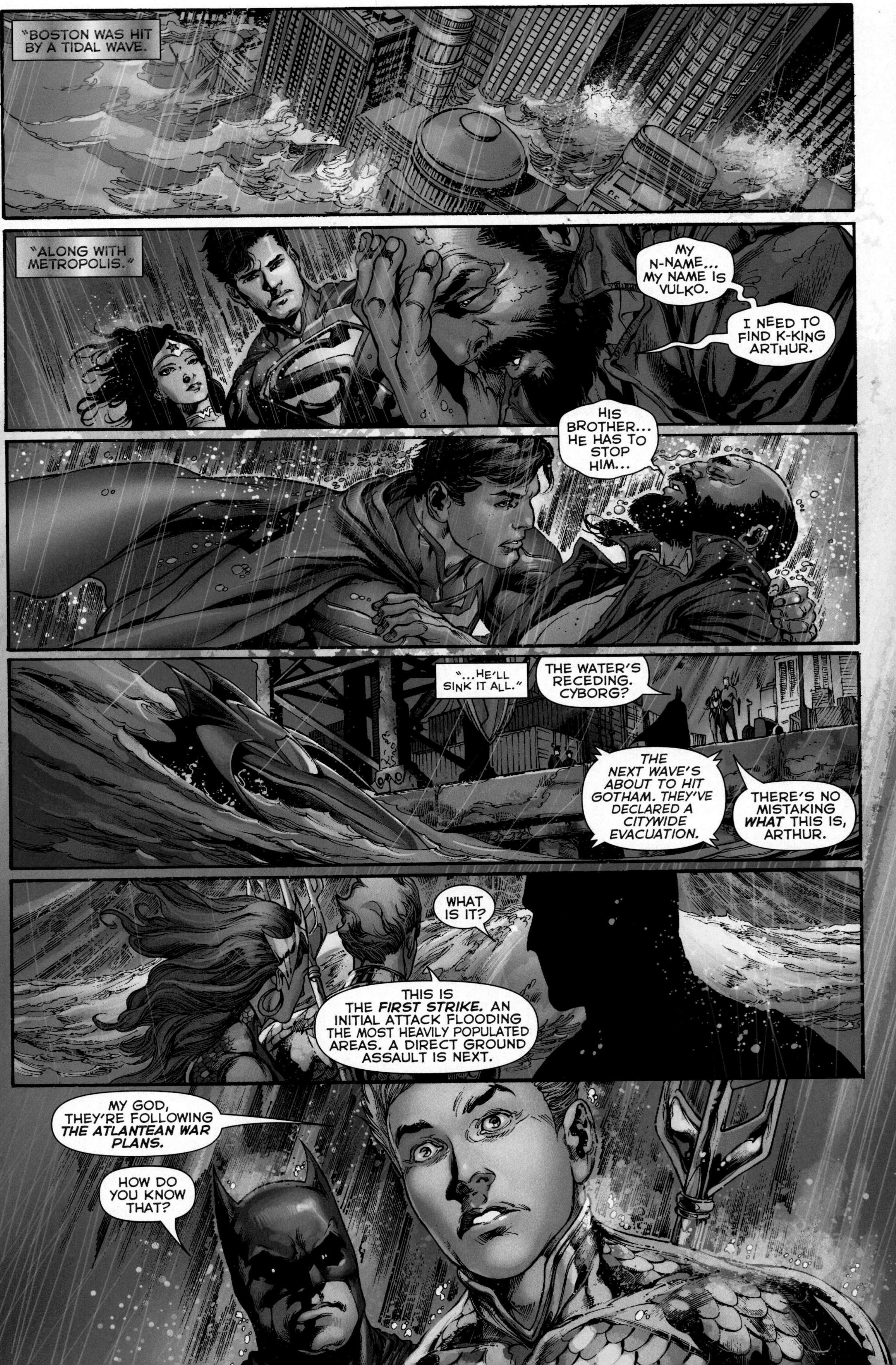
"BOSTON WAS HIT BY A TIDAL WAVE.
"ALONG WITH METROPOLIS."
MY N-NAME... MY NAME IS VULKO.
I NEED TO FIND K-KING ARTHUR.
HIS BROTHER... HE HAS TO STOP HIM...
"...HE'LL SINK IT ALL."
THE WATER'S RECEDING. CYBORG?
THE NEXT WAVE'S ABOUT TO HIT GOTHAM. THEY'VE DECLARED A CITYWIDE EVACUATION.
THERE'S NO MISTAKING WHAT THIS IS, ARTHUR.
WHAT IS IT?
THIS IS THE FIRST STRIKE. AN INITIAL ATTACK FLOODING THE MOST HEAVILY POPULATED AREAS. A DIRECT GROUND ASSAULT IS NEXT.
MY GOD, THEY'RE FOLLOWING THE ATLANTEAN WAR PLANS.
HOW DO YOU KNOW THAT?

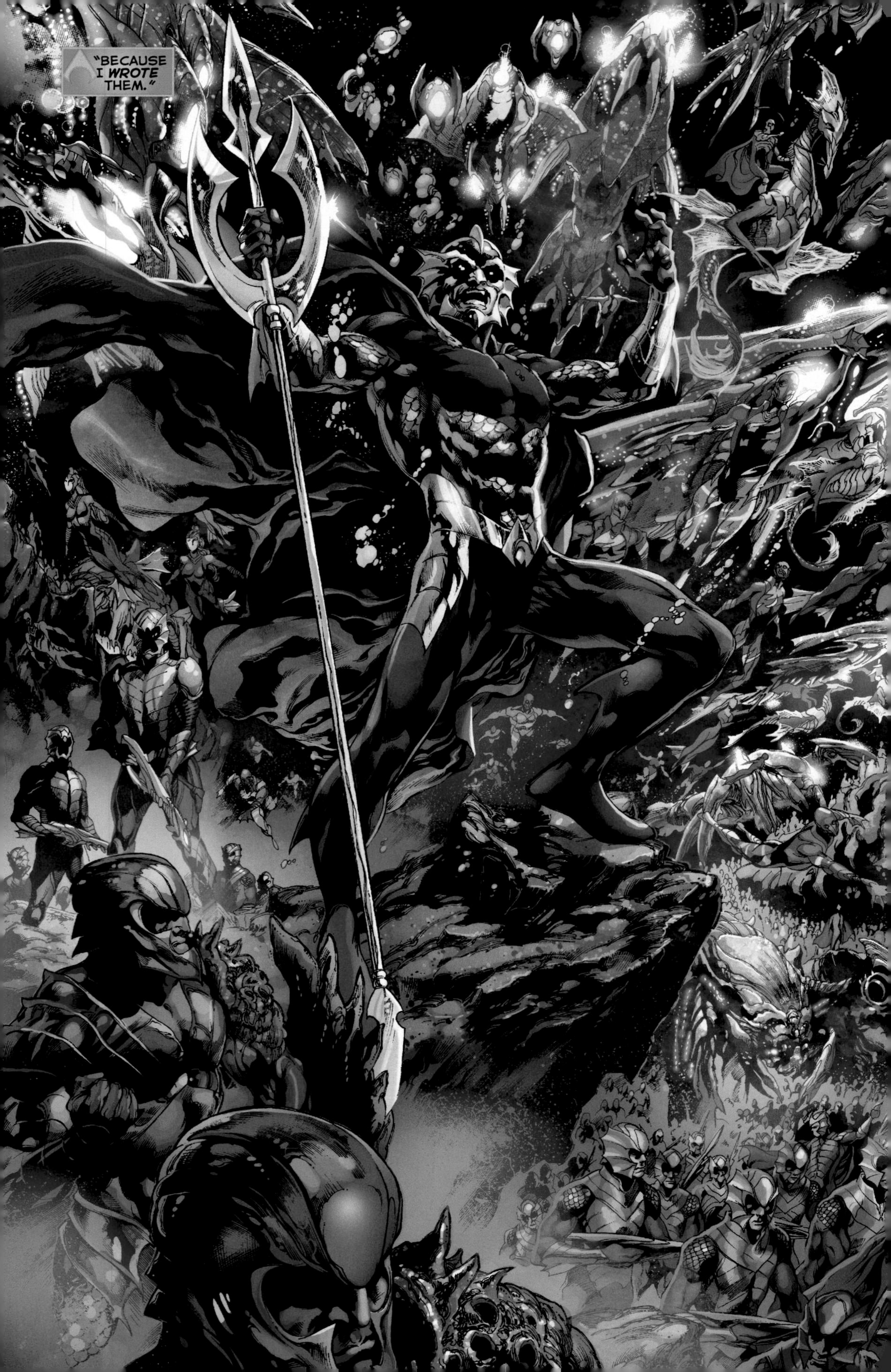
"BECAUSE I WROTE THEM."

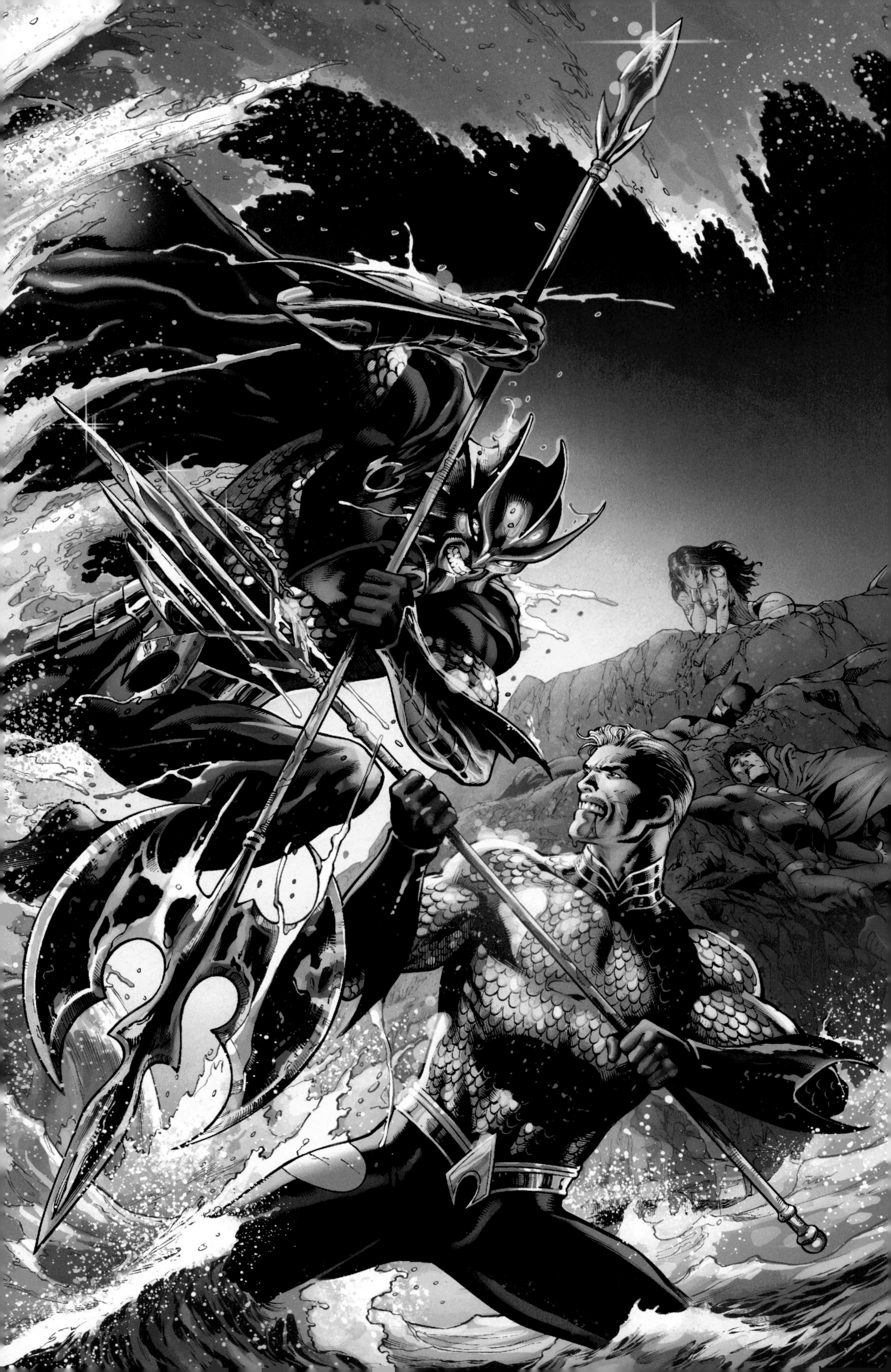

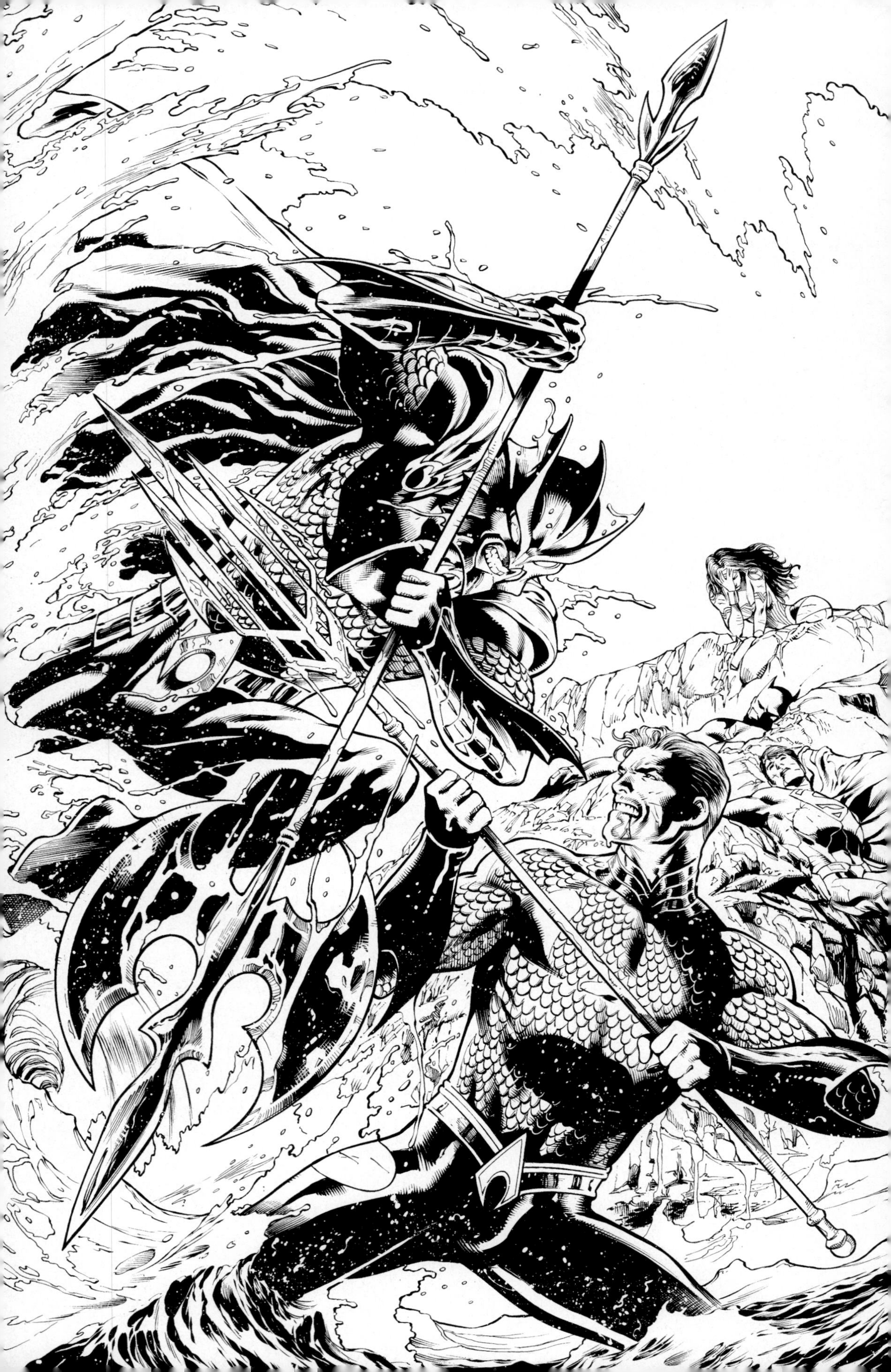

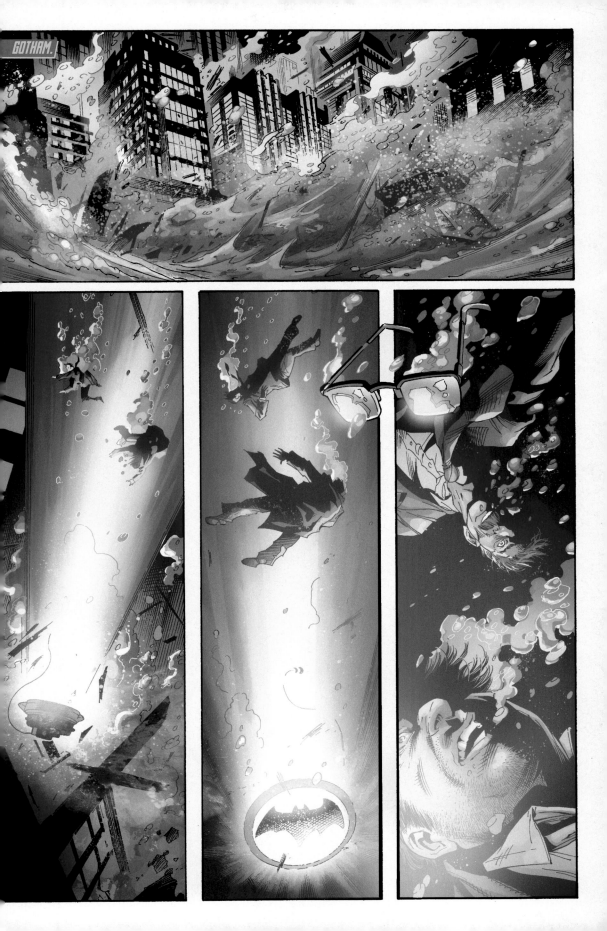

GOTHAM.

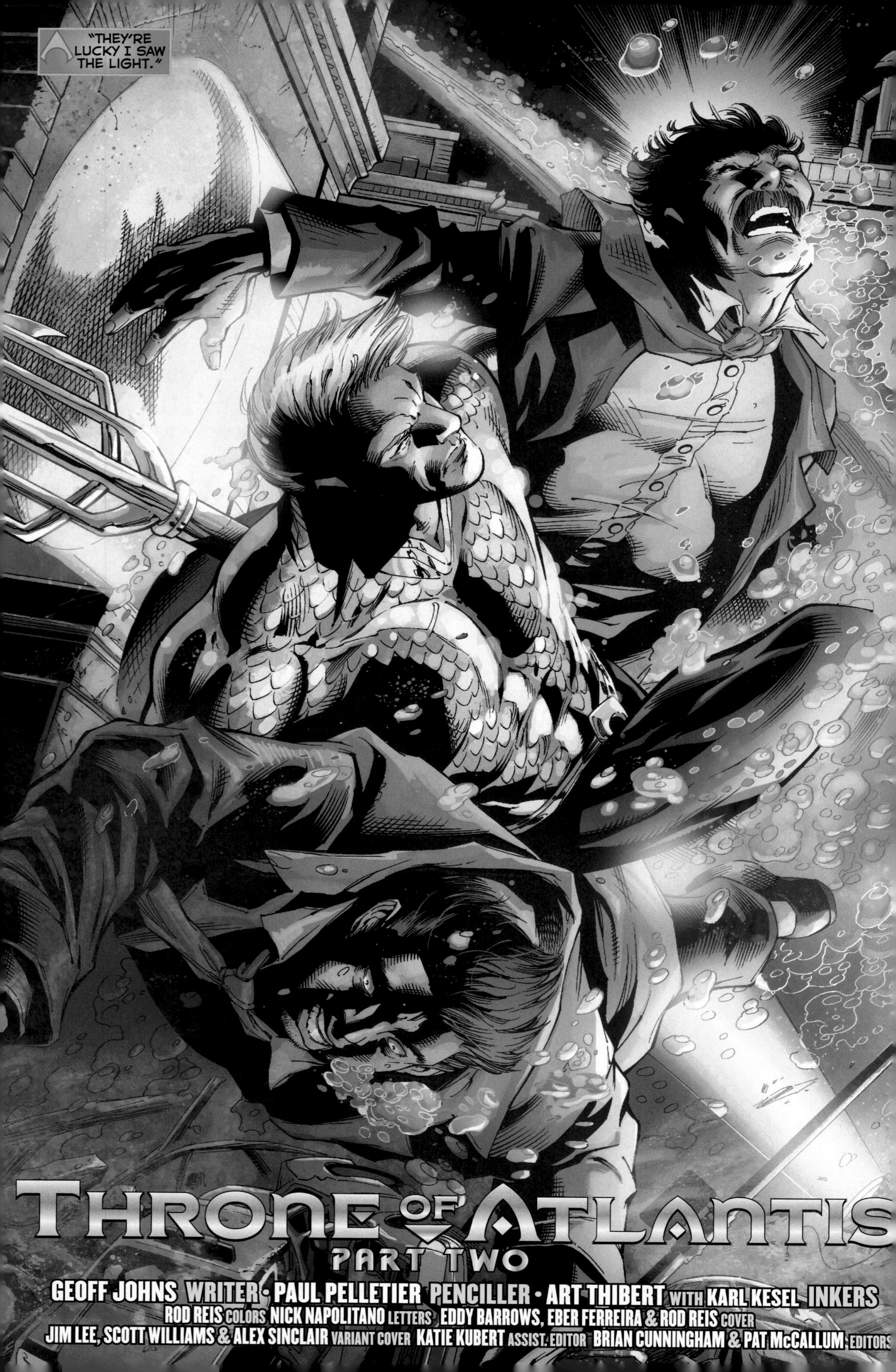
"THEY'RE LUCKY I SAW THE LIGHT."
THRONE OF ATLANTIS
PART TWO
GEOFF JOHNS WRITER · PAUL PELLETIER PENCILLER · ART THIBERT WITH KARL KESEL INKERS
ROD REIS COLORS NICK NAPOLITANO LETTERS EDDY BARROWS, EBER FERREIRA & ROD REIS COVER
JIM LEE, SCOTT WILLIAMS & ALEX SINCLAIR VARIANT COVER KATIE KUBERT ASSIST. EDITOR BRIAN CUNNINGHAM & PAT McCALLUM EDITORS

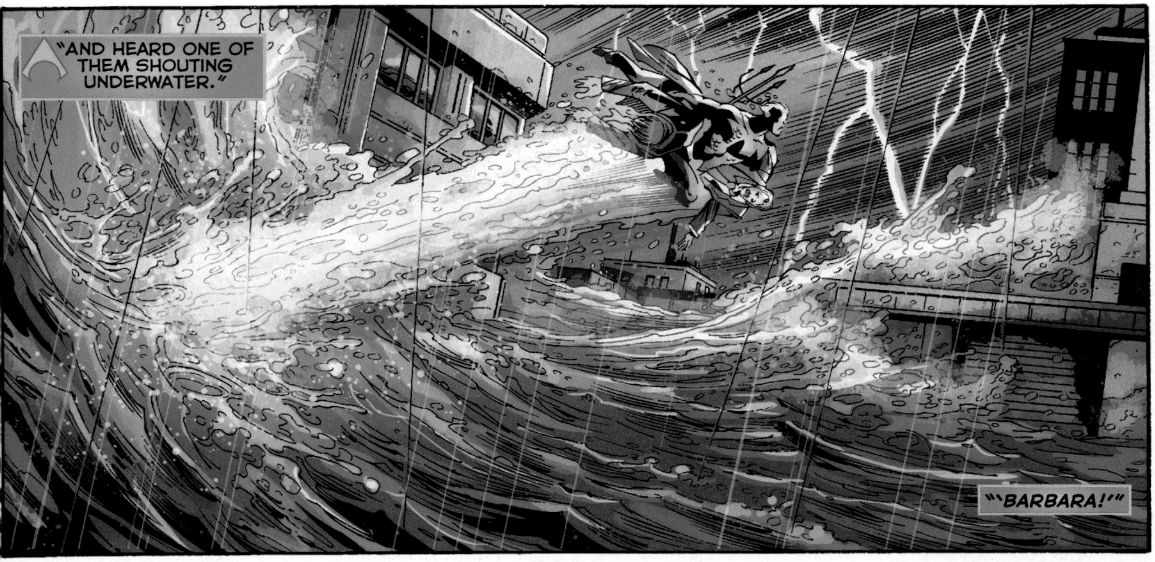
"AND HEARD ONE OF THEM SHOUTING UNDERWATER."
"'BARBARA!'"

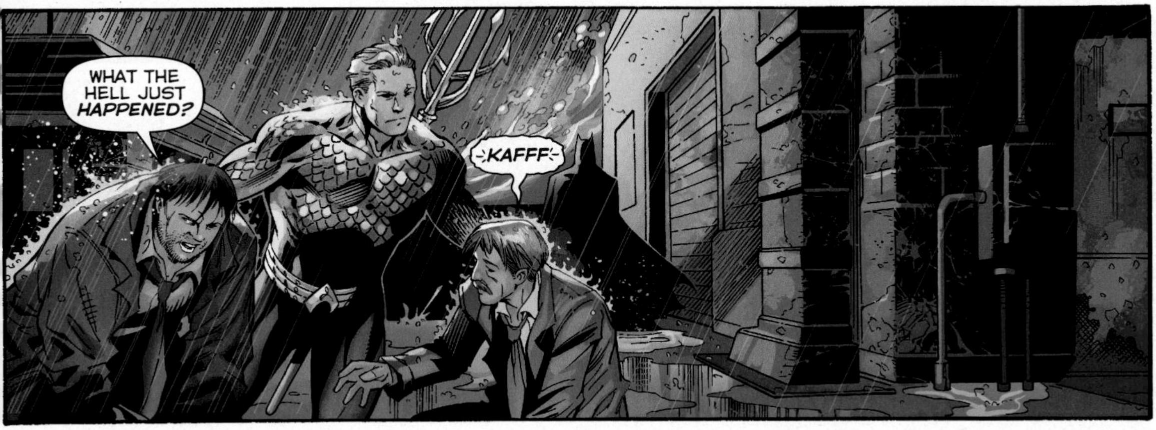
WHAT THE HELL JUST HAPPENED?
KAFFF

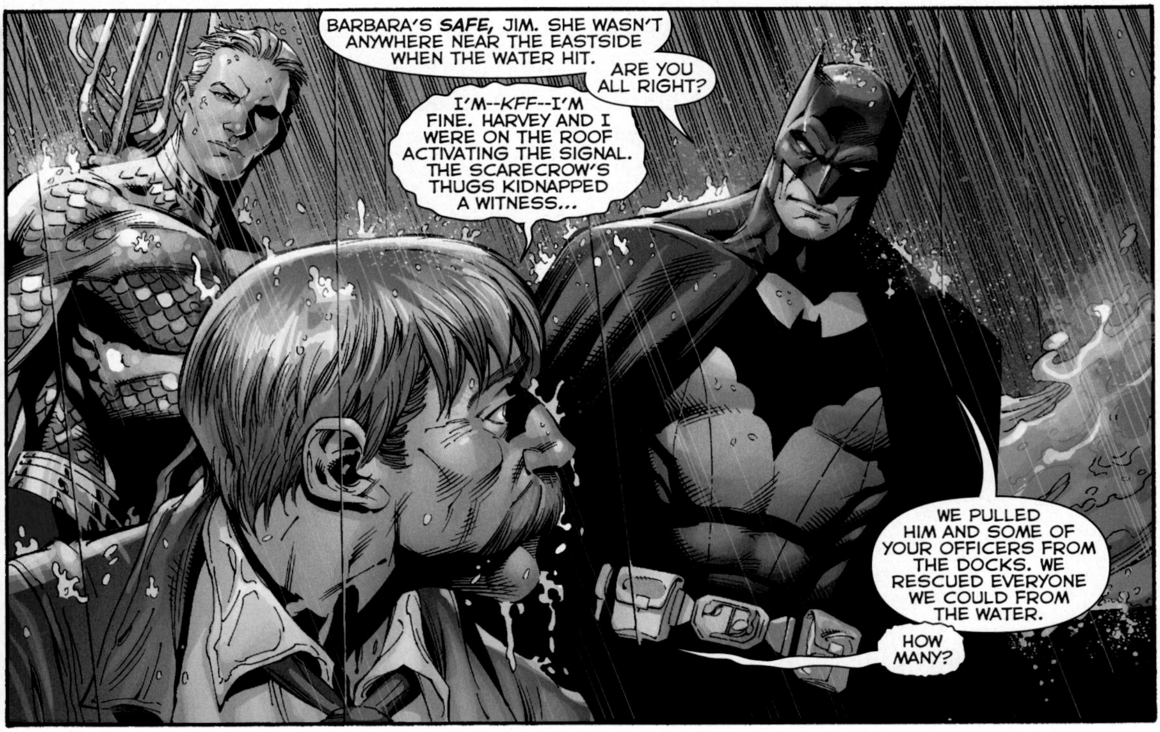
BARBARA'S SAFE, JIM. SHE WASN'T ANYWHERE NEAR THE EASTSIDE WHEN THE WATER HIT.
ARE YOU ALL RIGHT?
I'M--KFF--I'M FINE. HARVEY AND I WERE ON THE ROOF ACTIVATING THE SIGNAL. THE SCARECROW'S THUGS KIDNAPPED A WITNESS...
WE PULLED HIM AND SOME OF YOUR OFFICERS FROM THE DOCKS. WE RESCUED EVERYONE WE COULD FROM THE WATER.
HOW MANY?

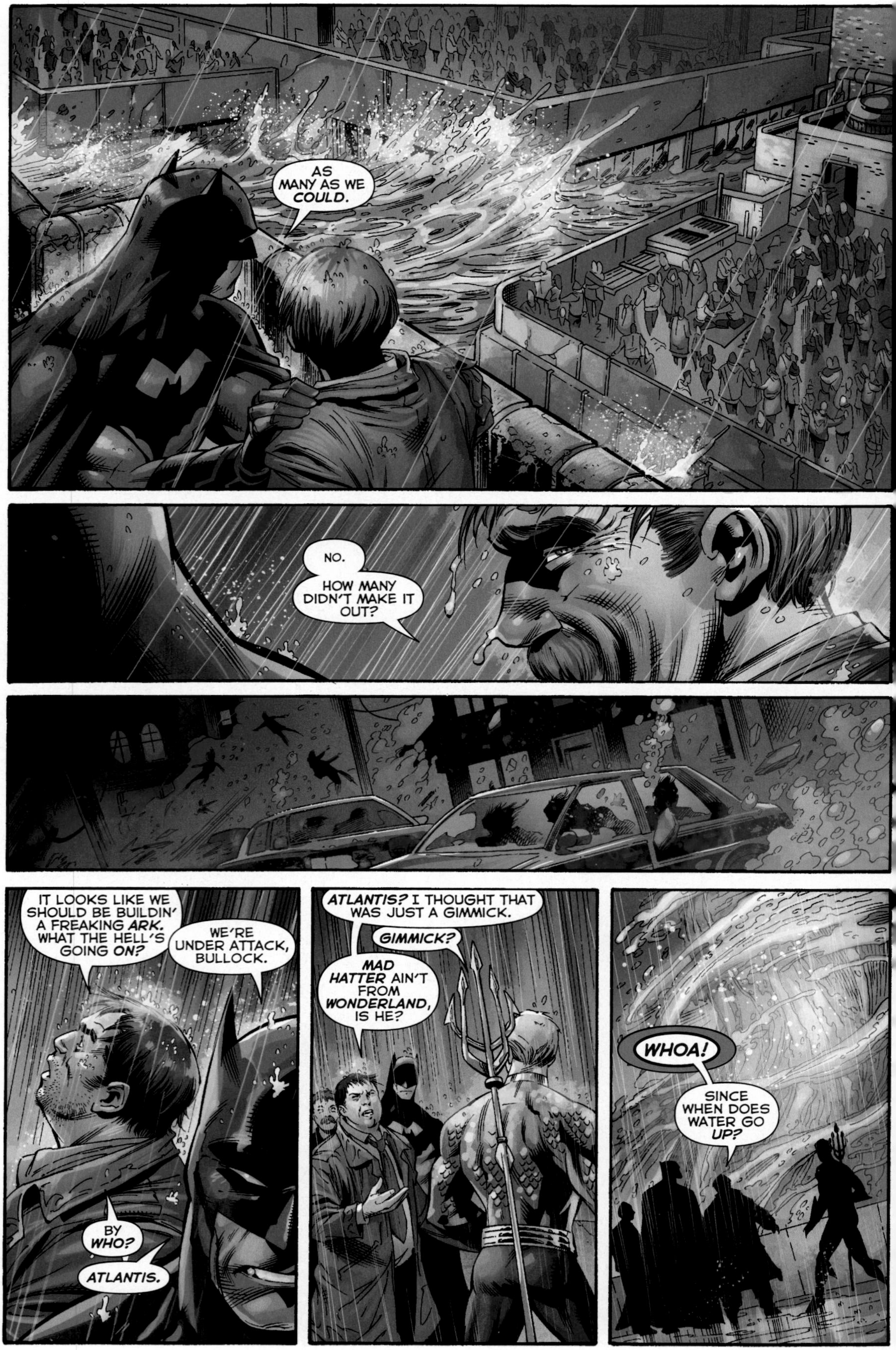
AS MANY AS WE COULD.
NO.
HOW MANY DIDN'T MAKE IT OUT?
IT LOOKS LIKE WE SHOULD BE BUILDIN' A FREAKING ARK. WHAT THE HELL'S GOING ON?
WE'RE UNDER ATTACK, BULLOCK.
BY WHO?
ATLANTIS.
ATLANTIS? I THOUGHT THAT WAS JUST A GIMMICK.
GIMMICK?
MAD HATTER AIN'T FROM WONDERLAND, IS HE?
WHOA!
SINCE WHEN DOES WATER GO UP?

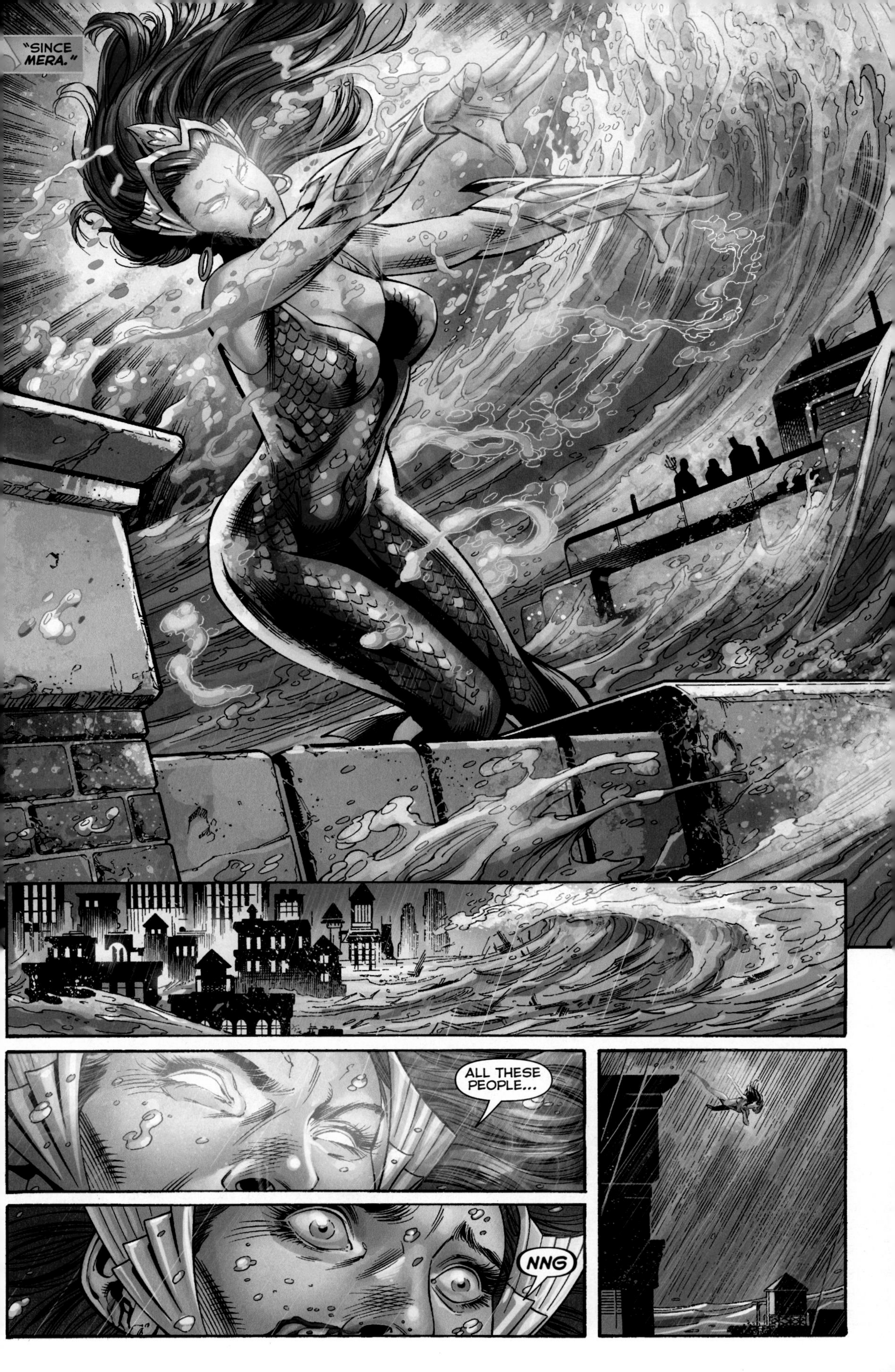
"SINCE MERA."
ALL THESE PEOPLE...
NNG

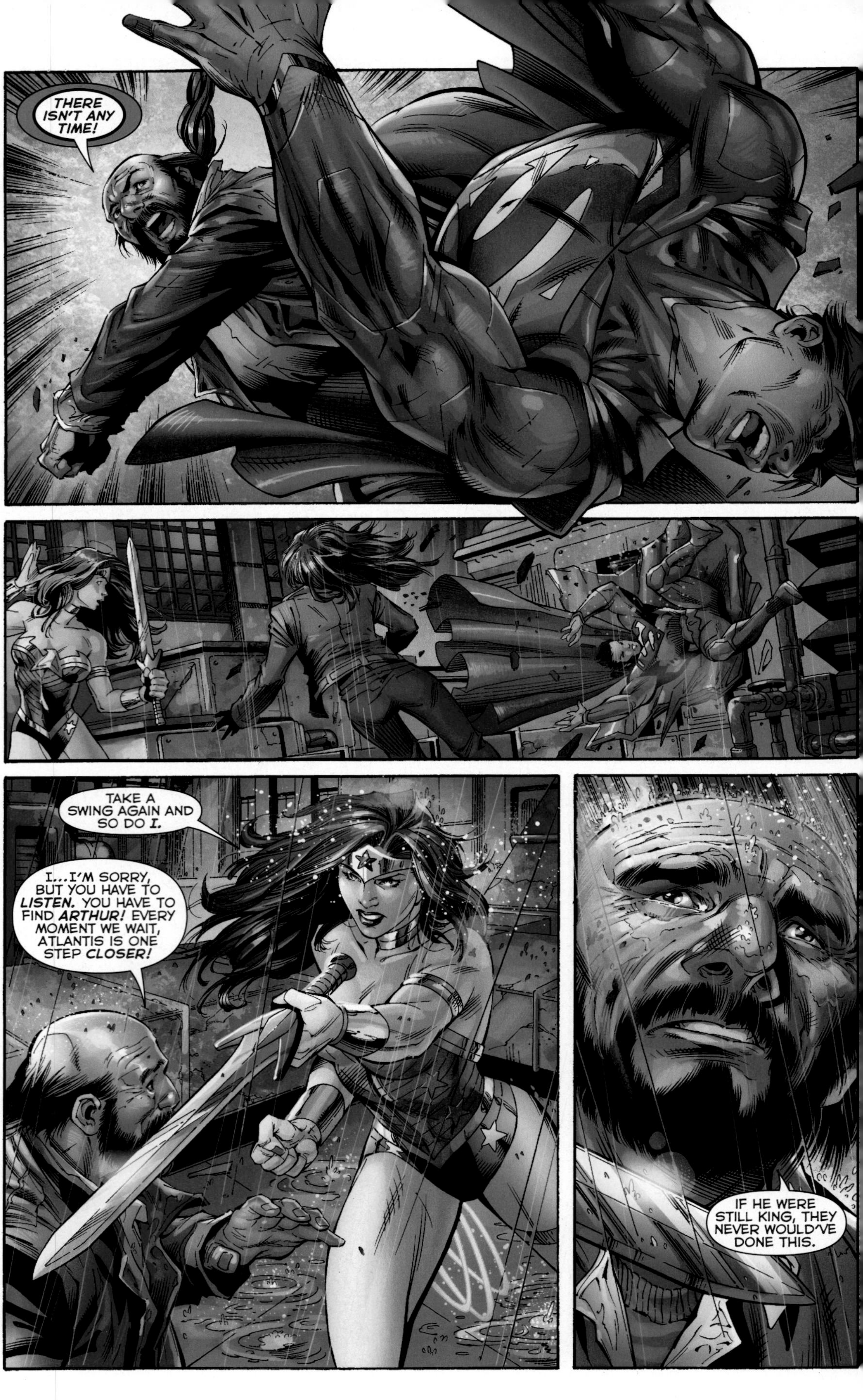
THERE ISN'T ANY TIME!
TAKE A SWING AGAIN AND SO DO *I*.
I...I'M SORRY, BUT YOU HAVE TO *LISTEN.* YOU HAVE TO FIND *ARTHUR!* EVERY MOMENT WE WAIT, ATLANTIS IS ONE STEP *CLOSER!*
IF HE WERE STILL KING, THEY NEVER WOULD'VE DONE THIS.

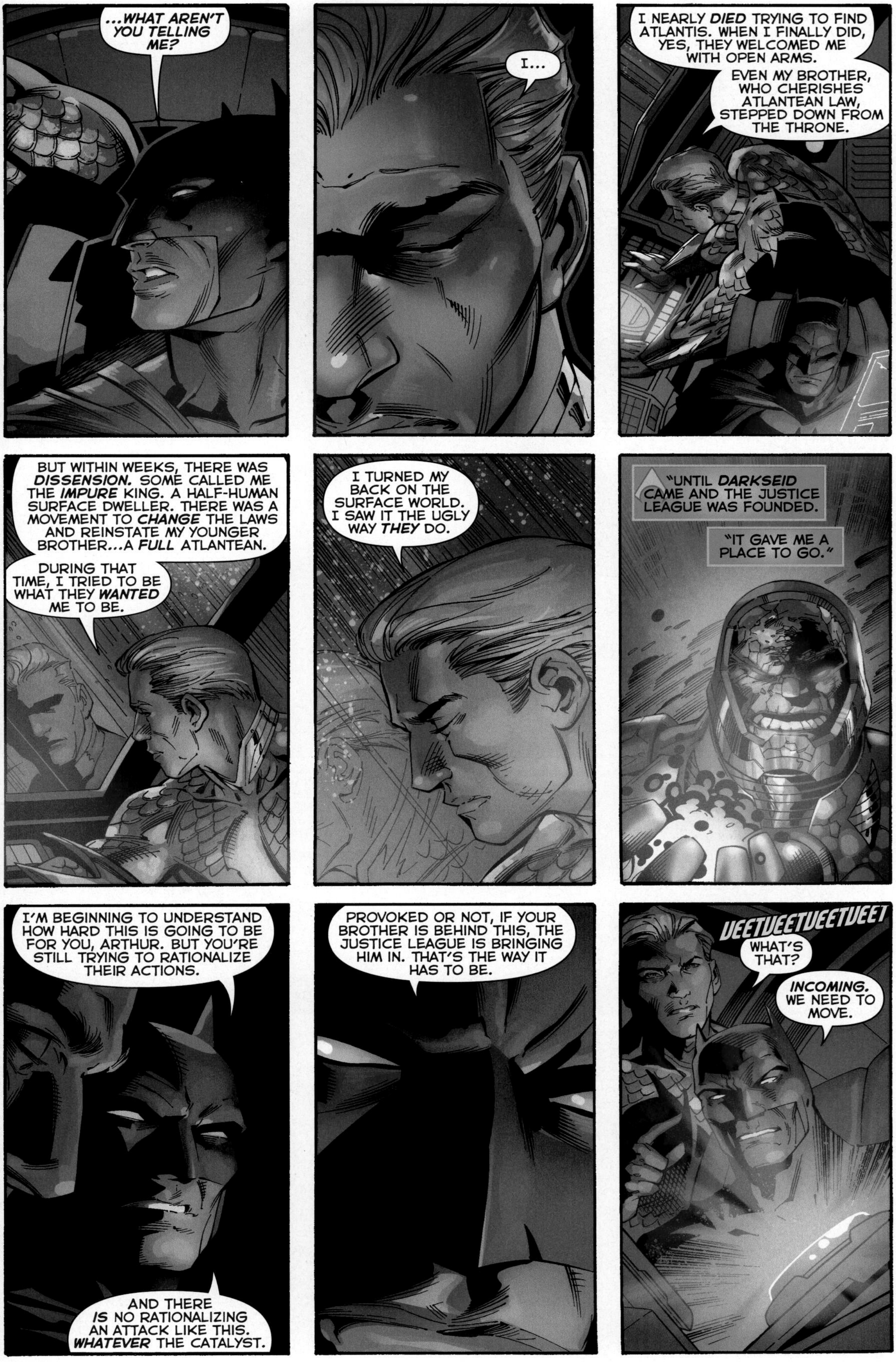
...WHAT AREN'T YOU TELLING ME?
I...
I NEARLY DIED TRYING TO FIND ATLANTIS. WHEN I FINALLY DID, YES, THEY WELCOMED ME WITH OPEN ARMS.
EVEN MY BROTHER, WHO CHERISHES ATLANTEAN LAW, STEPPED DOWN FROM THE THRONE.
BUT WITHIN WEEKS, THERE WAS DISSENSION. SOME CALLED ME THE IMPURE KING. A HALF-HUMAN SURFACE DWELLER. THERE WAS A MOVEMENT TO CHANGE THE LAWS AND REINSTATE MY YOUNGER BROTHER...A FULL ATLANTEAN.
DURING THAT TIME, I TRIED TO BE WHAT THEY WANTED ME TO BE.
I TURNED MY BACK ON THE SURFACE WORLD. I SAW IT THE UGLY WAY THEY DO.
"UNTIL DARKSEID CAME AND THE JUSTICE LEAGUE WAS FOUNDED.
"IT GAVE ME A PLACE TO GO."
I'M BEGINNING TO UNDERSTAND HOW HARD THIS IS GOING TO BE FOR YOU, ARTHUR. BUT YOU'RE STILL TRYING TO RATIONALIZE THEIR ACTIONS.
AND THERE IS NO RATIONALIZING AN ATTACK LIKE THIS. WHATEVER THE CATALYST.
PROVOKED OR NOT, IF YOUR BROTHER IS BEHIND THIS, THE JUSTICE LEAGUE IS BRINGING HIM IN. THAT'S THE WAY IT HAS TO BE.
VEETVEETVEETVEET
WHAT'S THAT?
INCOMING. WE NEED TO MOVE.

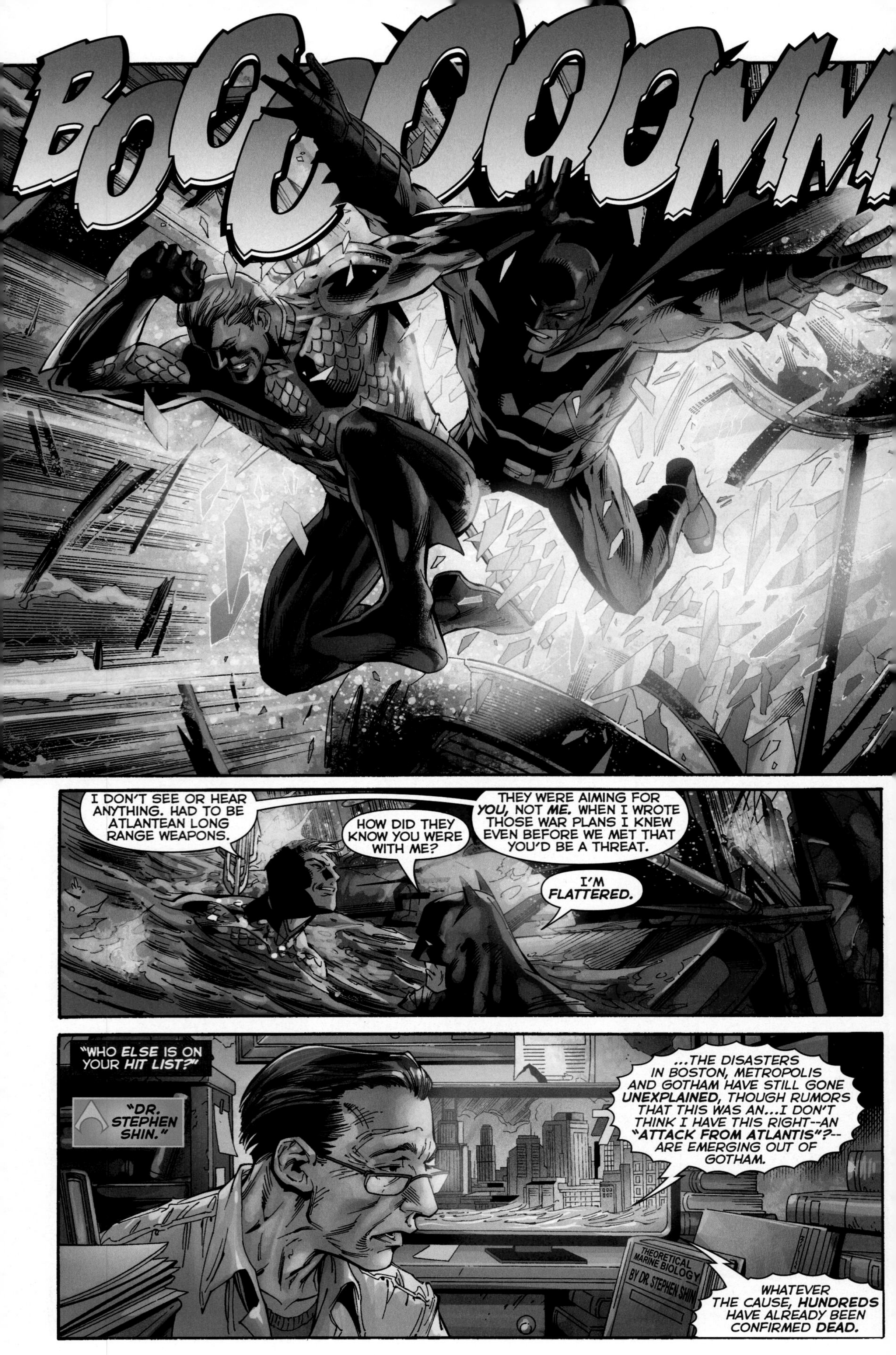
BOOOOOOMM
I DON'T SEE OR HEAR ANYTHING. HAD TO BE ATLANTEAN LONG RANGE WEAPONS.
HOW DID THEY KNOW YOU WERE WITH ME?
THEY WERE AIMING FOR YOU, NOT ME. WHEN I WROTE THOSE WAR PLANS I KNEW EVEN BEFORE WE MET THAT YOU'D BE A THREAT.
I'M FLATTERED.
"WHO ELSE IS ON YOUR HIT LIST?"
"DR. STEPHEN SHIN."
...THE DISASTERS IN BOSTON, METROPOLIS AND GOTHAM HAVE STILL GONE UNEXPLAINED, THOUGH RUMORS THAT THIS WAS AN...I DON'T THINK I HAVE THIS RIGHT--AN "ATTACK FROM ATLANTIS"?--ARE EMERGING OUT OF GOTHAM.
THEORETICAL MARINE BIOLOGY BY DR. STEPHEN SHIN
WHATEVER THE CAUSE, HUNDREDS HAVE ALREADY BEEN CONFIRMED DEAD.

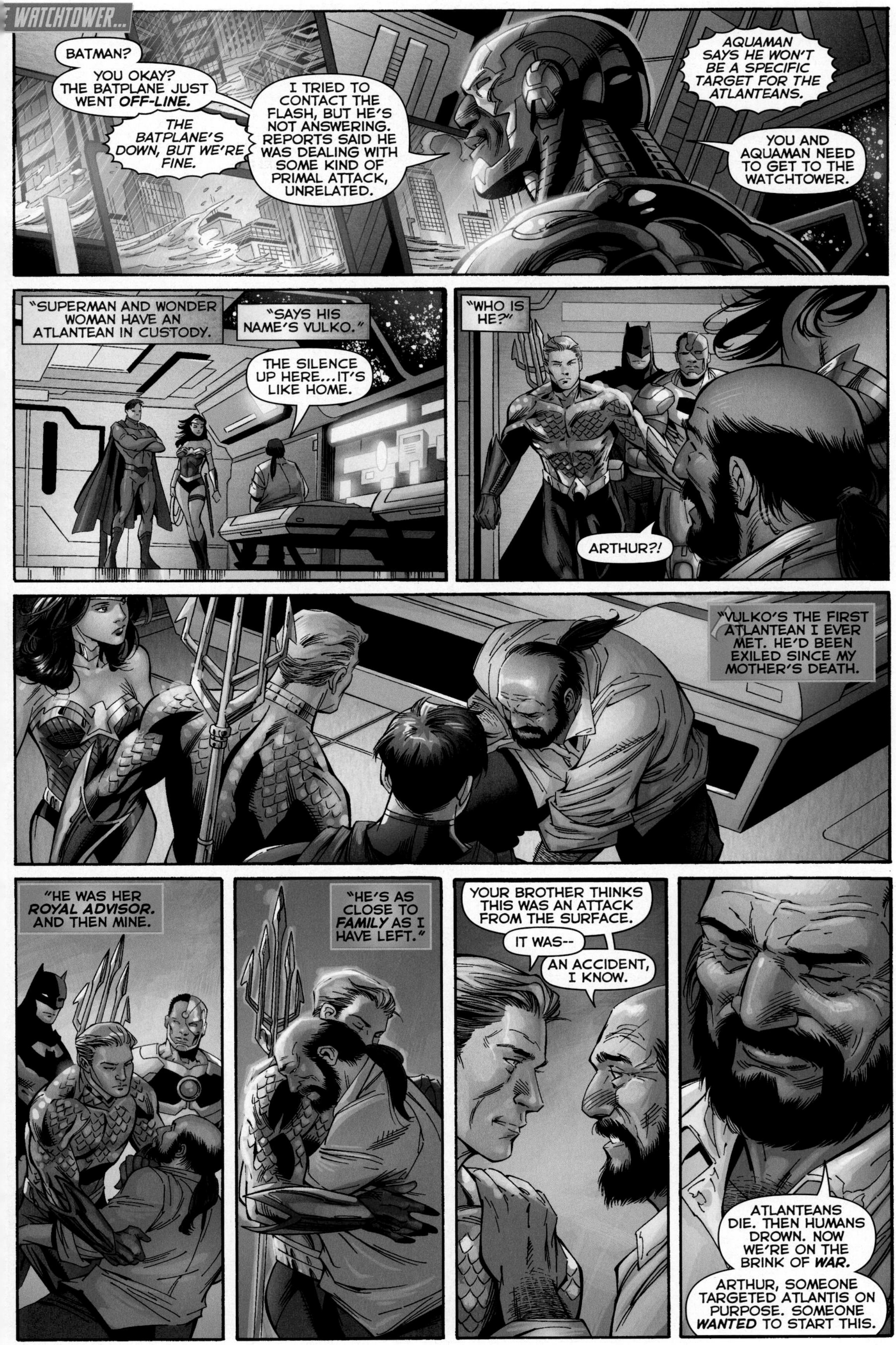
WATCHTOWER...
BATMAN?
YOU OKAY? THE BATPLANE JUST WENT OFF-LINE.
THE BATPLANE'S DOWN, BUT WE'RE FINE.
I TRIED TO CONTACT THE FLASH, BUT HE'S NOT ANSWERING. REPORTS SAID HE WAS DEALING WITH SOME KIND OF PRIMAL ATTACK, UNRELATED.
AQUAMAN SAYS HE WON'T BE A SPECIFIC TARGET FOR THE ATLANTEANS.
YOU AND AQUAMAN NEED TO GET TO THE WATCHTOWER.
"SUPERMAN AND WONDER WOMAN HAVE AN ATLANTEAN IN CUSTODY.
"SAYS HIS NAME'S VULKO."
THE SILENCE UP HERE...IT'S LIKE HOME.
"WHO IS HE?"
ARTHUR?!
"VULKO'S THE FIRST ATLANTEAN I EVER MET. HE'D BEEN EXILED SINCE MY MOTHER'S DEATH.
"HE WAS HER ROYAL ADVISOR. AND THEN MINE.
"HE'S AS CLOSE TO FAMILY AS I HAVE LEFT."
YOUR BROTHER THINKS THIS WAS AN ATTACK FROM THE SURFACE.
IT WAS--
AN ACCIDENT, I KNOW.
ATLANTEANS DIE. THEN HUMANS DROWN. NOW WE'RE ON THE BRINK OF WAR.
ARTHUR, SOMEONE TARGETED ATLANTIS ON PURPOSE. SOMEONE WANTED TO START THIS.

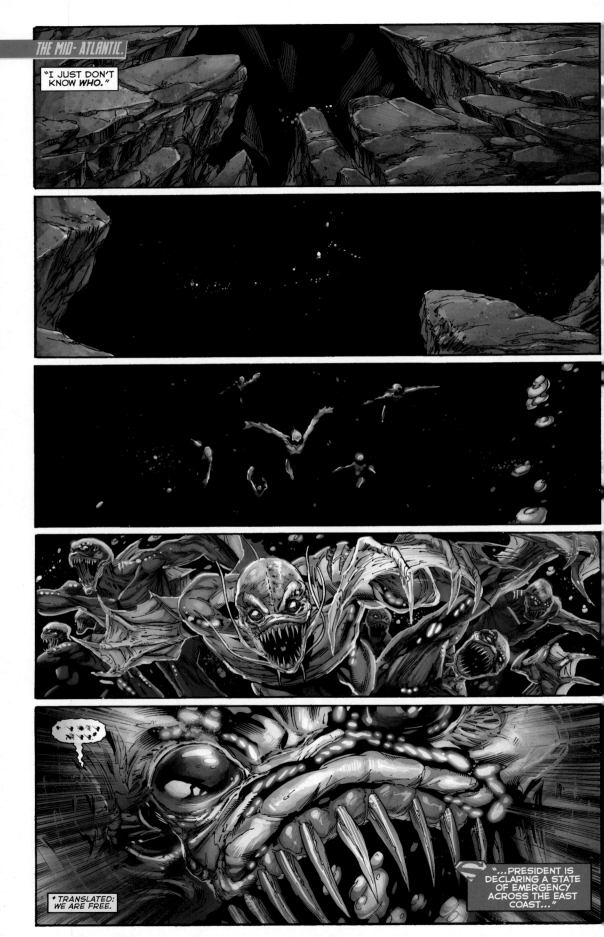

"I JUST DON'T KNOW *WHO*."

*TRANSLATED: WE ARE FREE.

"...PRESIDENT IS DECLARING A STATE OF EMERGENCY ACROSS THE EAST COAST..."

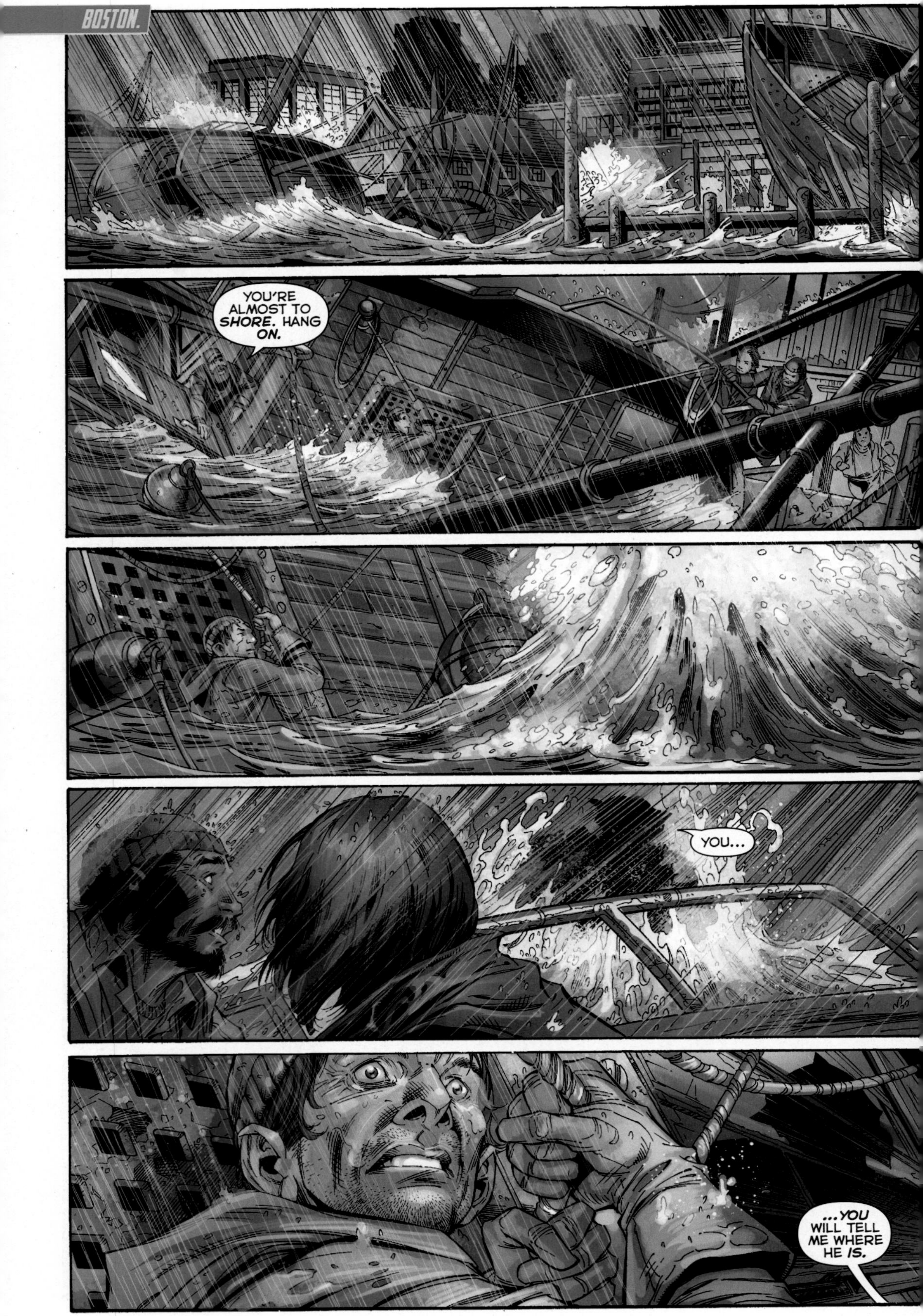
BOSTON.
YOU'RE ALMOST TO SHORE. HANG ON.
YOU...
...YOU WILL TELL ME WHERE HE IS.

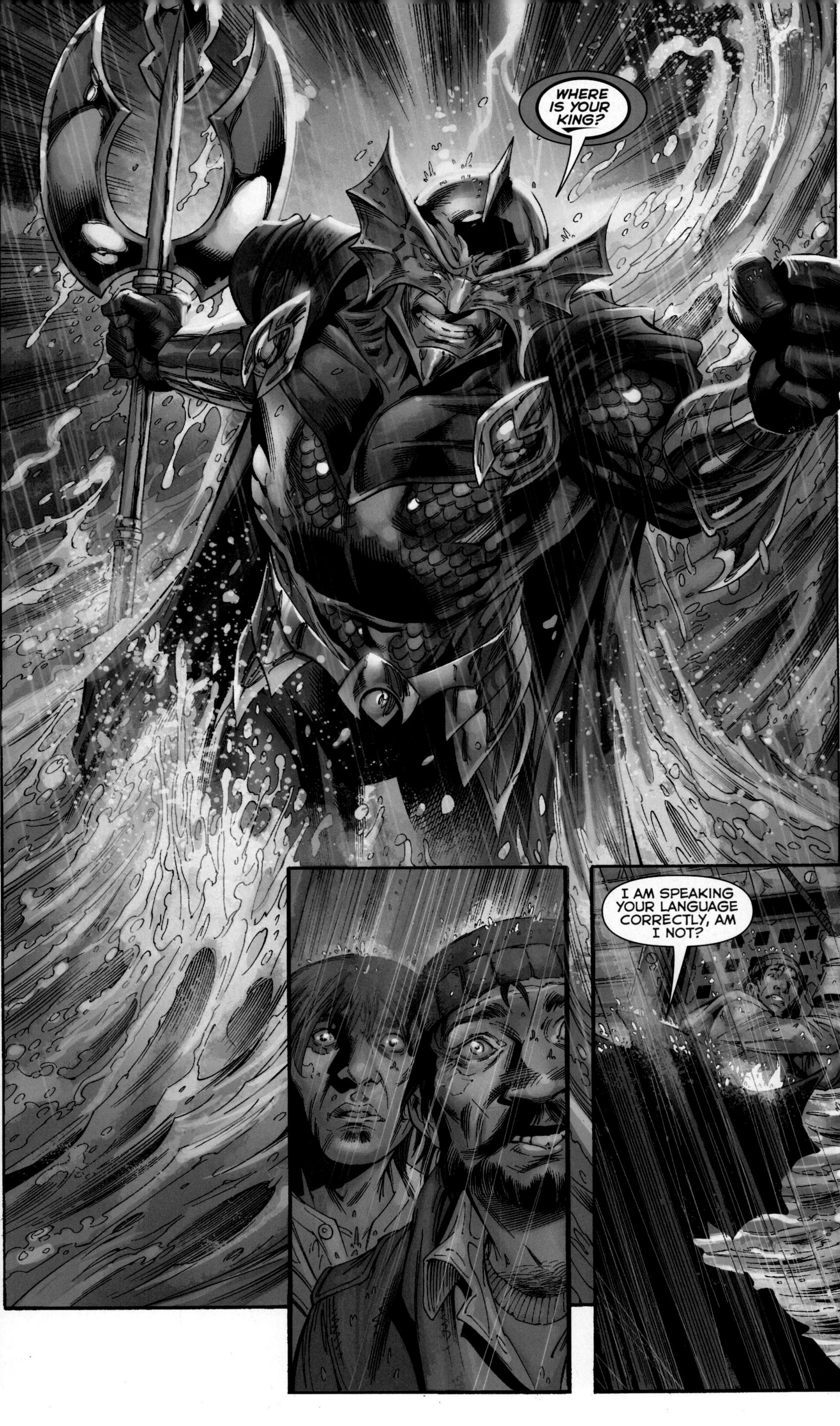
WHERE IS YOUR KING?
I AM SPEAKING YOUR LANGUAGE CORRECTLY, AM I NOT?

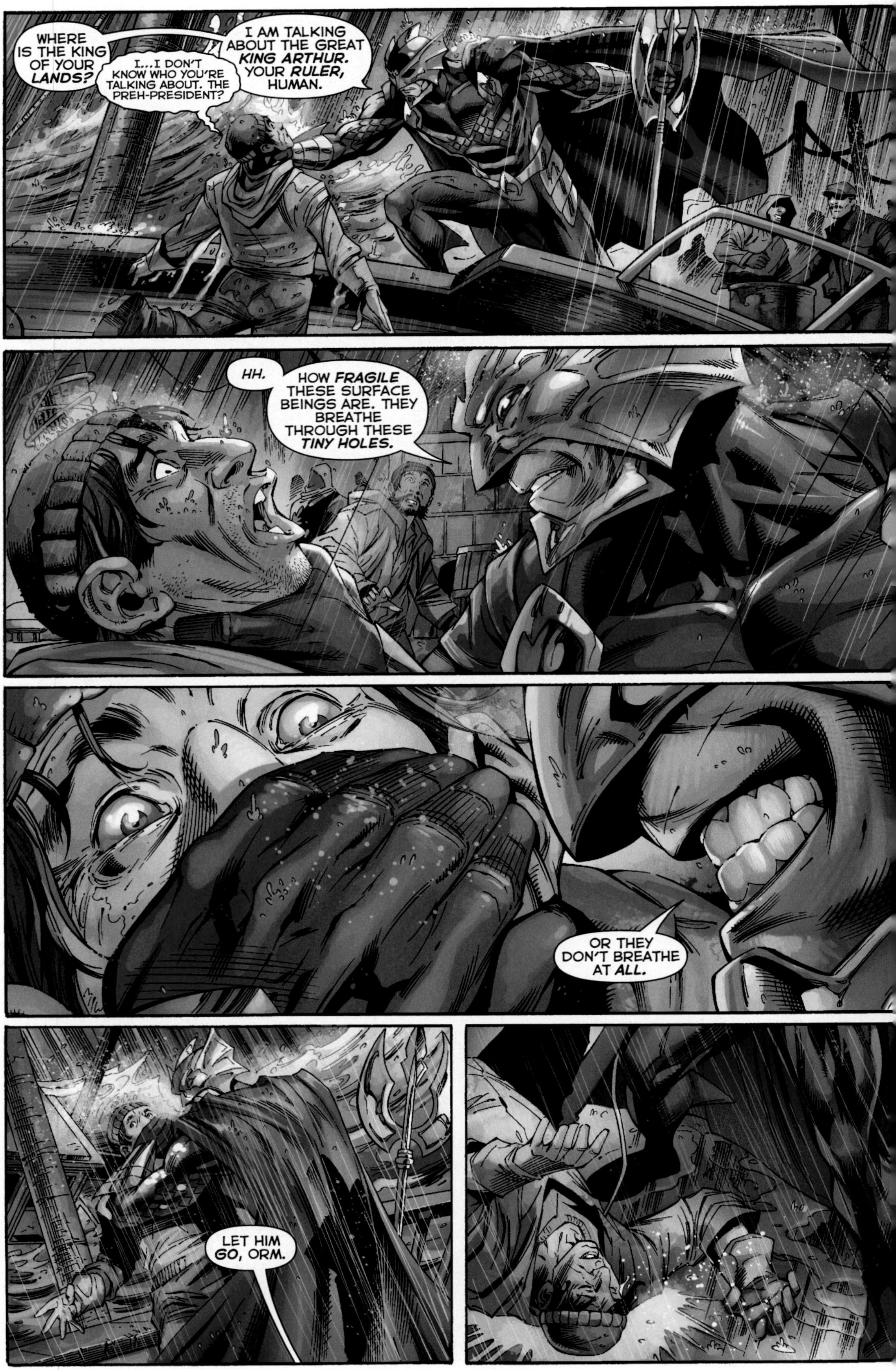
WHERE IS THE KING OF YOUR LANDS?
I AM TALKING ABOUT THE GREAT KING ARTHUR. YOUR RULER, HUMAN.
I...I DON'T KNOW WHO YOU'RE TALKING ABOUT. THE PREH-PRESIDENT?
HH.
HOW FRAGILE THESE SURFACE BEINGS ARE. THEY BREATHE THROUGH THESE TINY HOLES.
OR THEY DON'T BREATHE AT ALL.
LET HIM GO, ORM.

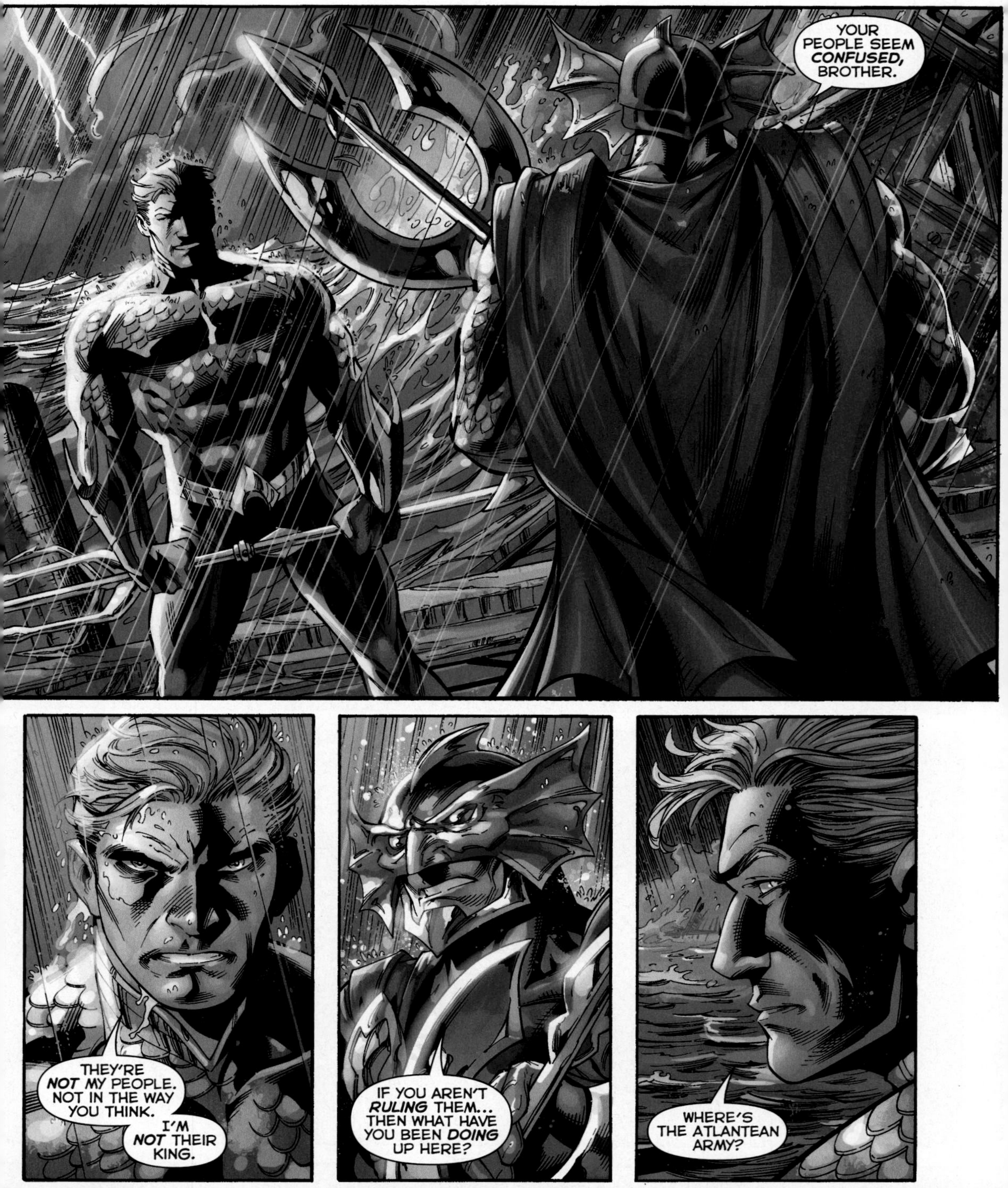
YOUR PEOPLE SEEM CONFUSED, BROTHER.
THEY'RE NOT MY PEOPLE. NOT IN THE WAY YOU THINK.
I'M NOT THEIR KING.
IF YOU AREN'T RULING THEM... THEN WHAT HAVE YOU BEEN DOING UP HERE?
WHERE'S THE ATLANTEAN ARMY?
JUST BENEATH THE SURFACE. WAITING FOR MY SIGNAL.

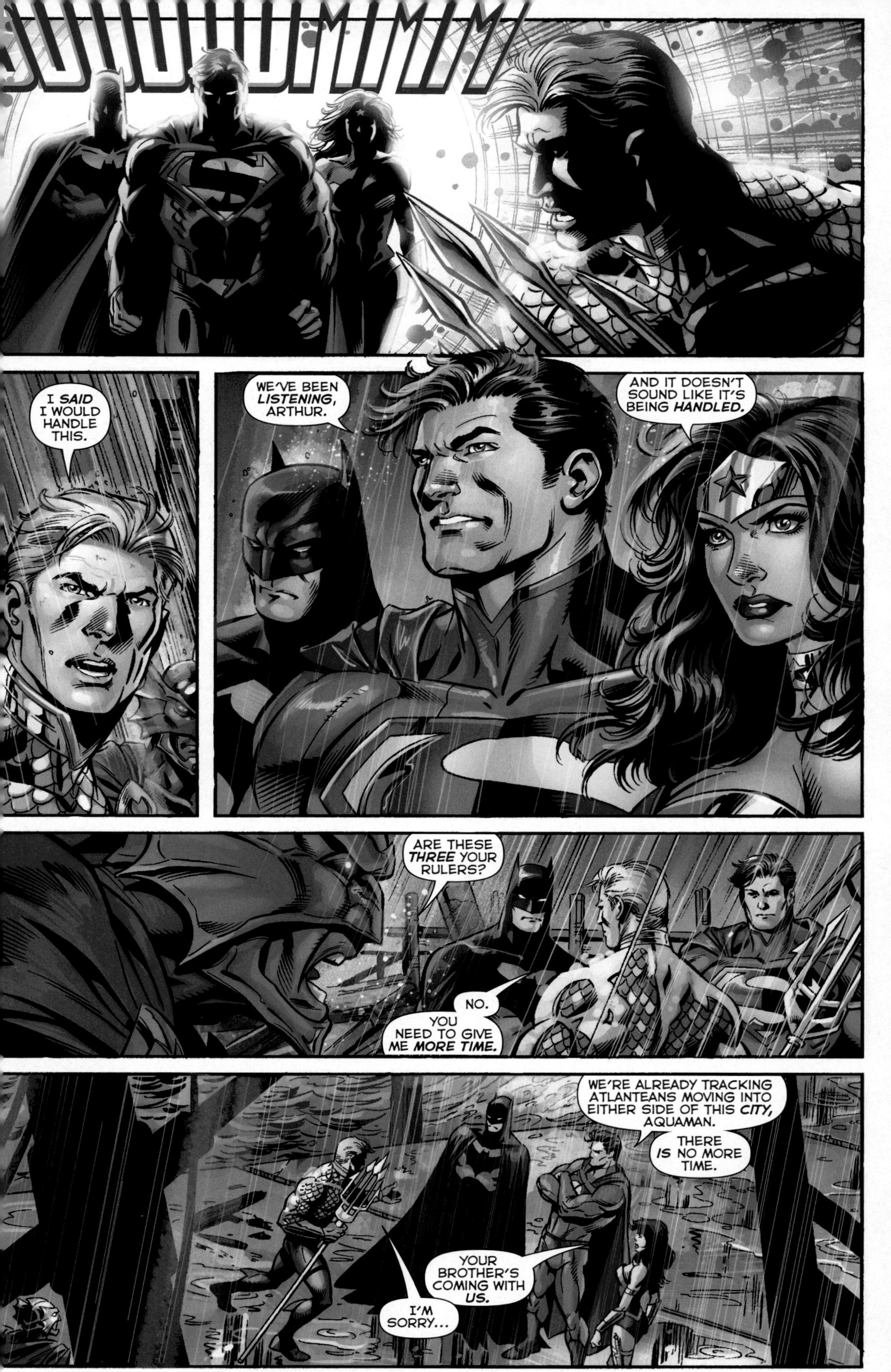

SHHHHMMMM
I SAID I WOULD HANDLE THIS.
WE'VE BEEN LISTENING, ARTHUR.
AND IT DOESN'T SOUND LIKE IT'S BEING HANDLED.
ARE THESE THREE YOUR RULERS?
NO.
YOU NEED TO GIVE ME MORE TIME.
WE'RE ALREADY TRACKING ATLANTEANS MOVING INTO EITHER SIDE OF THIS CITY, AQUAMAN.
THERE IS NO MORE TIME.
YOUR BROTHER'S COMING WITH US.
I'M SORRY...

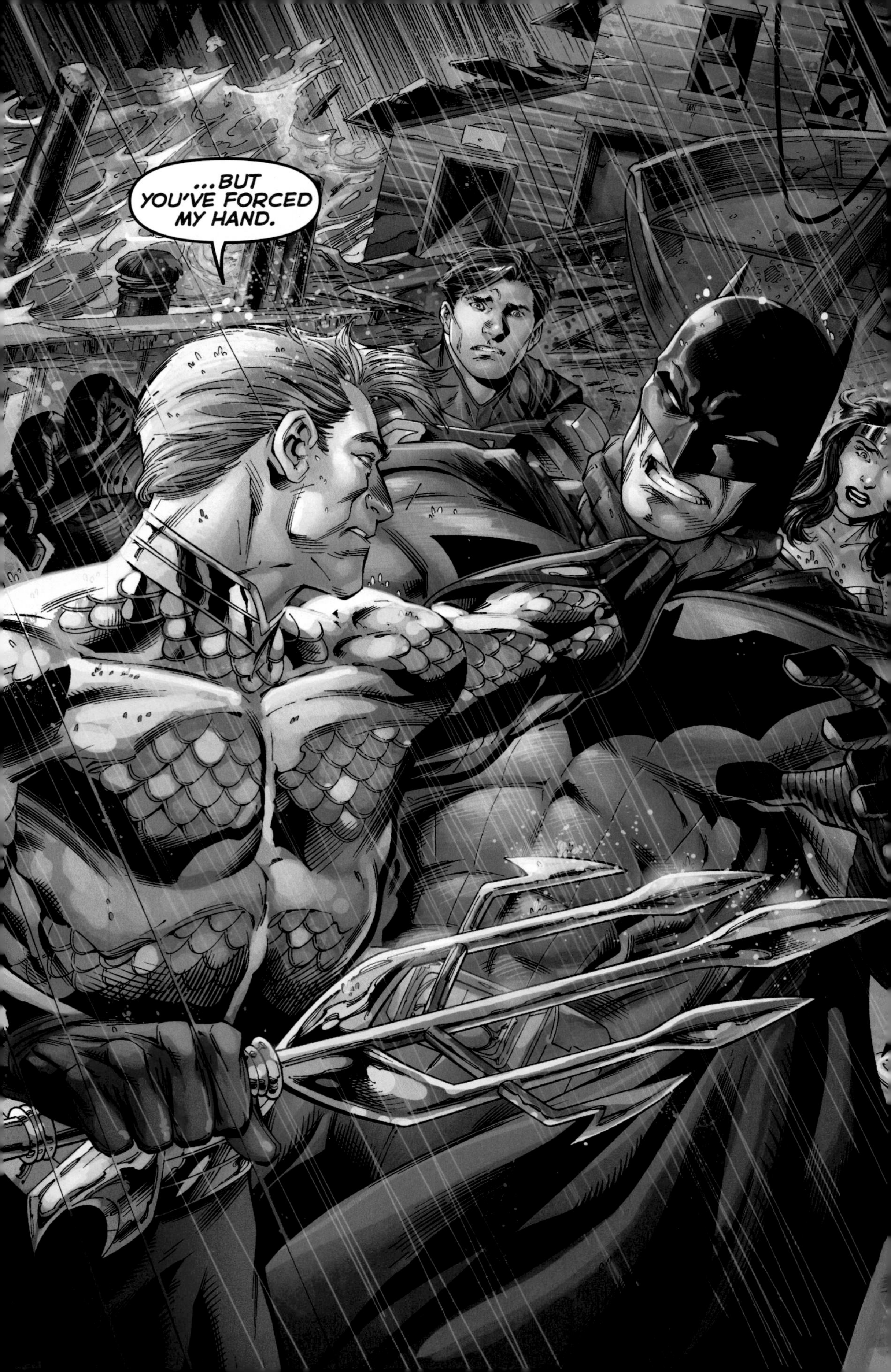
...BUT YOU'VE FORCED MY HAND.

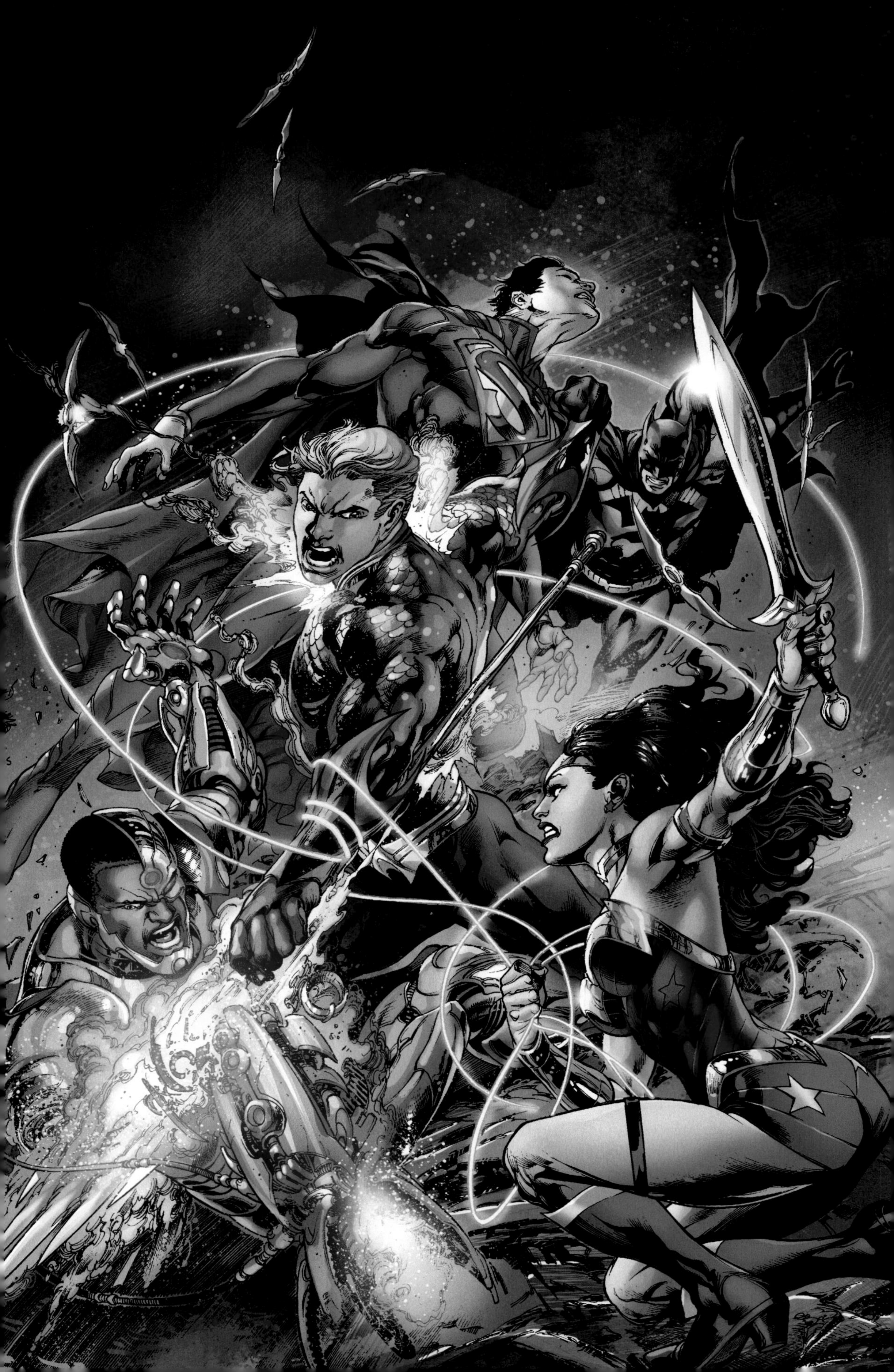

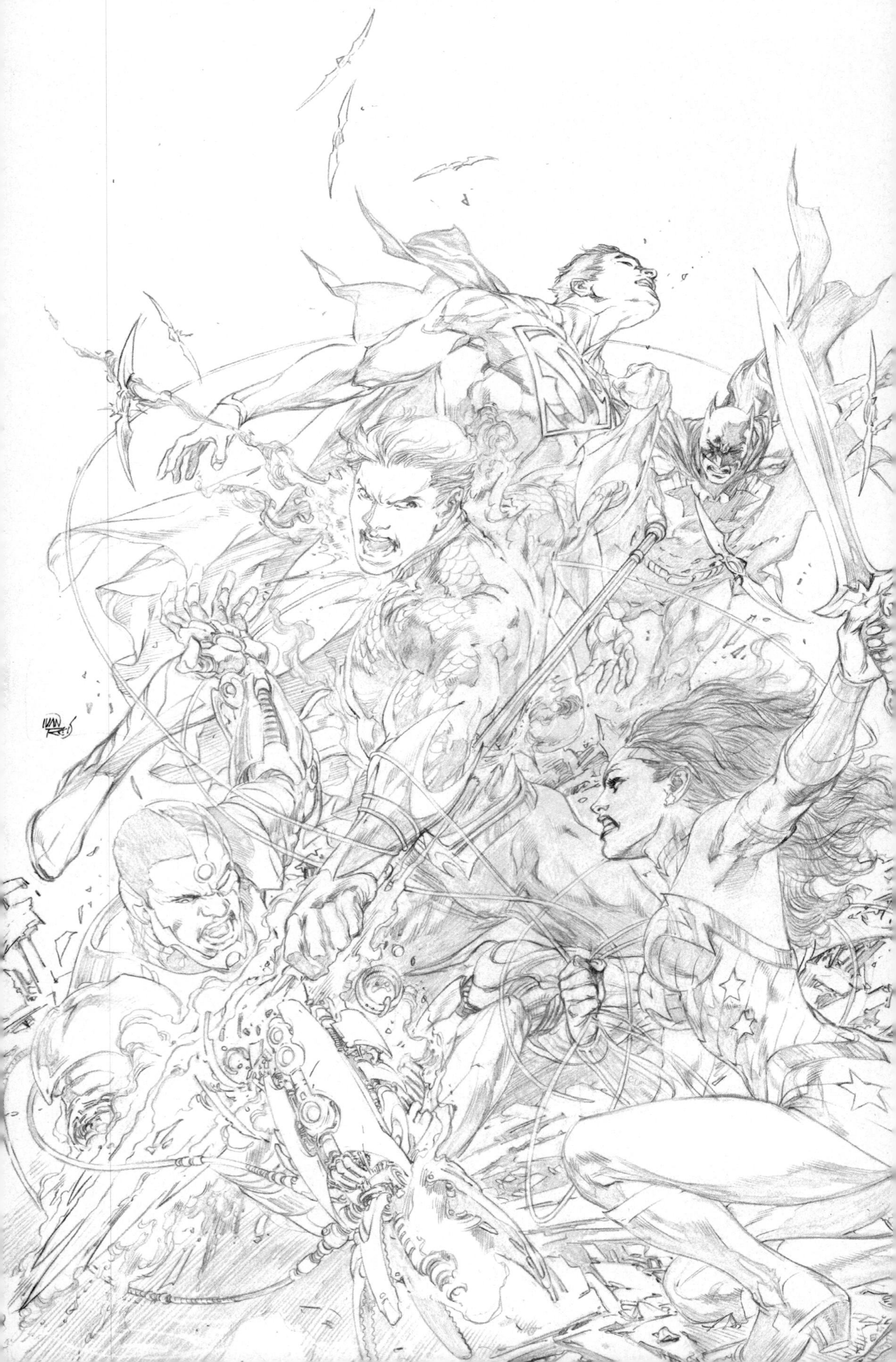

OUR *OCEANS* ARE AS ALIEN AS *OUTER SPACE.*

I READ 70% OF OUR PLANET IS COVERED IN WATER, BUT 95% OF THAT HAS *NEVER* BEEN EXPLORED.

EVER SINCE *DARKSEID,* WE'VE BEEN WORRIED ABOUT THREATS *OUTSIDE* OF OUR WORLD, BUT THE GREATEST ONES COULD BE *FROM* IT.

WHO THE HELL REALLY KNOWS *WHAT'S* IN THE OCEAN?

NOT A SINGLE ONE OF ORM'S SOLDIERS HAS RISEN FROM THE WATER AND ALREADY *HUNDREDS* ARE DEAD.

THE JUSTICE LEAGUE MUST LET ARTHUR REASON WITH ORM. THIS WAR WITH ATLANTIS *CANNOT* HAPPEN.

ARE THERE ANY SIGNS OF THE ATLANTEANS YET, CYBORG?

KING ARTHUR REFERRED TO ME AS ONE OF HIS *MENTORS?* I AM VERY HONORED.

NO, THANKFULLY, VULKO. AND I'VE LOCATED DR. SHIN. ARTHUR SAID HE WAS ONE OF HIS *MENTORS,* LIKE YOU, BUT--

BUT *WHY* WOULD THE ATLANTEANS WANT DR. SHIN *DEAD?*

"DR. SHIN STUDIED ARTHUR'S ATLANTEAN BIOLOGY FOR YEARS, CYBORG. AND HE IMMERSED HIMSELF IN ATLANTEAN HISTORY.

"HE KNOWS MORE ABOUT ATLANTIS AND ARTHUR THAN ANYONE ELSE ON THE SURFACE WORLD."

"BUT FROM WHAT I'VE DOWNLOADED AND SORTED THROUGH, DR. SHIN DIDN'T AMOUNT TO ANYTHING BUT A FEW *HEADLINES* IN THE TABLOIDS."

...MILITARY IS WATCHING THE WATERS CLOSELY NOW TO SEE IF *ATLANTIS* IS ACTUALLY BEHIND THESE TIDAL WAVES, BUT EFFORTS TO MOVE IN HAVE BEEN HINDERED BY THE STORM.

"HE MAY BE CONSIDERED LESS THAN A THREAT TODAY, BUT WHEN ARTHUR AND HIS BROTHER WROTE THE ATLANTEAN WAR PLANS, THEY THOUGHT DR. SHIN HAD THE POTENTIAL TO BECOME THEIR *GREATEST ENEMY.*"

THEY'LL BELIEVE ME NOW. THEY'LL *HAVE* TO.

"BUT WITH HIS KNOWLEDGE, HE MAY PROVE INVALUABLE IN *STOPPING* ATLANTIS."

"THEN I'LL GO GET HIM."

BABOOOM

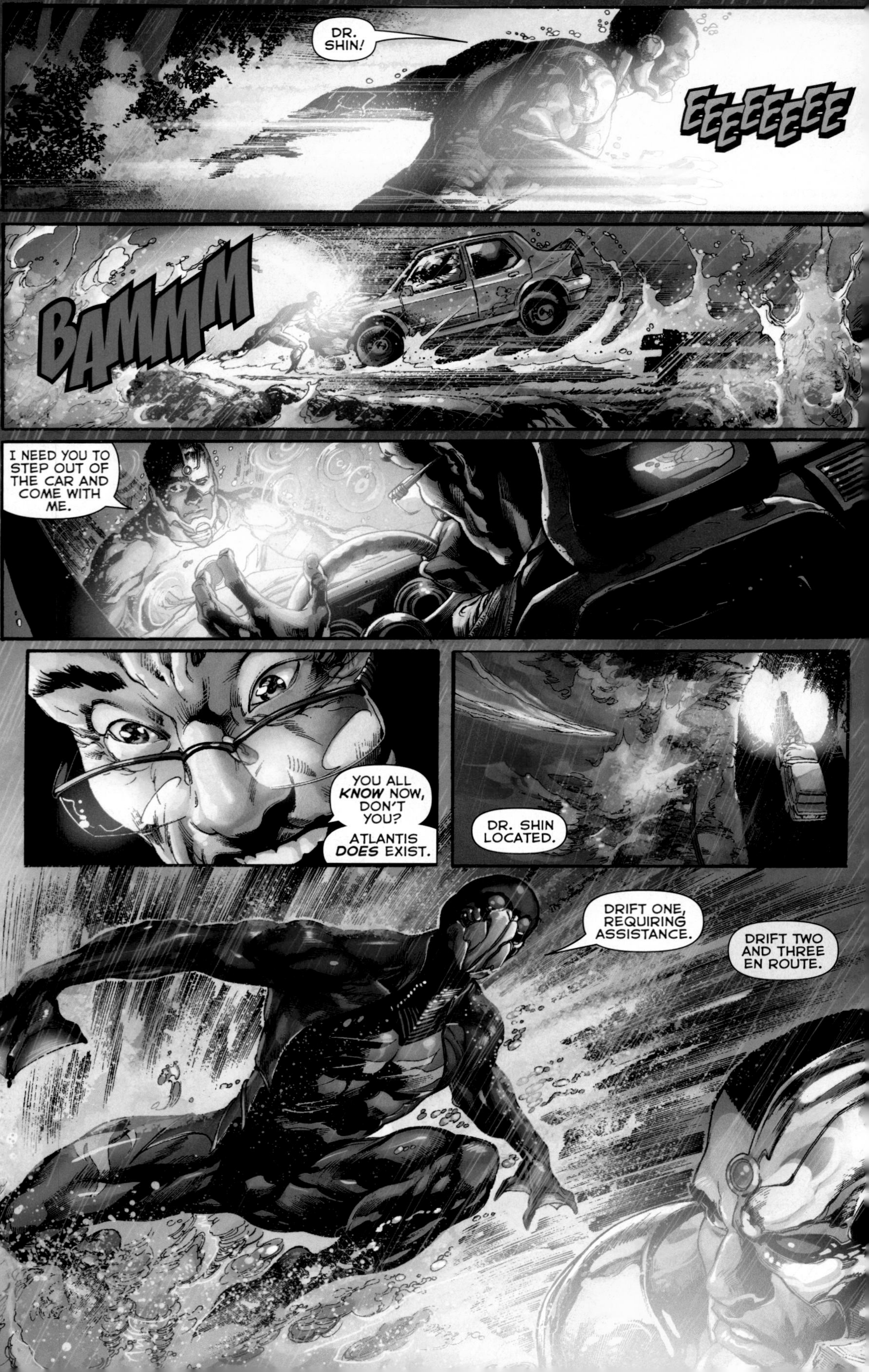
DR. SHIN!
EEEEEEEE
BAMMM
I NEED YOU TO STEP OUT OF THE CAR AND COME WITH ME.
YOU ALL KNOW NOW, DON'T YOU?
ATLANTIS DOES EXIST.
DR. SHIN LOCATED.
DRIFT ONE, REQUIRING ASSISTANCE.
DRIFT TWO AND THREE EN ROUTE.

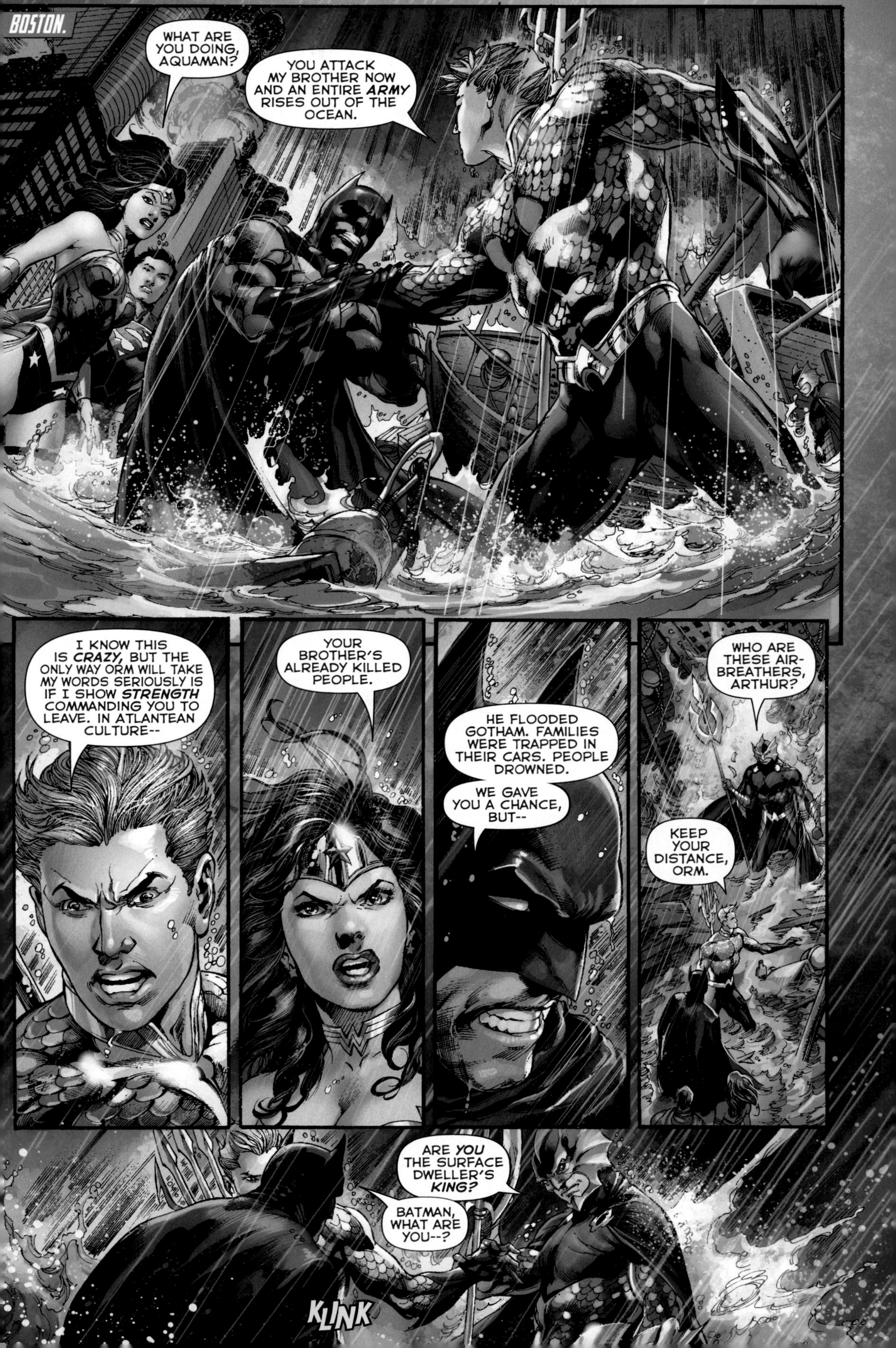
BOSTON.
WHAT ARE YOU DOING, AQUAMAN?
YOU ATTACK MY BROTHER NOW AND AN ENTIRE ARMY RISES OUT OF THE OCEAN.
I KNOW THIS IS CRAZY, BUT THE ONLY WAY ORM WILL TAKE MY WORDS SERIOUSLY IS IF I SHOW STRENGTH COMMANDING YOU TO LEAVE. IN ATLANTEAN CULTURE--
YOUR BROTHER'S ALREADY KILLED PEOPLE.
HE FLOODED GOTHAM. FAMILIES WERE TRAPPED IN THEIR CARS. PEOPLE DROWNED.
WE GAVE YOU A CHANCE, BUT--
WHO ARE THESE AIR-BREATHERS, ARTHUR?
KEEP YOUR DISTANCE, ORM.
ARE YOU THE SURFACE DWELLER'S KING?
BATMAN, WHAT ARE YOU--?
KLINK

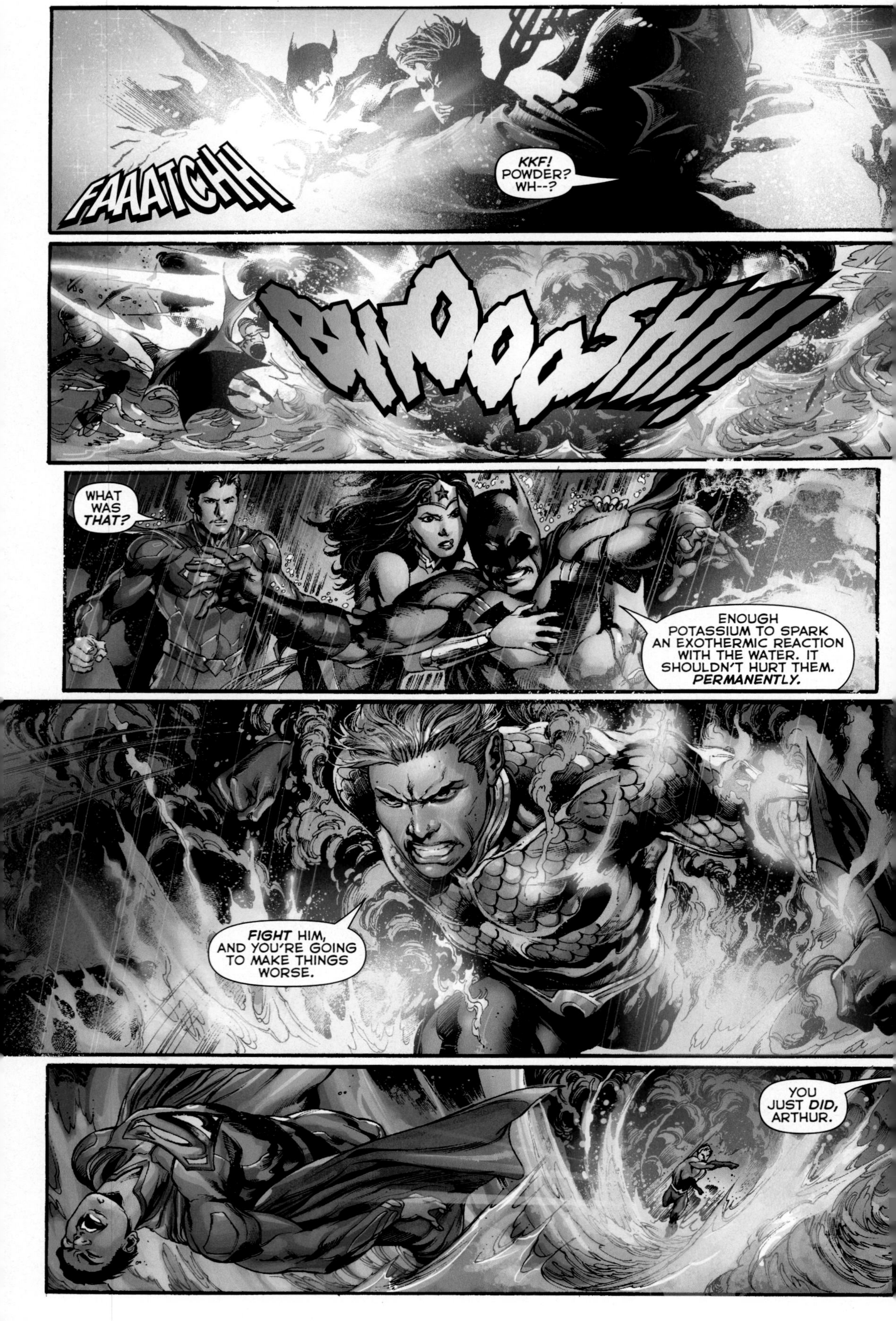
FAAATCHH
KKF! POWDER? WH--?
BWOOSHH
WHAT WAS THAT?
ENOUGH POTASSIUM TO SPARK AN EXOTHERMIC REACTION WITH THE WATER. IT SHOULDN'T HURT THEM. PERMANENTLY.
FIGHT HIM, AND YOU'RE GOING TO MAKE THINGS WORSE.
YOU JUST DID, ARTHUR.

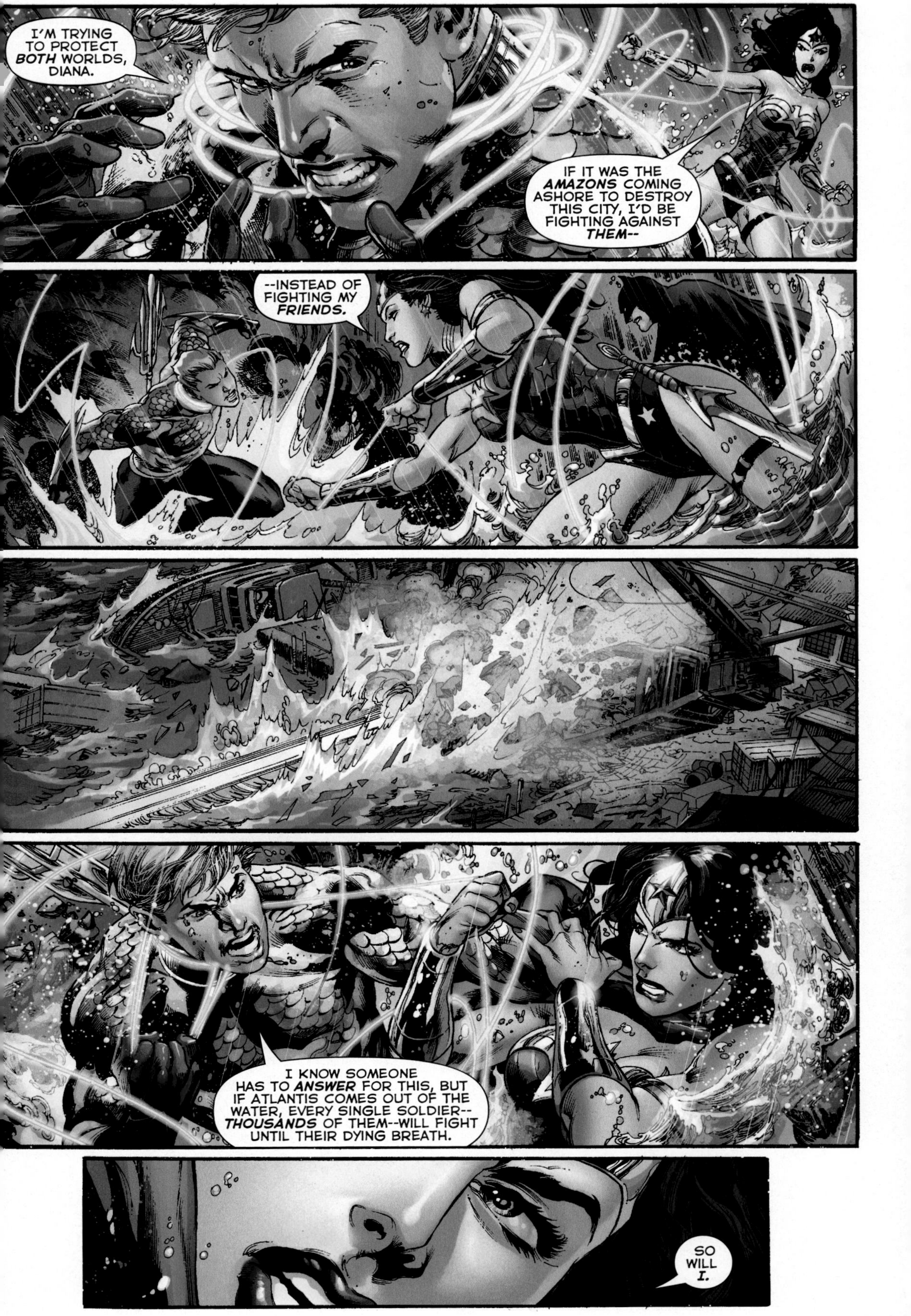
I'M TRYING TO PROTECT BOTH WORLDS, DIANA.
IF IT WAS THE AMAZONS COMING ASHORE TO DESTROY THIS CITY, I'D BE FIGHTING AGAINST THEM--
--INSTEAD OF FIGHTING MY FRIENDS.
I KNOW SOMEONE HAS TO ANSWER FOR THIS, BUT IF ATLANTIS COMES OUT OF THE WATER, EVERY SINGLE SOLDIER--THOUSANDS OF THEM--WILL FIGHT UNTIL THEIR DYING BREATH.
SO WILL I.

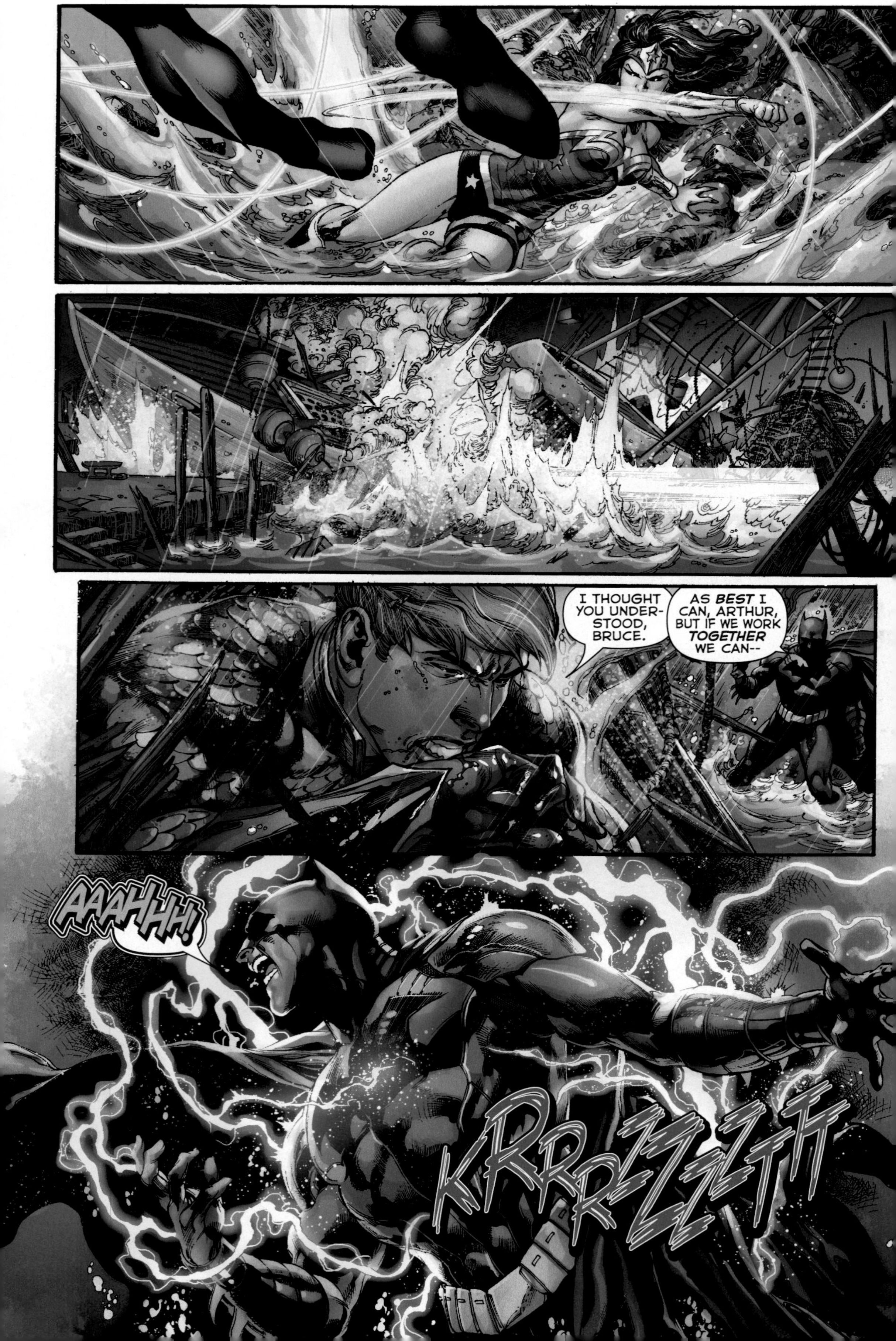
I THOUGHT YOU UNDER-STOOD, BRUCE.
AS BEST I CAN, ARTHUR, BUT IF WE WORK TOGETHER WE CAN--
AAAHHH!
KRRRZZZZTH

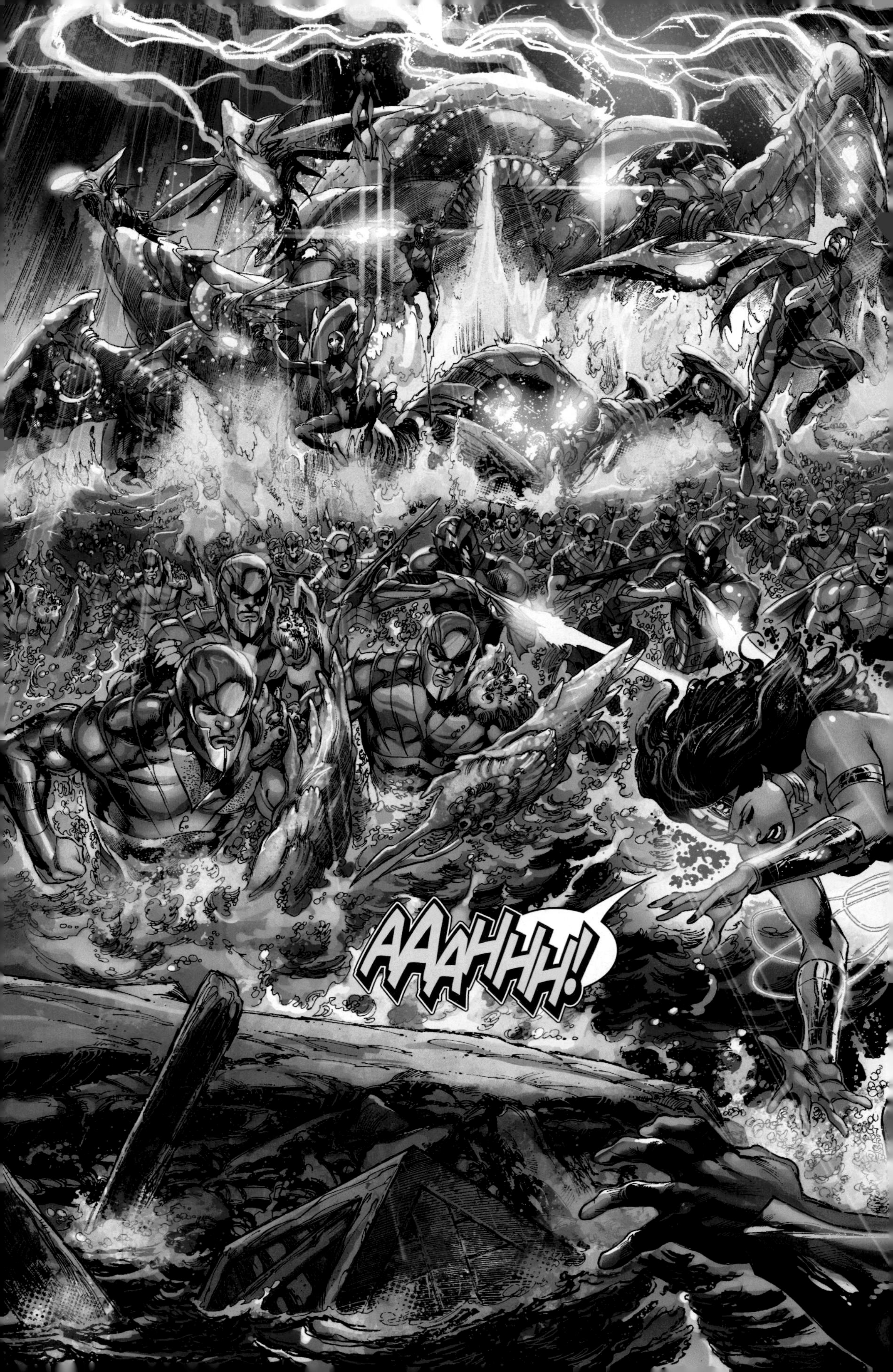
AAAHHH!

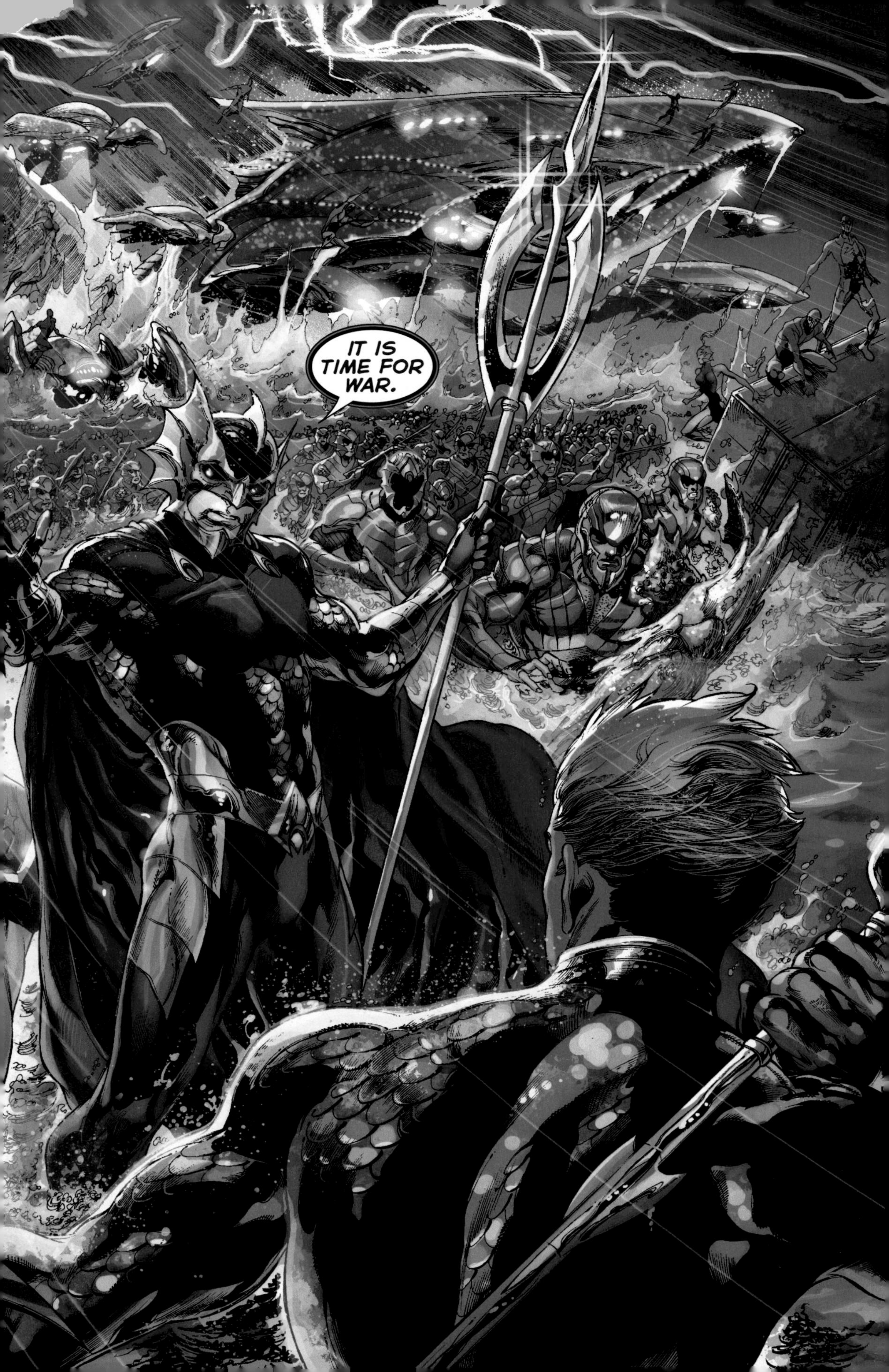
IT IS TIME FOR WAR.

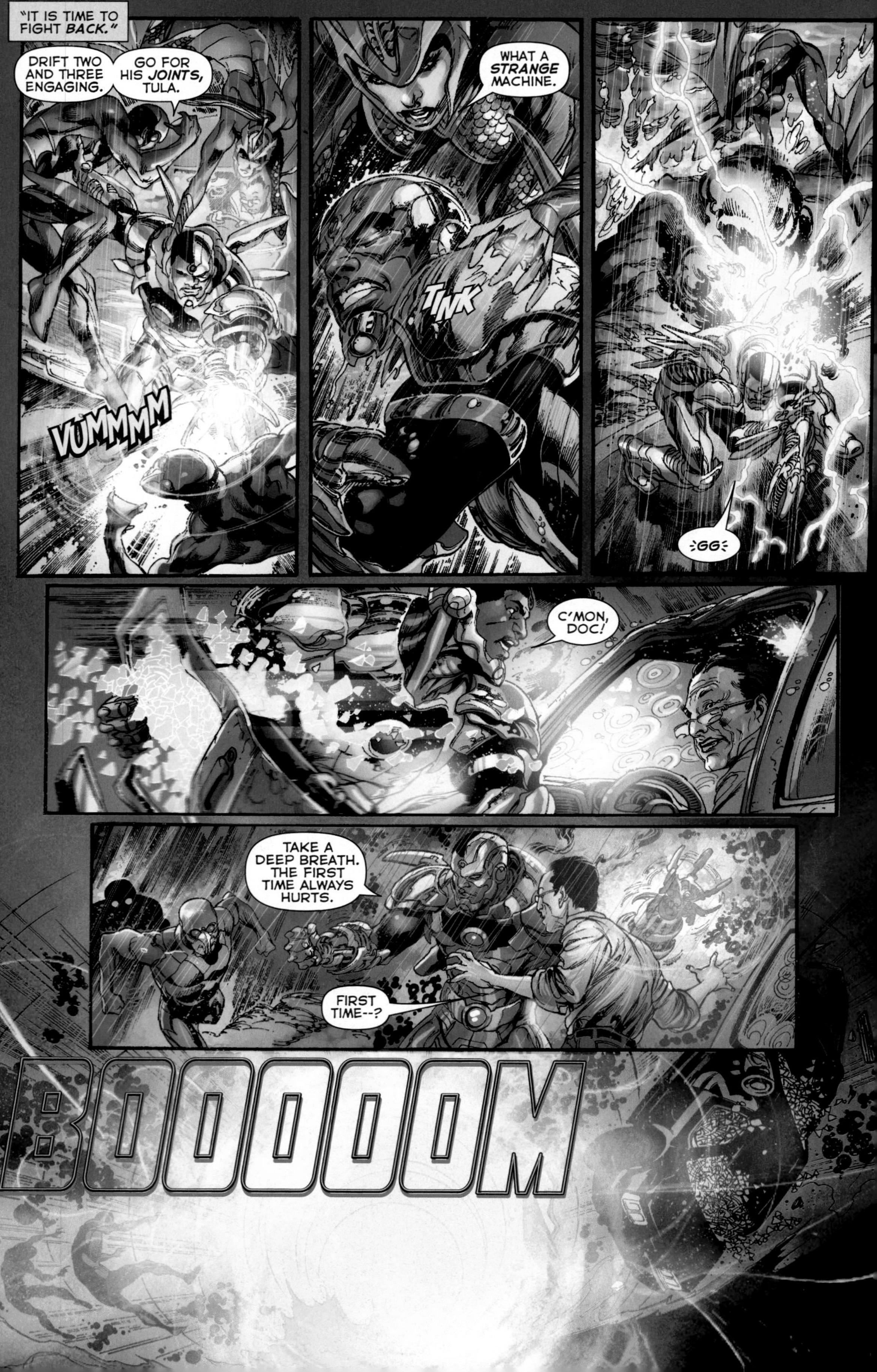
"IT IS TIME TO FIGHT BACK."
DRIFT TWO AND THREE ENGAGING.
GO FOR HIS JOINTS, TULA.
VUMMMM
WHAT A STRANGE MACHINE.
TINK
GG
C'MON, DOC!
TAKE A DEEP BREATH. THE FIRST TIME ALWAYS HURTS.
FIRST TIME--?
BOOOOOM

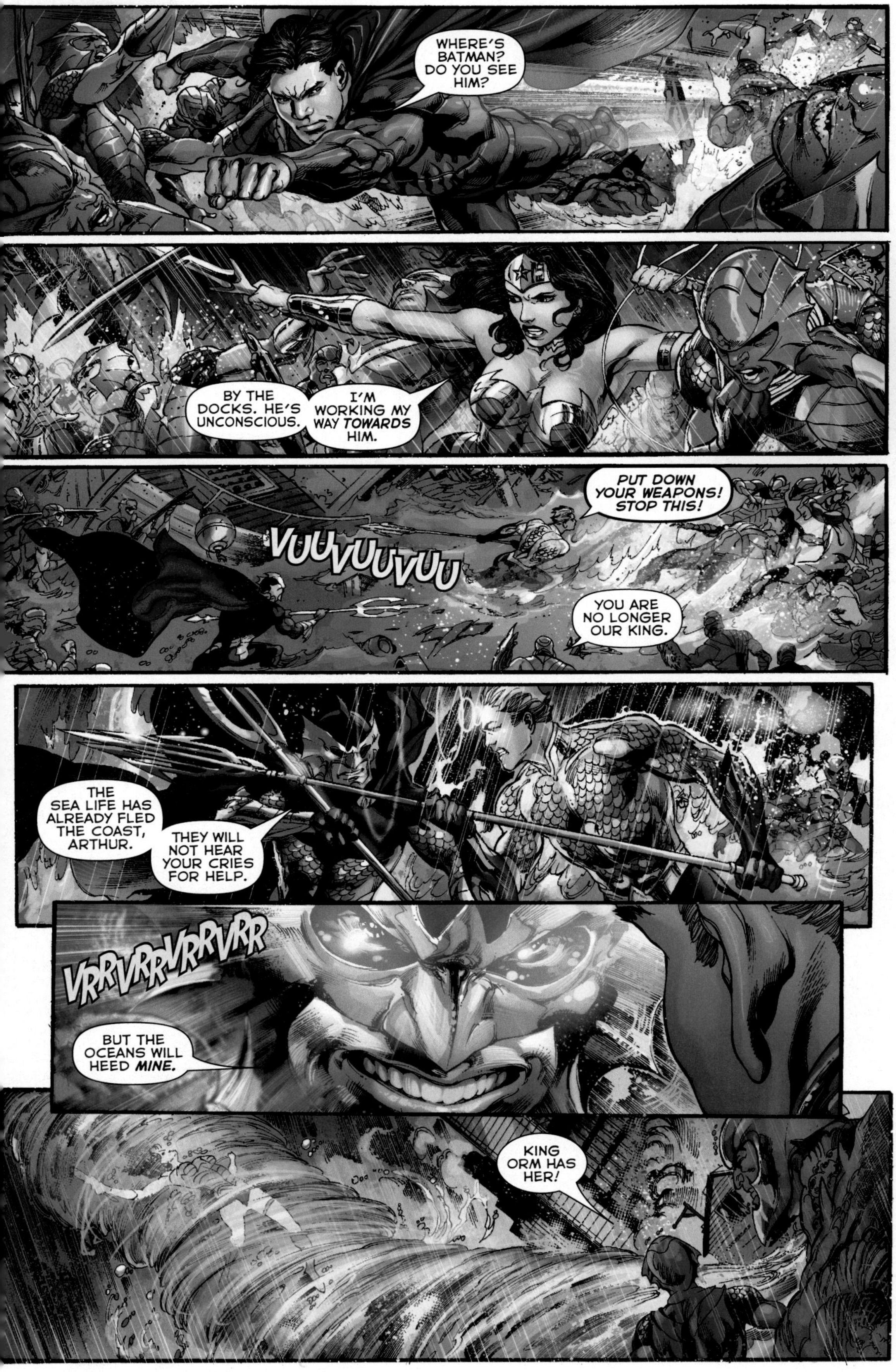
WHERE'S BATMAN? DO YOU SEE HIM?
BY THE DOCKS. HE'S UNCONSCIOUS.
I'M WORKING MY WAY *TOWARDS* HIM.
PUT DOWN YOUR WEAPONS! STOP THIS!
VUUVUUVUU
YOU ARE NO LONGER OUR KING.
THE SEA LIFE HAS ALREADY FLED THE COAST, ARTHUR.
THEY WILL NOT HEAR YOUR CRIES FOR HELP.
VRRVRRVRRVRR
BUT THE OCEANS WILL HEED *MINE.*
KING ORM HAS HER!

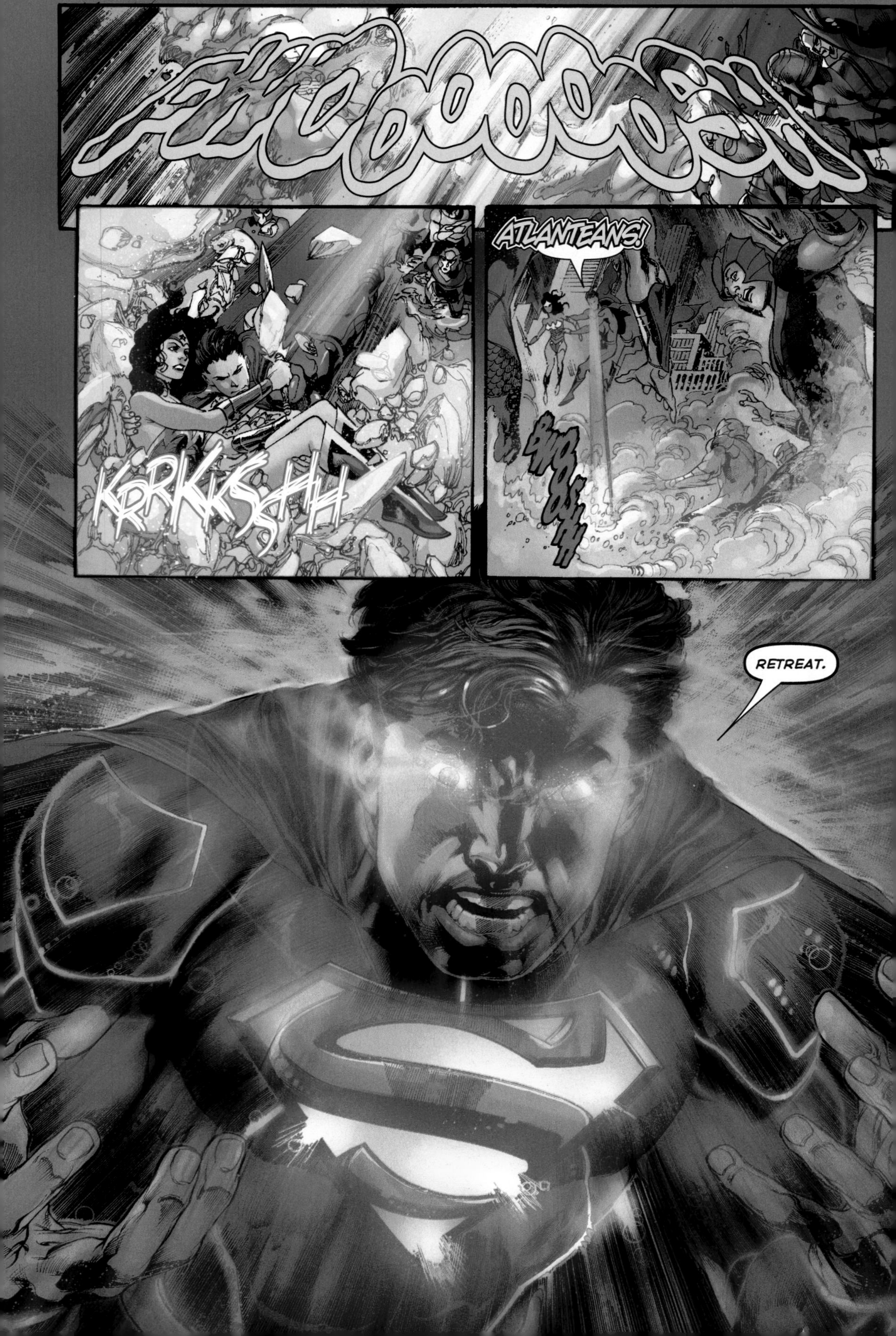

FZHOOOOOOM!!
KRRKKSHH
ATLANTEANS!
BWOOSHH
RETREAT.

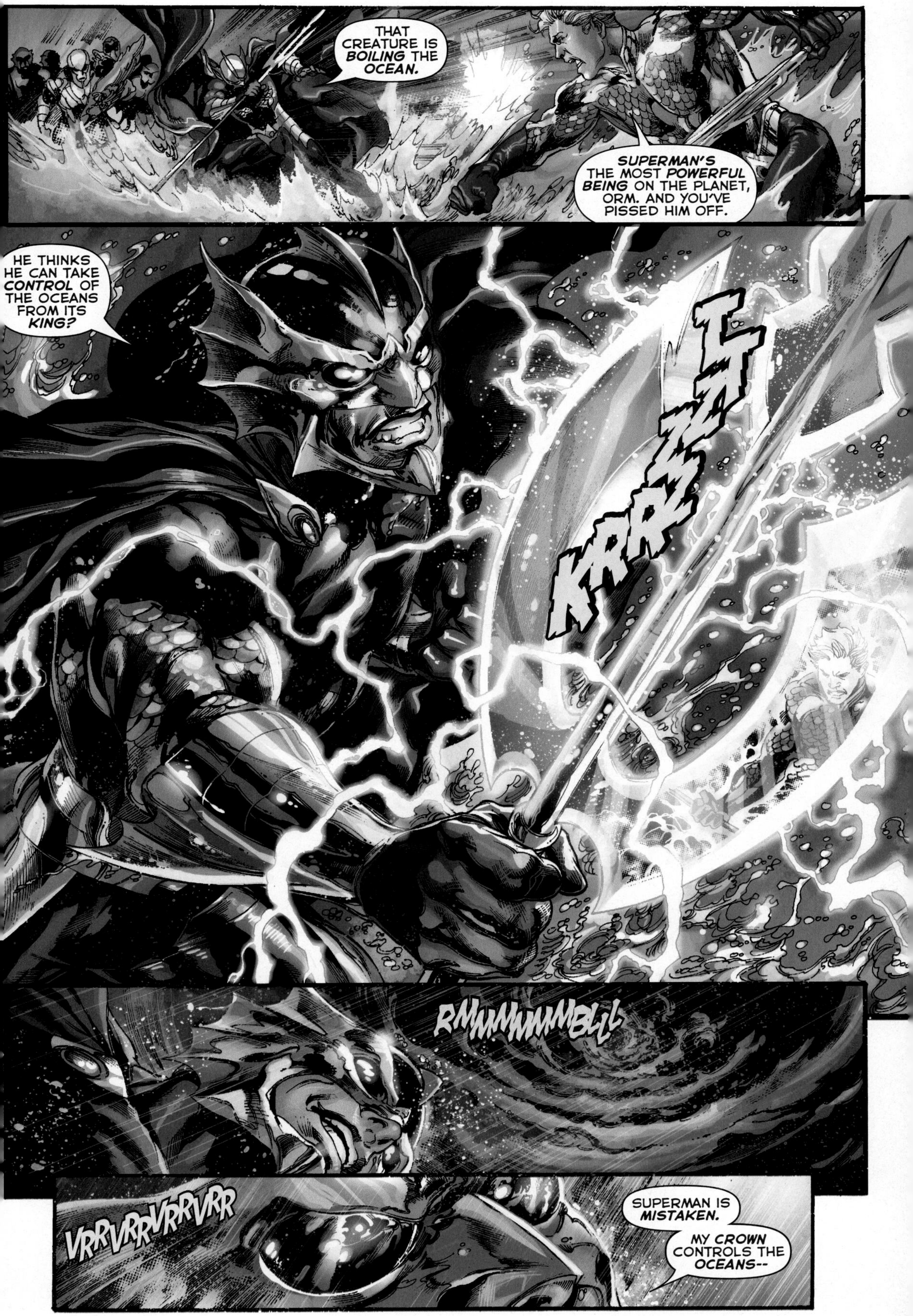
THAT CREATURE IS *BOILING* THE *OCEAN.*
SUPERMAN'S THE MOST *POWERFUL BEING* ON THE PLANET, ORM. AND YOU'VE PISSED HIM OFF.
HE THINKS HE CAN TAKE *CONTROL* OF THE OCEANS FROM ITS *KING?*
KRRZZZZT
RMMMMMMBLLL
VRRVRRVRRVRR
SUPERMAN IS *MISTAKEN.*
MY *CROWN* CONTROLS THE *OCEANS--*

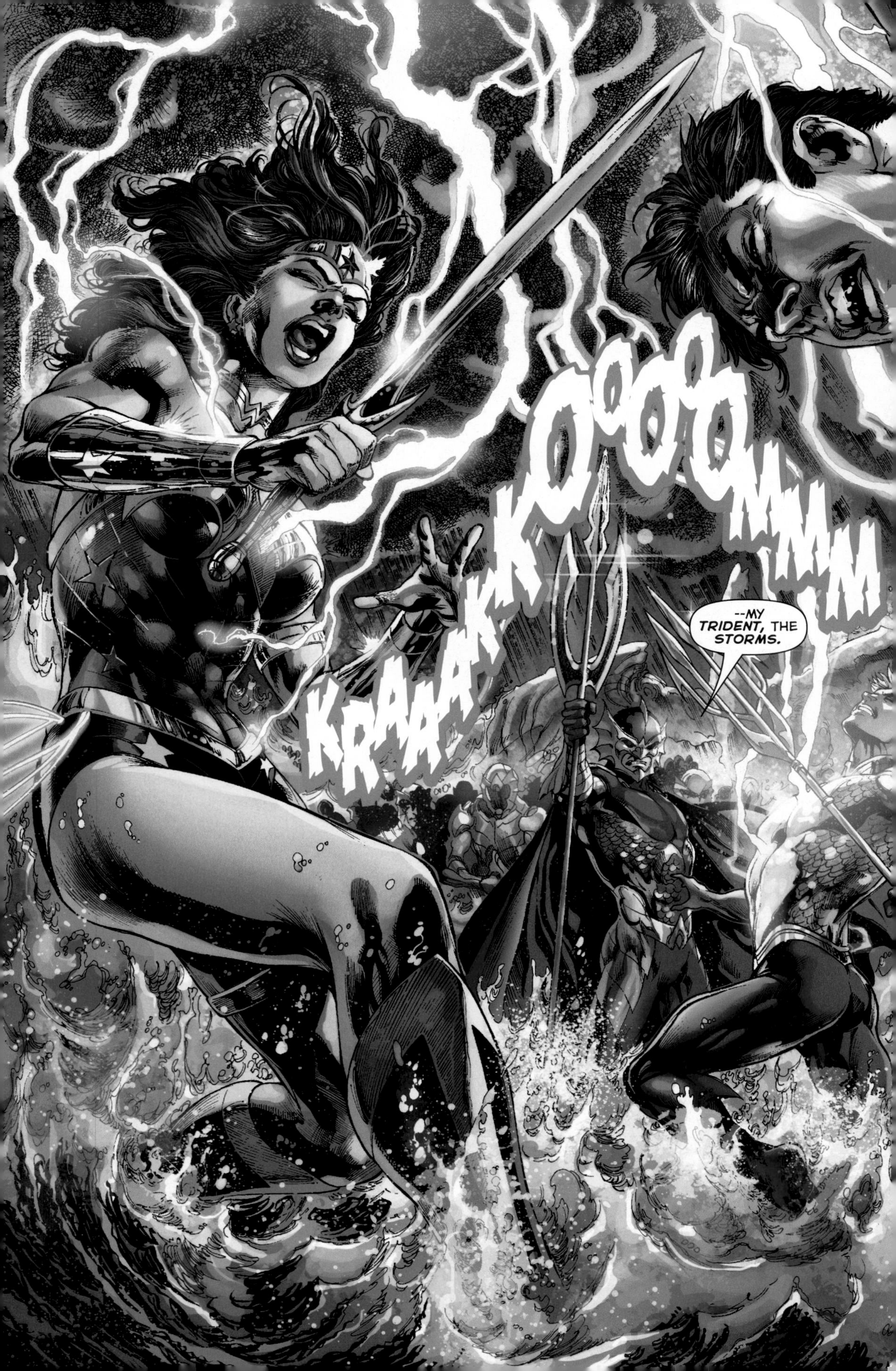
KRAAAKKOOOOMMMM
--MY TRIDENT, THE STORMS.

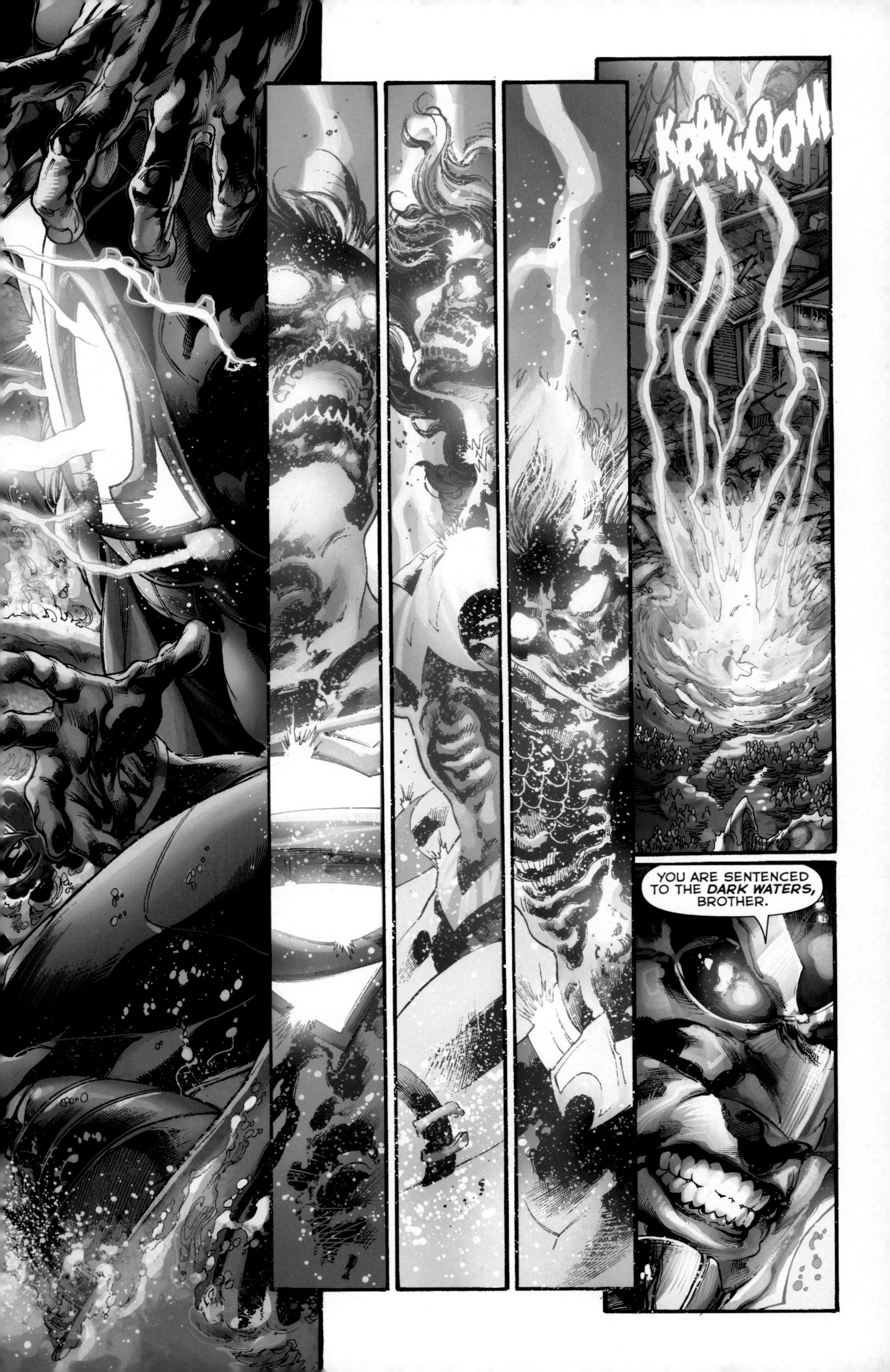
KRAKKOOM
YOU ARE SENTENCED TO THE *DARK WATERS,* BROTHER.

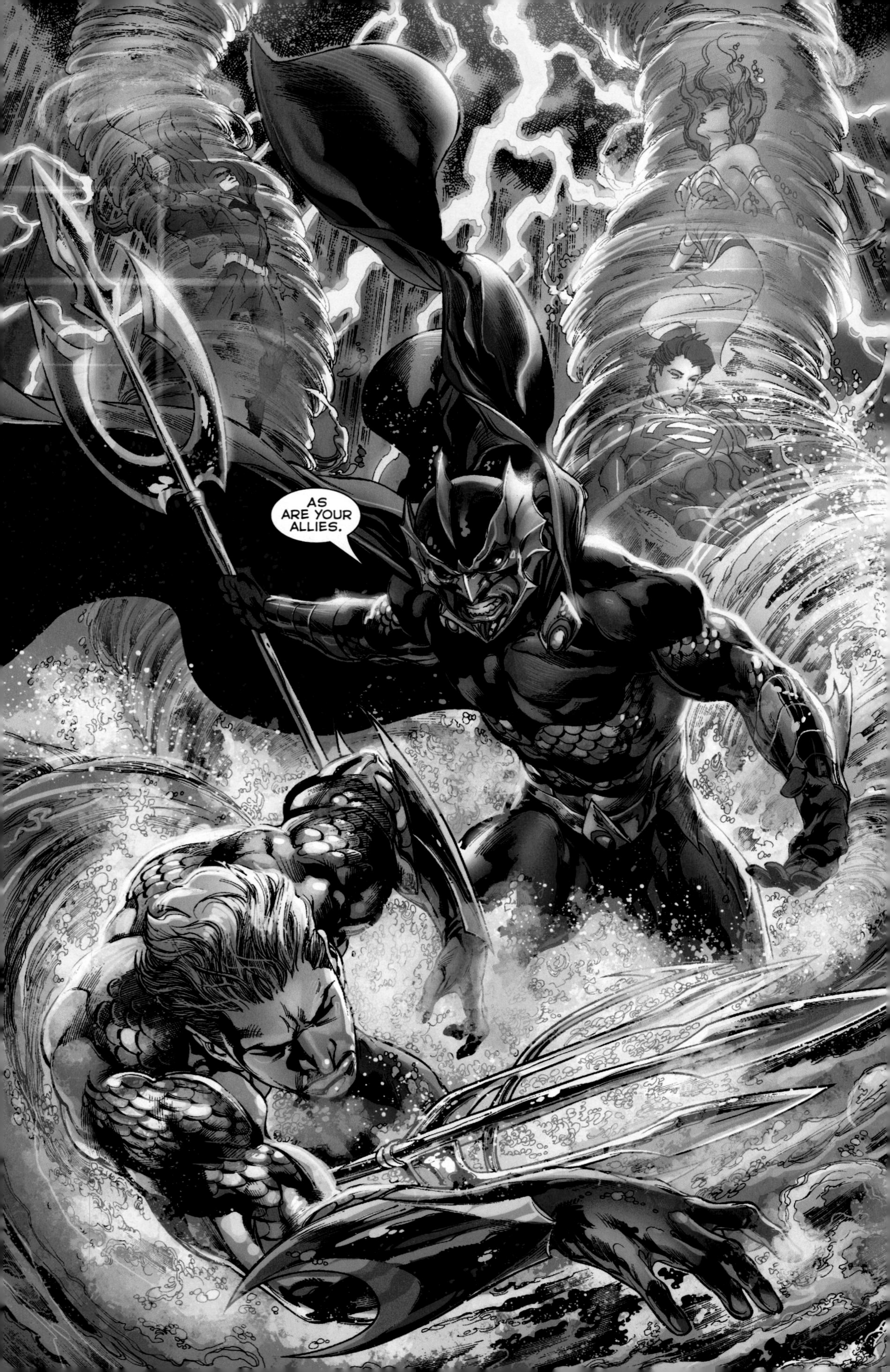
AS ARE YOUR ALLIES.

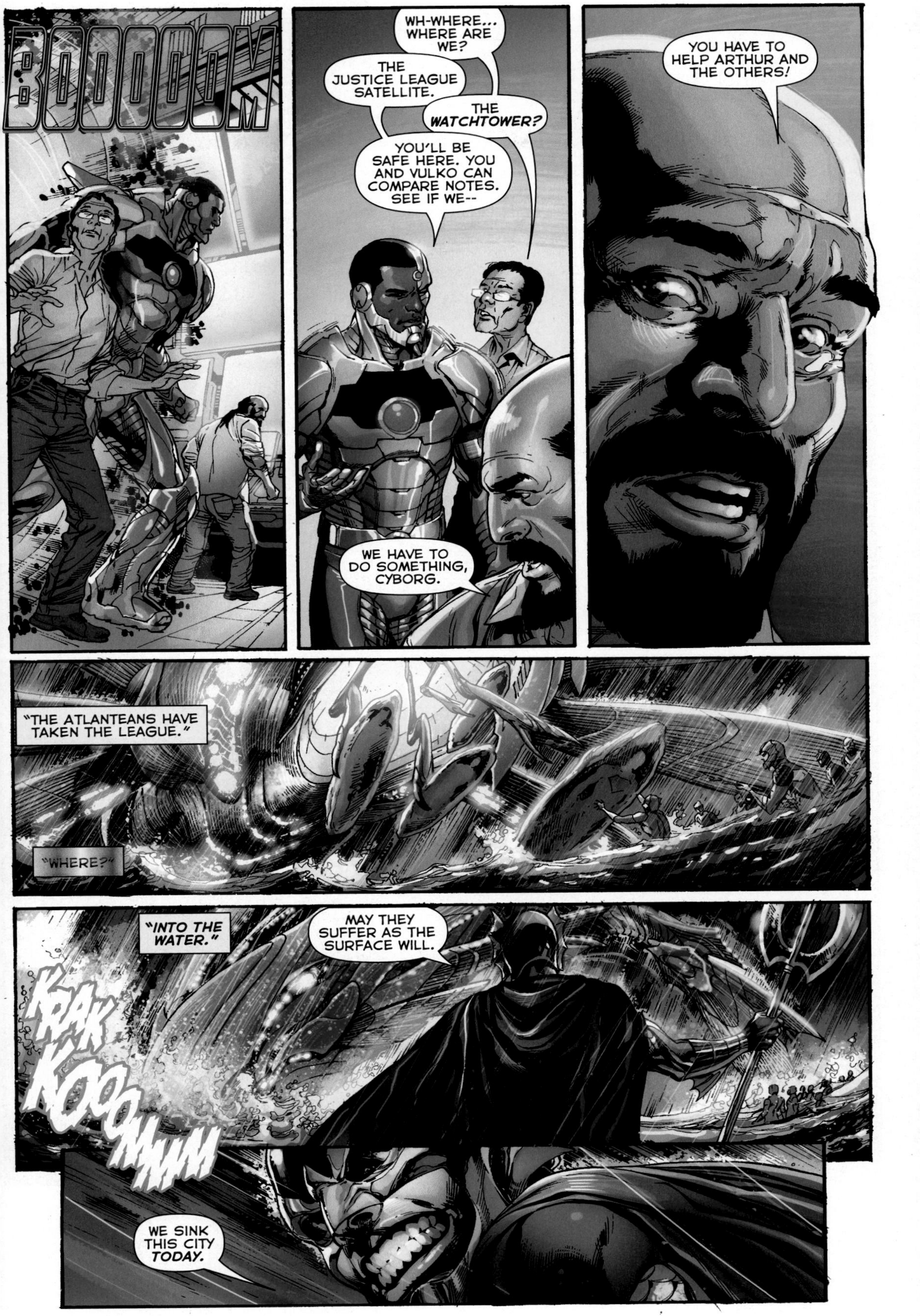
BOOOOOOM
WH-WHERE... WHERE ARE WE?
THE JUSTICE LEAGUE SATELLITE.
THE *WATCHTOWER?*
YOU'LL BE SAFE HERE. YOU AND VULKO CAN COMPARE NOTES. SEE IF WE--
WE HAVE TO DO SOMETHING, CYBORG.
YOU HAVE TO HELP ARTHUR AND THE OTHERS!
"THE ATLANTEANS HAVE TAKEN THE LEAGUE."
"WHERE?"
"INTO THE WATER."
MAY THEY SUFFER AS THE SURFACE WILL.
KRAK KOOOMMM
WE SINK THIS CITY *TODAY.*

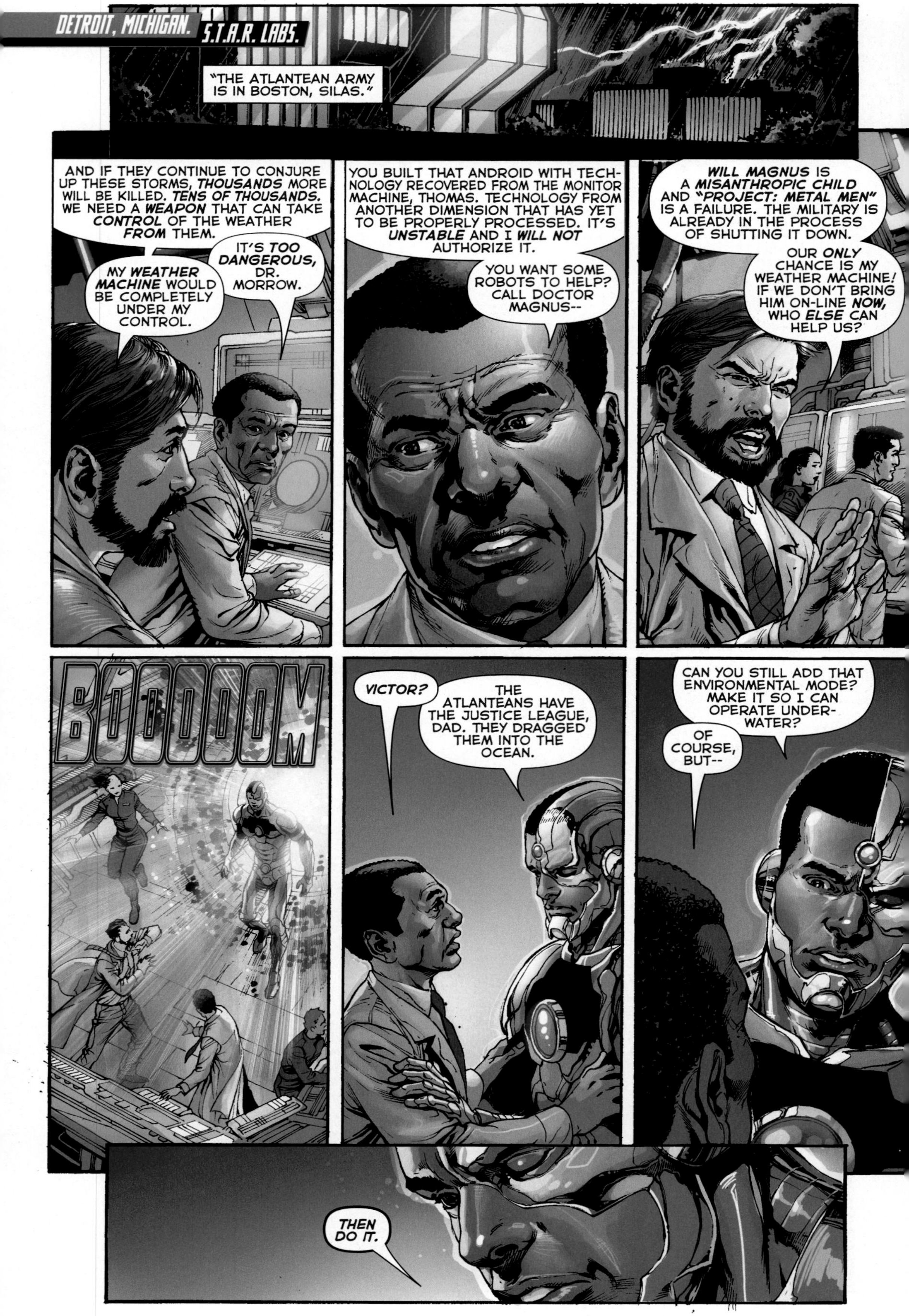

"THE ATLANTEAN ARMY IS IN BOSTON, SILAS."

AND IF THEY CONTINUE TO CONJURE UP THESE STORMS, *THOUSANDS* MORE WILL BE KILLED. *TENS OF THOUSANDS.* WE NEED A *WEAPON* THAT CAN TAKE *CONTROL* OF THE WEATHER *FROM* THEM.

MY *WEATHER MACHINE* WOULD BE COMPLETELY UNDER MY CONTROL.

IT'S *TOO DANGEROUS*, DR. MORROW.

YOU BUILT THAT ANDROID WITH TECHNOLOGY RECOVERED FROM THE MONITOR MACHINE, THOMAS. TECHNOLOGY FROM ANOTHER DIMENSION THAT HAS YET TO BE PROPERLY PROCESSED. IT'S *UNSTABLE* AND I *WILL NOT* AUTHORIZE IT.

YOU WANT SOME ROBOTS TO HELP? CALL DOCTOR MAGNUS--

WILL MAGNUS IS A *MISANTHROPIC CHILD* AND *"PROJECT: METAL MEN"* IS A FAILURE. THE MILITARY IS ALREADY IN THE PROCESS OF SHUTTING IT DOWN.

OUR *ONLY* CHANCE IS MY *WEATHER MACHINE!* IF WE DON'T BRING HIM ON-LINE *NOW*, WHO *ELSE* CAN HELP US?

BOOOOOM

VICTOR?

THE ATLANTEANS HAVE THE JUSTICE LEAGUE, DAD. THEY DRAGGED THEM INTO THE OCEAN.

CAN YOU STILL ADD THAT ENVIRONMENTAL MODE? MAKE IT SO I CAN OPERATE UNDER-WATER?

OF COURSE, BUT--

THEN DO IT.

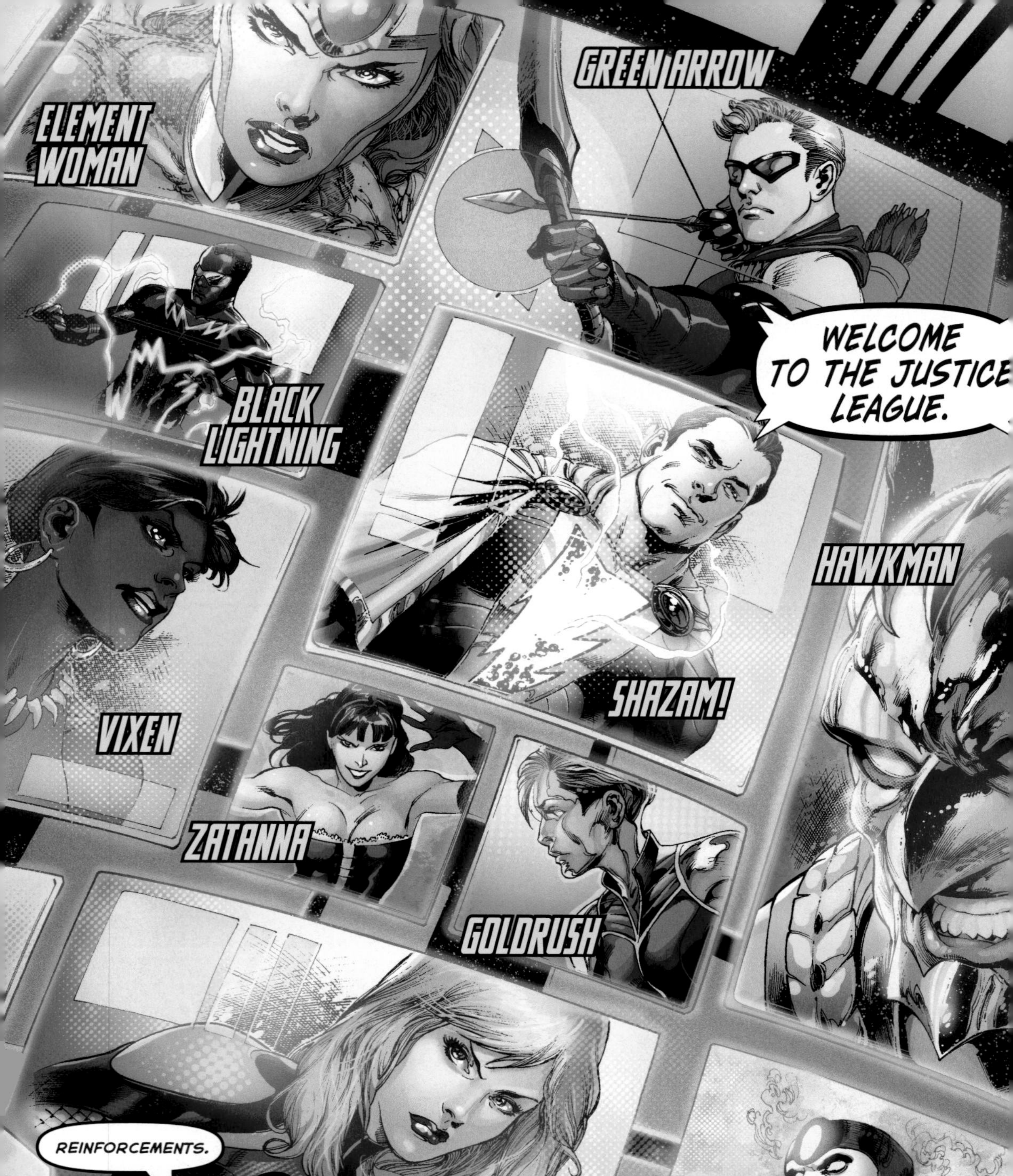
ELEMENT WOMAN
GREEN ARROW
BLACK LIGHTNING
WELCOME TO THE JUSTICE LEAGUE.
HAWKMAN
VIXEN
SHAZAM!
ZATANNA
GOLDRUSH
REINFORCEMENTS.
BLACK CANARY
FIRESTORM

THRONE OF ATLANTIS

CHAPTER THREE: FRIENDS AND ENEMIES

GEOFF JOHNS - WRITER IVAN REIS - PENCILLER
JOE PRADO AND IVAN REIS - INKERS ROD REIS - COLORIST
DAVE SHARPE - LETTERER IVAN REIS, JOE PRADO AND ROD REIS - COVER
LANGDON FOSS AND JOSE VILLARRUBIA - VARIANT COVER
KATIE KUBERT - ASSISTANT EDITOR BRIAN CUNNINGHAM - EDITOR

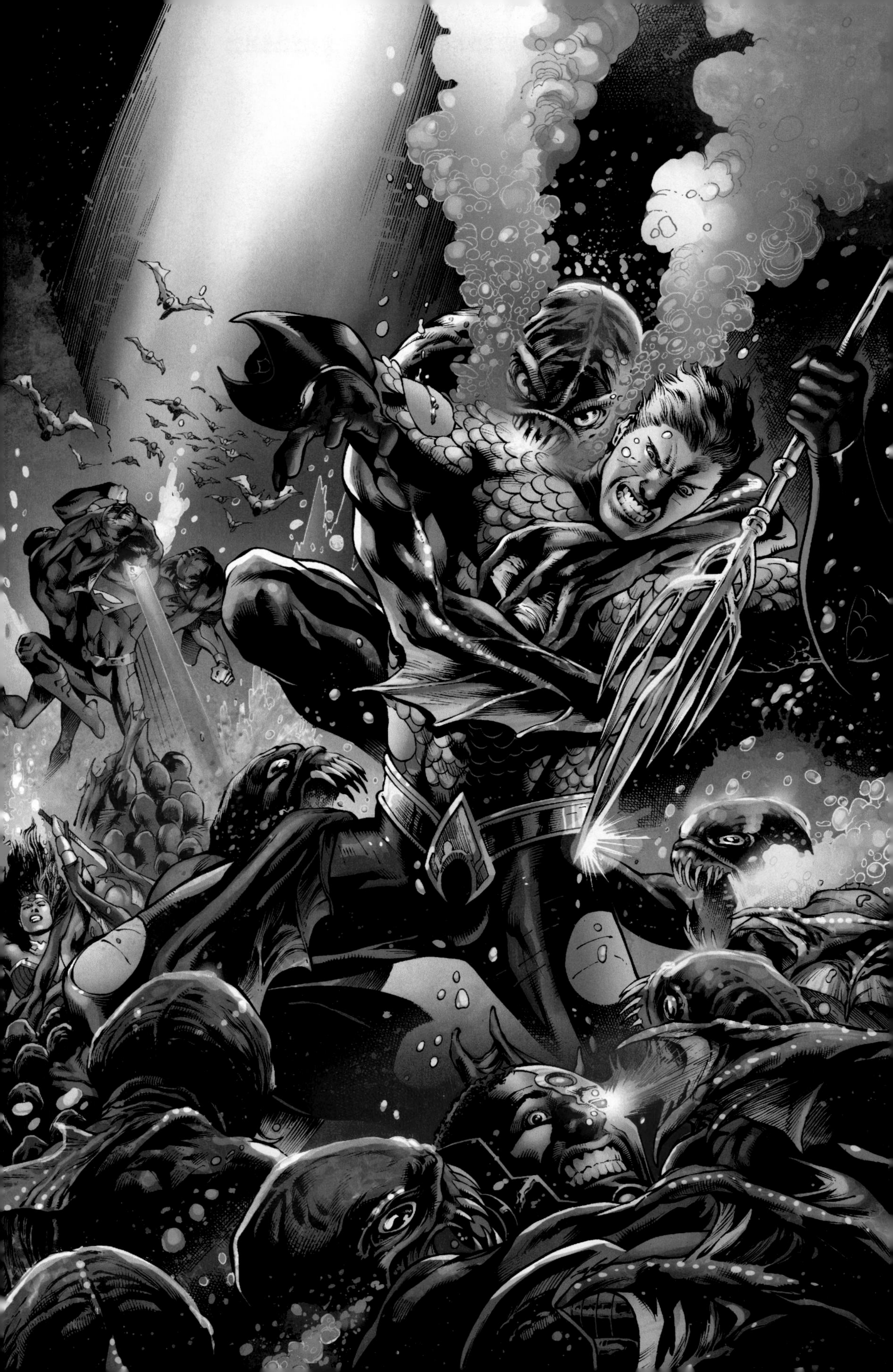

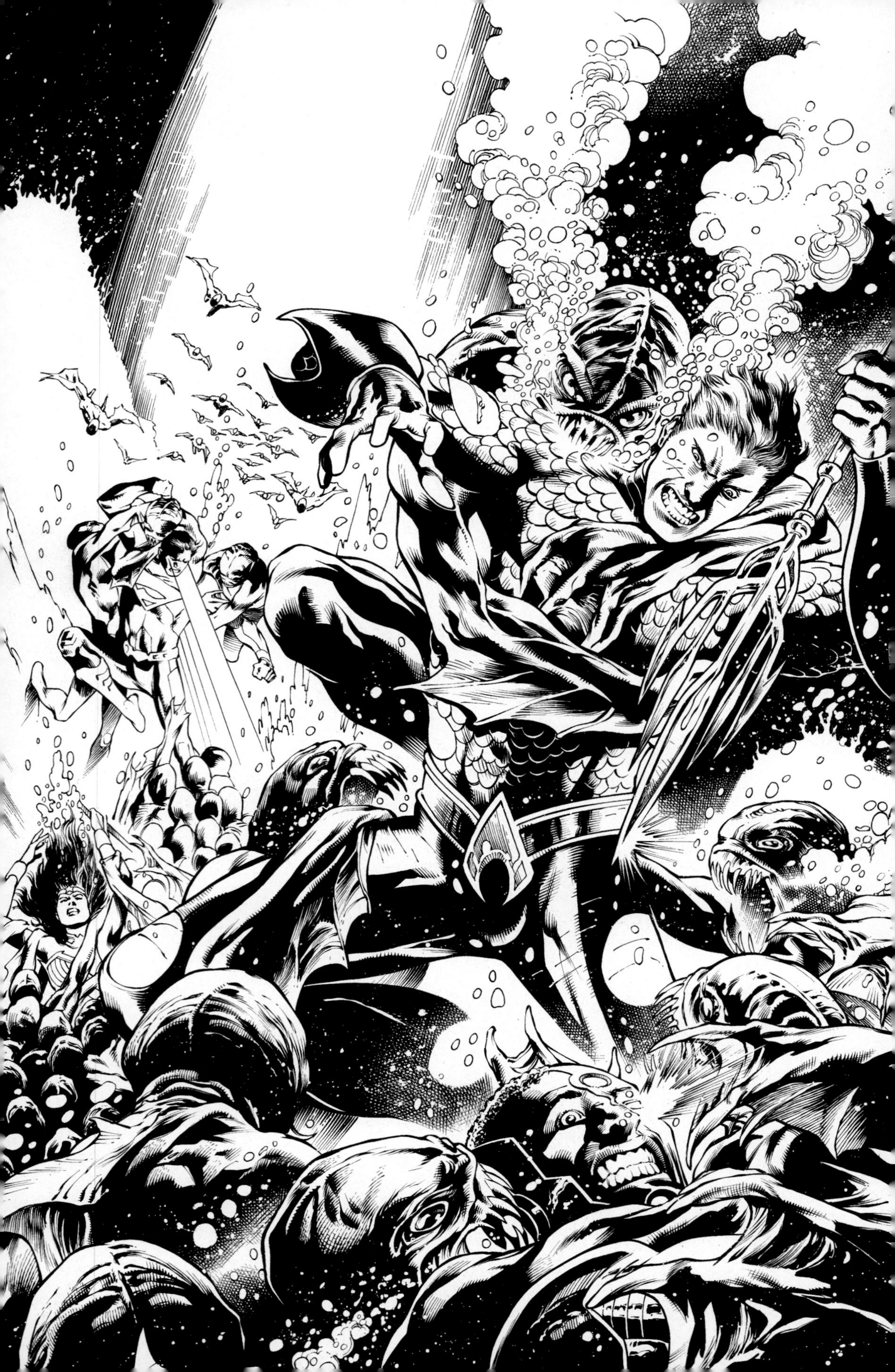

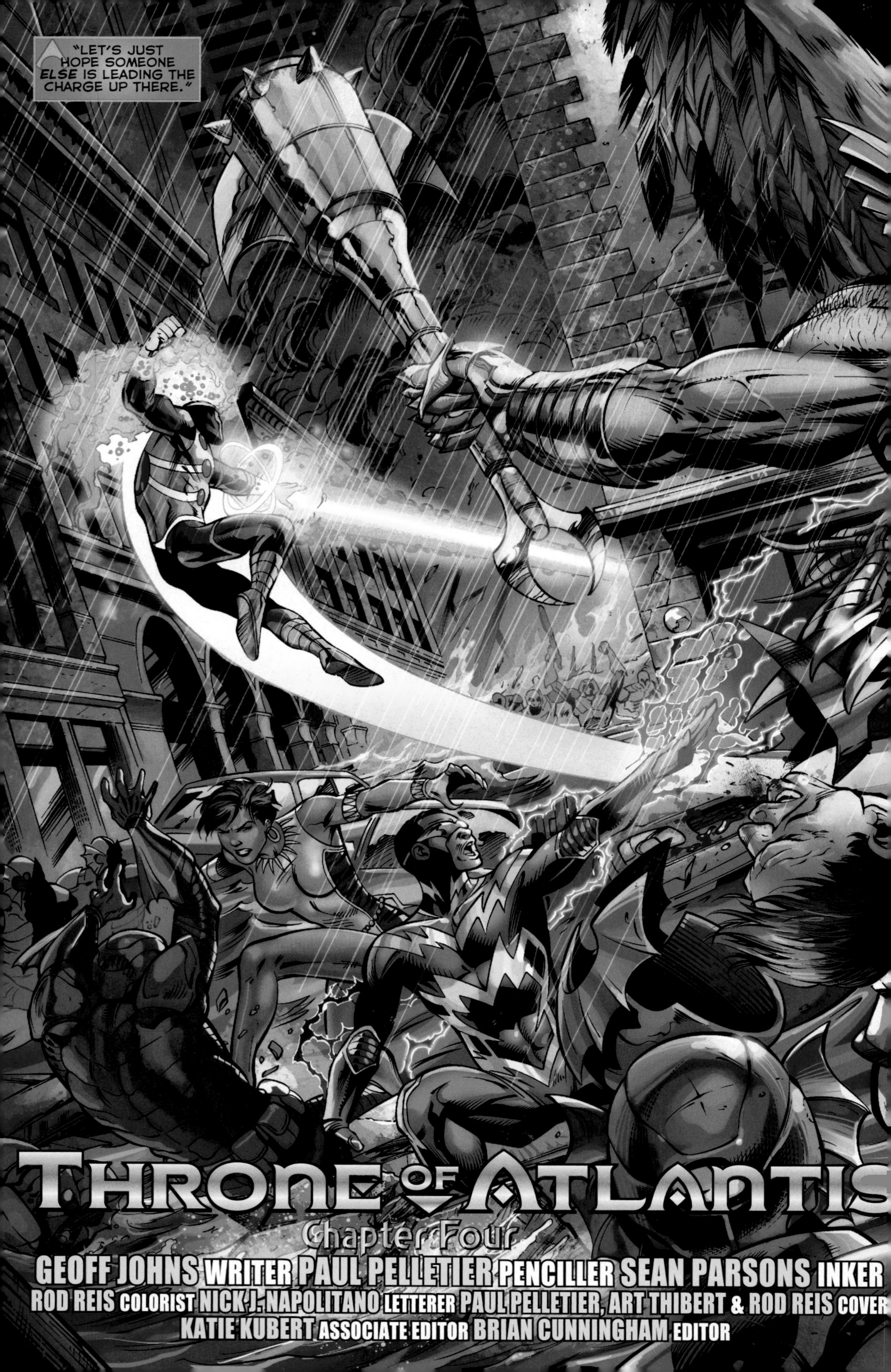
"LET'S JUST HOPE SOMEONE ELSE IS LEADING THE CHARGE UP THERE."
THRONE OF ATLANTIS
Chapter Four
GEOFF JOHNS WRITER PAUL PELLETIER PENCILLER SEAN PARSONS INKER
ROD REIS COLORIST NICK J. NAPOLITANO LETTERER PAUL PELLETIER, ART THIBERT & ROD REIS COVER
KATIE KUBERT ASSOCIATE EDITOR BRIAN CUNNINGHAM EDITOR

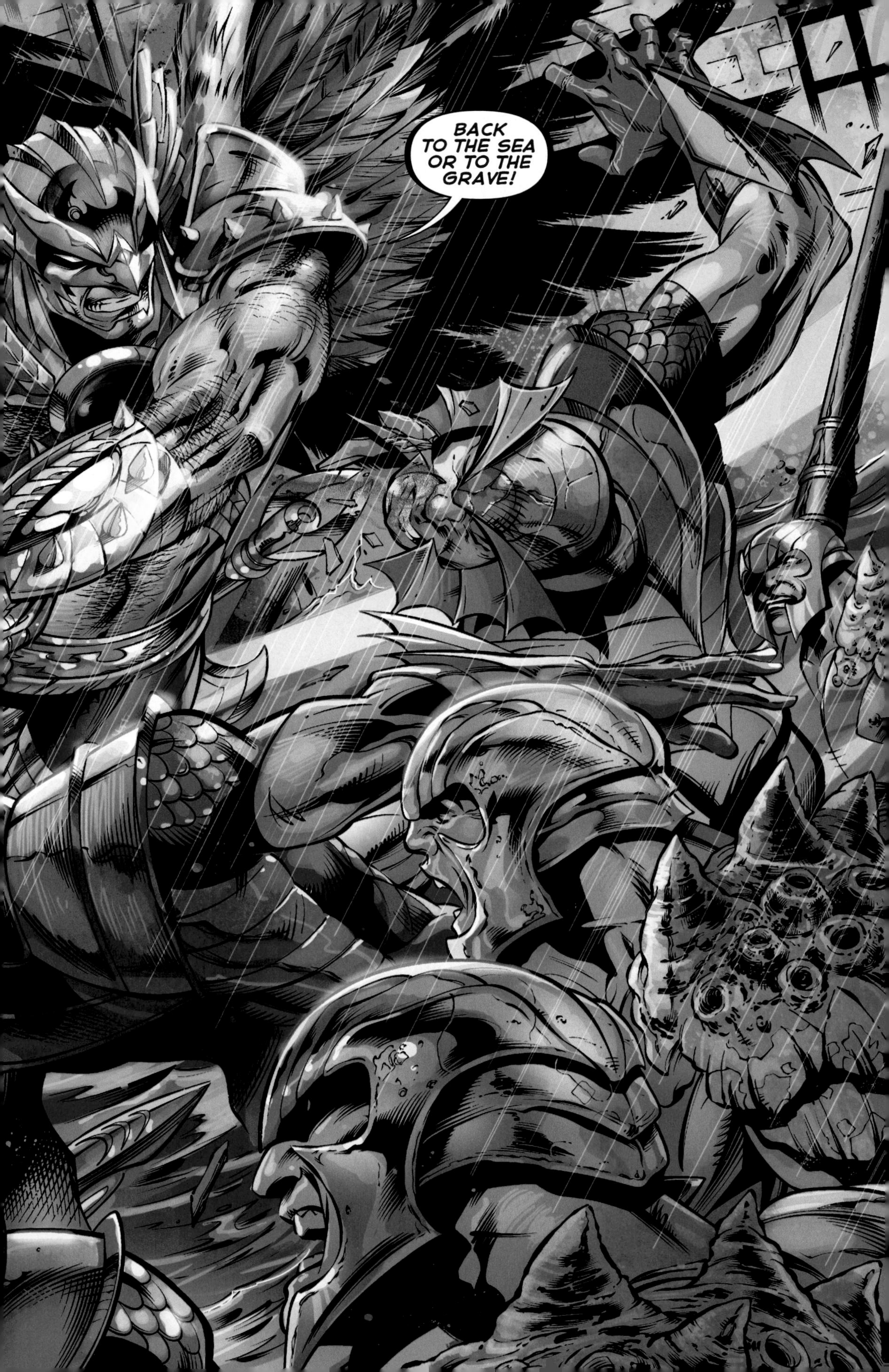
BACK TO THE SEA OR TO THE GRAVE!

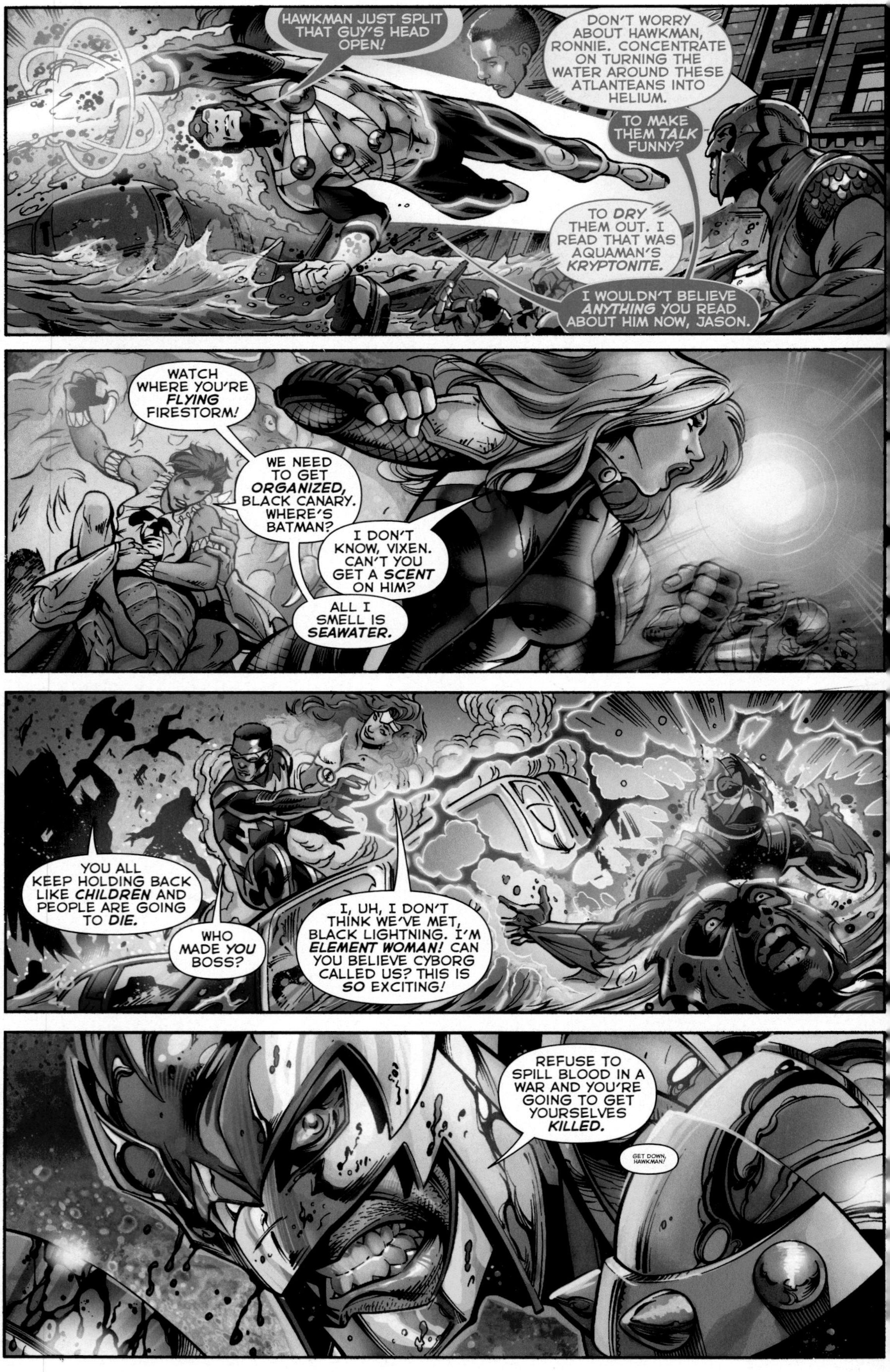
HAWKMAN JUST SPLIT THAT GUY'S HEAD OPEN!
DON'T WORRY ABOUT HAWKMAN, RONNIE. CONCENTRATE ON TURNING THE WATER AROUND THESE ATLANTEANS INTO HELIUM.
TO MAKE THEM *TALK* FUNNY?
TO *DRY* THEM OUT. I READ THAT WAS AQUAMAN'S ***KRYPTONITE.***
I WOULDN'T BELIEVE ***ANYTHING*** YOU READ ABOUT HIM NOW, JASON.
WATCH WHERE YOU'RE ***FLYING*** FIRESTORM!
WE NEED TO GET ***ORGANIZED,*** BLACK CANARY. WHERE'S BATMAN?
I DON'T KNOW, VIXEN. CAN'T YOU GET A ***SCENT*** ON HIM?
ALL I SMELL IS ***SEAWATER.***
YOU ALL KEEP HOLDING BACK LIKE ***CHILDREN*** AND PEOPLE ARE GOING TO ***DIE.***
WHO MADE *YOU* BOSS?
I, UH, I DON'T THINK WE'VE MET, BLACK LIGHTNING. I'M ***ELEMENT WOMAN!*** CAN YOU BELIEVE CYBORG CALLED US? THIS IS ***SO*** EXCITING!
REFUSE TO SPILL BLOOD IN A WAR AND YOU'RE GOING TO GET YOURSELVES ***KILLED.***
GET DOWN, HAWKMAN!

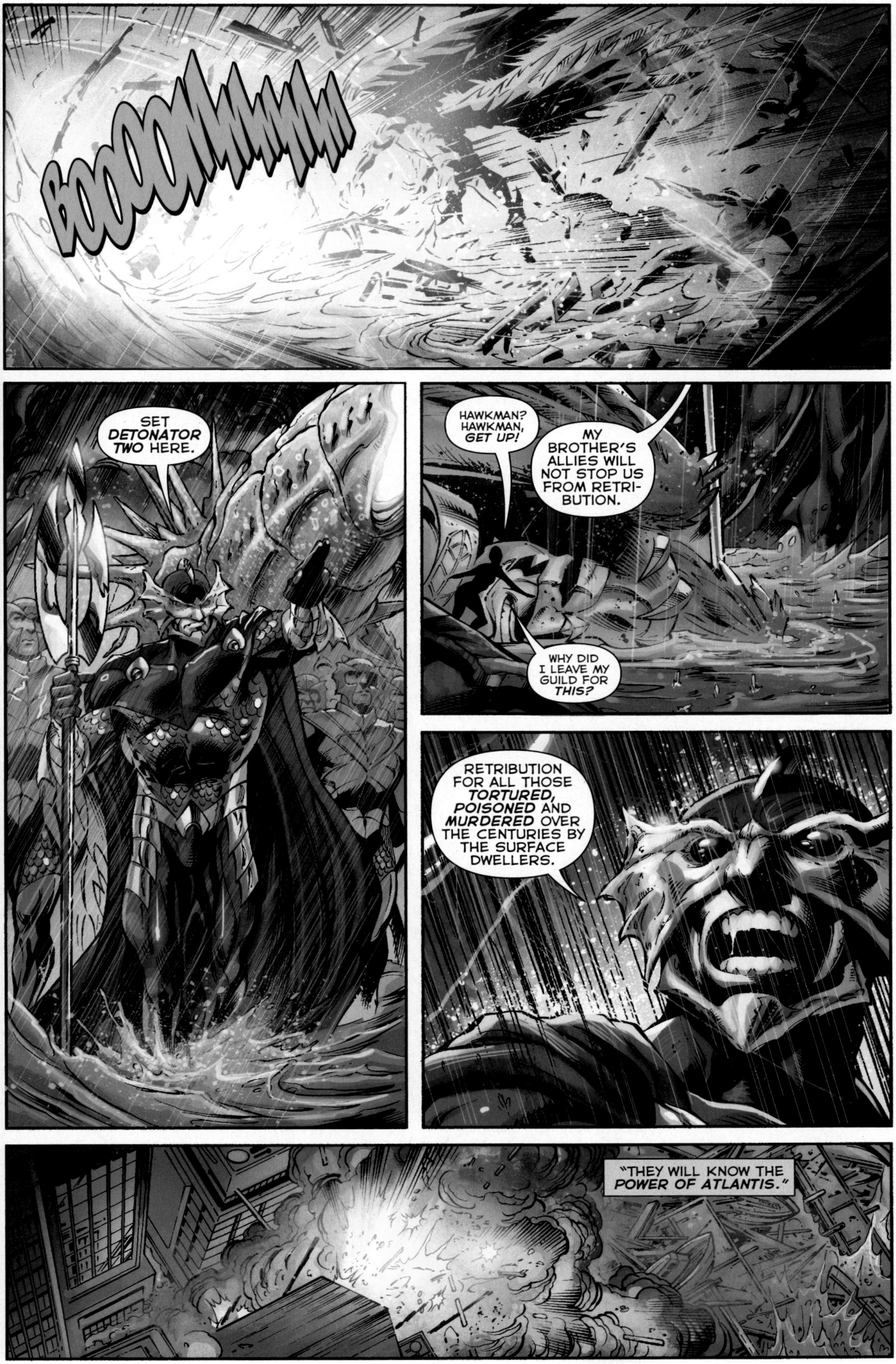
BOOOOMMMMM
SET DETONATOR TWO HERE.
HAWKMAN? HAWKMAN, GET UP!
MY BROTHER'S ALLIES WILL NOT STOP US FROM RETRIBUTION.
WHY DID I LEAVE MY GUILD FOR THIS?
RETRIBUTION FOR ALL THOSE TORTURED, POISONED AND MURDERED OVER THE CENTURIES BY THE SURFACE DWELLERS.
"THEY WILL KNOW THE POWER OF ATLANTIS."

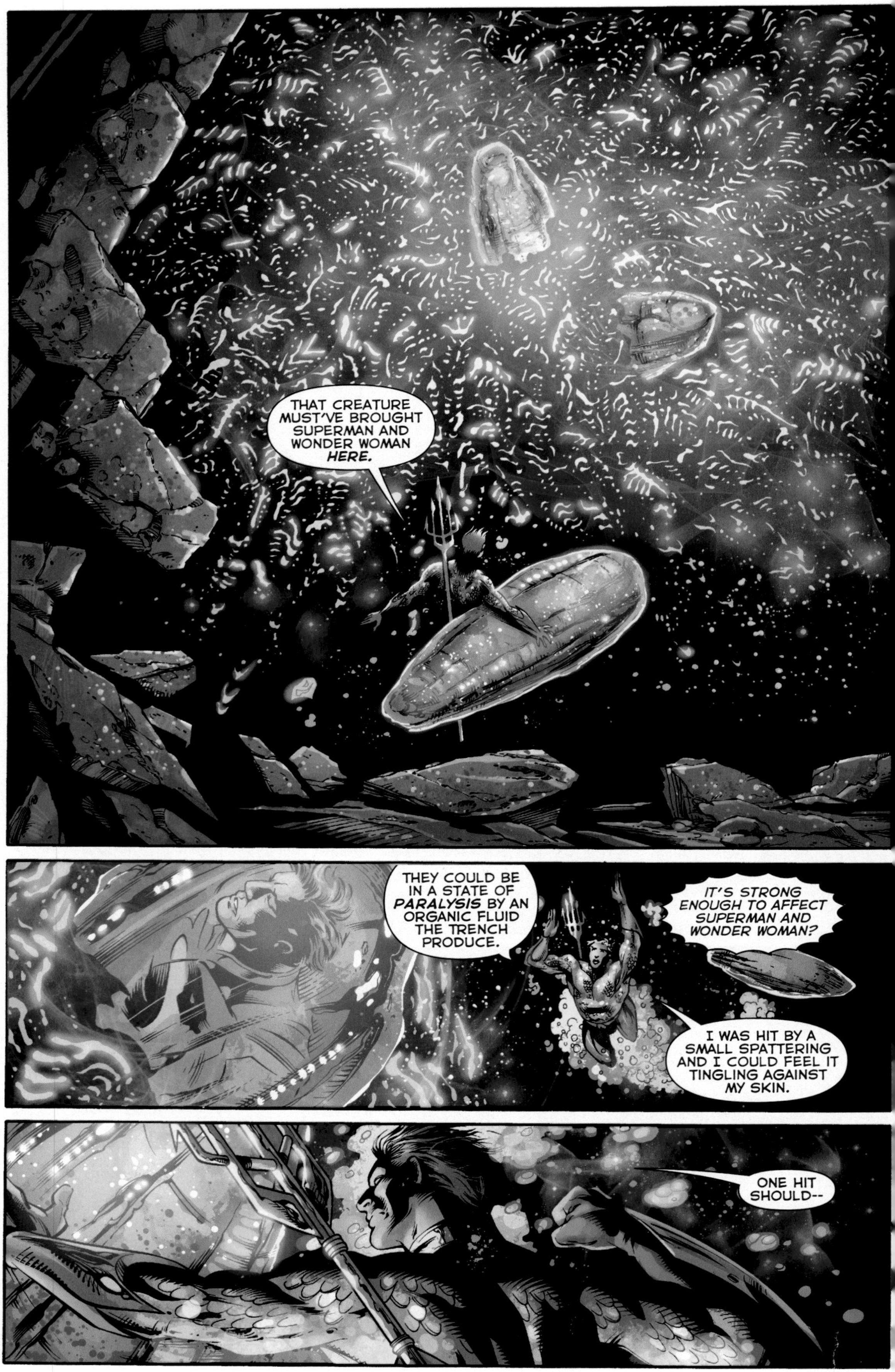
THAT CREATURE MUST'VE BROUGHT SUPERMAN AND WONDER WOMAN *HERE.*
THEY COULD BE IN A STATE OF *PARALYSIS* BY AN ORGANIC FLUID THE TRENCH PRODUCE.
IT'S STRONG ENOUGH TO AFFECT SUPERMAN AND WONDER WOMAN?
I WAS HIT BY A SMALL SPATTERING AND I COULD FEEL IT TINGLING AGAINST MY SKIN.
ONE HIT SHOULD--

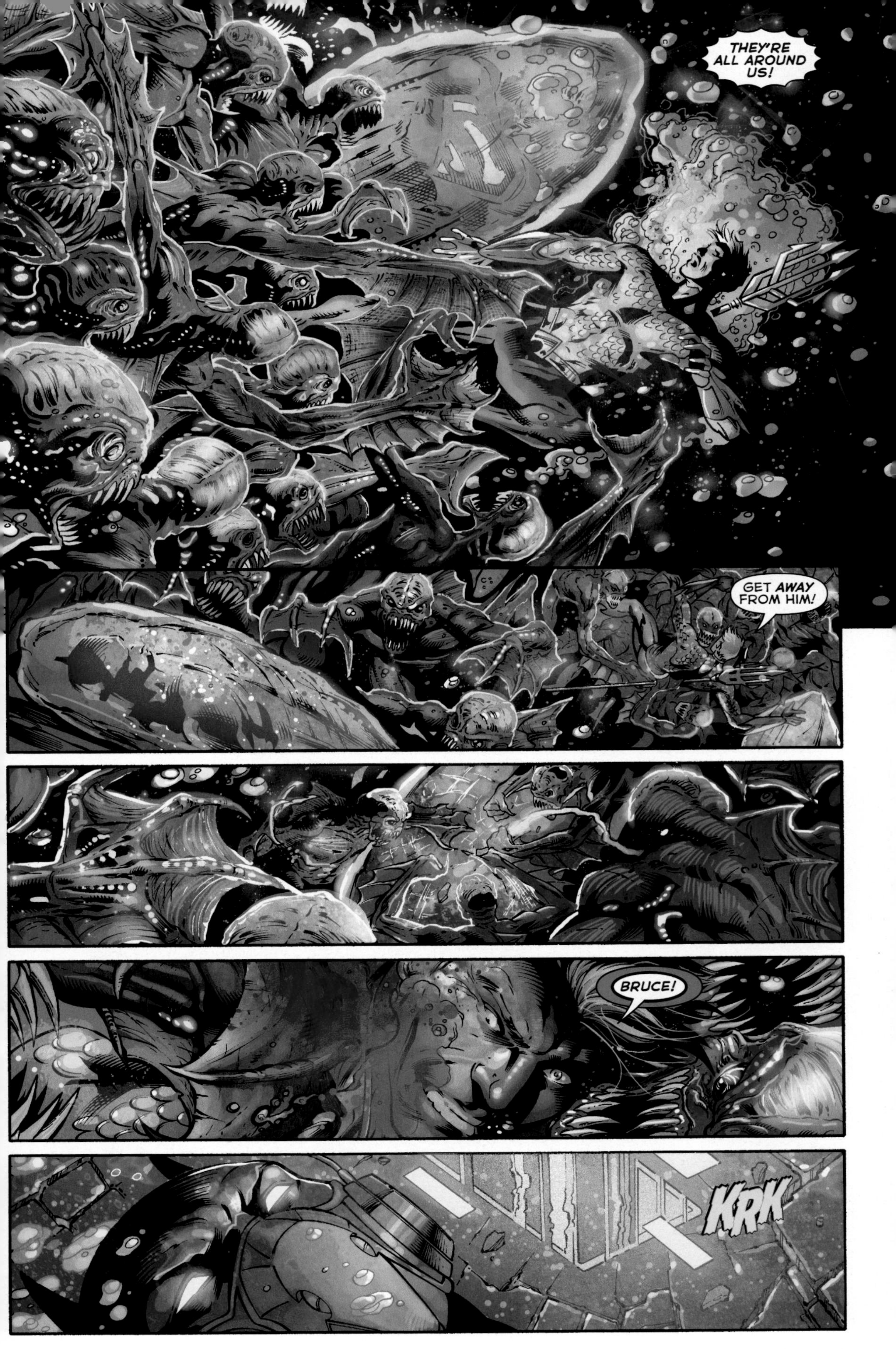
THEY'RE ALL AROUND US!
GET AWAY FROM HIM!
BRUCE!
KRK

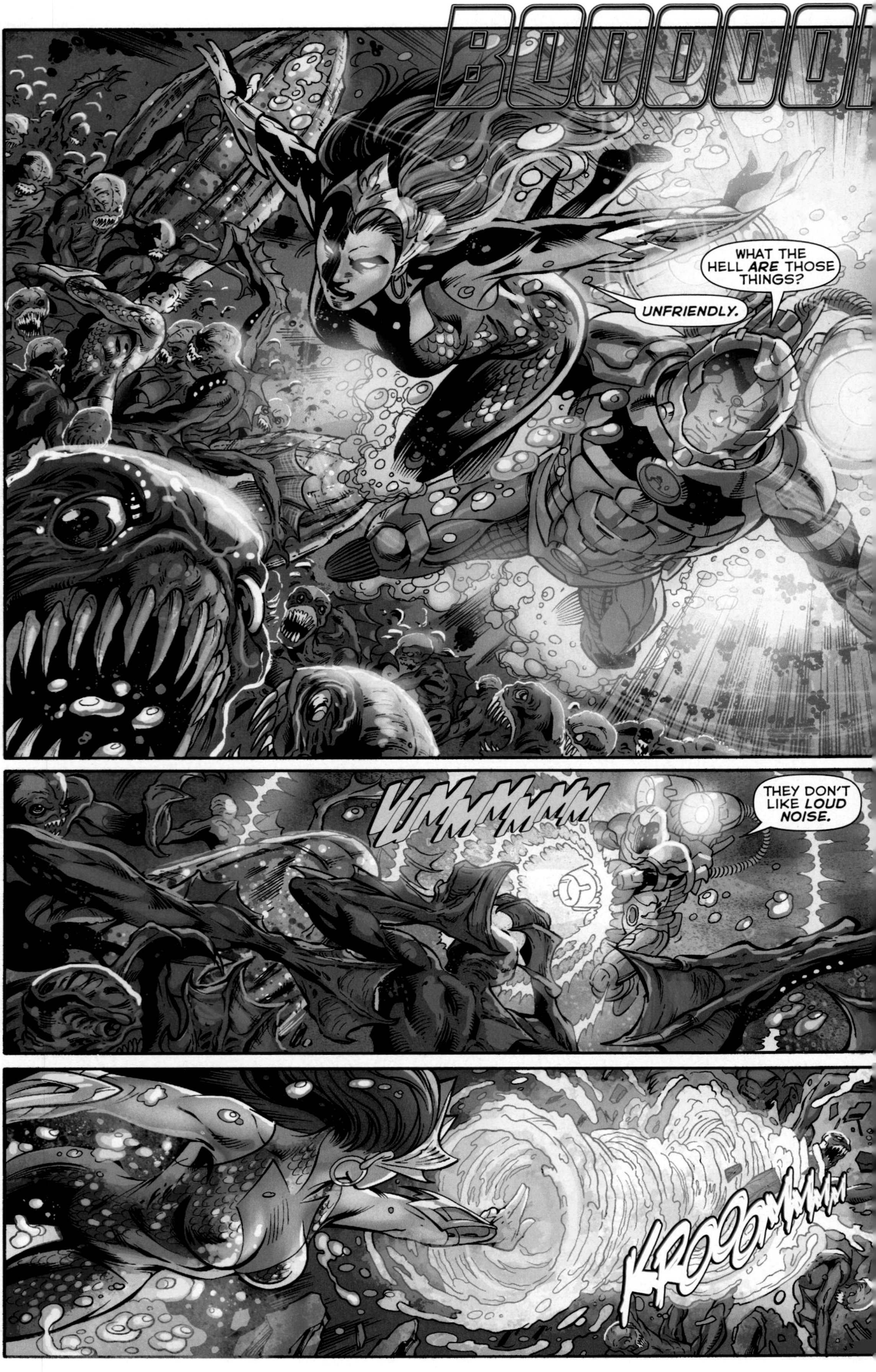
WHAT THE HELL *ARE* THOSE THINGS?
UNFRIENDLY.
THEY DON'T LIKE *LOUD NOISE.*

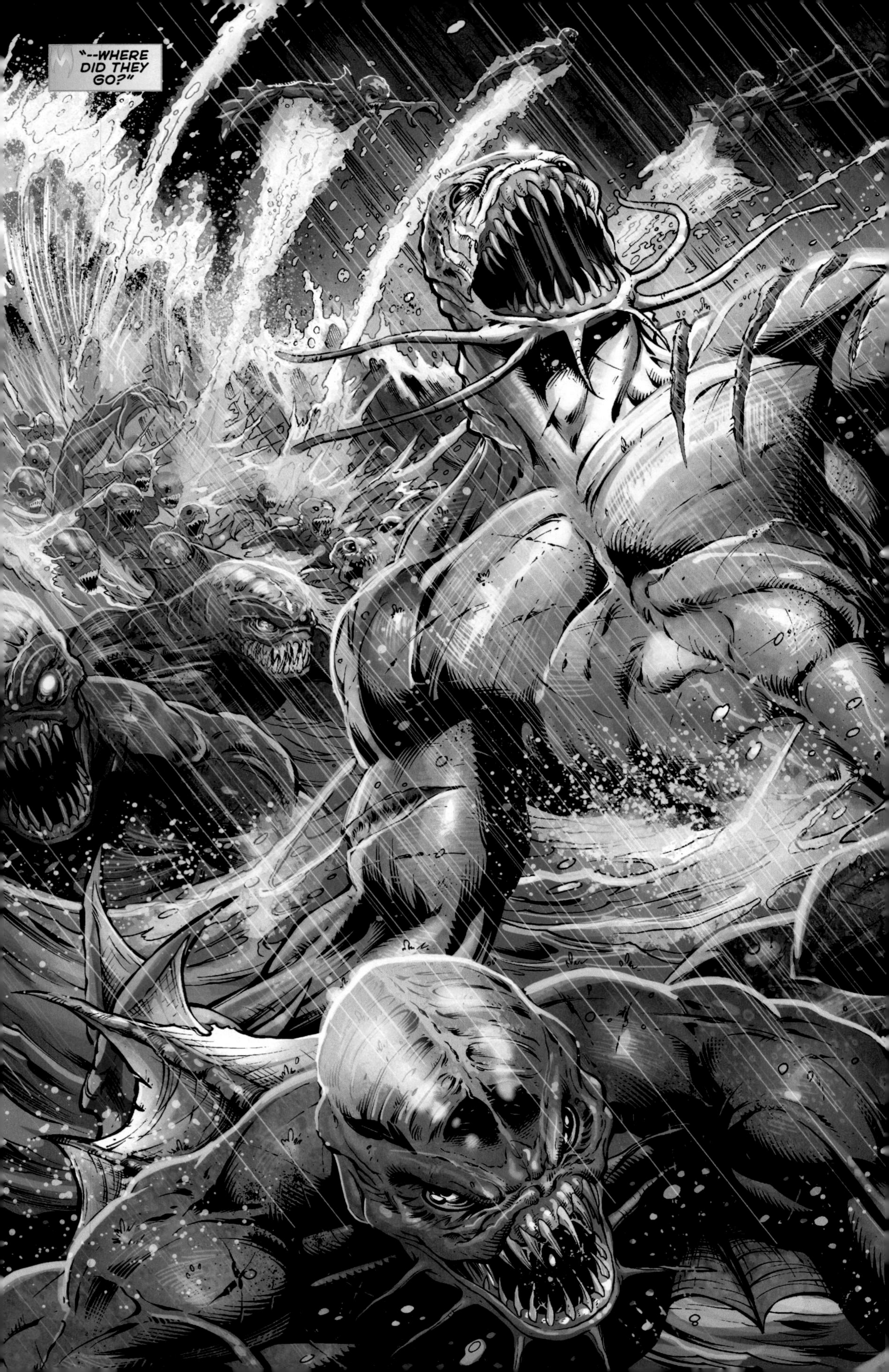
"--WHERE DID THEY GO?"

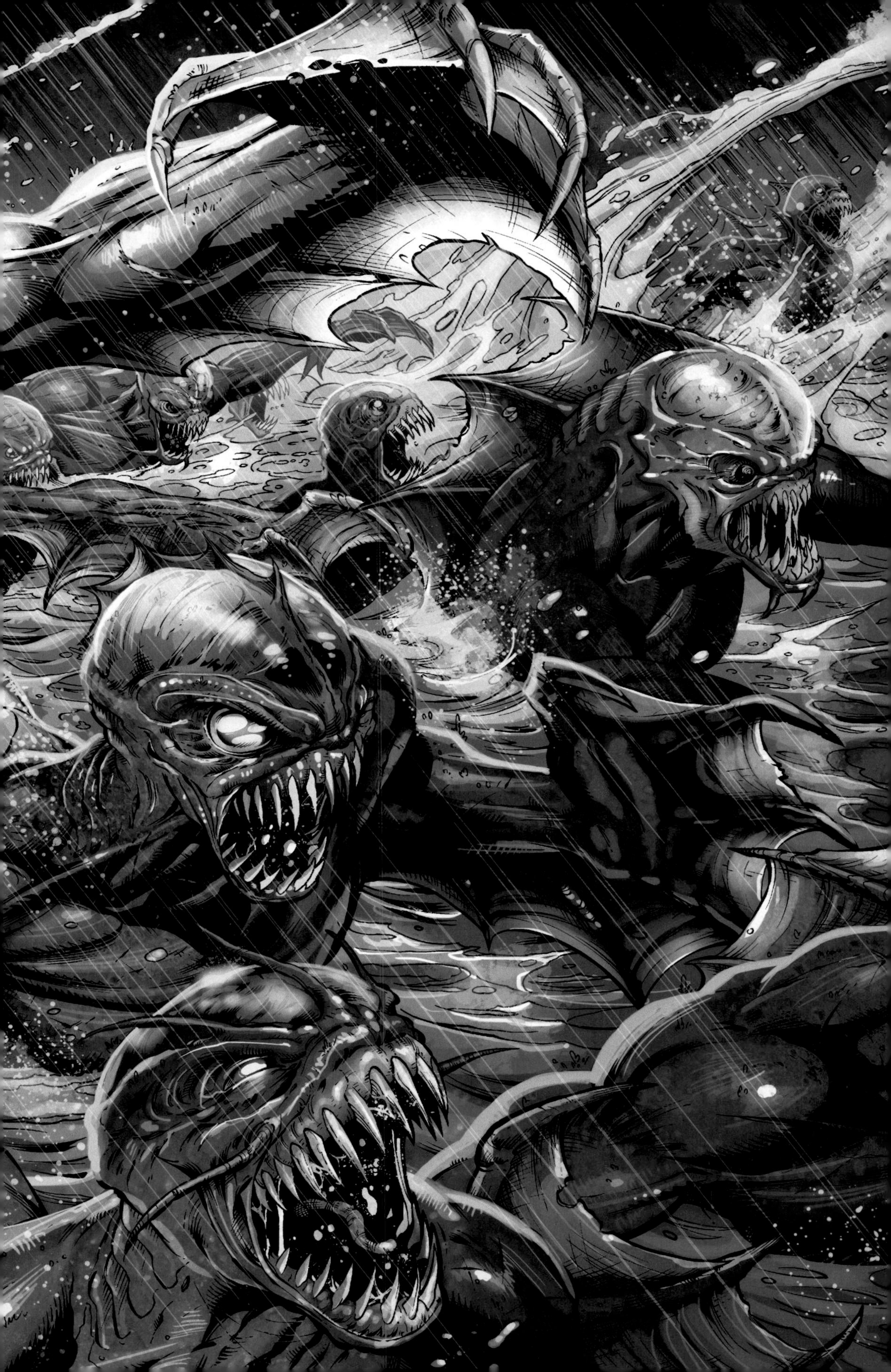

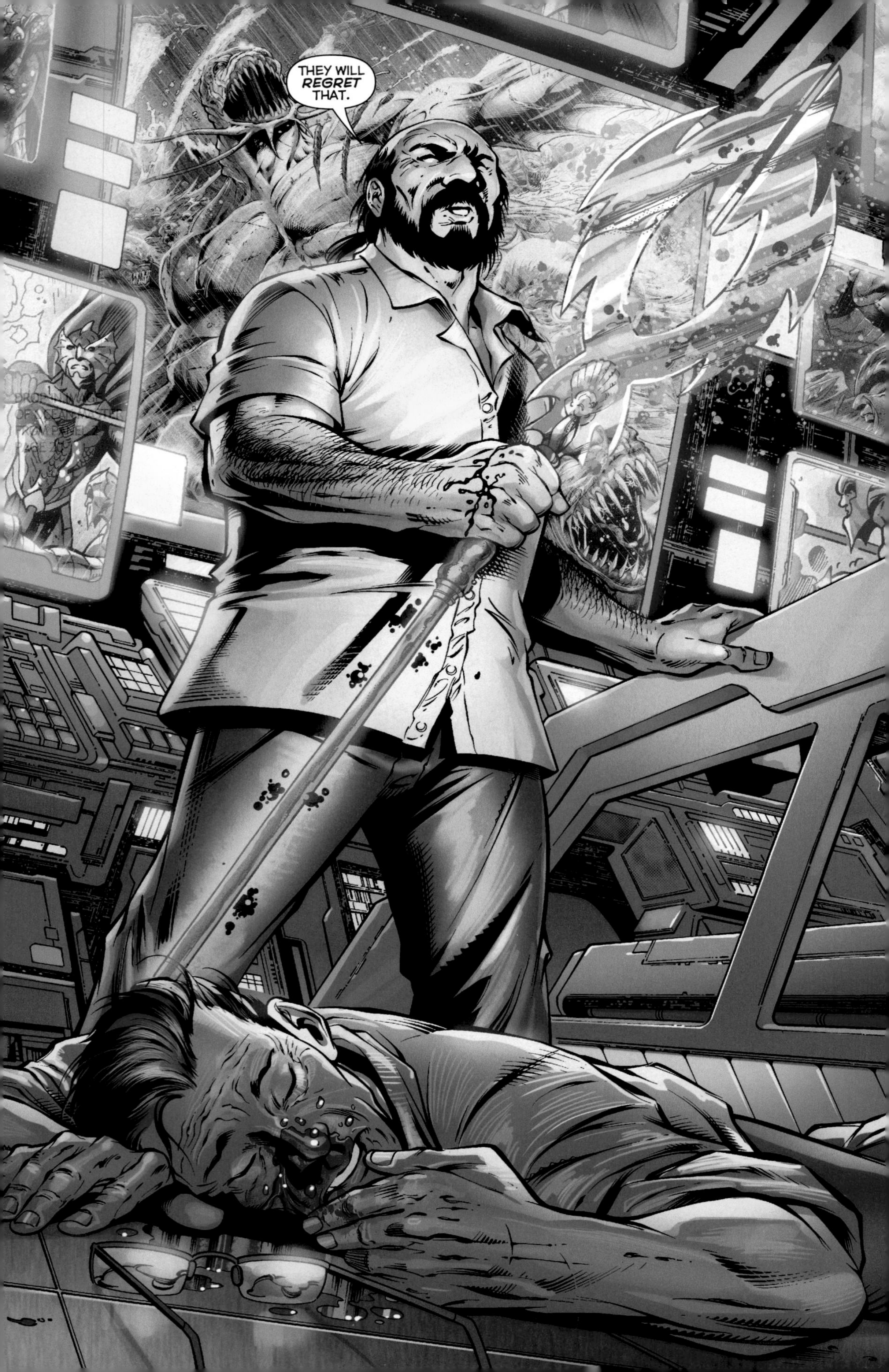
THEY WILL *REGRET* THAT.

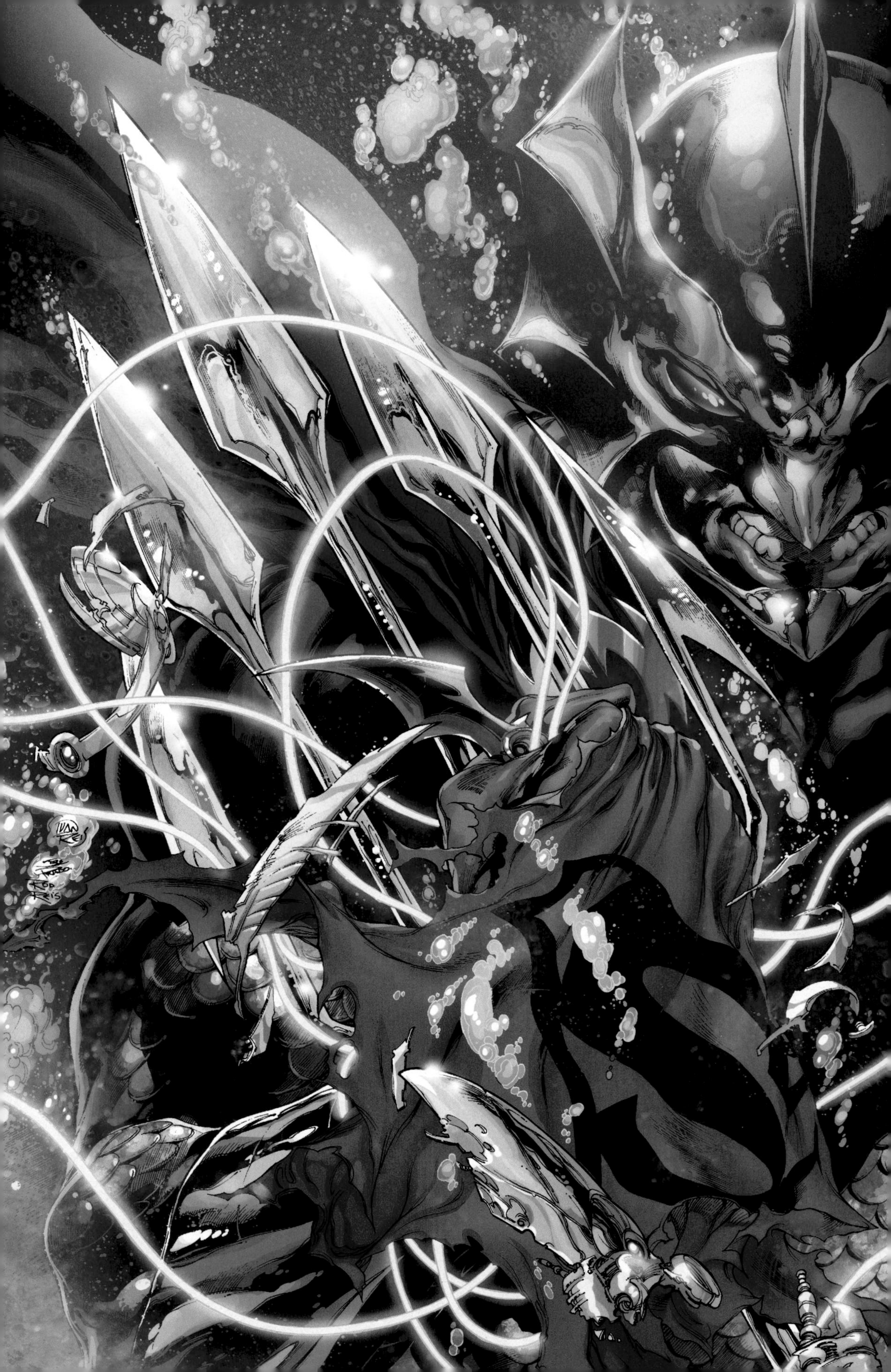

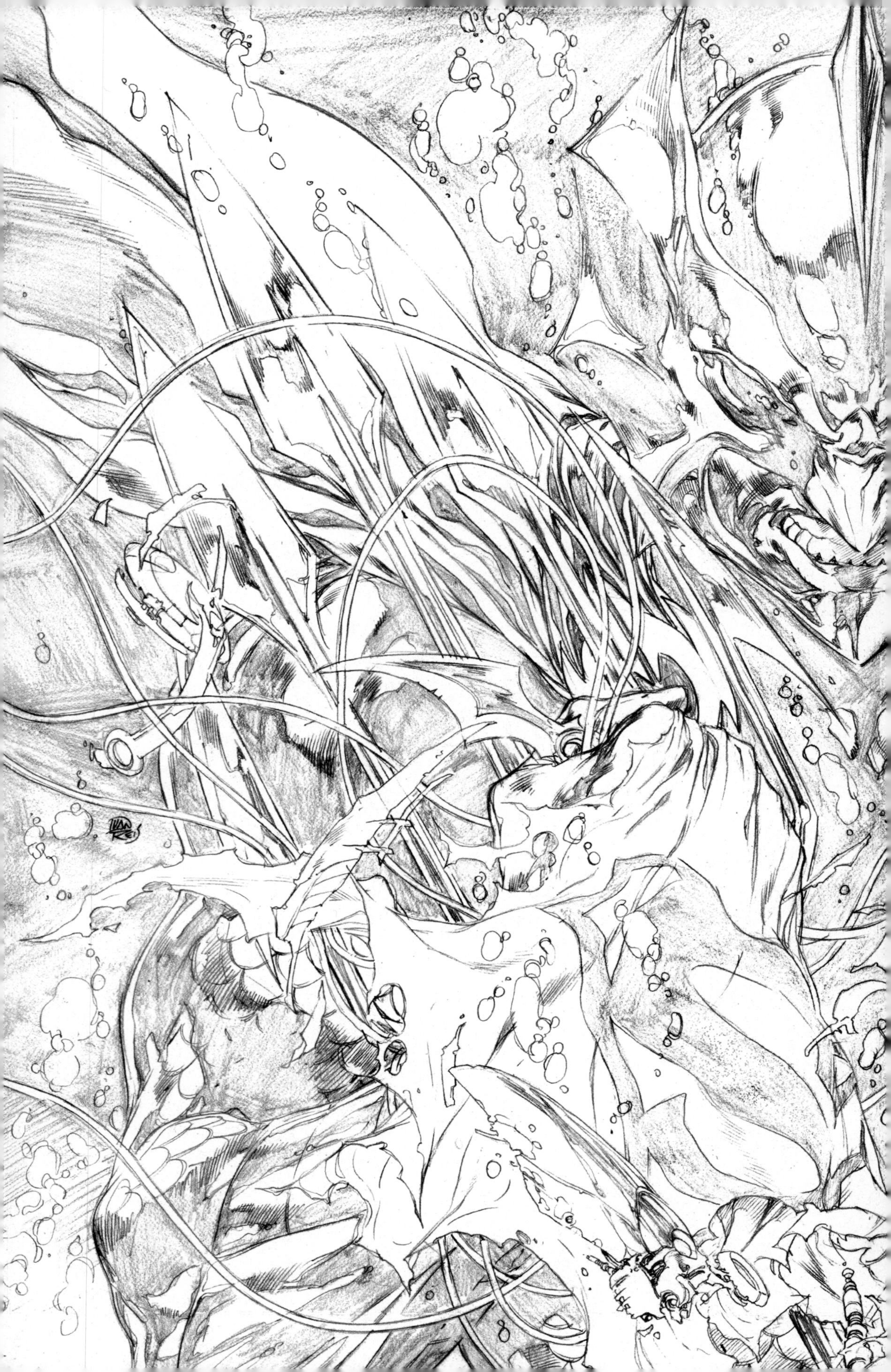

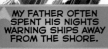

MY FATHER OFTEN SPENT HIS NIGHTS WARNING SHIPS AWAY FROM THE SHORE.

SOMETIMES HE'D CATCH ME STAYING AWAKE TO WATCH HIM WORK.

HE SEEMED *FRIGHTENED* OF SOMETHING. HE NEVER TOLD ME WHAT--

--UNTIL ONE NIGHT. WHEN THE WORST STORM WE'D EVER SEEN HIT AMNESTY BAY. HE LOOKED AT ME AND FINALLY ADMITTED, "I'M SCARED THEY'RE COMING FOR *YOU*, ARTHUR."

I'D NEVER BEEN MORE *TERRIFIED* IN MY LIFE.

MY FATHER ISN'T HERE TO WARN ANYONE ANYMORE.

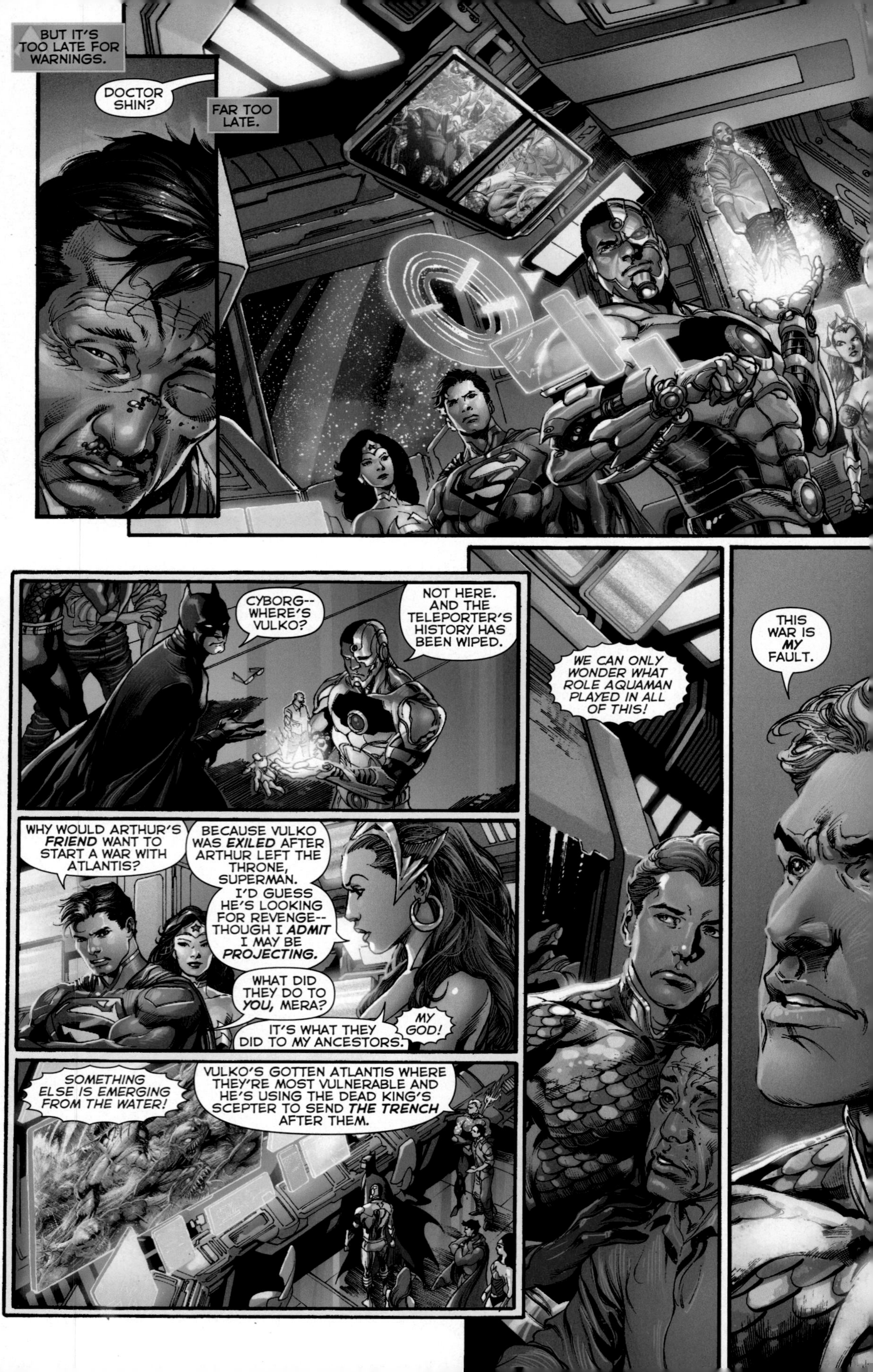
BUT IT'S TOO LATE FOR WARNINGS.
DOCTOR SHIN?
FAR TOO LATE.
CYBORG-- WHERE'S VULKO?
NOT HERE. AND THE TELEPORTER'S HISTORY HAS BEEN WIPED.
WHY WOULD ARTHUR'S FRIEND WANT TO START A WAR WITH ATLANTIS?
BECAUSE VULKO WAS EXILED AFTER ARTHUR LEFT THE THRONE, SUPERMAN.
I'D GUESS HE'S LOOKING FOR REVENGE-- THOUGH I ADMIT I MAY BE PROJECTING.
WHAT DID THEY DO TO YOU, MERA?
IT'S WHAT THEY DID TO MY ANCESTORS.
MY GOD!
SOMETHING ELSE IS EMERGING FROM THE WATER!
VULKO'S GOTTEN ATLANTIS WHERE THEY'RE MOST VULNERABLE AND HE'S USING THE DEAD KING'S SCEPTER TO SEND THE TRENCH AFTER THEM.
WE CAN ONLY WONDER WHAT ROLE AQUAMAN PLAYED IN ALL OF THIS!
THIS WAR IS MY FAULT.

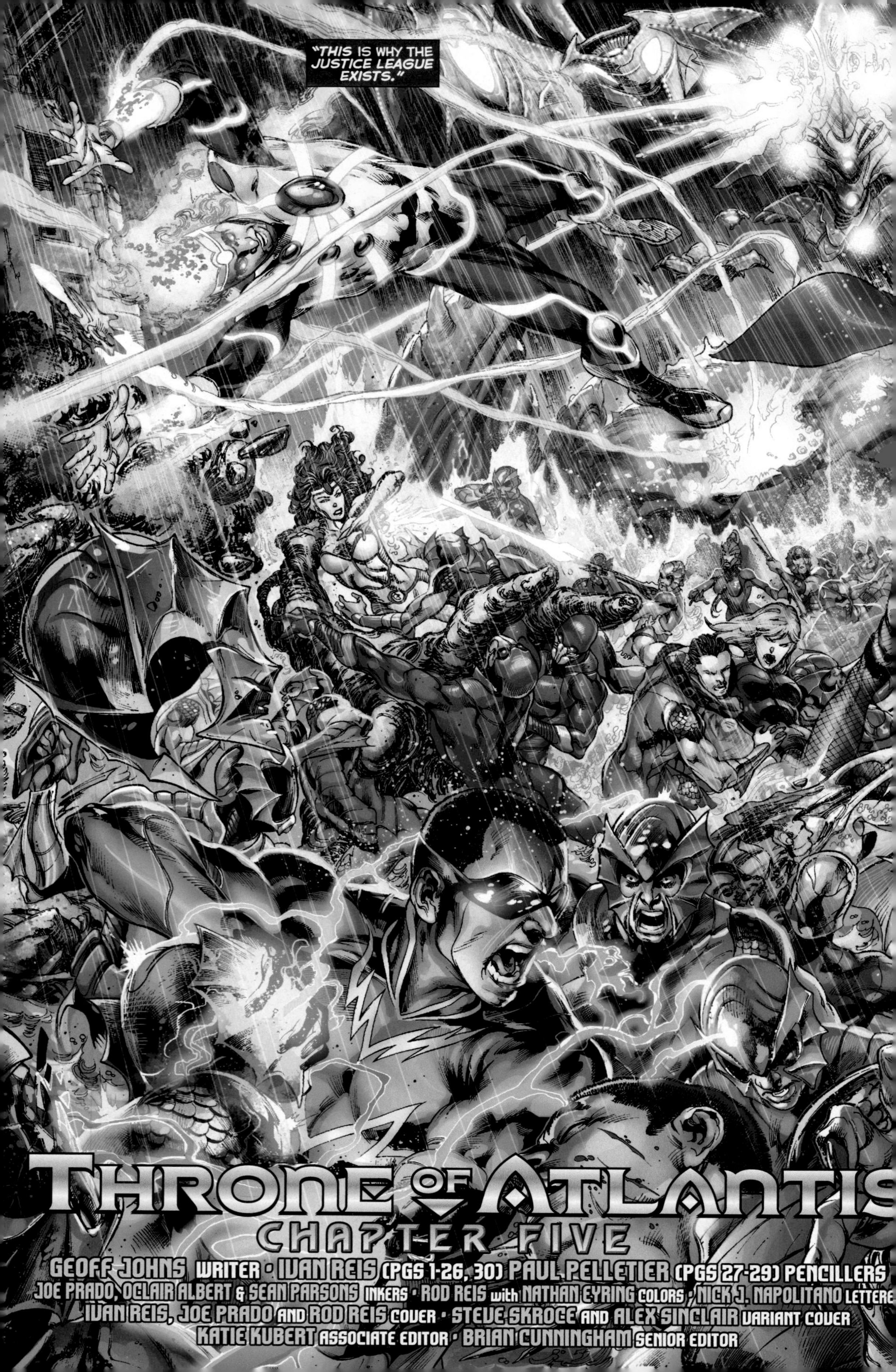
"THIS IS WHY THE JUSTICE LEAGUE EXISTS."
THRONE OF ATLANTIS
CHAPTER FIVE
GEOFF JOHNS WRITER · IVAN REIS (PGS 1-26, 30) PAUL PELLETIER (PGS 27-29) PENCILLERS
JOE PRADO, OCLAIR ALBERT & SEAN PARSONS INKERS · ROD REIS with NATHAN EYRING COLORS · NICK J. NAPOLITANO LETTERE
IVAN REIS, JOE PRADO AND ROD REIS COVER · STEVE SKROCE AND ALEX SINCLAIR VARIANT COVER
KATIE KUBERT ASSOCIATE EDITOR · BRIAN CUNNINGHAM SENIOR EDITOR

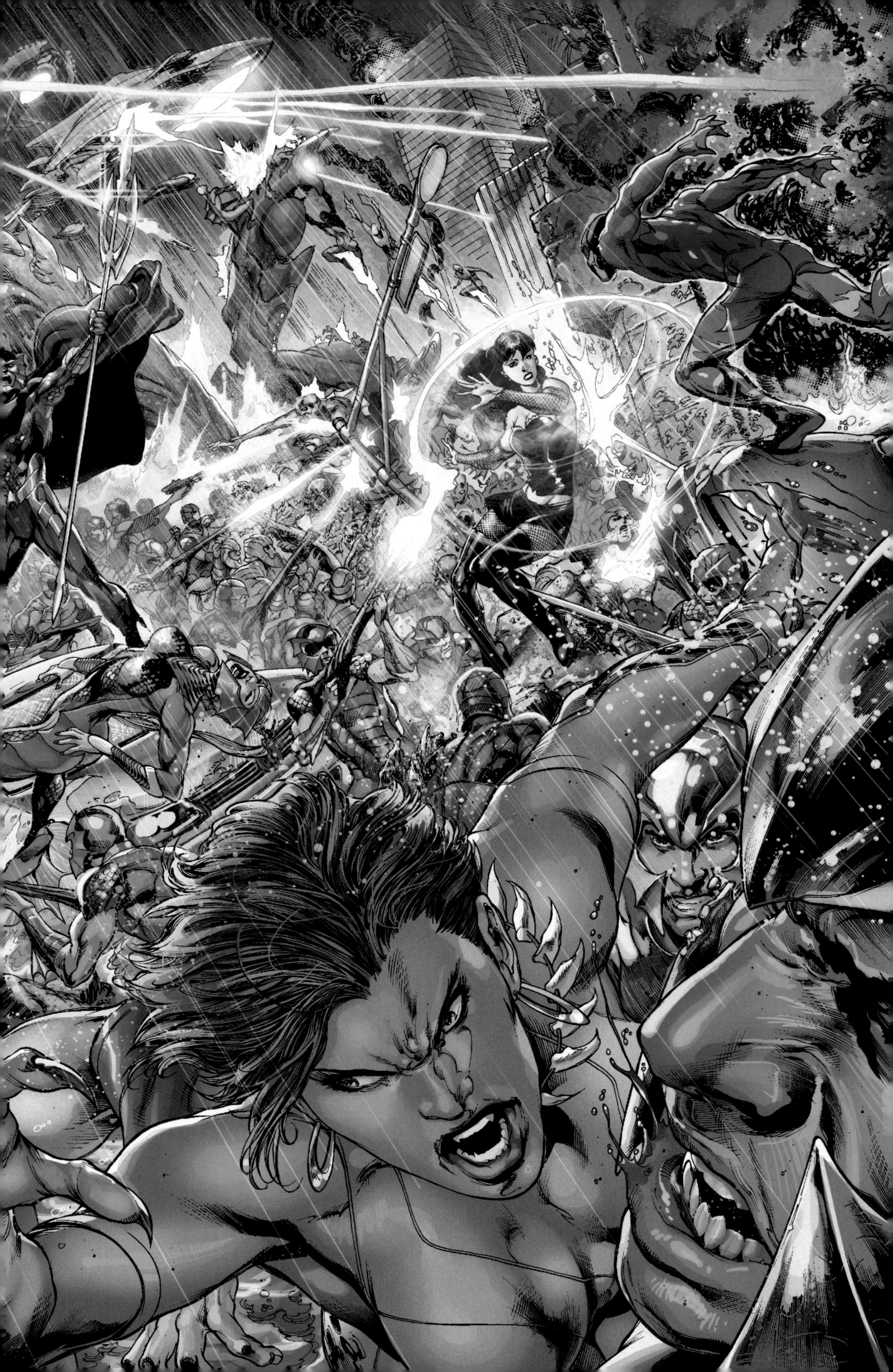

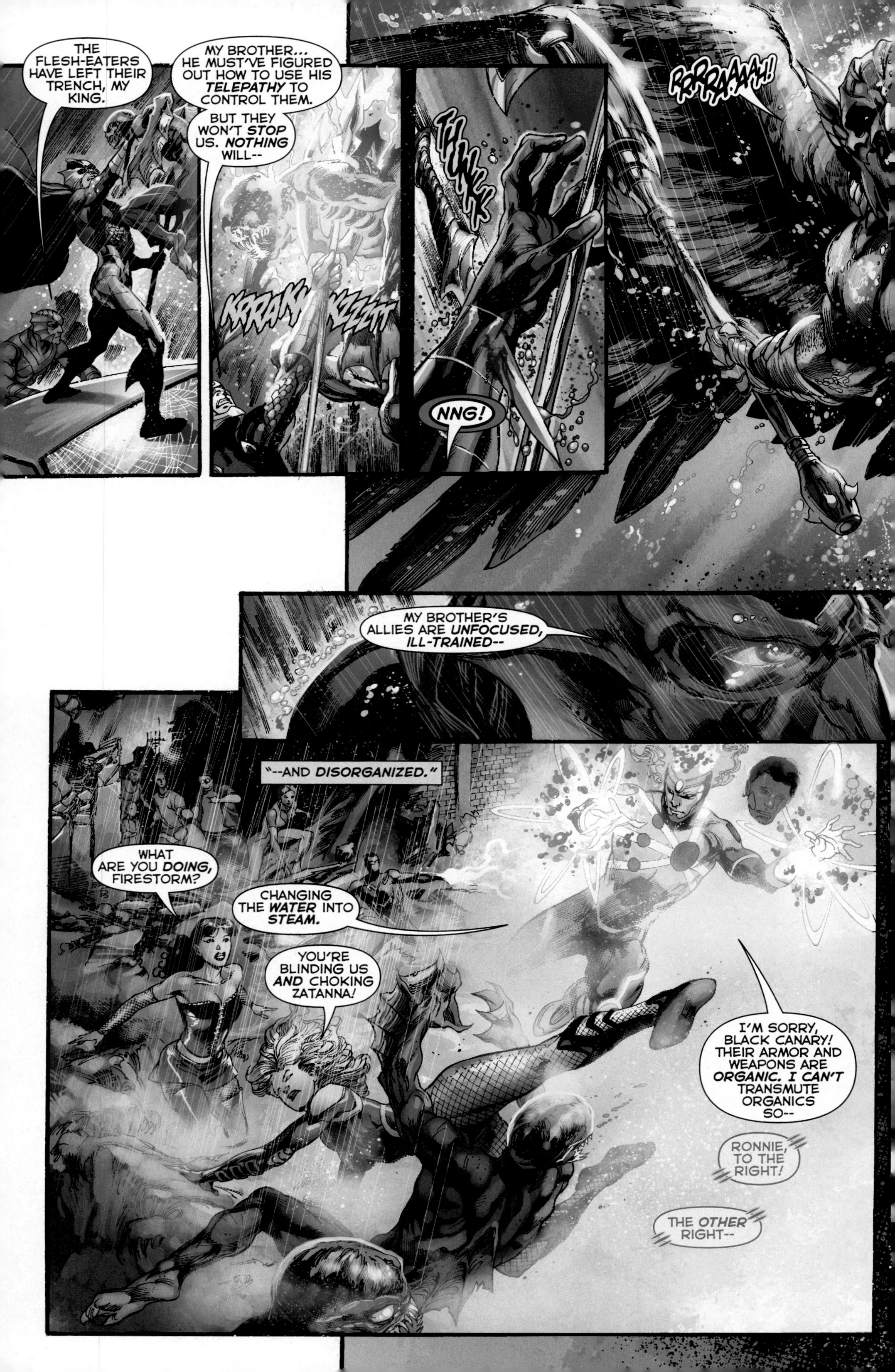
THE FLESH-EATERS HAVE LEFT THEIR TRENCH, MY KING.
MY BROTHER... HE MUST'VE FIGURED OUT HOW TO USE HIS *TELEPATHY* TO CONTROL THEM.
BUT THEY WON'T *STOP* US. *NOTHING* WILL--
KRRAKK
KZZZTT
THUNKK
NNG!
RRRRAAAAH!
MY BROTHER'S ALLIES ARE *UNFOCUSED, ILL-TRAINED*--
"--AND *DISORGANIZED.*"
WHAT ARE YOU *DOING,* FIRESTORM?
CHANGING THE *WATER* INTO *STEAM.*
YOU'RE BLINDING US *AND* CHOKING ZATANNA!
I'M SORRY, BLACK CANARY! THEIR ARMOR AND WEAPONS ARE *ORGANIC. I CAN'T* TRANSMUTE ORGANICS SO--
RONNIE, TO THE RIGHT!
THE *OTHER* RIGHT--

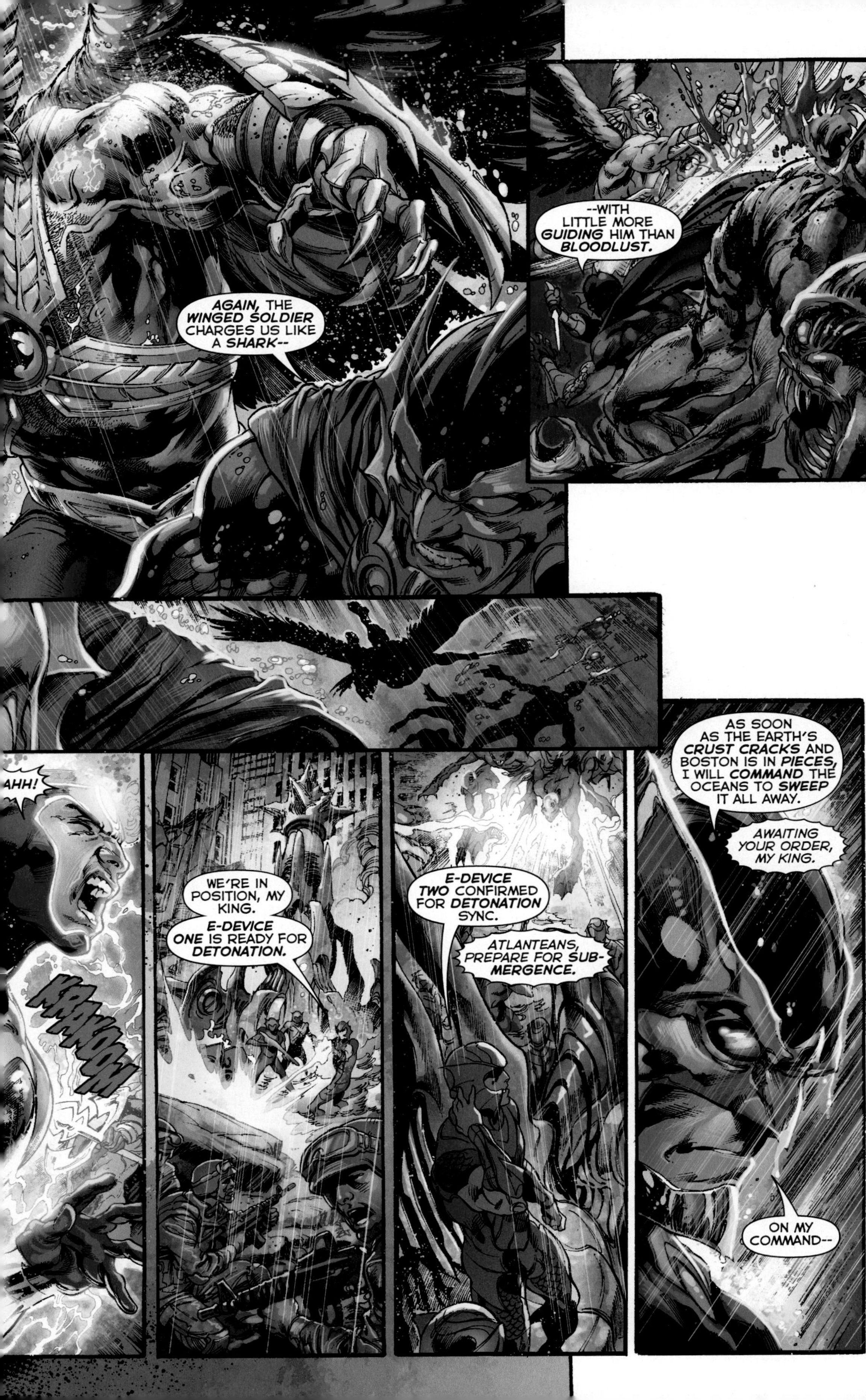
AGAIN, THE WINGED SOLDIER CHARGES US LIKE A SHARK--
--WITH LITTLE MORE GUIDING HIM THAN BLOODLUST.
AHH!
KRAKOOM
WE'RE IN POSITION, MY KING.
E-DEVICE ONE IS READY FOR DETONATION.
E-DEVICE TWO CONFIRMED FOR DETONATION SYNC.
ATLANTEANS, PREPARE FOR SUB-MERGENCE.
AS SOON AS THE EARTH'S CRUST CRACKS AND BOSTON IS IN PIECES, I WILL COMMAND THE OCEANS TO SWEEP IT ALL AWAY.
AWAITING YOUR ORDER, MY KING.
ON MY COMMAND--

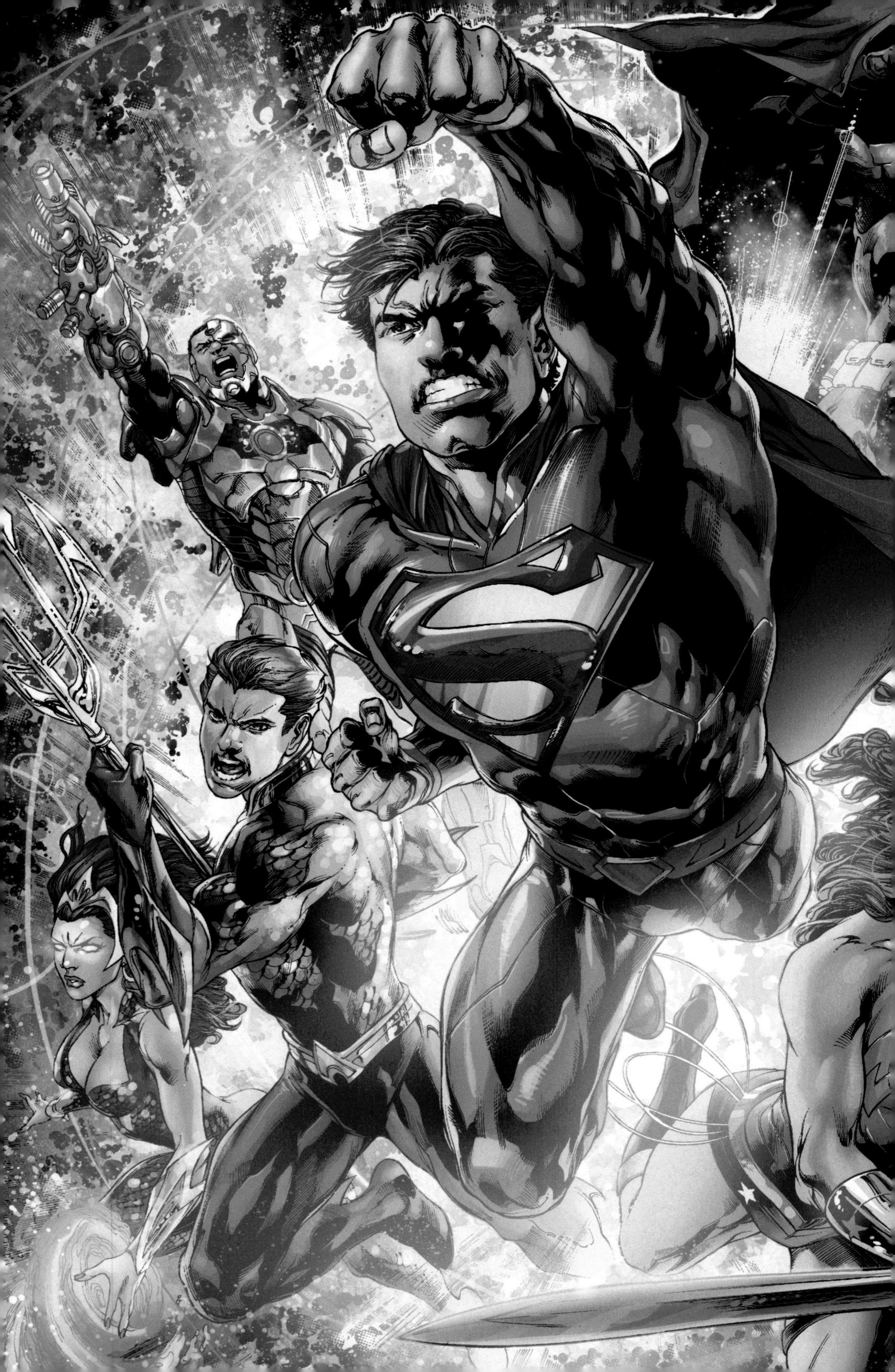

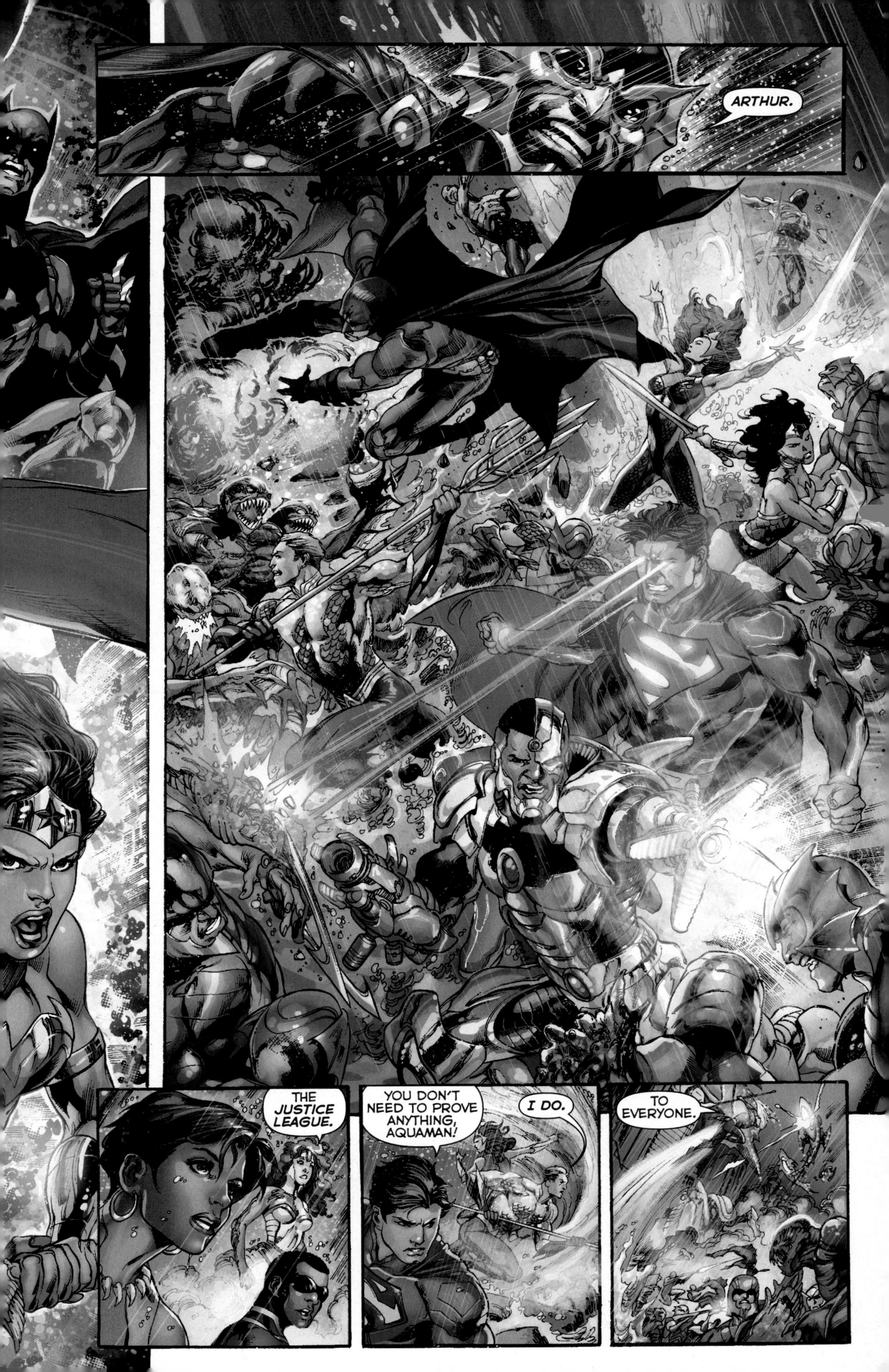
ARTHUR.
THE JUSTICE LEAGUE.
YOU DON'T NEED TO PROVE ANYTHING, AQUAMAN!
I DO.
TO EVERYONE.

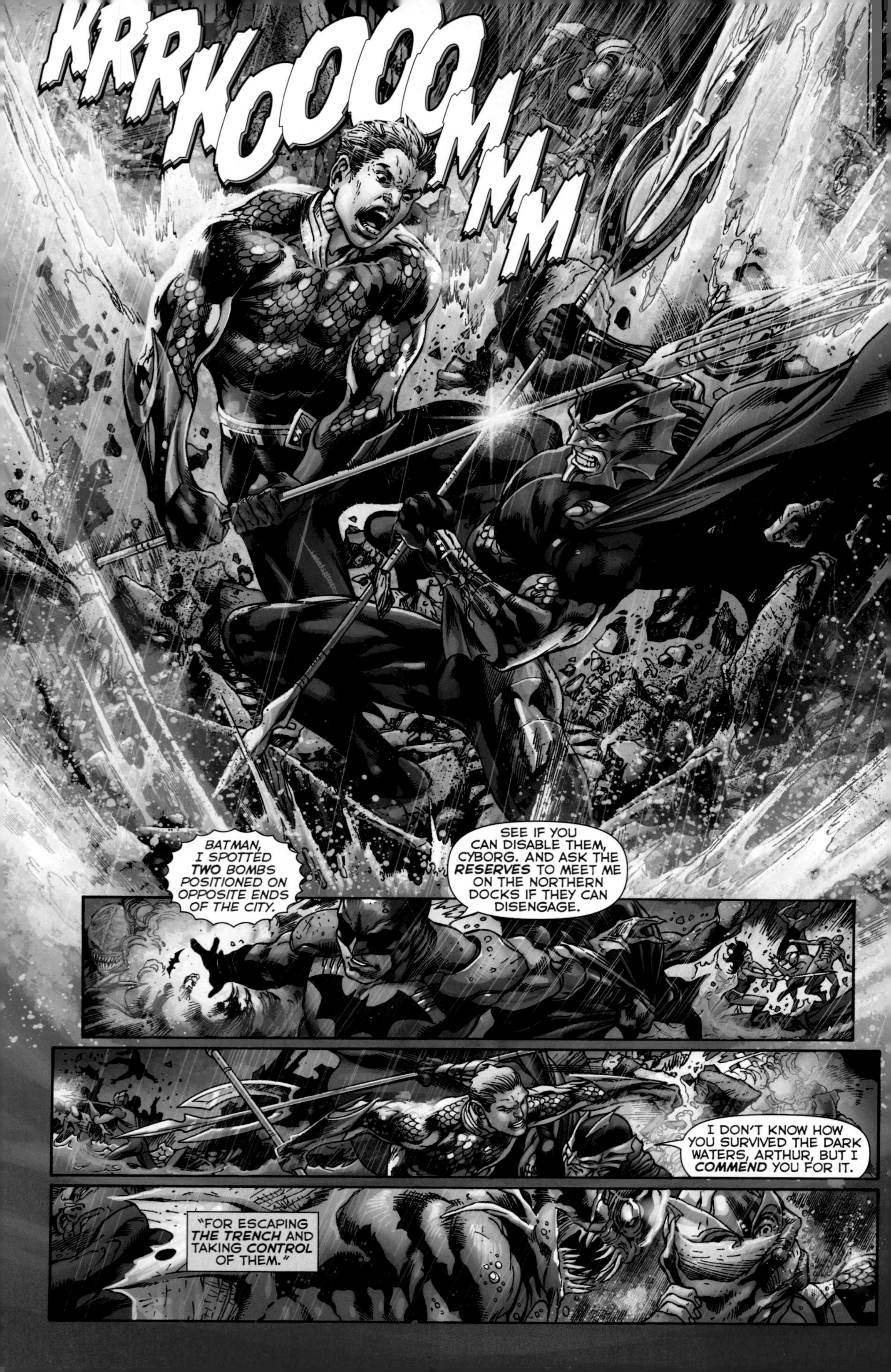
KRRKOOOOMMM
BATMAN, I SPOTTED TWO BOMBS POSITIONED ON OPPOSITE ENDS OF THE CITY.
SEE IF YOU CAN DISABLE THEM, CYBORG. AND ASK THE RESERVES TO MEET ME ON THE NORTHERN DOCKS IF THEY CAN DISENGAGE.
I DON'T KNOW HOW YOU SURVIVED THE DARK WATERS, ARTHUR, BUT I COMMEND YOU FOR IT.
"FOR ESCAPING THE TRENCH AND TAKING CONTROL OF THEM."

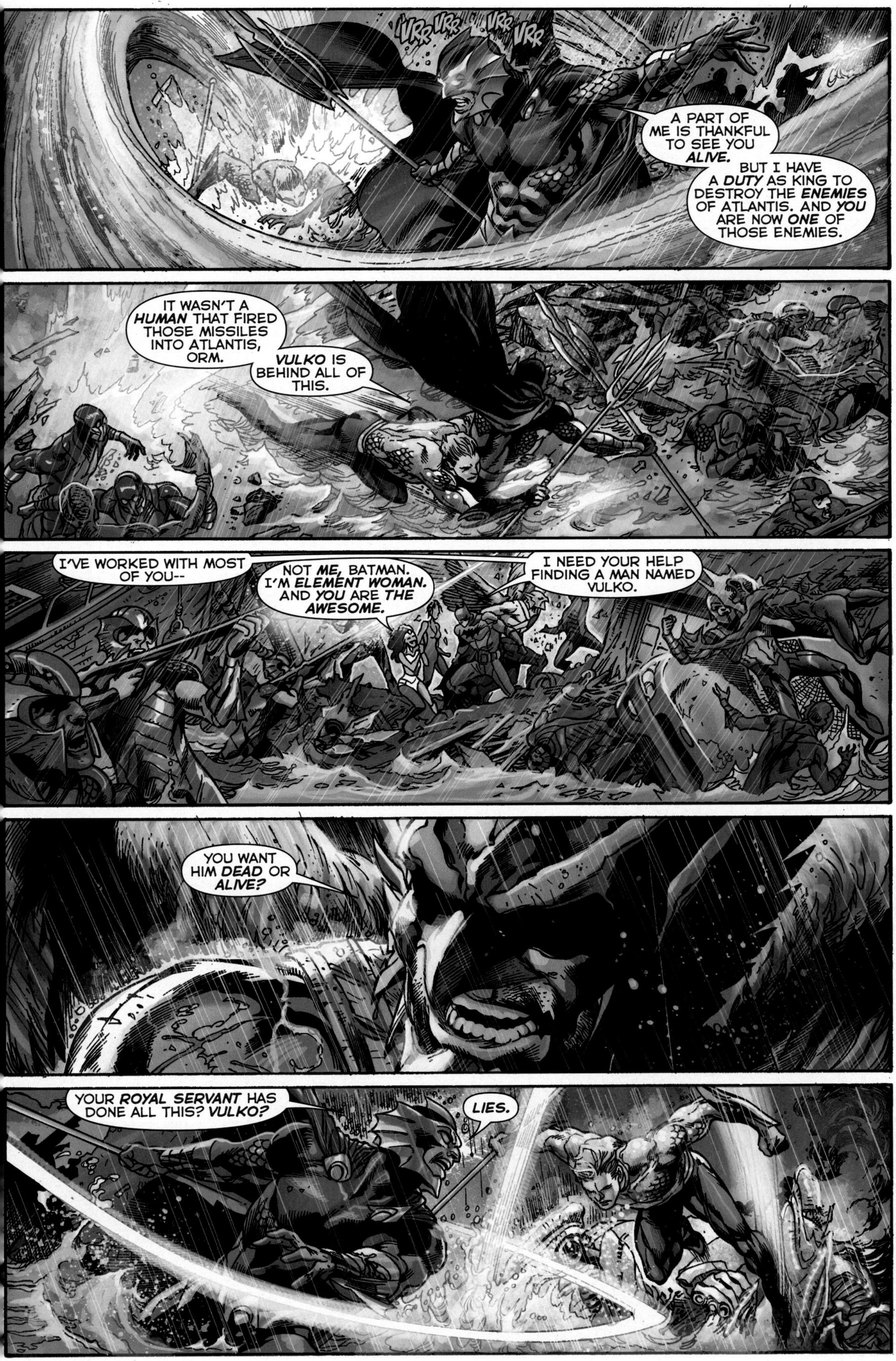
VRR VRR VRR VRR
A PART OF ME IS THANKFUL TO SEE YOU ALIVE.
BUT I HAVE A DUTY AS KING TO DESTROY THE ENEMIES OF ATLANTIS. AND YOU ARE NOW ONE OF THOSE ENEMIES.
IT WASN'T A HUMAN THAT FIRED THOSE MISSILES INTO ATLANTIS, ORM.
VULKO IS BEHIND ALL OF THIS.
I'VE WORKED WITH MOST OF YOU--
NOT ME, BATMAN. I'M ELEMENT WOMAN. AND YOU ARE THE AWESOME.
I NEED YOUR HELP FINDING A MAN NAMED VULKO.
YOU WANT HIM DEAD OR ALIVE?
YOUR ROYAL SERVANT HAS DONE ALL THIS? VULKO?
LIES.

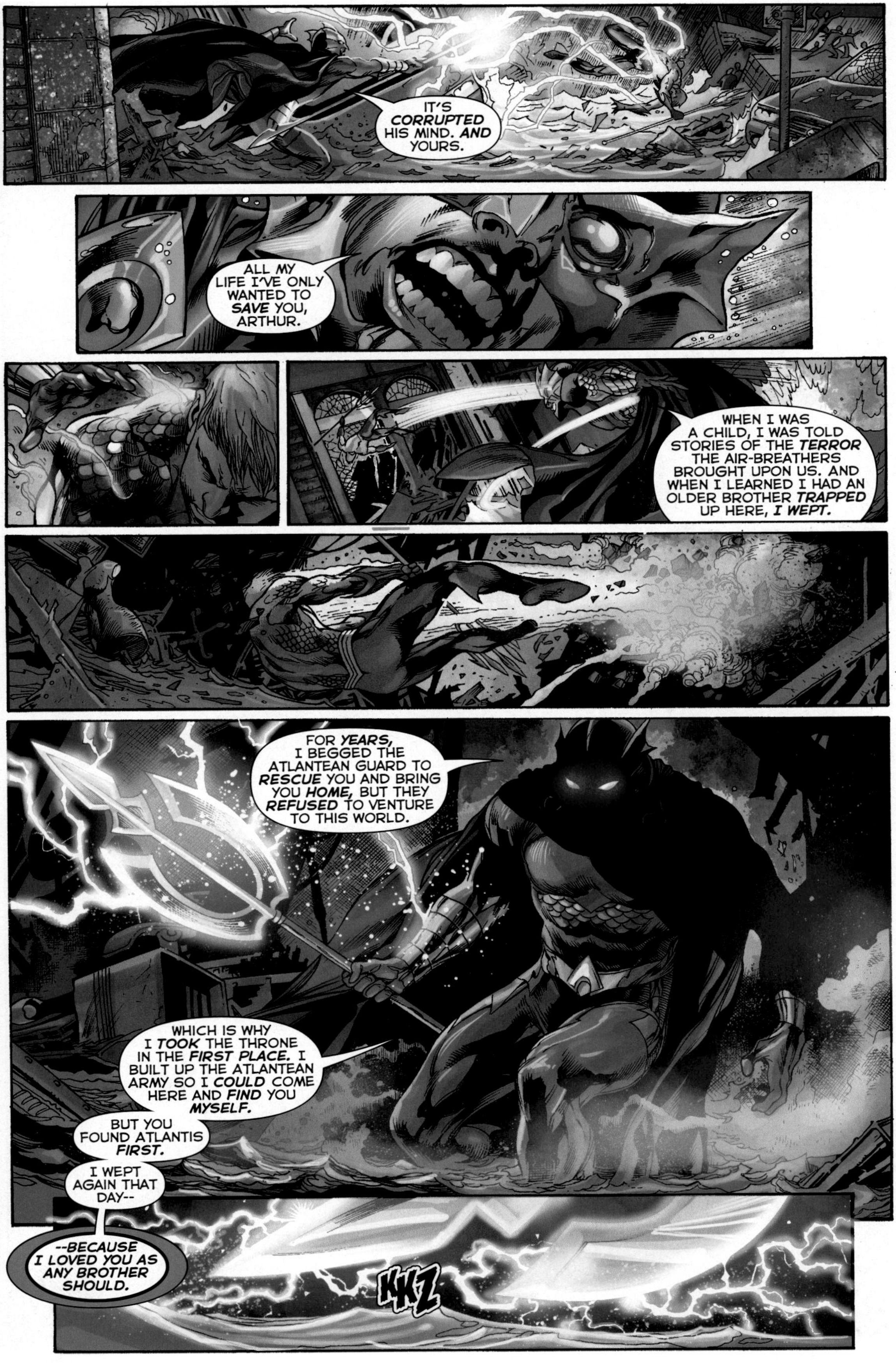
IT'S CORRUPTED HIS MIND. AND YOURS.
ALL MY LIFE I'VE ONLY WANTED TO SAVE YOU, ARTHUR.
WHEN I WAS A CHILD, I WAS TOLD STORIES OF THE TERROR THE AIR-BREATHERS BROUGHT UPON US. AND WHEN I LEARNED I HAD AN OLDER BROTHER TRAPPED UP HERE, I WEPT.
FOR YEARS, I BEGGED THE ATLANTEAN GUARD TO RESCUE YOU AND BRING YOU HOME, BUT THEY REFUSED TO VENTURE TO THIS WORLD.
WHICH IS WHY I TOOK THE THRONE IN THE FIRST PLACE. I BUILT UP THE ATLANTEAN ARMY SO I COULD COME HERE AND FIND YOU MYSELF.
BUT YOU FOUND ATLANTIS FIRST.
I WEPT AGAIN THAT DAY--
--BECAUSE I LOVED YOU AS ANY BROTHER SHOULD.
KKZ

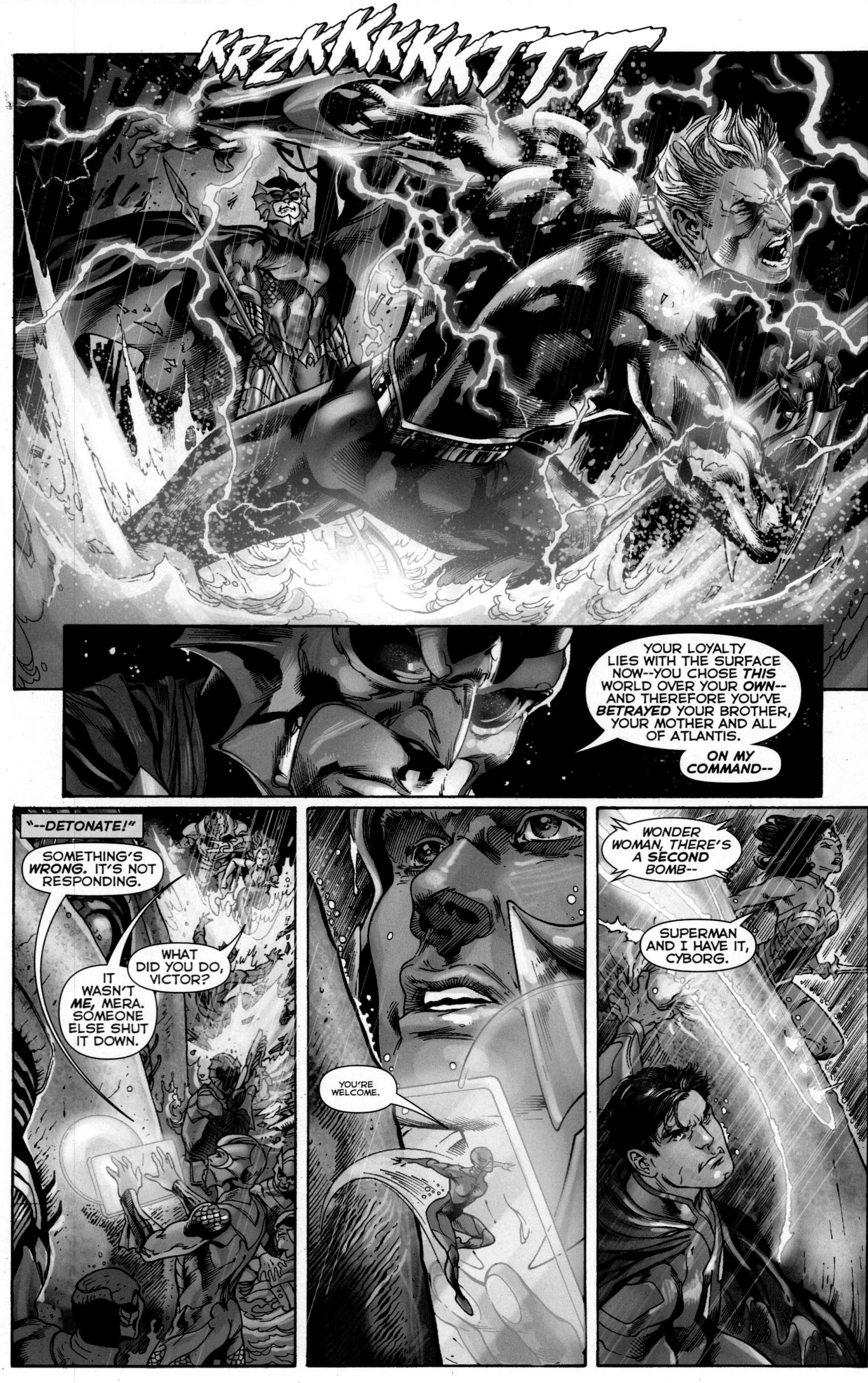
KRZKKKKKKTTTT
YOUR LOYALTY LIES WITH THE SURFACE NOW--YOU CHOSE THIS WORLD OVER YOUR OWN--AND THEREFORE YOU'VE BETRAYED YOUR BROTHER, YOUR MOTHER AND ALL OF ATLANTIS.
ON MY COMMAND--
"--DETONATE!"
SOMETHING'S WRONG. IT'S NOT RESPONDING.
WHAT DID YOU DO, VICTOR?
IT WASN'T ME, MERA. SOMEONE ELSE SHUT IT DOWN.
YOU'RE WELCOME.
WONDER WOMAN, THERE'S A SECOND BOMB--
SUPERMAN AND I HAVE IT, CYBORG.

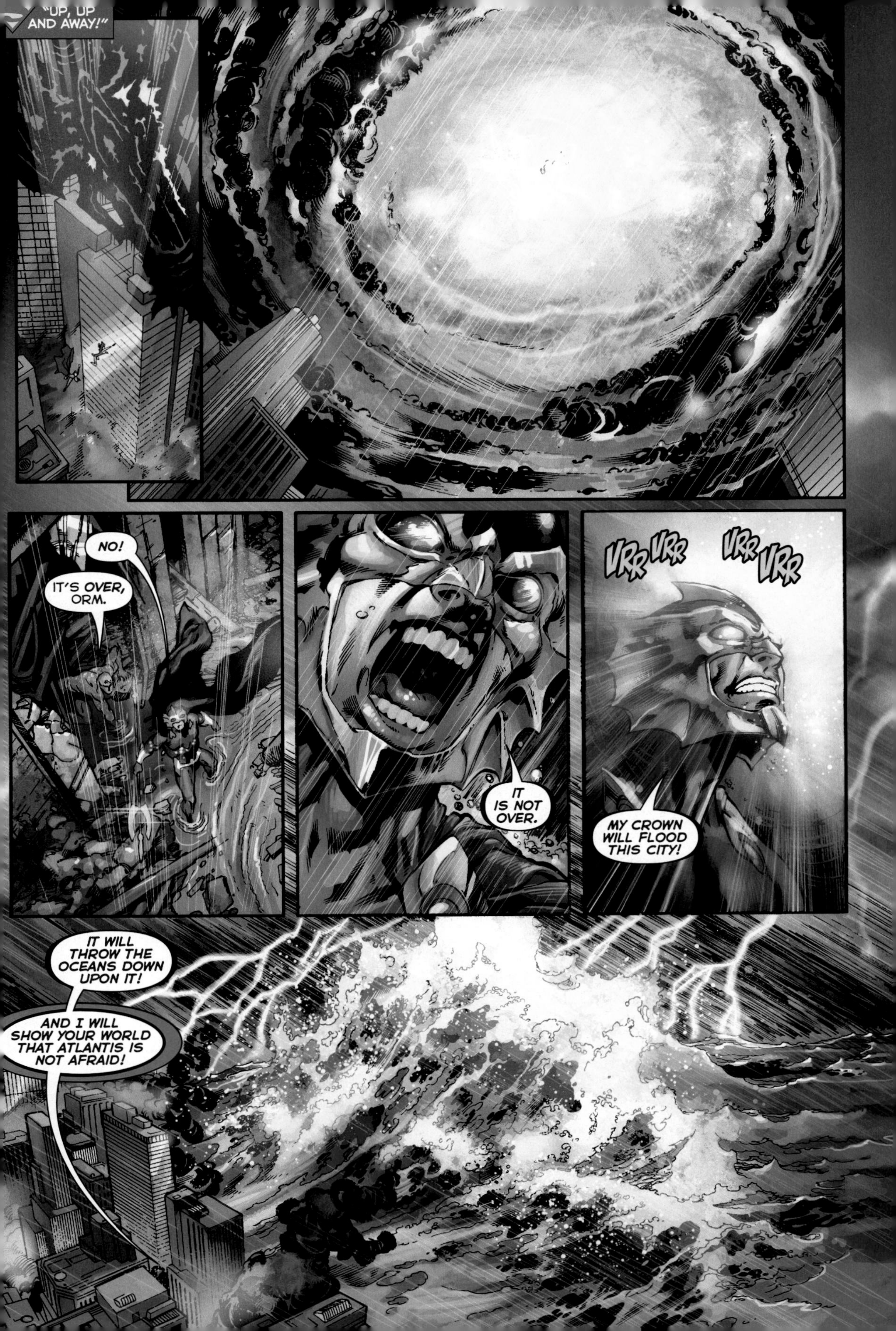
"UP, UP AND AWAY!"
NO!
IT'S OVER, ORM.
IT IS NOT OVER.
VRR VRR VRR VRR
MY CROWN WILL FLOOD THIS CITY!
IT WILL THROW THE OCEANS DOWN UPON IT!
AND I WILL SHOW YOUR WORLD THAT ATLANTIS IS NOT AFRAID!

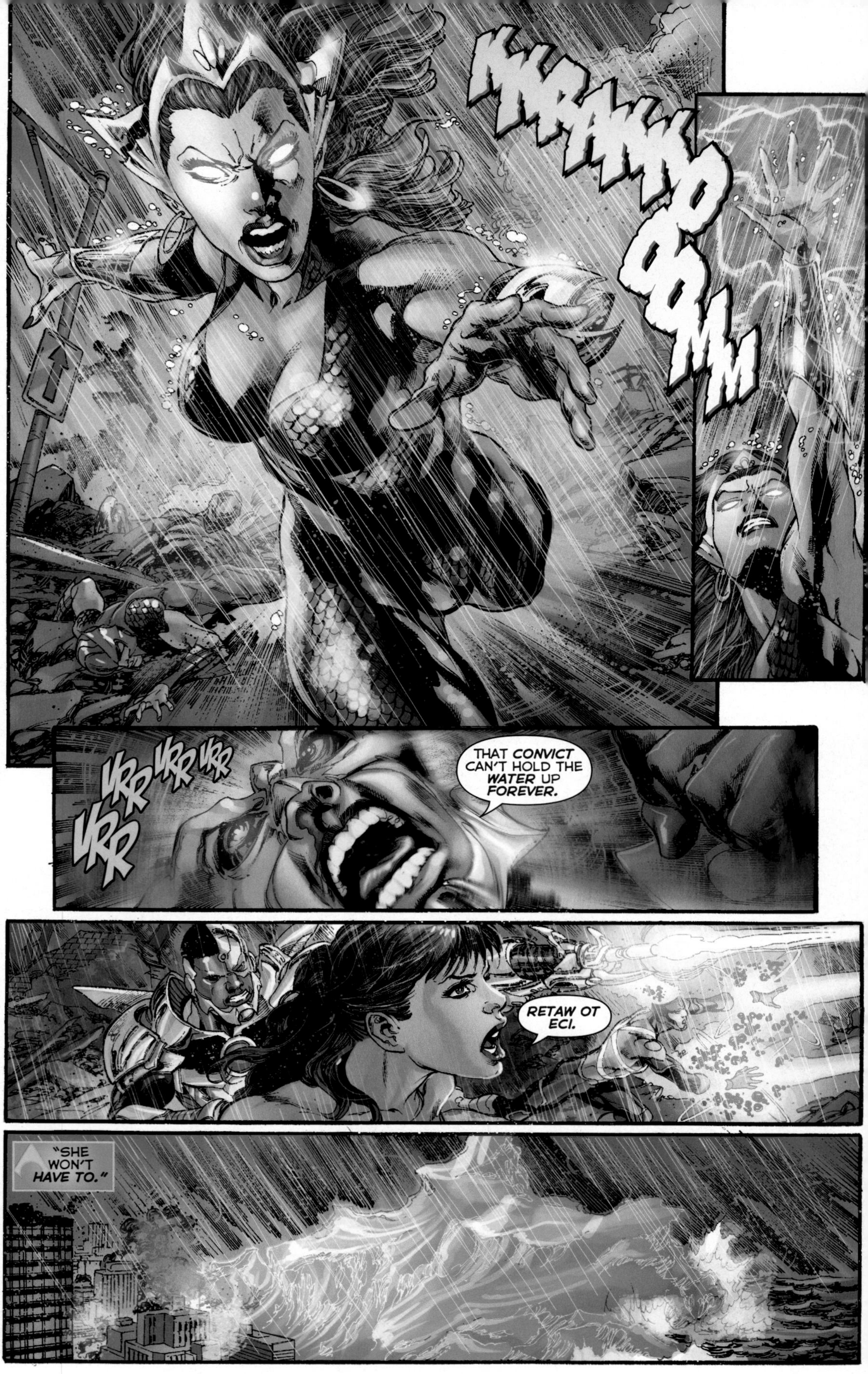
KKRAKKOOOMM
URR URR URR URR
THAT CONVICT CAN'T HOLD THE WATER UP FOREVER.
RETAW OT ECI.
"SHE WON'T HAVE TO."

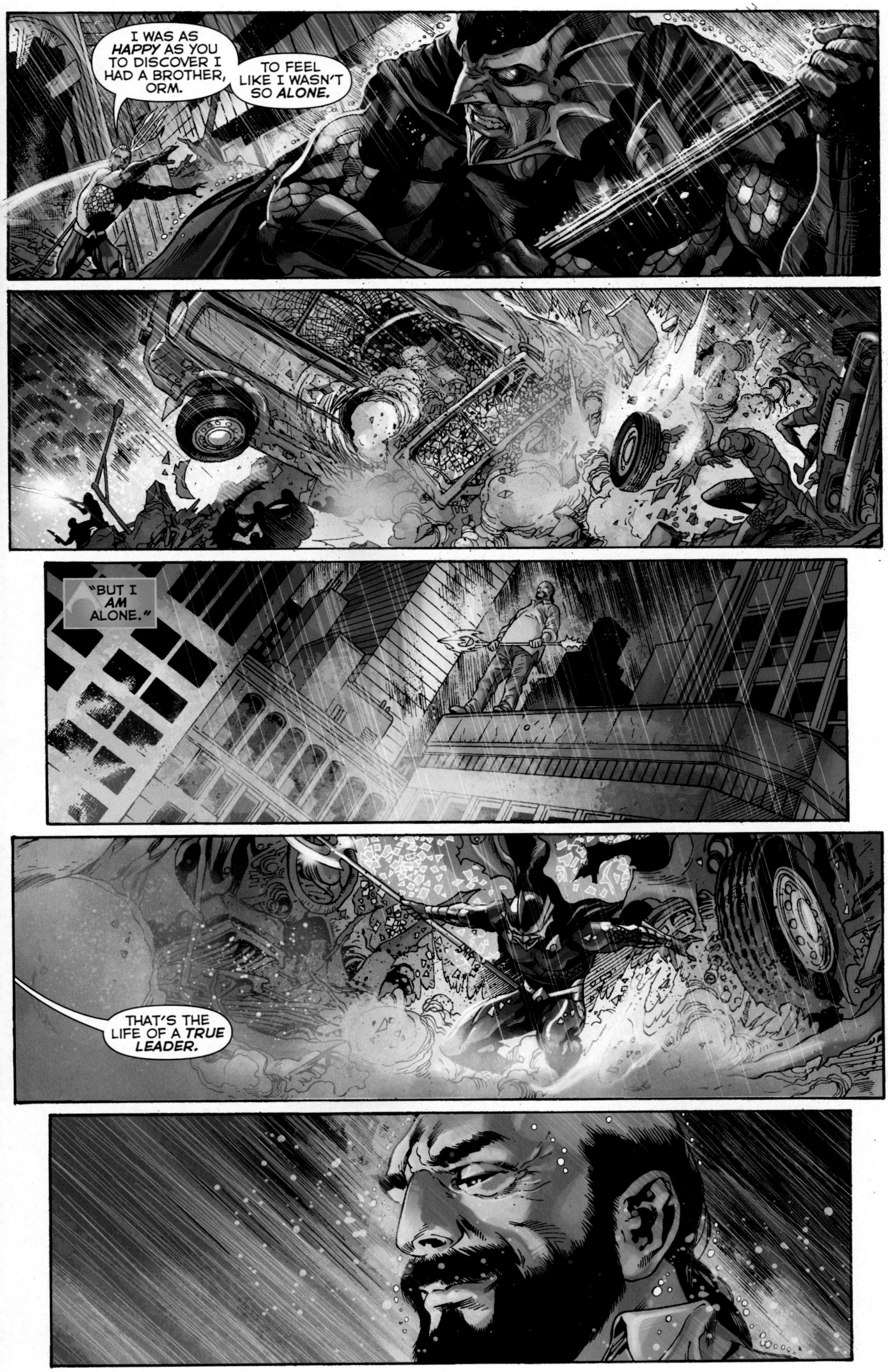
I WAS AS HAPPY AS YOU TO DISCOVER I HAD A BROTHER, ORM.
TO FEEL LIKE I WASN'T SO ALONE.
"BUT I AM ALONE."
THAT'S THE LIFE OF A TRUE LEADER.

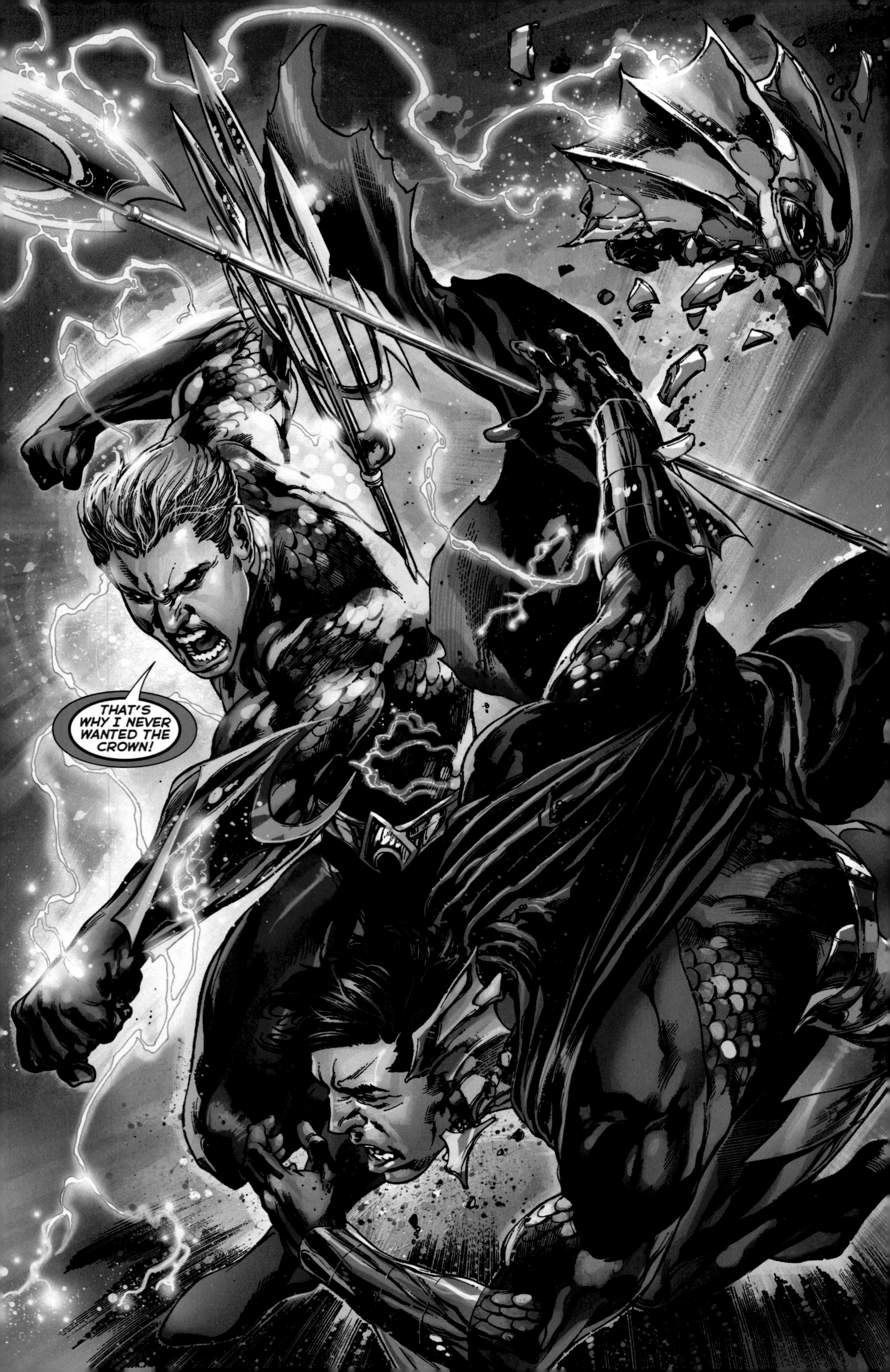
THAT'S WHY I NEVER WANTED THE CROWN!

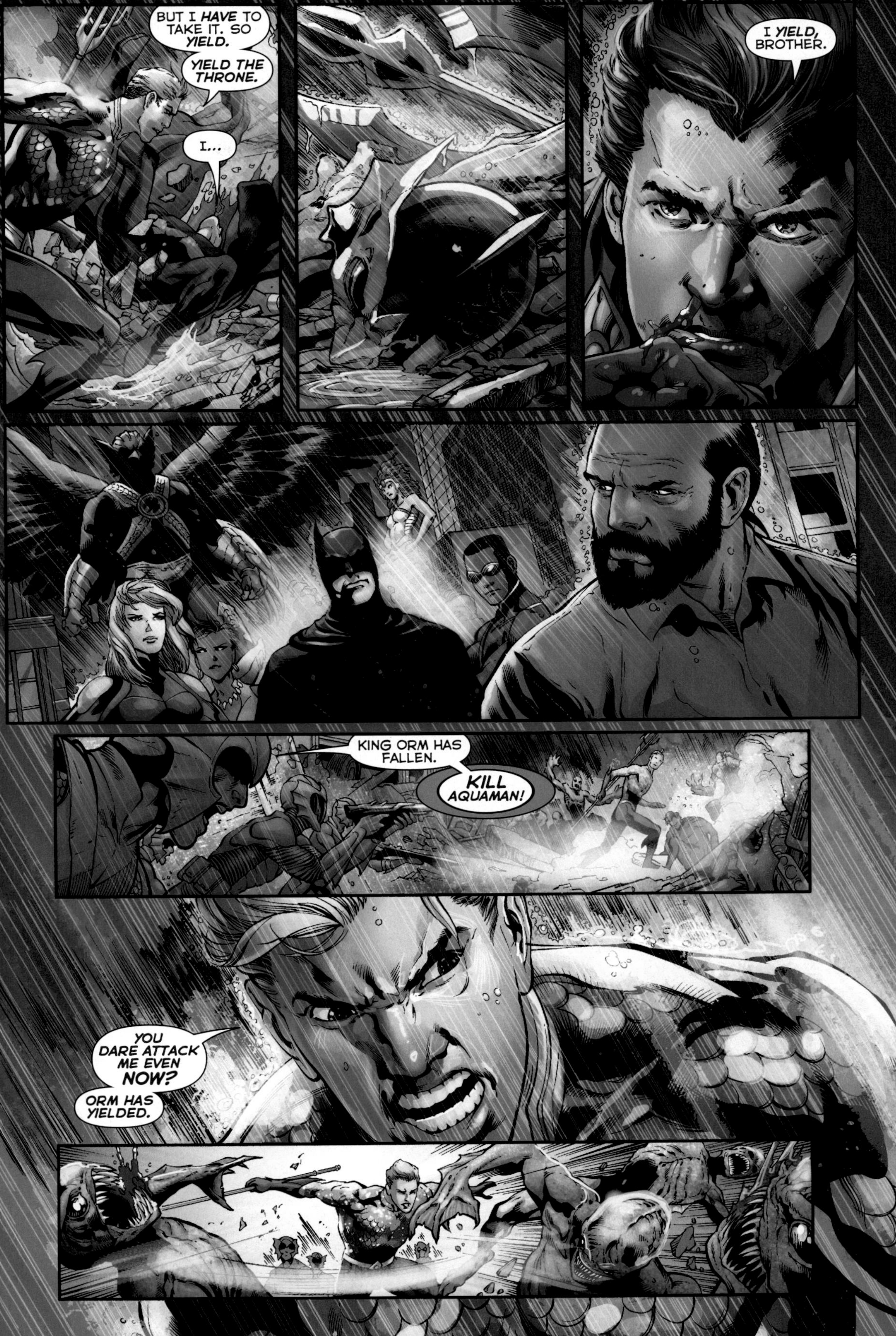

BUT I HAVE TO TAKE IT. SO YIELD.
YIELD THE THRONE.
I...
I YIELD, BROTHER.
KING ORM HAS FALLEN.
KILL AQUAMAN!
YOU DARE ATTACK ME EVEN NOW?
ORM HAS YIELDED.

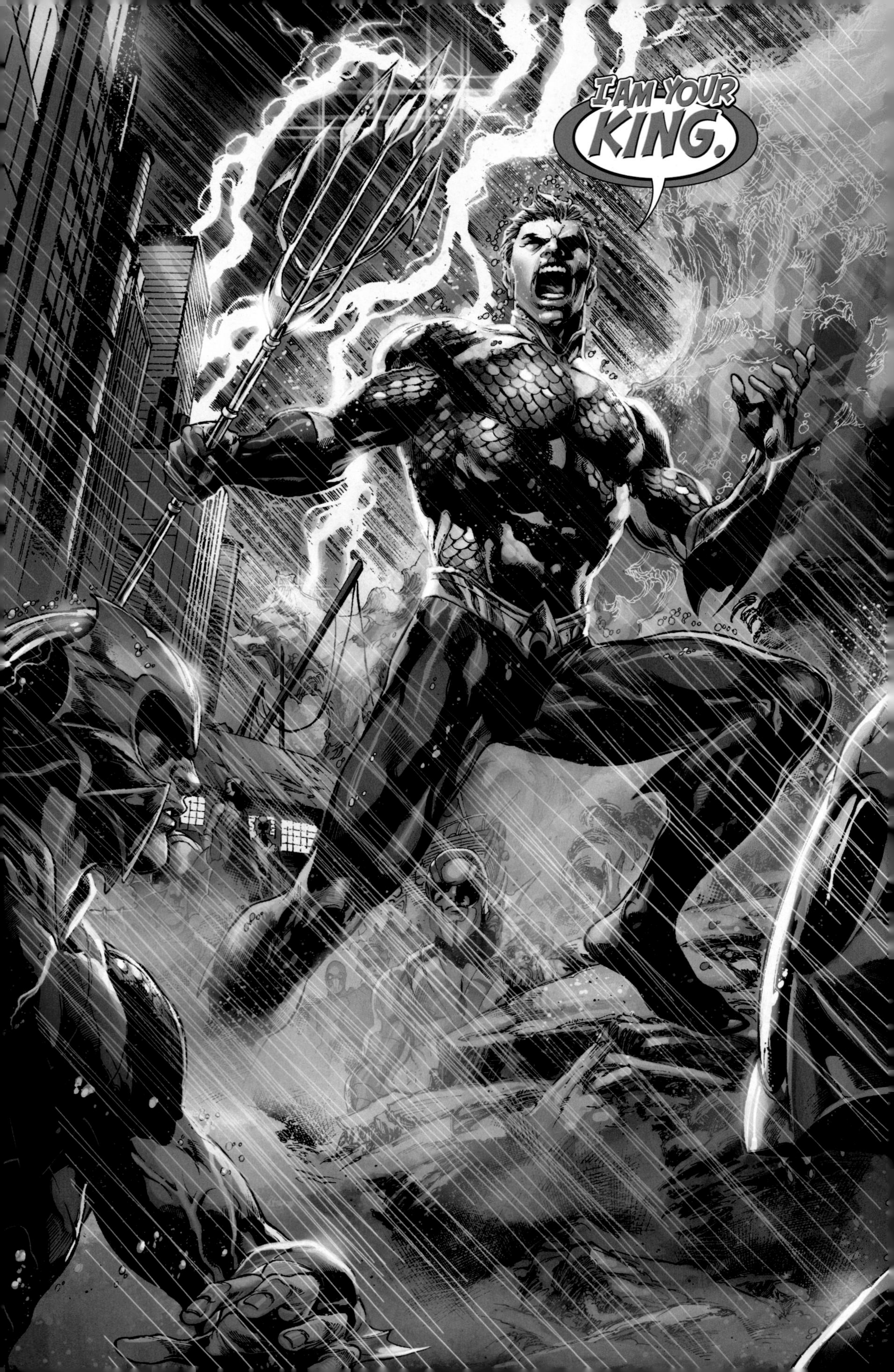
I AM YOUR KING.

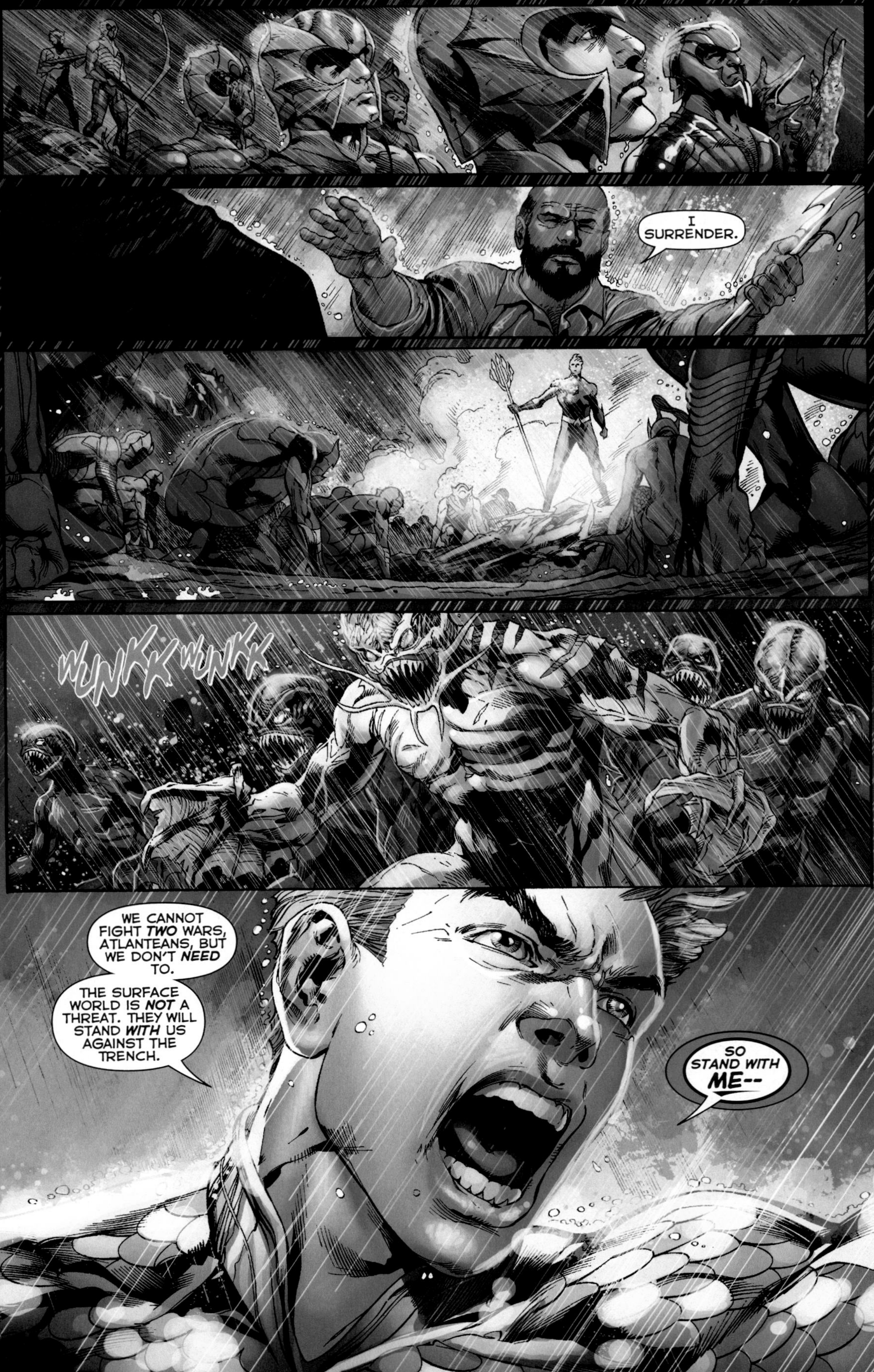
I SURRENDER.
WUNKK WUNKK
WE CANNOT FIGHT TWO WARS, ATLANTEANS, BUT WE DON'T NEED TO.
THE SURFACE WORLD IS NOT A THREAT. THEY WILL STAND WITH US AGAINST THE TRENCH.
SO STAND WITH ME--

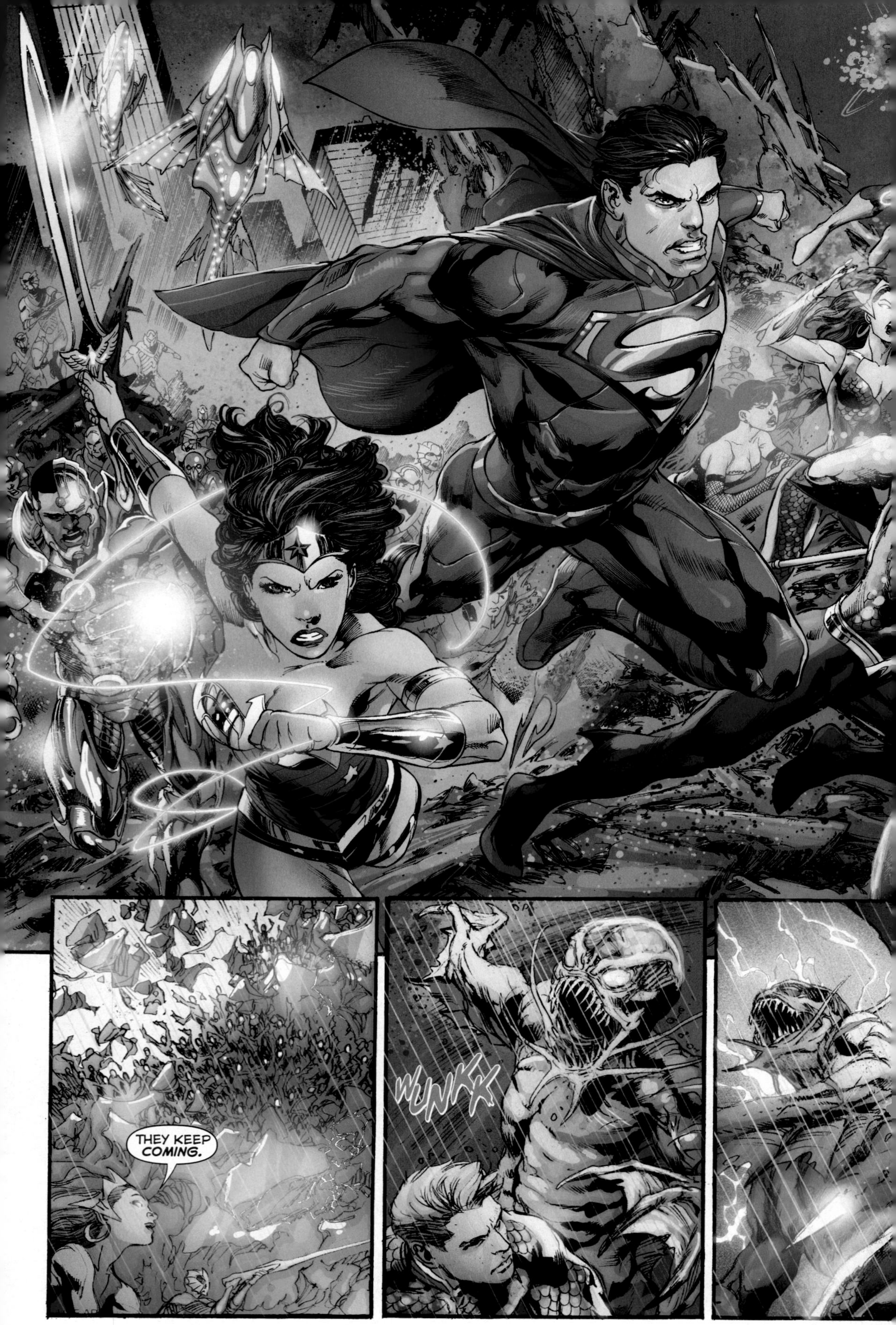
THEY KEEP COMING.
WUNKK

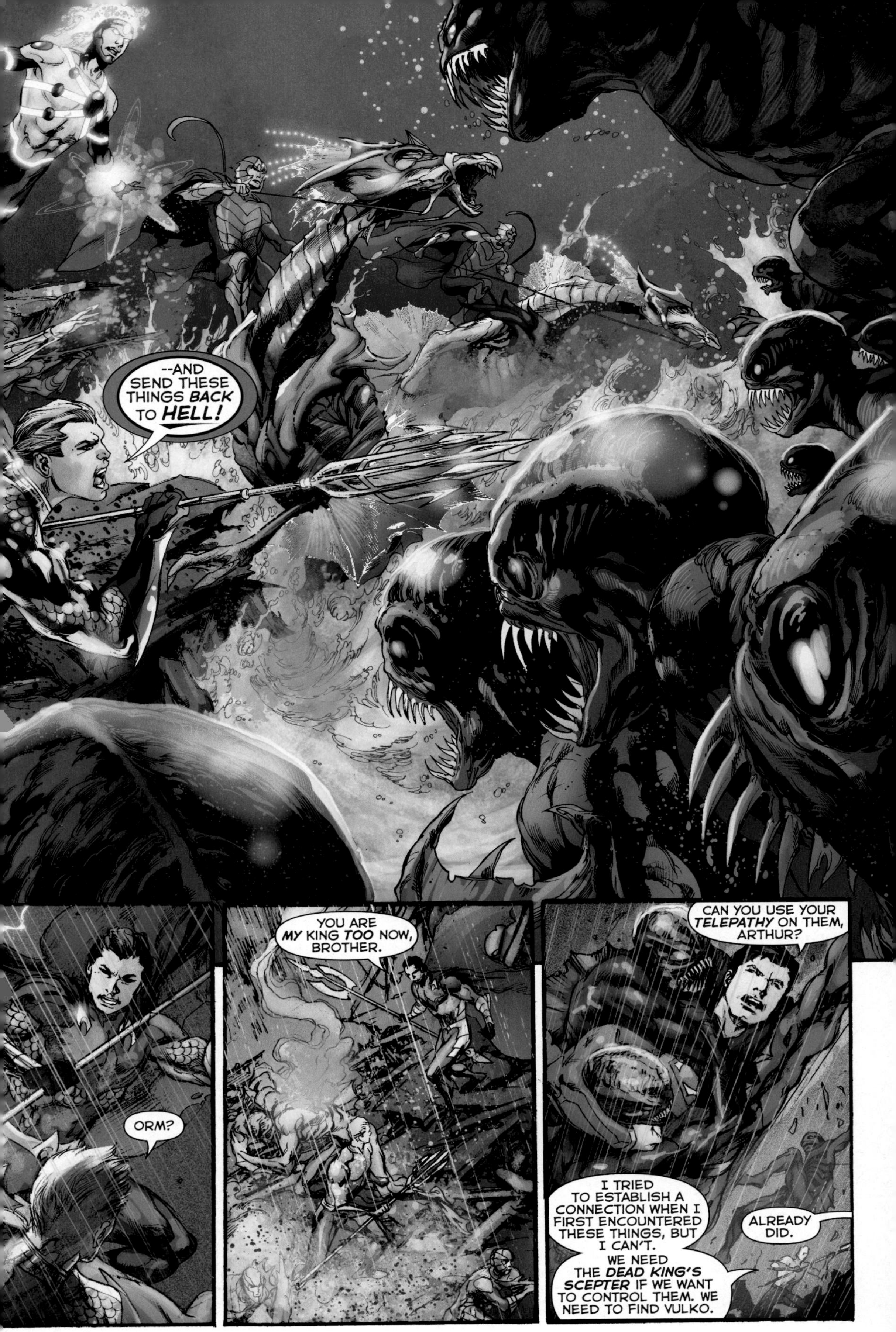
--AND SEND THESE THINGS BACK TO HELL!
ORM?
YOU ARE MY KING TOO NOW, BROTHER.
CAN YOU USE YOUR TELEPATHY ON THEM, ARTHUR?
ALREADY DID.
I TRIED TO ESTABLISH A CONNECTION WHEN I FIRST ENCOUNTERED THESE THINGS, BUT I CAN'T.
WE NEED THE DEAD KING'S SCEPTER IF WE WANT TO CONTROL THEM. WE NEED TO FIND VULKO.

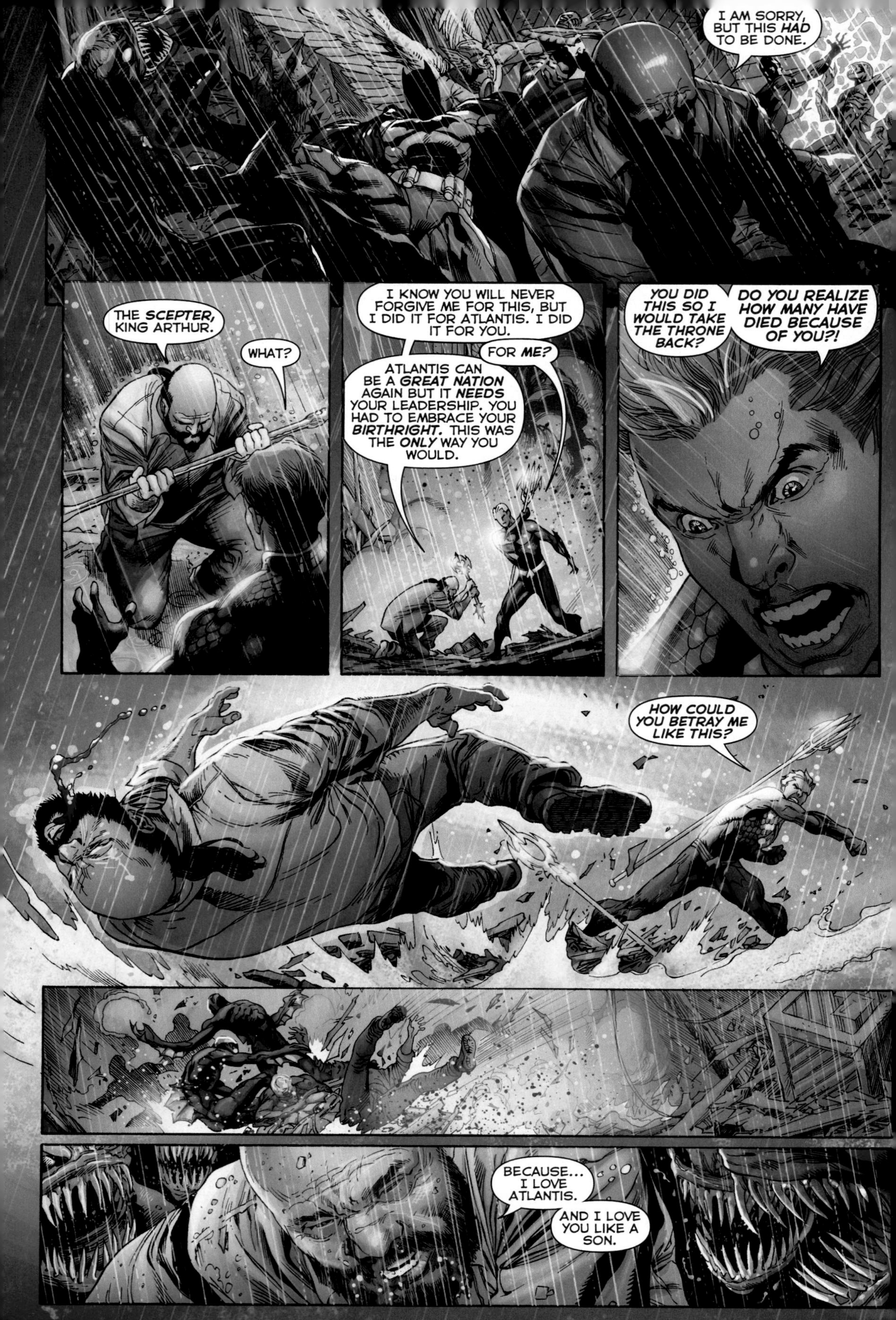
I AM SORRY, BUT THIS HAD TO BE DONE.
THE SCEPTER, KING ARTHUR.
WHAT?
I KNOW YOU WILL NEVER FORGIVE ME FOR THIS, BUT I DID IT FOR ATLANTIS. I DID IT FOR YOU.
FOR ME?
ATLANTIS CAN BE A GREAT NATION AGAIN BUT IT NEEDS YOUR LEADERSHIP. YOU HAD TO EMBRACE YOUR BIRTHRIGHT. THIS WAS THE ONLY WAY YOU WOULD.
YOU DID THIS SO I WOULD TAKE THE THRONE BACK?
DO YOU REALIZE HOW MANY HAVE DIED BECAUSE OF YOU?!
HOW COULD YOU BETRAY ME LIKE THIS?
BECAUSE... I LOVE ATLANTIS.
AND I LOVE YOU LIKE A SON.

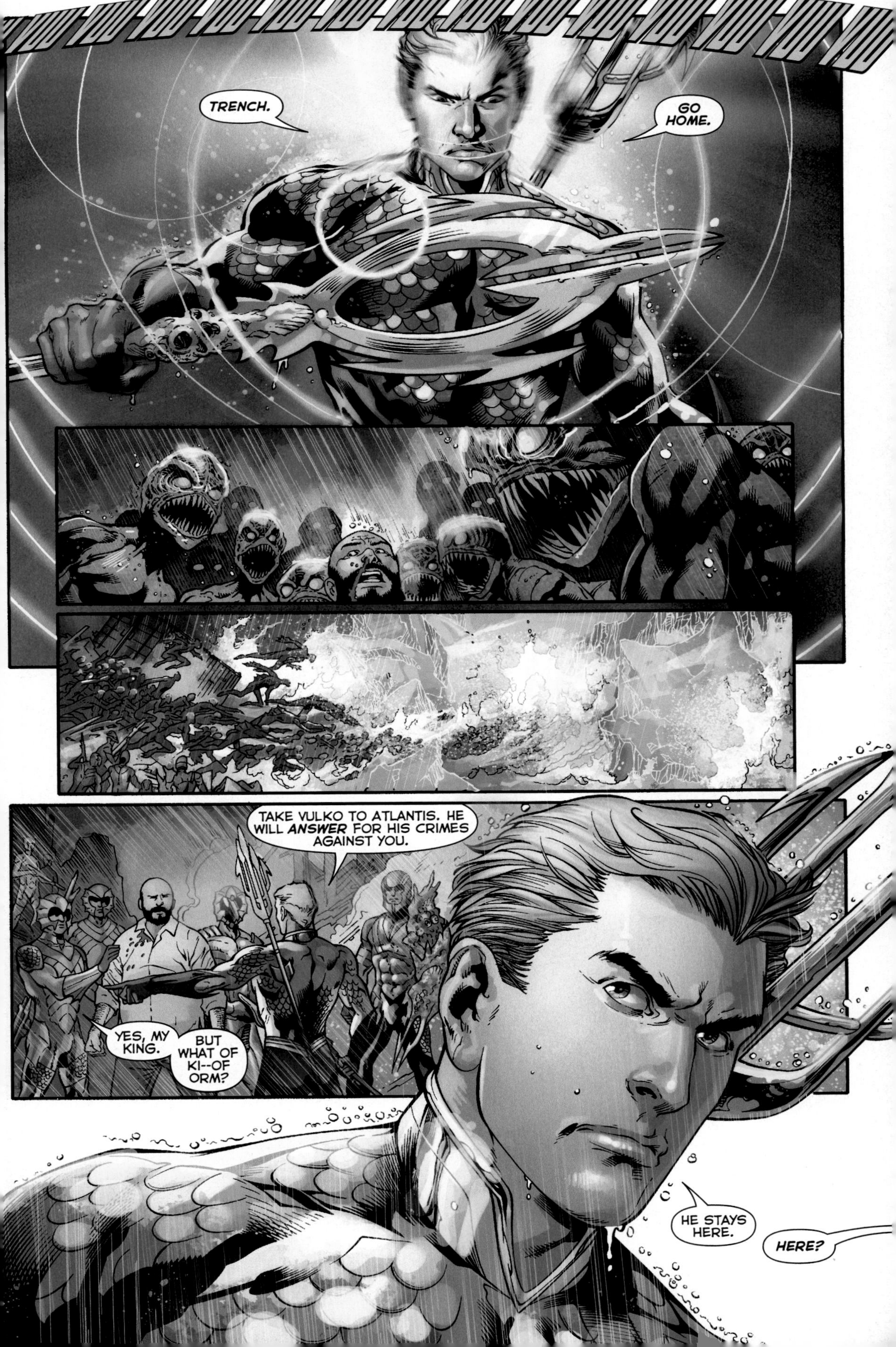
TRENCH.
GO HOME.
TAKE VULKO TO ATLANTIS. HE WILL ANSWER FOR HIS CRIMES AGAINST YOU.
YES, MY KING.
BUT WHAT OF KI--OF ORM?
HE STAYS HERE.
HERE?

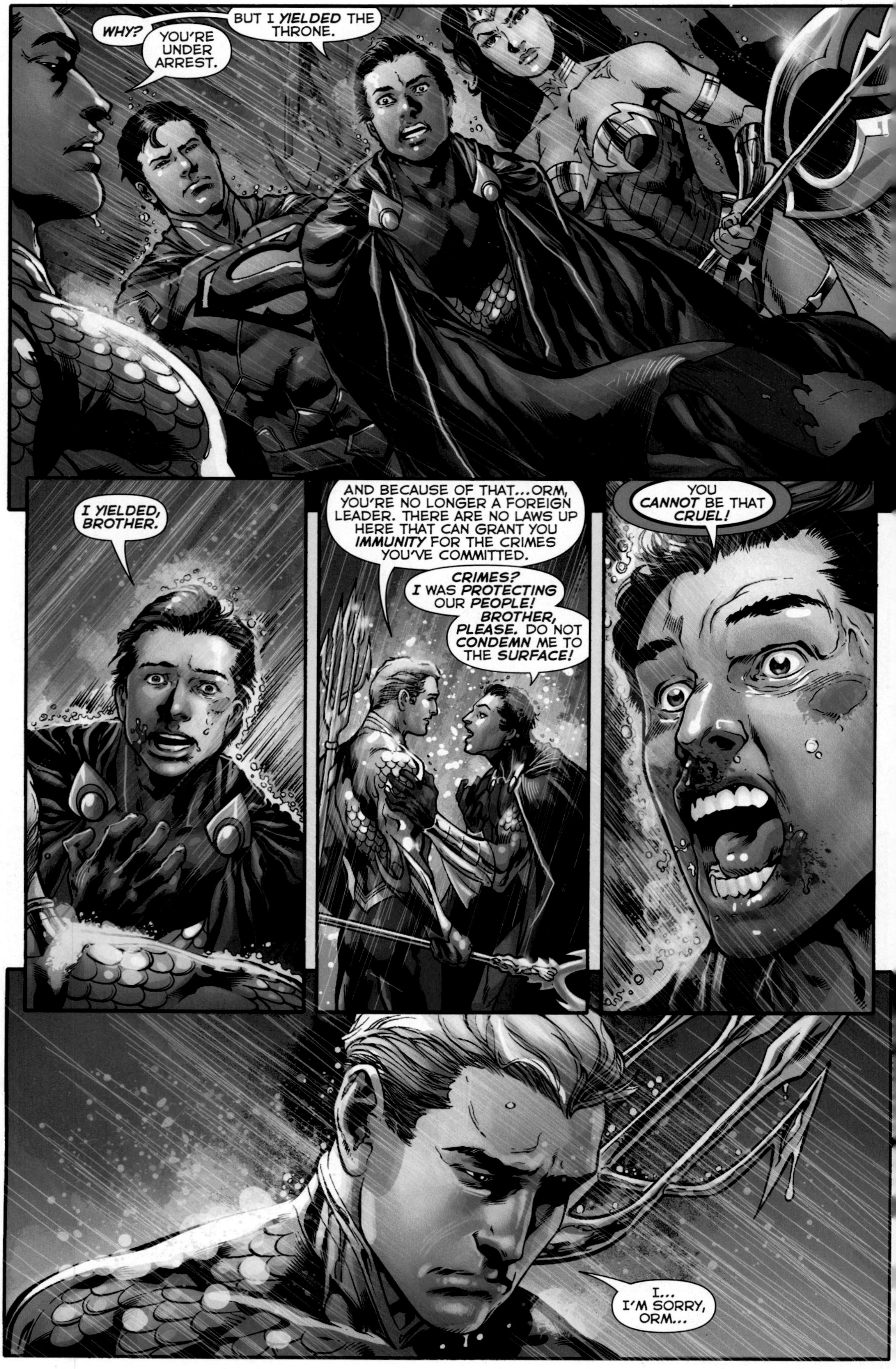
WHY?
YOU'RE UNDER ARREST.
BUT I YIELDED THE THRONE.
I YIELDED, BROTHER.
AND BECAUSE OF THAT...ORM, YOU'RE NO LONGER A FOREIGN LEADER. THERE ARE NO LAWS UP HERE THAT CAN GRANT YOU IMMUNITY FOR THE CRIMES YOU'VE COMMITTED.
CRIMES? I WAS PROTECTING OUR PEOPLE! BROTHER, PLEASE. DO NOT CONDEMN ME TO THE SURFACE!
YOU CANNOT BE THAT CRUEL!
I... I'M SORRY, ORM...

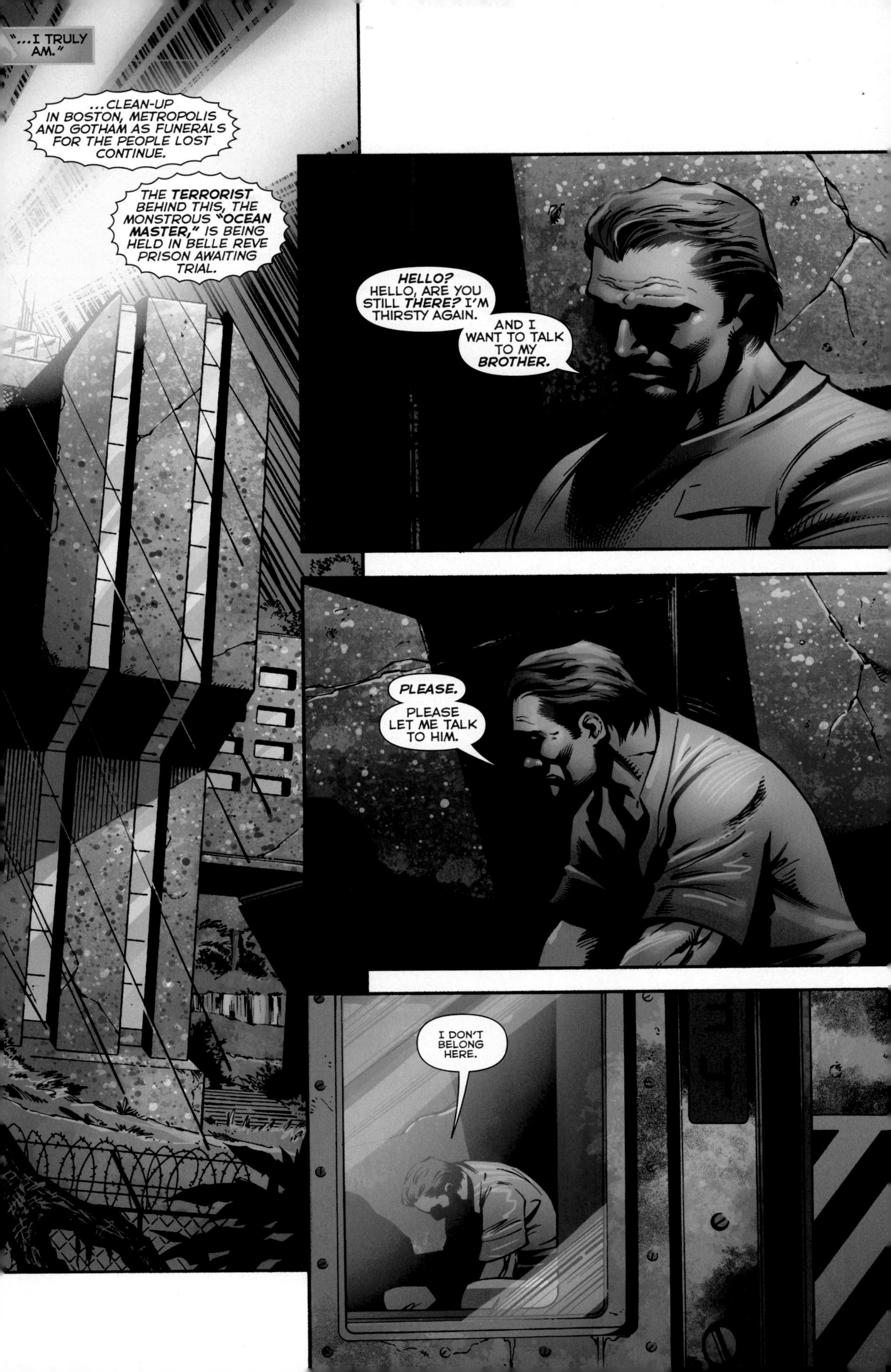
"...I TRULY AM."
...CLEAN-UP IN BOSTON, METROPOLIS AND GOTHAM AS FUNERALS FOR THE PEOPLE LOST CONTINUE.
THE TERRORIST BEHIND THIS, THE MONSTROUS "OCEAN MASTER," IS BEING HELD IN BELLE REVE PRISON AWAITING TRIAL.
HELLO? HELLO, ARE YOU STILL THERE? I'M THIRSTY AGAIN.
AND I WANT TO TALK TO MY BROTHER.
PLEASE. PLEASE LET ME TALK TO HIM.
I DON'T BELONG HERE.

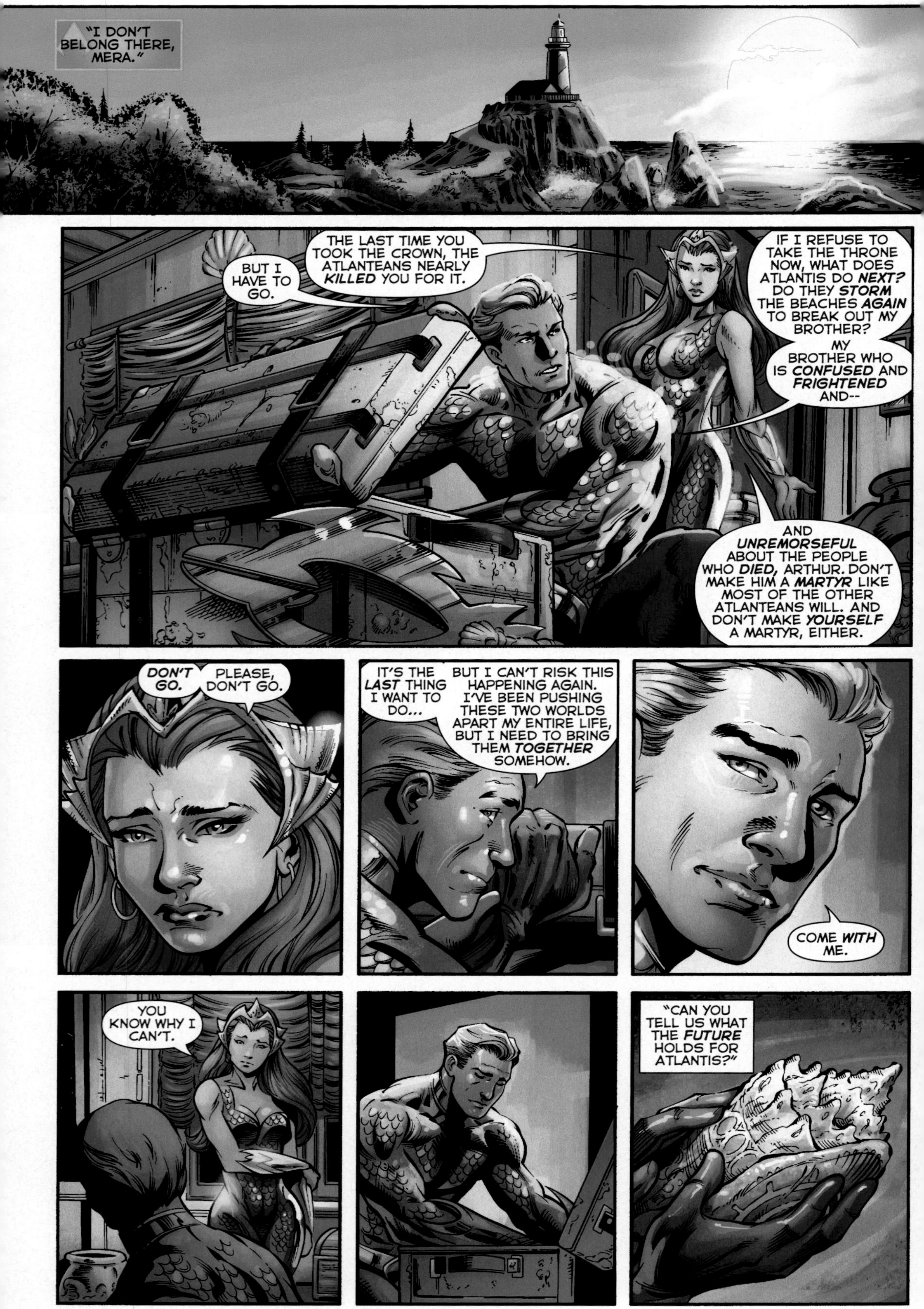
"I DON'T BELONG THERE, MERA."
THE LAST TIME YOU TOOK THE CROWN, THE ATLANTEANS NEARLY KILLED YOU FOR IT.
BUT I HAVE TO GO.
IF I REFUSE TO TAKE THE THRONE NOW, WHAT DOES ATLANTIS DO NEXT? DO THEY STORM THE BEACHES AGAIN TO BREAK OUT MY BROTHER?
MY BROTHER WHO IS CONFUSED AND FRIGHTENED AND--
AND UNREMORSEFUL ABOUT THE PEOPLE WHO DIED, ARTHUR. DON'T MAKE HIM A MARTYR LIKE MOST OF THE OTHER ATLANTEANS WILL. AND DON'T MAKE YOURSELF A MARTYR, EITHER.
DON'T GO.
PLEASE, DON'T GO.
IT'S THE LAST THING I WANT TO DO...
BUT I CAN'T RISK THIS HAPPENING AGAIN. I'VE BEEN PUSHING THESE TWO WORLDS APART MY ENTIRE LIFE, BUT I NEED TO BRING THEM TOGETHER SOMEHOW.
COME WITH ME.
YOU KNOW WHY I CAN'T.
"CAN YOU TELL US WHAT THE FUTURE HOLDS FOR ATLANTIS?"

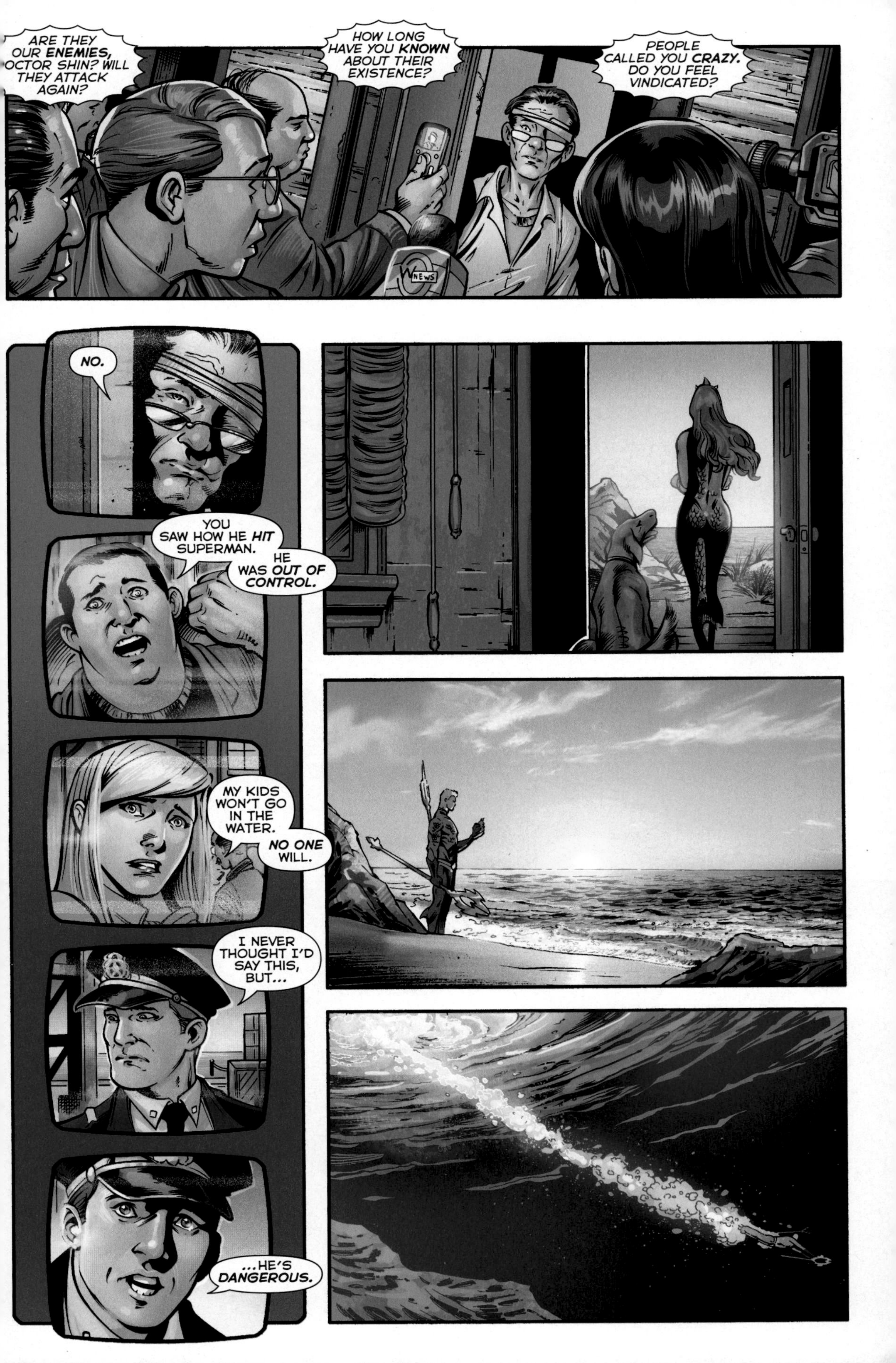
ARE THEY OUR **ENEMIES,** DOCTOR SHIN? WILL THEY ATTACK AGAIN?
HOW LONG HAVE YOU **KNOWN** ABOUT THEIR EXISTENCE?
PEOPLE CALLED YOU **CRAZY.** DO YOU FEEL VINDICATED?
NEWS
NO.
YOU SAW HOW HE ***HIT*** SUPERMAN.
HE WAS ***OUT OF CONTROL.***
MY KIDS WON'T GO IN THE WATER.
NO ONE WILL.
I NEVER THOUGHT I'D SAY THIS, BUT...
...HE'S ***DANGEROUS.***

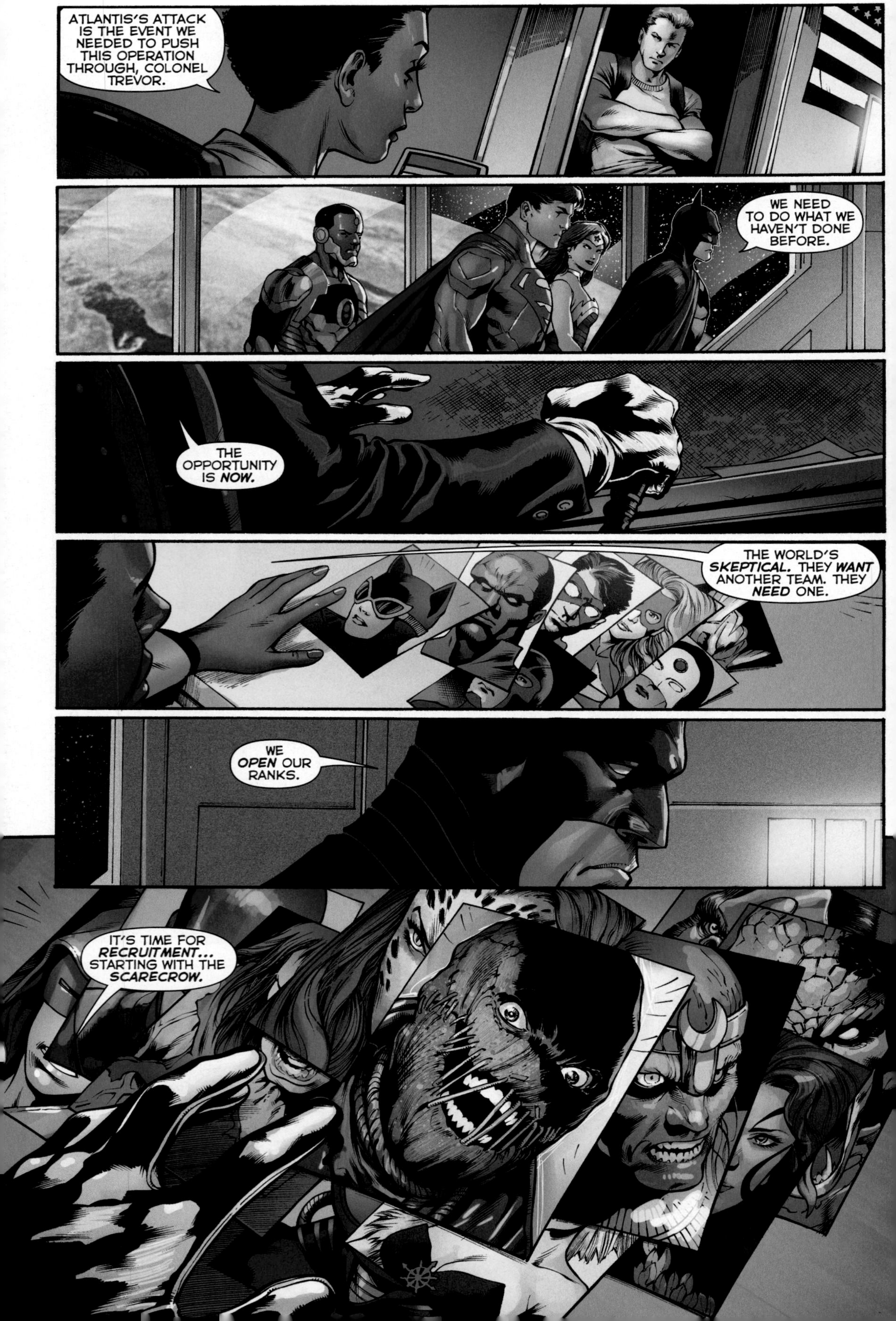
ATLANTIS'S ATTACK IS THE EVENT WE NEEDED TO PUSH THIS OPERATION THROUGH, COLONEL TREVOR.
WE NEED TO DO WHAT WE HAVEN'T DONE BEFORE.
THE OPPORTUNITY IS *NOW.*
THE WORLD'S *SKEPTICAL.* THEY *WANT* ANOTHER TEAM. THEY *NEED* ONE.
WE *OPEN* OUR RANKS.
IT'S TIME FOR *RECRUITMENT*... STARTING WITH THE *SCARECROW.*

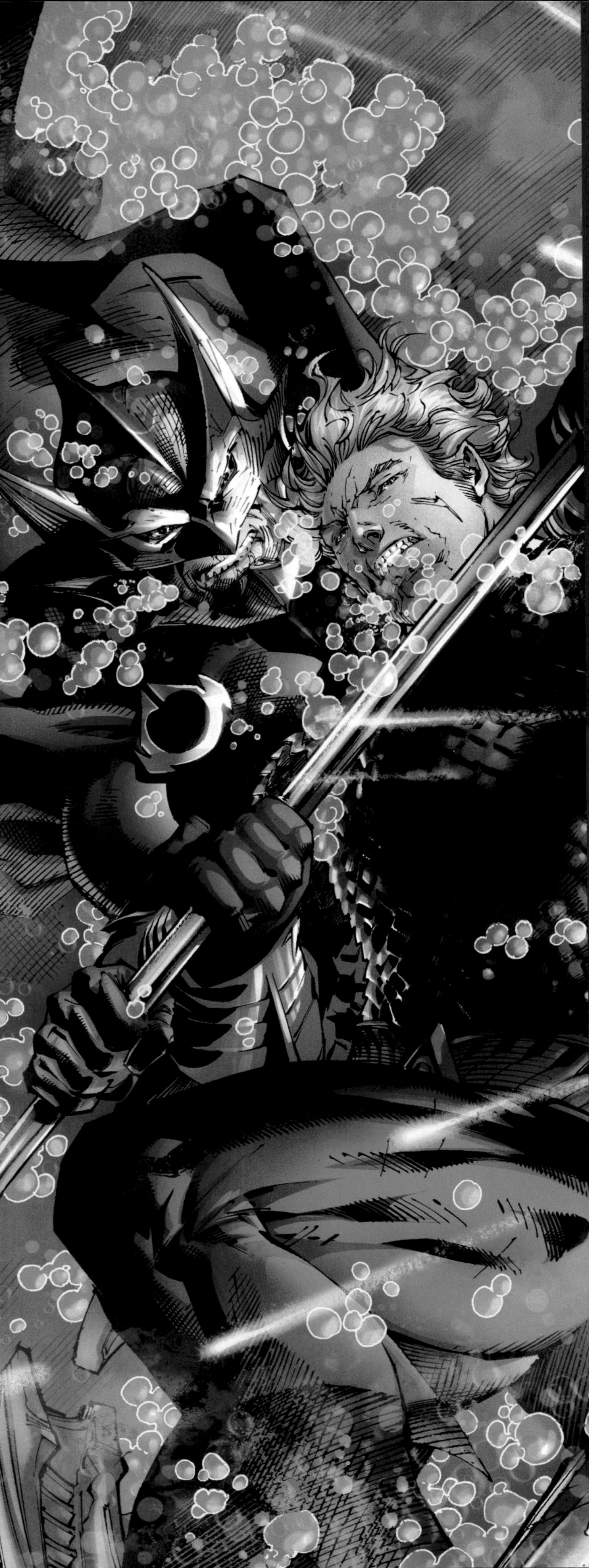

VARIANT COVER GALLERY

AQUAMAN №15 *and* **JUSTICE LEAGUE №15**

Connecting variant covers by Jim Lee, Scott Williams & Alex Sinclair

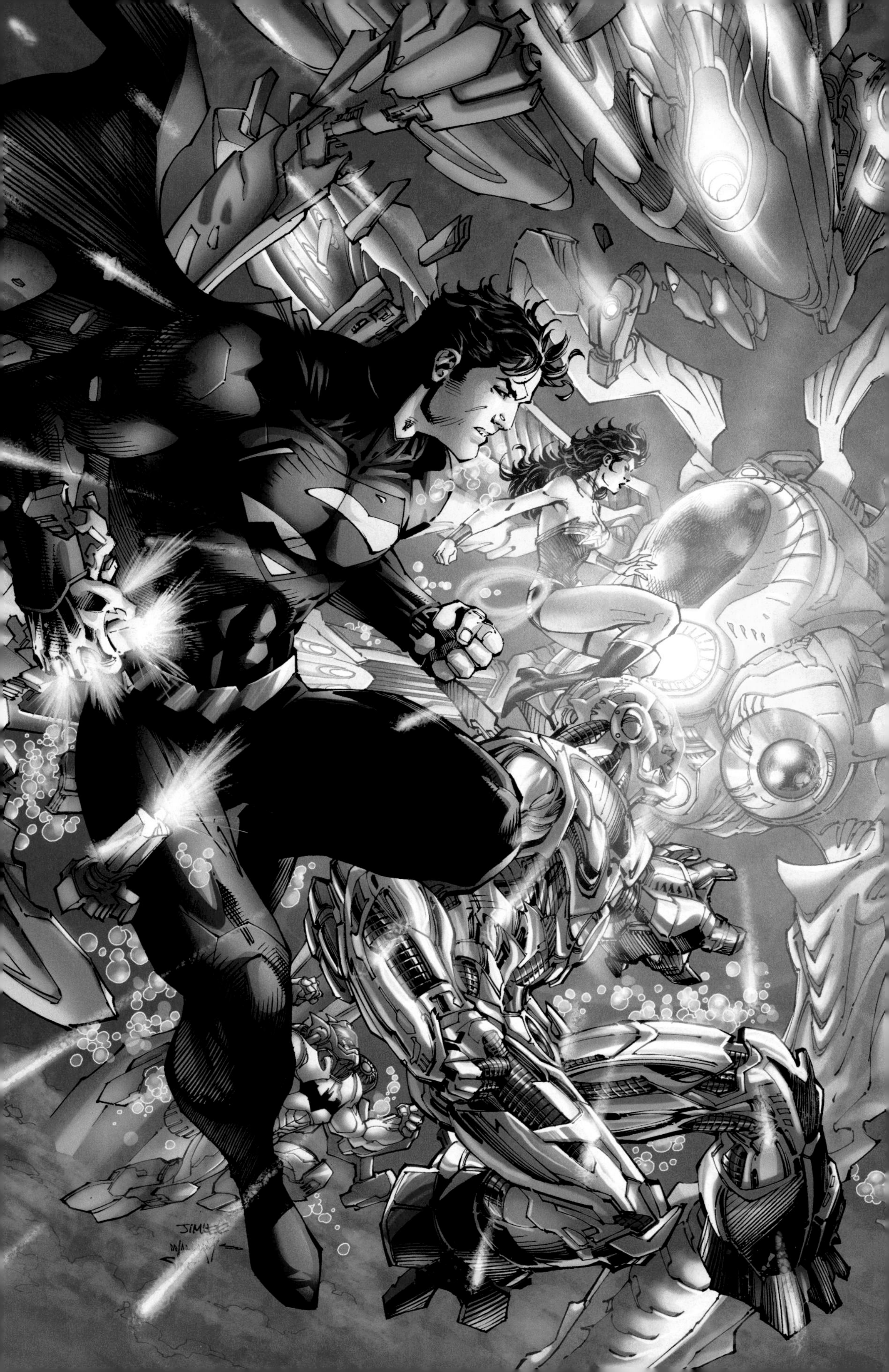

JUSTICE LEAGUE №15
Variant cover by Billy Tucci & Hi-Fi

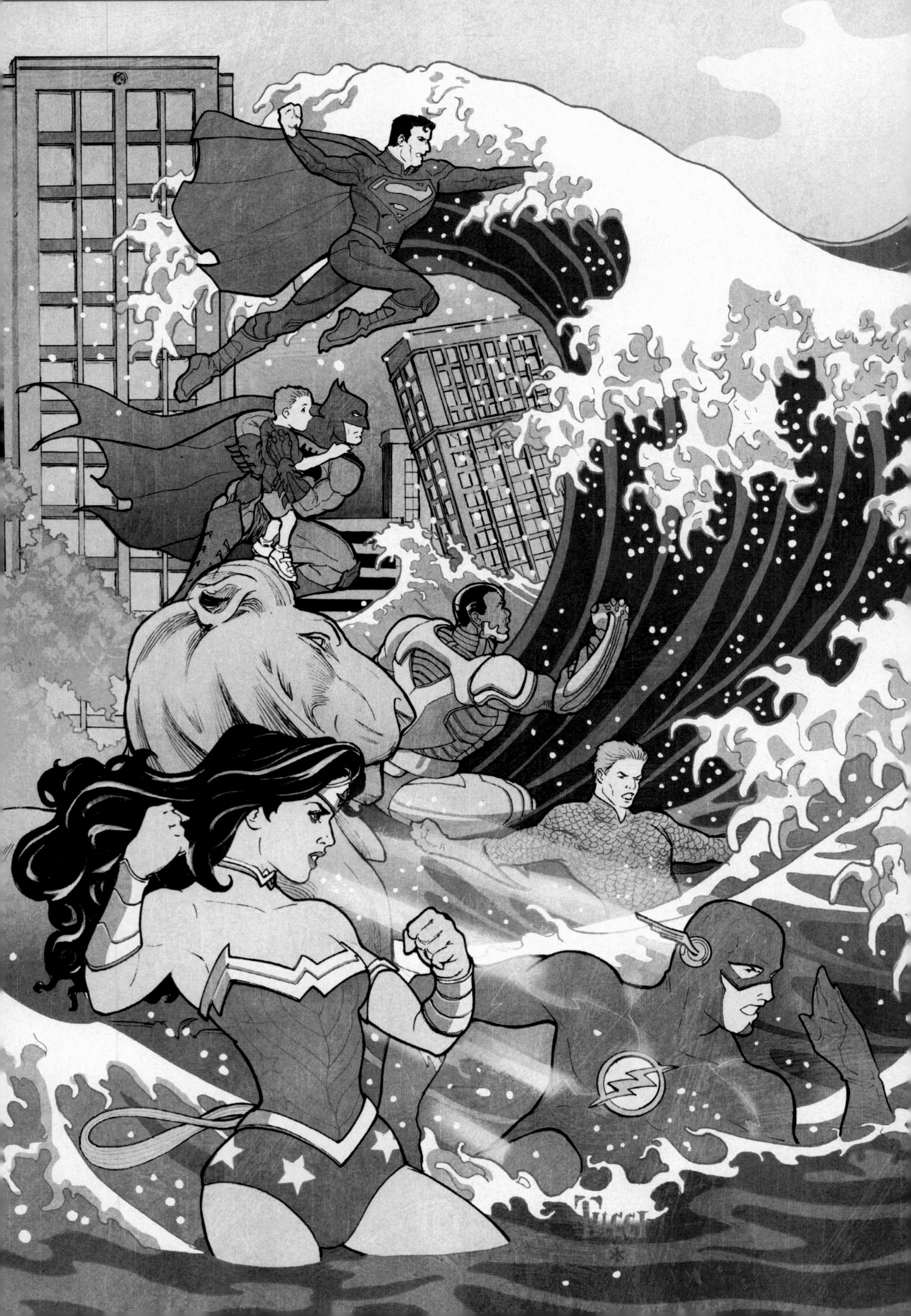

JUSTICE LEAGUE №16
Variant cover by Langdon Foss & José Villarrubia

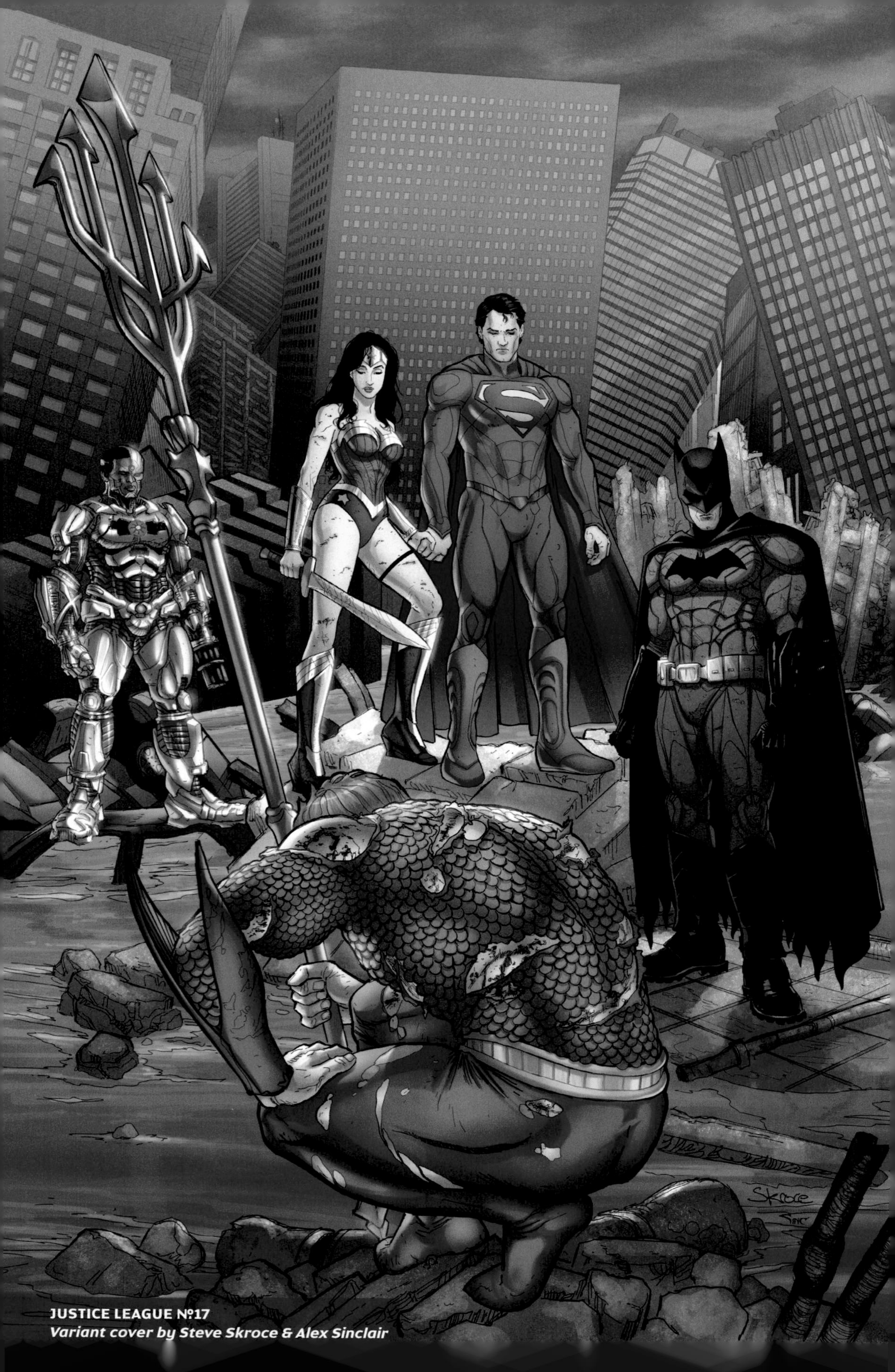

JUSTICE LEAGUE №17
Variant cover by Steve Skroce & Alex Sinclair

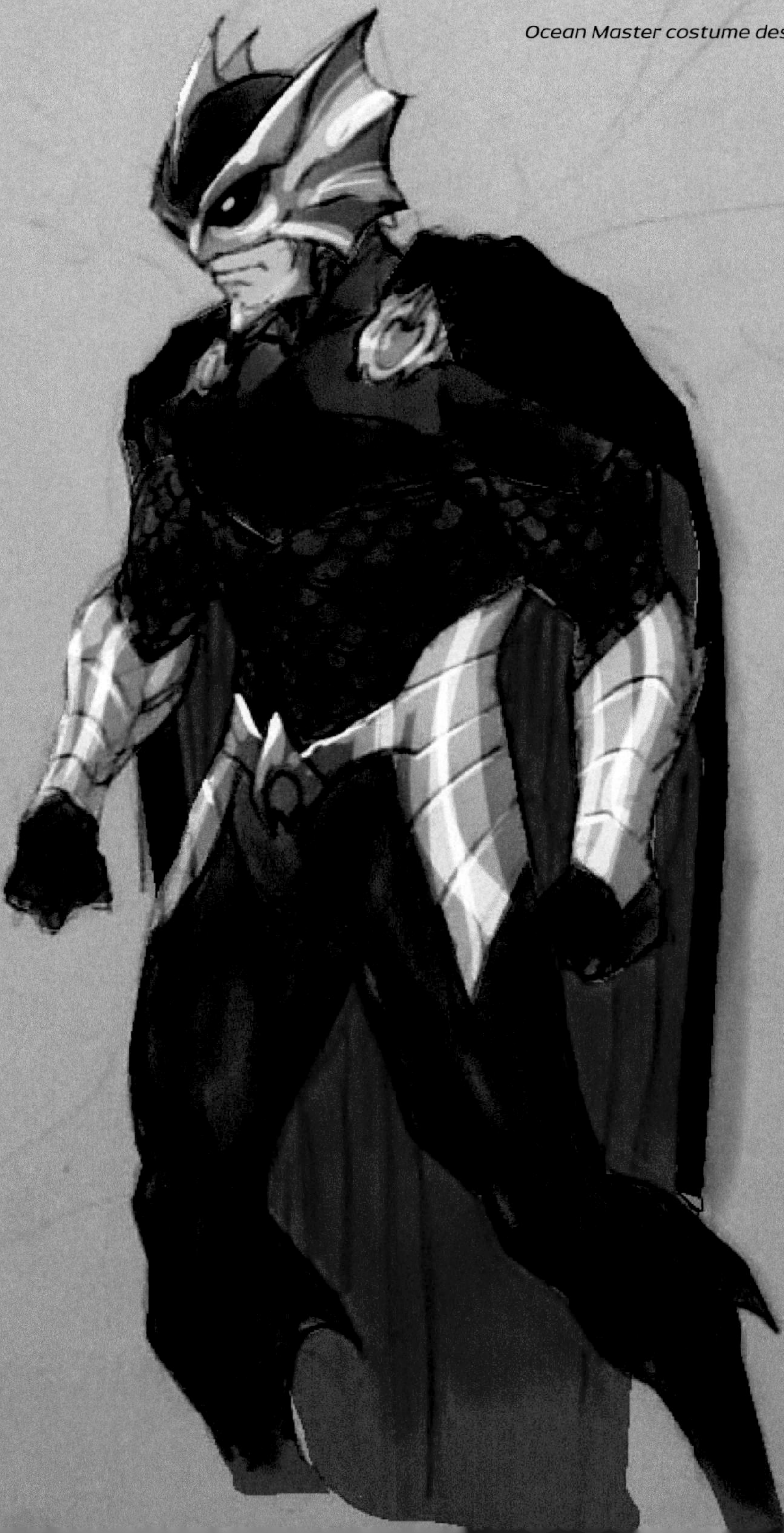

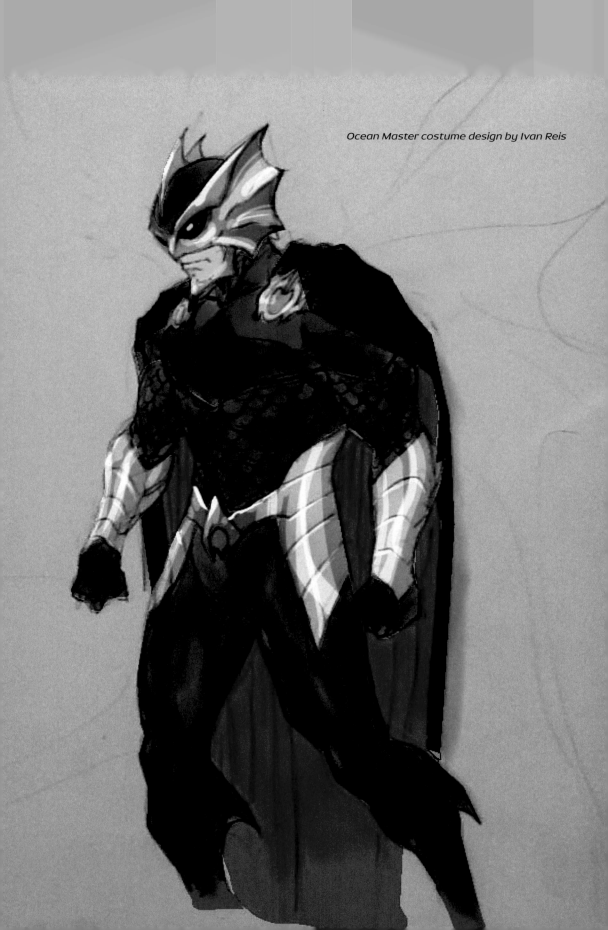

Ocean Master costume design by Ivan Reis

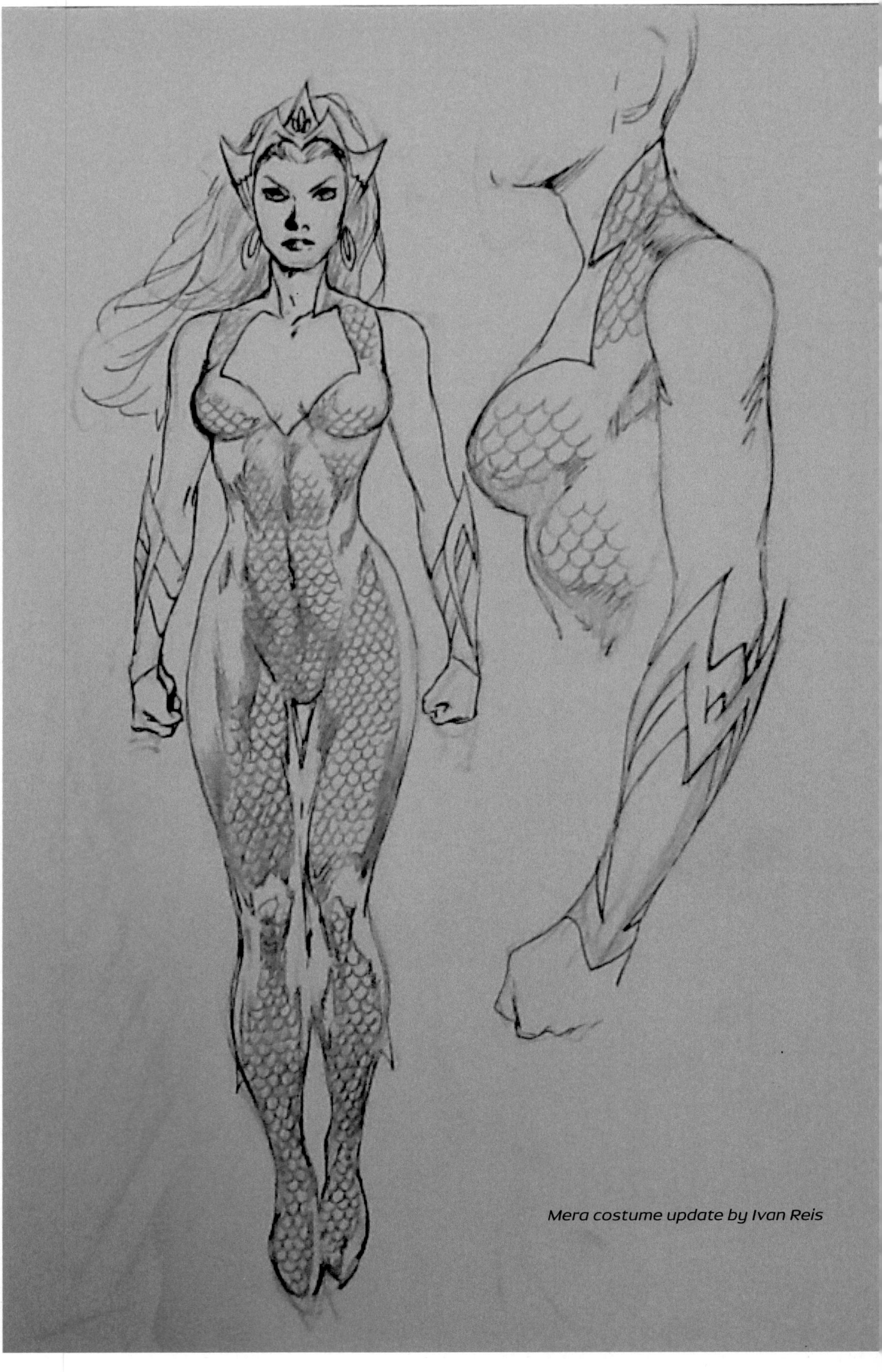

Mera costume update by Ivan Reis

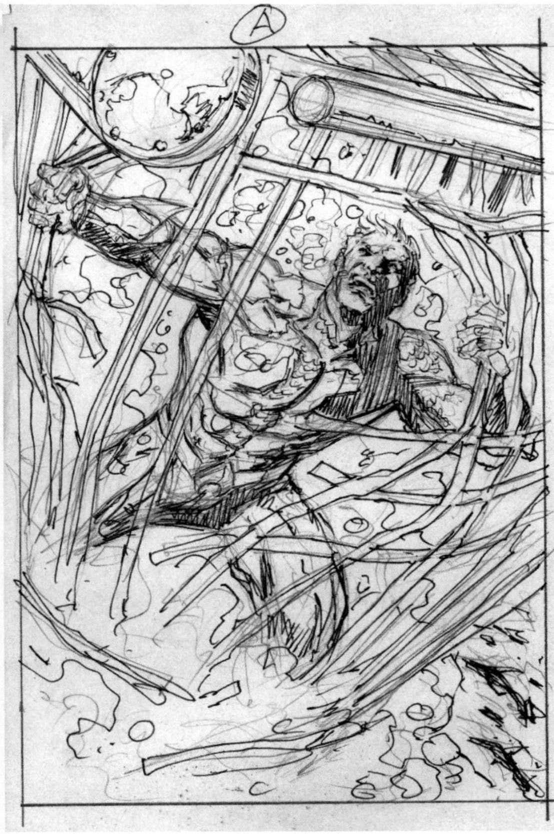
A

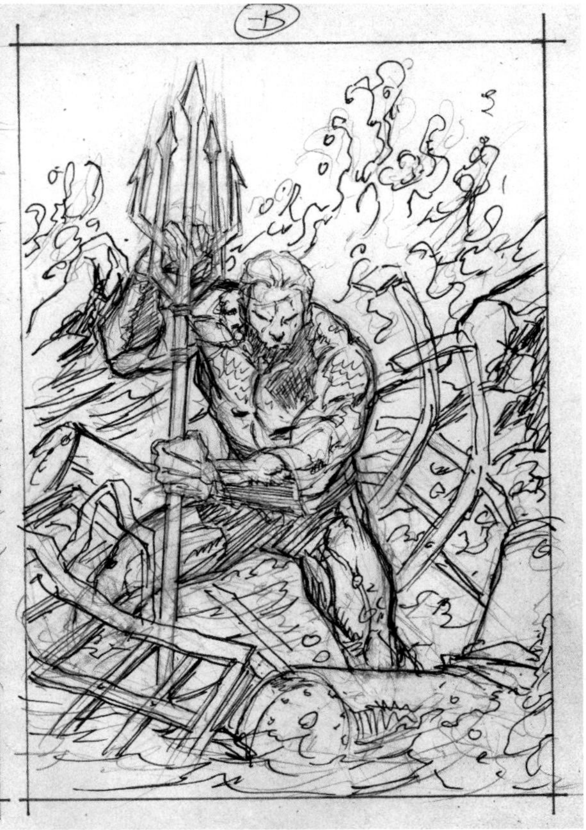
B

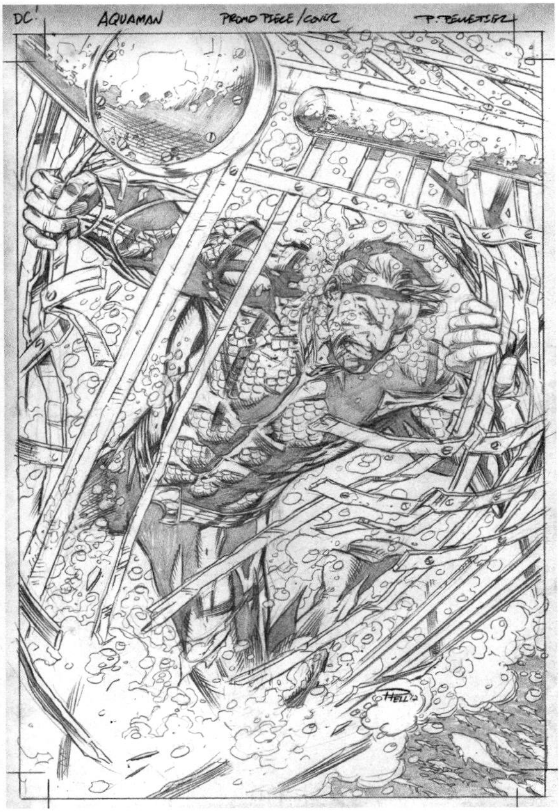
DC
AQUAMAN

Step-by-step progression of New York Comic Con AQUAMAN promo piece by Paul Pelletier, Art Thibert & Gabe Eltaeb.

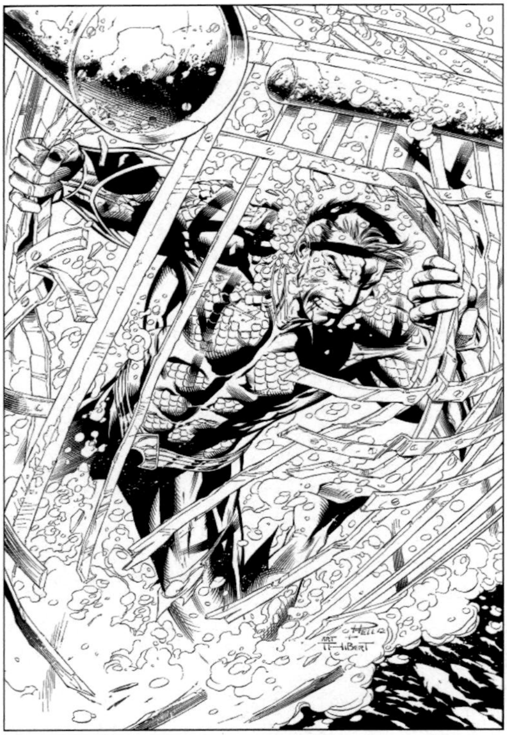

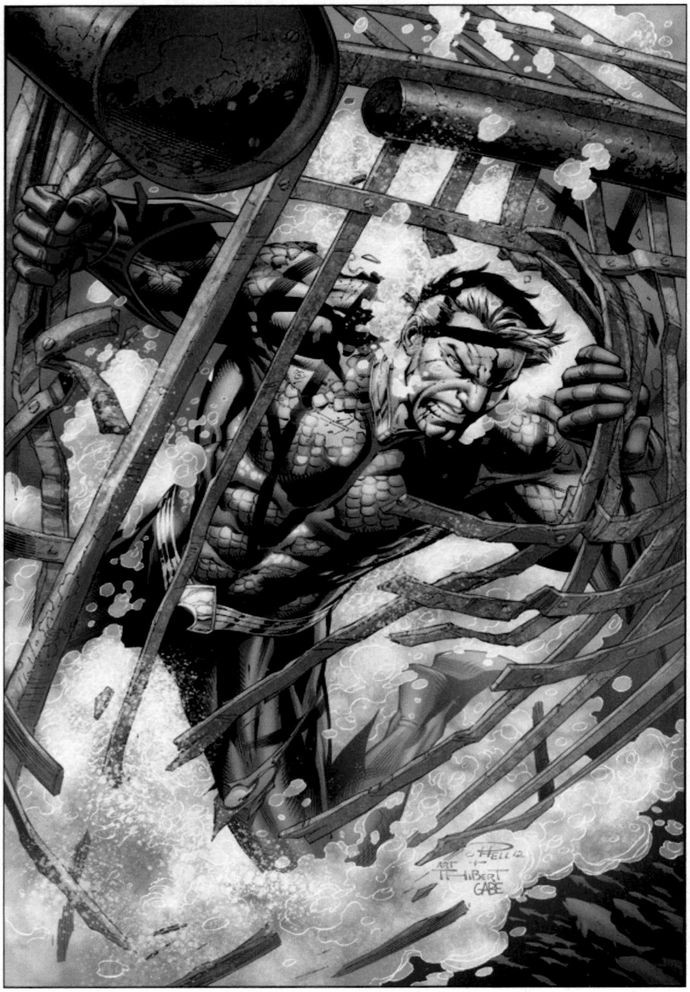

AQUAMAN Nº15 cover sketches by Pete Woods

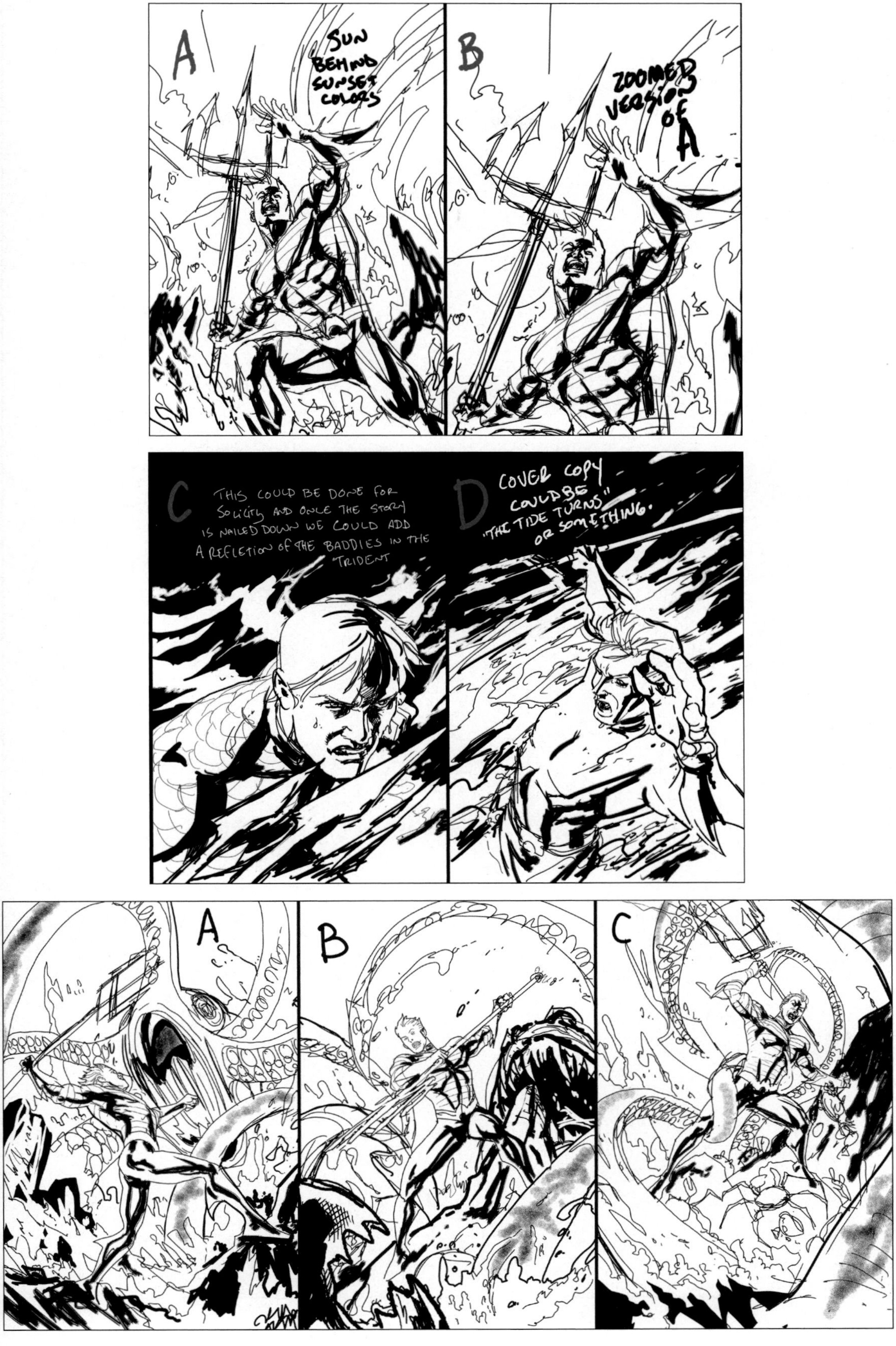
A
SUN BEHIND SUNSET COLORS
B
ZOOMED VERSION OF A
C
THIS COULD BE DONE FOR SOLICITY AND ONCE THE STORY IS NAILED DOWN WE COULD ADD A REFLETION OF THE BADDIES IN THE TRIDENT
D
COVER COPY COULD BE "THE TIDE TURNS" OR SOMETHING.
A
B
C

Pencils for AQUAMAN №15 variant cover by Jim Lee

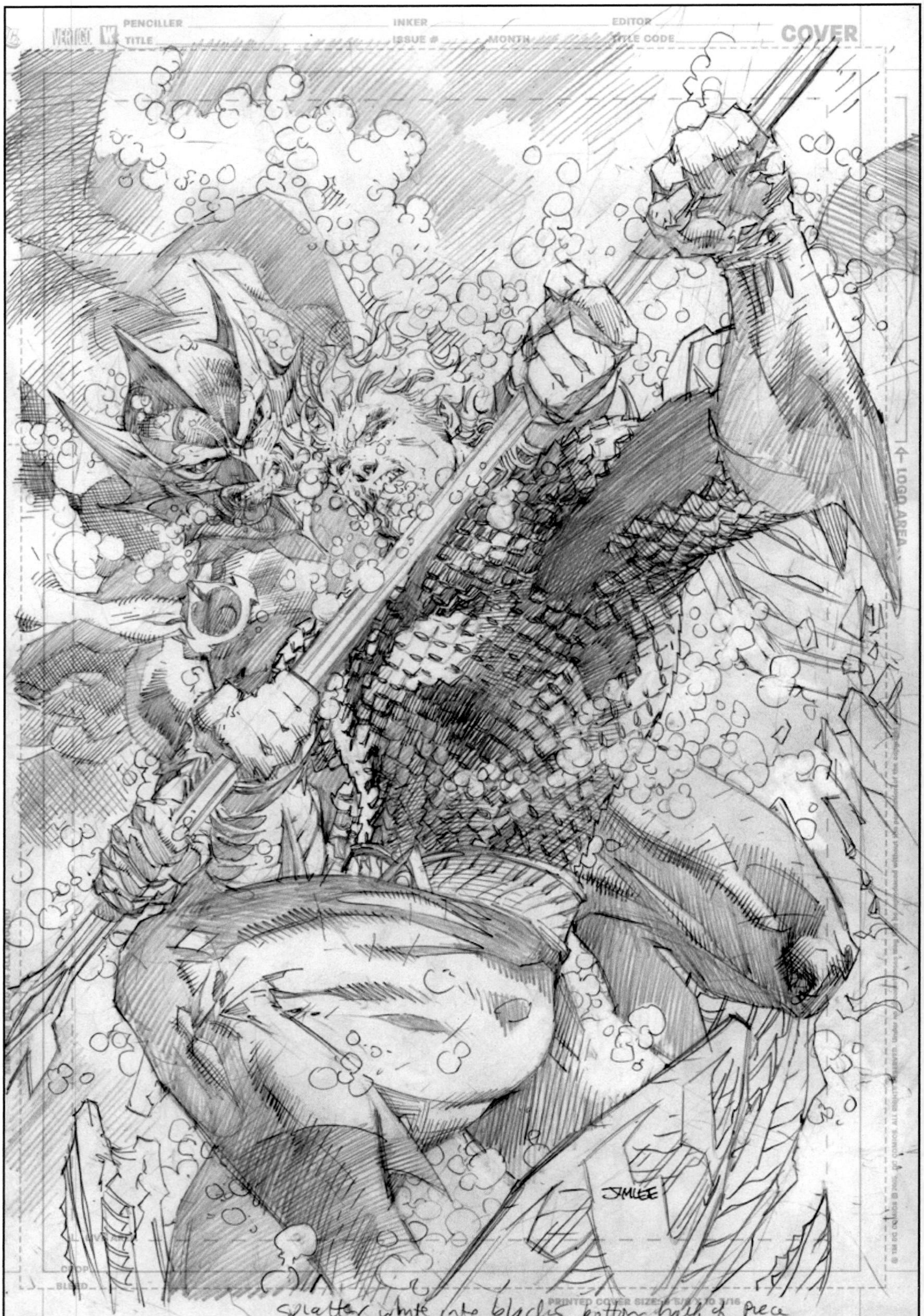
PENCILLER
INKER
EDITOR
TITLE
ISSUE #
MONTH
TITLE CODE
COVER
LOGO AREA
JIMLEE
Splatter white into blacks bottom half of piece

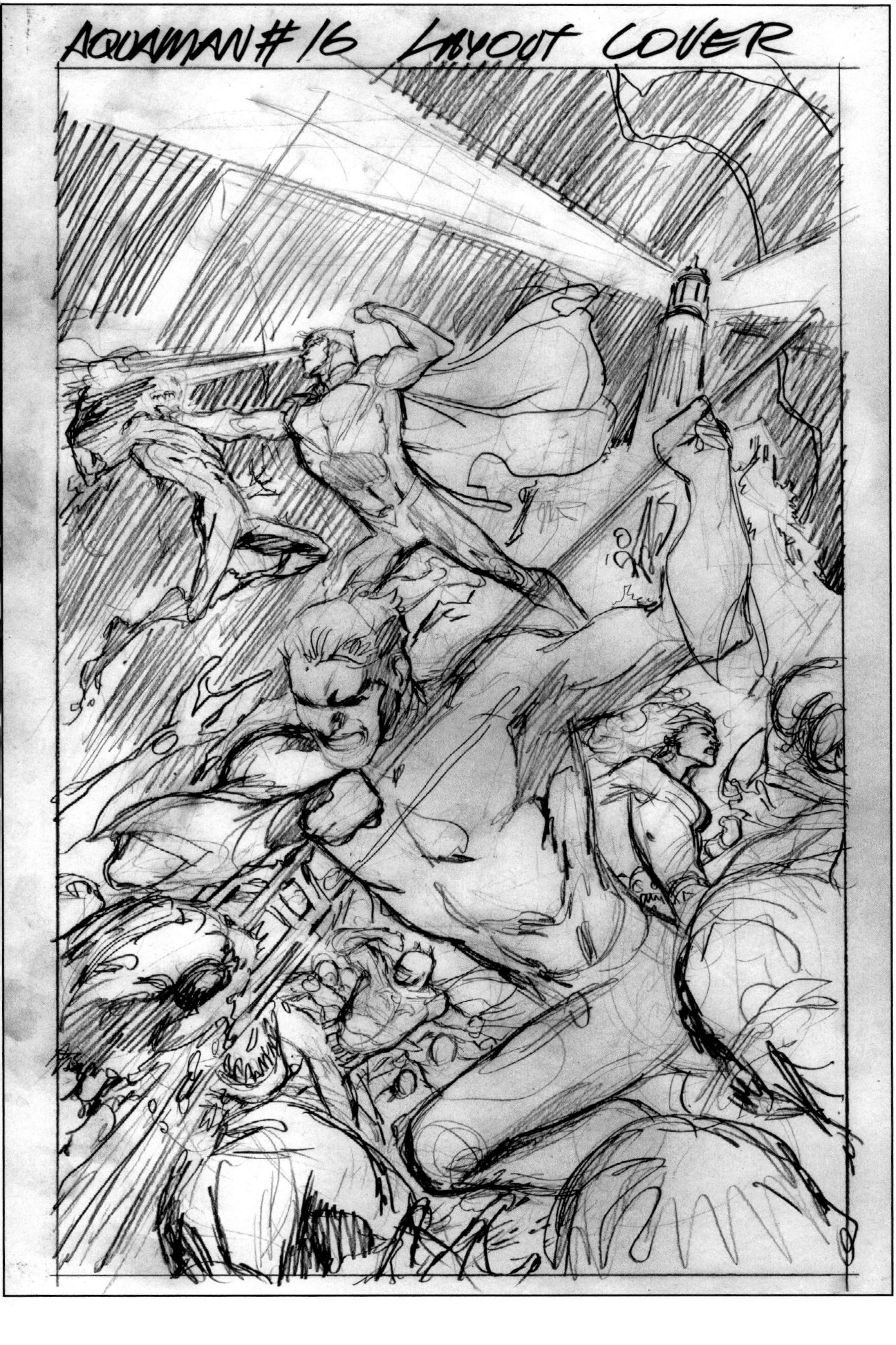
AQUAMAN #16 LAYOUT COVER

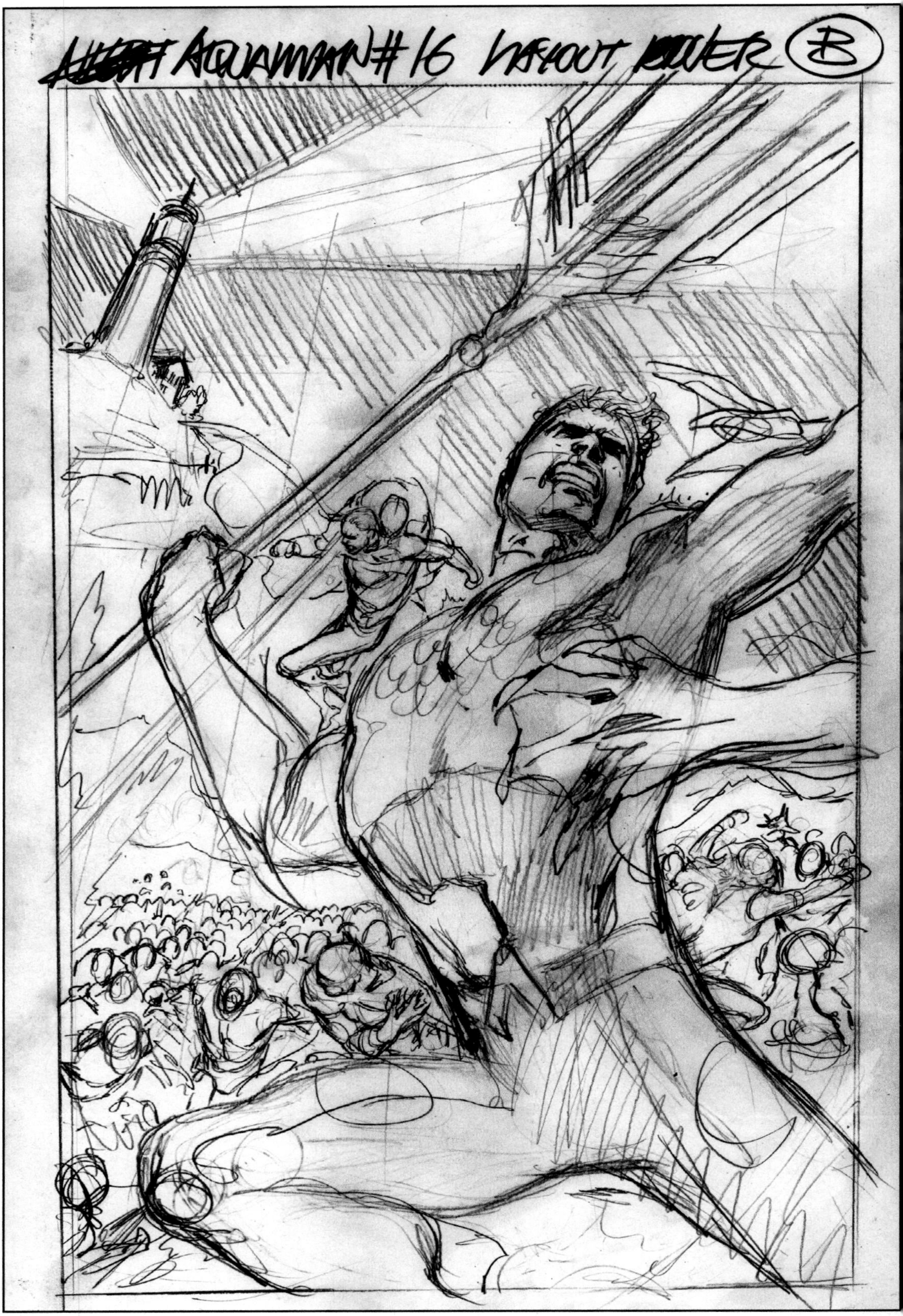
AQUAMAN #16 WITHOUT POWER
B

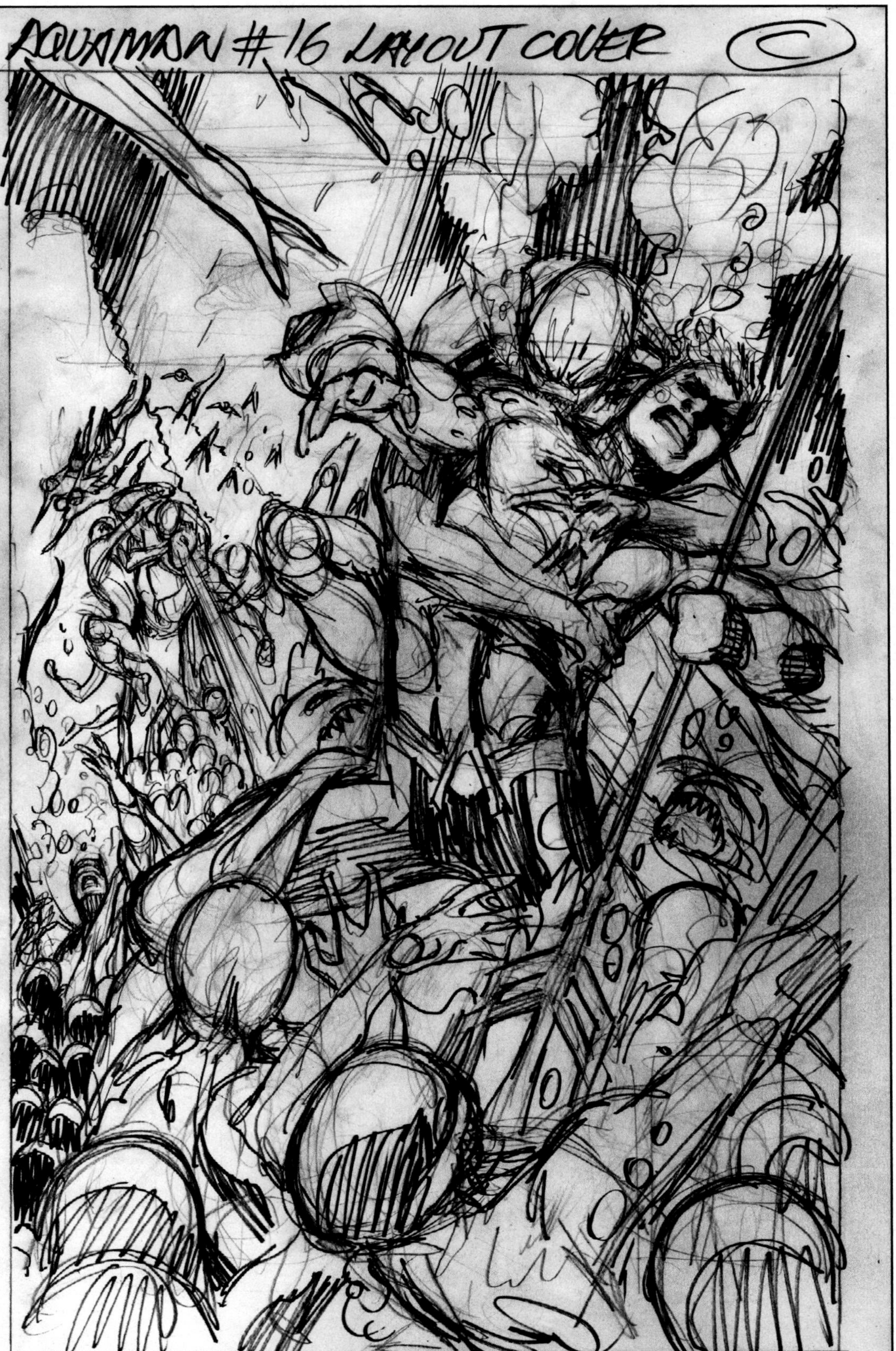
AQUAMAN #16 LAYOUT COVER

“AQUAMAN has been a rollicking good ride so far… The mythology Johns has been building up here keeps getting teased out at just the right rate, like giving a junkie their fix.” **– MTV GEEK**

“With Reis on art and Johns using his full creative juices, AQUAMAN is constantly setting the bar higher and higher.”
– CRAVE ONLINE

THE #1 NEW YORK TIMES BESTSELLER
THE NEW 52!
AQUAMAN
VOLUME 1
THE TRENCH
"ACTUALLY, THIS MIGHT BE [GEOFF JOHNS'] MOST IMPRESSIVE FEAT TO DATE. GENIUS."
— USA TODAY
GEOFF JOHNS IVAN REIS JOE PRADO

AQUAMAN
VOL. 1: THE TRENCH
GEOFF JOHNS
with IVAN REIS

THE #1 NEW YORK TIMES BEST-SELLING SERIES
THE NEW 52!
AQUAMAN
VOLUME 2
THE OTHERS
GEOFF JOHNS IVAN REIS JOE PRADO

AQUAMAN VOL. 2: THE OTHERS

THE #1 NEW YORK TIMES BEST-SELLING SERIES
THE NEW 52!
AQUAMAN
VOLUME 3
THRONE OF ATLANTIS
"IT'S DRAMATIC, ENGAGING, AND EXPERTLY RENDERED."
— IGN
GEOFF JOHNS PAUL PELLETIER IVAN REIS

AQUAMAN VOL. 3: THRONE OF ATLANTIS

READ THE ENTIRE EP

AQUAMAN VOL
DEATH OF A K

AQUAMAN VOL
SEA OF STOR

AQUAMAN VOL
MAELSTR

AQUAMAN VOL
EXIL

AQUAMAN VOL
OUT OF DARKNE